Crossing a Line

Crossing a Line

*Laws, Violence, and Roadblocks
to Palestinian Political Expression*

Amahl A. Bishara

Stanford University Press
Stanford, California

Stanford University Press
Stanford, California

Printed in the United States of America on acid-free, archival-quality paper

Library of Congress Cataloging-in-Publication Data

Names: Bishara, Amahl A., 1976– author.

Title: Crossing a line : laws, violence, and roadblocks to Palestinian political expression / Amahl A. Bishara.

Description: Stanford, California : Stanford University Press, [2022] | Includes bibliographical references and index.

Identifiers: LCCN 2021051786 (print) | LCCN 2021051787 (ebook) | ISBN 9781503631373 (cloth) | ISBN 9781503632097 (paperback) | ISBN 9781503632103 (ebook)

Subjects: LCSH: Palestinian Arabs—Israel—Politics and government. | Palestinian Arabs—West Bank—Politics and government.

Classification: LCC DS113.6 .B57 2022 (print) | LCC DS113.6 (ebook) | DDC 956.94/0049274—dc23/eng/20211025

LC record available at https://lccn.loc.gov/2021051786

LC ebook record available at https://lccn.loc.gov/2021051787

Cover design: Rob Ehle
Cover art: Majid Alaa Eldeen
Typeset by Newgen in 10/14 Minion

For Zaha and Ziad, and all their cousins.

Contents

Acknowledgments

It is strange indeed to write acknowledgements at a time when I have not been in the field for two years due to the COVID emergency, and yet, completing this book—even gathering the photo permissions—has been a fulfilling process of reconnecting. I could never have done this work without the love and support of the Bisharas and the Al-Azraqs. I am especially grateful to my aunts and uncles and my parents-in-law who have always taken such tremendous care of me during my stays and made me feel at home again and again. I am still moved by the many ways, large and small, that my aunts and uncles in the Galilee have found connections with my world in the West Bank: coming to visit, letting me know when they saw someone we knew on Palestine TV, making meals to greet people who make the journey north, and much more. Sweeter verandas I have never known than those in Tarshiha. And I deeply appreciate my loved ones in the West Bank who have received guests from Tarshiha with such warmth and generosity. I am grateful to my bold, brilliant, hardworking, and generous female cousins and sisters-in-law: Palestinian women whose commitment to love and justice inspire me year after year, and whose friendship I am so fortunate to enjoy. These were also intense child nurturing years, so I am grateful to all those with whom I shared the joys of caregiving while doing this field research, all of whom opened their homes to me and shared their ideas as well.

As a Palestinian-American researcher, I am especially appreciative of the gifts of insights and time of Palestinians who are deeply rooted in Palestinian communities in Palestine, folks like Sa'ed Abu-Hijleh, Salah Al-Ajarma (may he rest in peace), Nisreen Al-Azza, Nidal Al-Azza, Mohammad Al-Azza, Bassim

Bishara, Rana Bishara, Ghousoon Bisharat, Sami Bukhari, Diana Buttu, Rula Nasr-Mazzawi, Nidal Rafa, and many others. As a person who has never been incarcerated, I am deeply grateful to those who have shared with me their experiences and analysis of prison bravely and wisely for this book and in the past, including Khaled Al-Azraq, Khawla Al-Azraq, Mukhlis Burghal, Mohammad Hamada, Mohammad Al-Qeeq, Khalida Jarrar, Dareen Tatour, and many others. I am grateful to all of those who participated in the photography projects in Aida and Jaffa for their perspectives and for the pleasure of walking, looking, and talking together in two cherished communities. I am grateful to everyone who traveled across the Green Line with me, especially when this meant putting up with my driving, and to everyone who attended the protests and commemorations discussed in this volume.

In the academic world, I'm grateful to a rock-star crew of fellow travelers who help me to keep walking through the trying terrain of US academia and who have offered me incisive reads on parts of this manuscript. They include the unstoppable Southwest Asia North African anthropology crowd, the publics and crowds crowd, and my colleagues from NYU who continue to inspire creativity and commitment in scholarship, including Diana Allan, Lori Allen, Jessica Cattelino, Julie Chu, Frank Cody, Lara Deeb, Ilana Feldman, Andy Graan, Sherine Hamdy, Eleana Kim, Tim Loh, Julie Norman, Alejandro Paz, Shira Robinson, Naomi Schiller, Rebecca Stein, Winifred Tate, and Jessica Winegar. For reads on early drafts, I am grateful to Leila Farsakh and a patient writing group that included wise friends: Safa Abu Rabia, Sarah Ihmoud, Areej Sabbagh-Khoury, Randa Wahbe, and Alex Winder.

I appreciated the camaraderie I found at the Radcliffe Institute, where I completed my ACLS fellowship under the deft leadership of Judith Vichniac (may she rest in peace) and the intellectual fellowship of scholars working across disciplines and continents, especially Rebecca Carter, Erica Edwards, Jonathan Guyer, Shireen Hassim, Aisha Khan, Adela Pinch, Tulasi Srinivas, Conevery Valencius, and Patricia Williams. Though it was a trying time for both me and the world, they and others made me and my project feel seen. The CHAT community at Tufts—led by Lisa Lowe and then Kamran Rastegar—was a stimulating location for developing big ideas and welcoming close reads. I am grateful to a manuscript workshop in 2019 that included Tatiana Chudakova, Sarah Ihmoud, Lisa Lowe, Ayşe Parla, Sarah Pinto, and Ajantha Subramanian. Insaniyyat, the Society of Palestinian Anthropologists, has been a crucial space of learning for me, and I thank especially Nayrouz Abu Hatoum, Khaled Furani, Rema Hammami, and Nadeem Karkabi for their tireless work and vision in creating and maintaining this space. I also thank the wonderful research assistants Halah Ahmad, Shireen Boshar, Marshall Hanig, and Isabel Rosenbaum, all of whom are inspiring thinkers of a new generation. The rigor and creativity of Lila Abu-Lughod, Steven Feld, Faye Ginsburg, and Rosalind Shaw continue to shape my work here. I might not have finished this manuscript without the vital reads of most or all of the manuscript at critical times by the brilliant J. Kēhaulani Kauanui, Suhad Bishara, and Paul Beran. Rana Barakat, Lana Tatour, and Maha Nassar were new and cherished interlocutors at a crucial time.

I am grateful for the creative, warm, and engaged academic spaces collectively nurtured in the Tufts Department of Anthropology and the Department for the Studies of Race, Colonialism, and Diaspora. The Tufts Faculty Research Awards Committee, the Wenner-Gren Foundation, the Palestinian American Research Center (PARC), and especially a PARC-NEH grant, made possible a large part of this field research. I also appreciate others who work hard to make a space for this kind of scholarship and writing, despite the many obstacles we face, especially Kate Wahl of Stanford University Press, Beshara Doumani through the New Directions in Palestinian Studies workshops, Penelope Mitchell at PARC, Rashid Khalidi, Sherene Seikaly, Maia Tabet, Salim Tamari, and others at the Institute for Palestine Studies, friends at the Columbia Center for Palestine Studies, and those who run important blogs like *Mondoweiss*, +972, and *Electronic Intifada*. And I appreciate those whose writing and research year after year offer intrepid and eloquent chronicles and resources, like the staff of Adalah, Defense for Children International-Palestine, Addameer, and B'Tselem, as well as journalists like Amira Hass. I appreciate two insightful reviewers and the wonderful people at Stanford University Press for all their thinking and hard work.

As I look at these lists of names, and think of other astute interlocutors who remain unnamed, I also write with the humility of knowing that I have so much more to learn from all of these people.

In the Boston area, I'm so appreciative of all of the teachers and caregivers who have made it possible for me to take the time to write this book. I am deeply thankful for friends and community members who share the struggles in which I find myself: those involved with 1for3.org, the Alliance for Water Justice, Jewish Voice for Peace Boston, the Palestinian Community of Boston,

Anthropologists for the Boycott of Israeli Academic Institutions, and the United American Indians of New England. And I am grateful to my oldest friends who are anchors to all I do, especially Jenny, Carolyn, Judy, and Jay. For their patient friendship, proclivity for adventure, and smart conversation over these many years, I thank Lori Allen, Mohammad Al-Azza, Paul Beran, Sherine Hamdy, Alejandro Paz, and Hilary Rantisi.

I thank my parents, June and Ghassan Bishara, for their positivity, unflappability, and super caregiving to my whole household. It is a tremendous comfort to have their encouragement and confidence and a joy to have their company and conversation. I'm grateful to Zaha and Ziad for their insights large and small, for the delight they express and elicit, and for the compassion with which they approach me each day. Without Nidal Al-Azraq and his vision, kindness, and care, I could never have undertaken this project, neither logistically, nor intellectually and politically. I'm grateful that he gives me the space and time to explore, yet is always present when I need him. What magic is that?

Note on Transliteration and Translation

I have provided transliterations of Arabic when it is important for the reader's understanding or appreciation of the material. I have followed IJMES's style guide to the extent possible and used colloquial transliterations when most appropriate, as with protest chants. I have omitted *ayins* and *hamzas* in the case of placenames and individuals' names commonly written in English without them, and otherwise followed common English spellings for places. Most interviews were conducted in Arabic, and I have provided English translations of them.

Prologue

In early 2011, I became a frequent visitor to the Israeli Ministry of the Interior in Acre, the Galilee, in an effort to obtain the Israeli passport to which I always had a legal right, because my father is a Palestinian citizen of Israel. At first, my uncle drove me there and made sure I found a Palestinian clerk whom he knew through his years as a nurse in Acre. He knew how to share with her a little joke and a smile, or to ask after a common acquaintance, putting us all at ease. But after a while I made these trips on my own. I would pass through the metal detector and bag check into the undistinguished mall and go up the cramped elevator to the office only to pass through another metal detector and another bag check.

The Ministry of Interior reflected the population of the Galilee, the northernmost part of Israel's 1948 territories. There were as many Palestinians as Jewish Israelis, it seemed,[1] and also a great diversity of those in urban or rural styles of clothing, observant Muslims, Palestinian Christians wearing necklaces with prominent crosses, Orthodox Jews, Arab Jews, Russians—and many, many children. Often I had to scramble for a seat. One time I met someone who told me she was the first female Palestinian clown. She pulled out her red nose to entertain my nine-month-old daughter as we waited. Eventually, I would meet with the special clerk in her small office. She handled more complex cases than those dealt with at the line of service windows that ran the length of the room, and she always, it seemed, had a line of Palestinians waiting to meet her. These bureaucratic exchanges were a reminder of Palestinian presence throughout the spaces of Israeli public life.

I would return to Aida Refugee Camp in the West Bank, where my husband was born and raised. This had become my primary home base during fieldwork because Israeli closure prohibited my husband from entering Israel legally since he carries a West Bank identity card. Each time I would return, my father-in-law would ask about the progress of the passport. He oversaw the goings on of his eleven children and dozens of grand- and great-grandchildren as he reclined on a mattress in front of his house. This summer setup was a convenient adaptation of a traditional Arab seating that benefited from the several extra mattresses this large family always had on hand. A few hundred meters away was the military base from which Israeli soldiers could enter the refugee camp at any time, but we felt relatively sheltered from it in the small courtyard. When he asked about the passport, I would usually report that it was still in progress: We needed more documents, or more time, or another meeting.

One day, when he inquired again, "Is it done?" I flashed him the sky-blue passport. It felt odd to see it in the refugee camp—I suddenly had a closer relationship with the soldiers in that watchtower. But he did not miss a beat. "Congratulations!" he exclaimed. "You've become Palestinian." We both laughed loudly. All these years after he was pushed out of his own lands, he allowed that attaining an Israeli passport made me more Palestinian than I had been when I had only my US passport. Having identity documents that are complicated, problematic—that facilitate some things but undercut others—is indeed distinctly Palestinian.[2] Palestinians on both sides of what is called the Green Line that divides Israel's 1948 territories from the 1967 occupied territories of the West Bank know this well, though they know it differently. The dynamics of political expression shaped by this line and those identity documents are the topic of this book.

The next year, the clerk remembered me when I came back to register my marriage so that we could apply for a permit for my husband to visit my family in the Galilee. She all too quickly found my husband's name in the computer. This time, it seemed strange that we were so far north in a little office in Acre and my husband's information was so readily available—that, nearly twenty years after the establishment of the Palestinian Authority (PA), the entity that was to become a Palestinian state, there was not even a pretense of a border between the system for Israeli citizens and that for Palestinians in the West Bank. This time there was no shared laughter, only a long look, and her finger pointing at the screen. I wondered what else she could see about my husband and his politically active family. Meanwhile, my husband applied for a magnetic card, a precursor necessary for applying for a permit, and then he applied for the permit itself, only to be denied. When I told my family in the Galilee, they asked why he had been declined. I did not know how to answer them. I knew they might be anxious about proximity to a Palestinian somehow regarded as a "terrorist."[3] Yet, in 2007, Israel categorized about 20 percent of the male population of the West Bank between the ages of 16 and 55 as security threats, such that, as Yael Berda has asserted, "the restriction was applied broadly across a wide range of risk levels, not only in cases where information actually existed."[4] It was hardly a surprise that this included my husband, a refugee who had relatives who were political prisoners. One of my relatives in the Galilee—himself active in a Palestinian political party in Israel—offered to contact a high-ranking Palestinian in the Israeli army who might help. I quickly declined the offer. This would have been both odious and alarming from the perspective of my husband: One avoids asking the Israeli security system for help. Moments of interaction with the Israeli security system are often opportunities for Israel to coerce Palestinians into collaborating.[5] Certainly, in many Palestinian communities inside Israel's 1948 territories, Palestinians are also suspicious of contact with Israeli authorities,[6] but this sense is even more pervasive in the West Bank. In any case, for years, whether my husband did or did not visit with me, the question of his permits loomed.

As these stories show, my own personal history as someone with beloved relatives inside Israel's 1948 territories and in the West Bank both encouraged me to ask questions about Palestinian relationships across the Green Line and actively shaped this research. Throughout the project, my identity was a factor, in particular that I am a middle class, cis-gendered woman with higher education and a professional job in the United States, who speaks good Arabic and fluent, first-language English. Yet, my apparent identity read differently on either side of the Green Line. In the West Bank, most people assumed when looking at me that I was white American or European, while in Israel's 1948 territories many first thought I was Jewish Israeli, depending on the context. Moreover, as the above demonstrates, my own legal identity shifted as I was doing the project. I took on the Israeli passport both because it was my right to do so and so that I would have better access to my field site, rather than having to worry about being prevented from entering any territory controlled by Israeli authorities, as has happened to many Palestinians and activists.[7]

It was not only my social position and legal status that shaped this research; it was also my embodied experience. Knowledge production about a highly militarized colonial setting is especially situated or embodied.[8] My own experiences of risk and fear flared up and faded based on the political situation and my physical location either in Israel, the West Bank, or even the United States. I noted when I felt tense, as when, after a protest in Al-Lidd / Lod, I was both hesitant and eager to ask police officers leaning on my car to step away from it. I noted the way I flinched when the first stun grenade would punctuate a calm afternoon in Aida Refugee Camp, the West Bank. This, in turn, made me remember the booms that filled my chest as a child in the Galilee, when Israeli warplanes flew over our village to bomb Lebanon. But of course there were pleasures in the field as well. I felt satiated and grateful when a spring meal of 'akoub (thistle-like gundelia) offered a sense of Palestinian cultural and agricultural continuity. I enjoyed my walks through the olive groves of the Al-Walaja hills in the West Bank and the olive groves on the hills around my father's village.

All the while I recognized how the experiences of those Palestinians permanently and irrevocably impacted by these forms of violence were different from my own: the sisters and brothers of prisoners and the parents of someone in a Jerusalem hospital, both applying for military permits to visit; those who live with no end in sight to the threat of military or police violence and in the shadow of Israel's rule that is never concerned with the well-being of Palestinians. Palestinians living under Israeli rule grow up with it, celebrate graduations and weddings at its whims, raise children with it, manage illnesses within its capricious illogics, bury loved ones at its conditions. This is a difficult and immense fact to take in; perhaps it has only been as I have spent almost two decades doing fieldwork—raising my own children, mourning the dead—that I begin to grasp the enormity of this toll. Slowly I witness how "someone's ordinary can endure or can sag defeated,"[9] or how people assemble bluster or joy or determined routine to make it through the year, again and again. As other feminist women of color have written on the practice of activist fieldwork:

> Centering the body in the stakes of activist research advances the path toward the project of decolonizing anthropology . . . A critical feminist activist anthropology . . . holds us politically accountable to our interlocutors as well as to our own embodied reality, as part of the same liberatory struggle, albeit differentially located.[10]

That is, centering the body does not mean focusing inward; it is a means toward an ethical engagement in the field and beyond.

Writing about my own experience in a way that takes into account embodied and emotional dimensions is also helpful as a complement to writing
about other Palestinians' political affect. I found that as I traveled across the
Green Line, my senses needed to be constantly retuned, almost like the radio
station did as I swerved around a curve on the road out of Bethlehem toward
Al-Walaja Checkpoint and toward Jerusalem. Neither the West Bank nor Palestinian communities inside the Green Line felt like a comfort zone to me, both
because of the frequent threats of political tension or outright violence, and
because I am a partial outsider. Moving between them, I often felt off balance,
like I needed to adjust my accent or my posture. If I am interested, here, in how
Palestinian citizens of Israel and Palestinians under military occupation often
experience politics through different affective lenses, then I must also recognize
my own distinct location as a Palestinian American who is differently socially
comfortable in the West Bank than Israel, and who has quite specific ties to the
two locations. It does not escape me that I am related to one side of the Green
Line through my father and the other through my husband, and that each of
these relations can hold weighty assumptions in prevailingly patriarchal societies. But I also appreciated that there were parts of both areas that I explored on
my own, and that many of my field relationships were mediated through my
female cousins and my sisters-in-law, because of their own activism, creativity,
and prominence.[11] I also explore in this volume how traditional kin modalities can be expanded toward liberation through deeply Palestinian practices of
hosting and caring, and my family members have been models for this, too.

Fear, outrage, and despair, along with senses of solidarity and love for Palestine as an idea or a territory or both, and the smaller places within it all motivate Palestinians' political expression and action. While there are similarities
across the Green Line—and while there are certainly important differences
within Palestinian societies in Israel's 1948 territories and the West Bank—Palestinian citizens of Israel and subjects of Israeli occupation do, I assert, have
differences in their political habitus, or embodied ways of living in political
and social structures,[12] and their structures of feeling, or inchoate senses of
social structures and political experience.[13] These motivate political life. With
my senses tuned by my own movement through space, I do my best to attend
to these differences.

To write of affect is also to write of embodied senses that are not fully
formed, that can shift. Or perhaps, in these Palestinian places, it is to write
about underlying senses of similarity that haunt public political stances. The

forms of violence that Palestinians face in various polities are not as distinct as they might seem. Palestinian citizens of Israel know that they, too, could be shot like Palestinians in the West Bank, because on key occasions, Israeli authorities have indeed shot Palestinian citizens of Israel at demonstrations. Palestinians in the West Bank know that they, too, could be bombed from the air as are Palestinians in Gaza, since they were bombed from the air during the second Intifada.

Especially in this project, movement is an important embodied epistemic experience. Ethnographic approaches to infrastructure—especially the road—are rich sites for considering the intersection of social, legal, and affective dimensions of experience.[14] This is particularly true at and around places construed as borders.[15] I watched how others controlled their tempers or bluffed their way through checkpoints, and sometimes I could feel my own pulse change as I approached checkpoints. Through movement Palestinians register their senses of safety or danger, and they apprehend how Israeli and other authorities regard them: as a threat, as irrelevant, as subjects that need to be taught their own irrelevance.[16] This is why I include "passages" between chapters, accounts of mobility that give a sense of the texture of politics, the feel of geography, and the experience of fieldwork. All of the passages chronicle travels across the Green Line or between Israeli-annexed East Jerusalem and the rest of the West Bank. They are examples of what I think of as "knowledge made in motion."

It should be clear that I do not claim to speak "objectively," because such a claim is inevitably a power play. Instead, my writing asserts its credibility from its grounding in experience and research, from a careful attention to perspective itself: to where I was standing when I saw something and to where I was sitting when I wrote it. I write as a person vested in Palestinian futures on multiple levels: first, as a Palestinian whose life has been conditioned by the dispossession of the Nakba and racism of Israel that eventually brought my father to the United States and who has reconnected to Palestinian societies through the people I have chosen to love as an adult, including many who continue to be on the front lines experiencing Israeli violence and racism; second, as an anthropologist who cares deeply about my field site as anthropologists are expected to do; and third, as a person who believes in justice for all those dispossessed or devastated by colonialism, militarism, patriarchy, and capitalism. These three dimensions are, of course, interrelated.

The reader will already have recognized a third location in this book: the United States. To the extent that state sovereignty is always relational among different states,[17] sovereignty in its current conception is necessarily rooted in an imperial history and present,[18] especially for Israel. Palestinian political expression is also shaped by international—and especially US—assumptions and definitions about Palestinians. Being a Palestinian American, I have been aware of this my entire life. Just as there are no comfort zones in the field, there are no comfort zones in writing about Palestine in the United States, in particular in the academy.[19] I have never been an anthropologist without the backdrop of the 9/11 attacks and the so-called US War on Terror, or the deeper histories of Orientalism and anti-Arab racisms.[20] It is all too engrained in the work of so many anthropologists of Southwest Asia and North Africa that our readers will open our books with tacit assumptions about engrained Arab violence, the universal good of US democratic values, and a watchful eye for who the "good" and "bad" Arabs are, including those who might be teaching them in the United States.[21] The context of the War on Terror has helped shape Israeli justifications for violence against Palestinians, and vice versa.[22] We write around and within these expectations, and, sometimes, we take them head on.

Still, anthropology's reflexive turn, movements to decolonize my discipline, a growing field of anthropology of Palestine,[23] and perhaps most of all my experiences with my Palestinian interlocutors give me the courage to write. I write also as a person who lives and works today in the territory of the Pennacook and Massachusett people. While it is important to recognize the specificity of that genocide and that dispossession, it is also crucial to recognize that my life in the United States has been shaped by the ongoing dispossession of many, many other Indigenous nations, in their interconnection and interrelationship with each other. I also witness US police and other violence against Black people with both an awareness of the white privilege I often harbor and with the stark outrage of recognition, because, as many others have recognized, US and Israeli mechanisms of racism and violence resemble each other,[24] though the structural and historical circumstances that have created anti-Black racism in the United States are distinct from those that have created anti-Palestinian racism in Israel. All of this makes me heartily agree with Aisha Beliso-De Jesús and Jemima Pierre that anthropologists' tendency to focus on the particular and the small scale can make it more difficult to identify and trace global white supremacy.[25] This is all to say, I write about the US in this book because it is a related settler colony, with its own dynamics of racialized violence and logics of elimination of Indigenous peoples, and with its own imperial politics in relation to the Arab world.

This project has helped me to think about practices of solidarity in the field and as a writer. The concept of solidarity is relevant here on multiple levels. First, in one sense, I am analyzing solidarity. While Palestinians sometimes distanced themselves from the label of "solidarity" for activism across the Green Line, preferring to assert that they were simply part of a shared political project, there are elements of solidarity in their practices, since often one group would advocate on behalf of another that was apparently more vulnerable. Denying "solidarity" might have more performative than analytic value. Second, there is my relationship as a Palestinian-American anthropologist to those with whom I worked. Third, there are forms of political solidarity between Palestinians and other non-Palestinians, especially, today, in the US and Europe, and especially Indigenous and Black activists. Another crucial form of solidarity today is between Jewish activists and Palestinians (in Israel, the United States, and beyond), all of whom have different stakes in building toward justice for Palestinians and Israelis, and all of whom carry different historical burdens of struggle, suffering, and responsibility. An activist ethnographic approach encourages us to attend to historical and structural similarities across relations of solidarity and similarities of experience, with an awareness that in finding these similarities we are never asserting sameness, that highlighting difference in nuanced ways will only make stories and bridges stronger. This book is a practice in doing just this. I will explore how people can, in speaking, recognize cross-cutting power hierarchies and multiple vulnerabilities, how they can speak with the goal not of achieving unison but with the goal of making space for more voices that may illuminate interrelationships among groups.

If this book is centrally about a comparison-as-relation[26] between Palestinians in Israel and those in the West Bank that reveals history and power rather than holds apart two isolated groups, I also aim for this book to reach beyond this small place. Palestinian scholars defined Israel as a settler colony decades ago;[27] scholarly interest in this perspective has only expanded in recent years. Alongside this, Palestinians and others have had renewed debates in recent years about whether Palestinians should use the framework of apartheid or assert Indigenous identity,[28] a discussion that has been shaped not only by critical Indigenous studies but also by conceptions of the political limitations of struggle for Indigenous self-determination under law as well as by preconceptions about indigeneity as a cultural category. Scholarly attention relating to Black-Palestinian solidarity has been approached through the frame of colonialism and through a lens of racism and militarism.[29] This volume contributes to these discussions by looking at distinct experiences of dispossession and their inter-relatedness. Palestinians who hold Israeli citizenship and Palestinians in the occupied territories are both dispossessed through Israeli settler colonialism, yet they exhibit subtle differences in (1) their experiences of state violence, (2) their political aspirations, and (3) how they historically relate to these different analytic lenses or kinds of solidarity. Palestinian history may structurally align them closer to analogies with Indigenous struggles, while there may in some cases seem to be more of a resemblance in terms of the politics of everyday life with Black Americans' experiences of racism. How do we match theoretical frames and ethnography in ways that account for these distinctions? Ethnography is an important method for this work. This angle on the study of Palestinians—looking at two Palestinian locations—is distinctly positioned to enrich a conversation about the relationships among settler colonialism, empire, racism, and militarism as ongoing—distinct, but related—processes.

Finally, we should note that these analogies are primarily US-centered. This is partly because I am a US-based scholar. But is it also another dimension of US empire that turns the heads of scholars of Palestine and Palestinian activists in the direction of the US? As Samar Al-Bulushi, Sahana Ghosh, and Madiha Tahir argue, US academy also needs to be provincialized as we work to decolonize our discipline.[30] We should be concerned about what we lose, politically and analytically, from tacitly centering the United States, these decades after Bandung and after the Palestinian Revolution firmly located itself in alignment with other anticolonial struggles. It is worth looking at how Palestinian histories and experiences of state violence resemble or connect to other Indigenous or racialized groups—or other groups living under foreign military rule—in Southwest Asia and North Africa and beyond. What remainders of nationalism as a de facto analytic—and Arab nationalism as a political movement—inform a relative lack of conversation between scholars writing with and about Sahrawis, Berbers, Armenians, and Kurds, and scholars of Palestine?

Perhaps the US focus is an anticipation of my audience, since my most obvious audience is made up of scholars of Palestine and the Middle East and colleagues and students in US anthropology who are concerned with state power, settler colonialism, and political expression and action. I have also written this book for anyone with the time and English-reading chops to tackle a full-length book on Palestine. For these readers, I hope I offer a sense of the texture of politics for Palestinians and the value of an ethnographic approach to political expression, broadly conceived. Perhaps my most treasured audience for this project is Palestinian readers. I recognize that Palestinian activists and writers who are citizens of Israel or subjects of Israeli occupation will find some part of this volume thin. Yet, I hope that some part of it will also be novel to most of these readers because of the very fact of Palestinian fragmentation. It is, after all, a result of my own privileged position as a diasporic Palestinian with an Israeli passport and a university position in the United States that I have been able to experience these occasions of Palestinian life on two sides of the Green Line. As an approach to the effects of geopolitical fragmentation on Palestinian political life, this book is by necessity partial, because of the great multiplicity of Palestinian places, because of the broadness of the framing of this book, and because it does not robustly address Palestinians in Gaza or the diaspora. Nevertheless, especially for Palestinian readers, I hope it will be evocative, demonstrating what an adjustment in perspective—actively decentering and looking constantly at more than one Palestinian location—can do for our understandings of our Palestinian present. Palestinian diversity has always been something to marvel at: from cuisines to lifeways to environments. An ethnographer is bound to appreciate that "differentiation is not after all contained—it runs riot."[31] Yet, the fragmentation of settler colonialism makes it difficult to embrace and maintain these diversities, and the violence of dispossession can exacerbate forms of oppression more internal to Palestinian societies. I hope to show that Palestinians can fight fragmentation with an awareness of each of our strengths and challenges and a willingness to struggle for connection, even when we do not speak from one experience. More generally, I hope this volume offers a vision of politics and action—and a way of writing about them—that embraces a multivocality rooted in experience and cognizant of difference, that honors those willing to attempt eloquence and bravery despite the many obstacles they face in doing so.

Crossing a Line

Introduction

ON ONE SUMMER EVENING IN HAIFA, in 2011, a small group of Palestinian citizens of Israel protested in solidarity with Palestinian political prisoners who were on a hunger strike for better living conditions. Protesters held framed photos of political prisoners whom the vast majority of Israeli society viewed as terrorists. Most of us had never met any of these striking prisoners in person. We had no easy way to capture or communicate the experiences of those prisoners who had not eaten for days, who lived in the prison of those who regarded them not just as criminals but as enemies. Some protesters blindfolded themselves and held their hands behind their backs as they kneeled in the cobblestone median of the main street. It was a different kind of vulnerability than that of hunger: visible solidarity with hated figures, bringing bodies low and close to traffic, denying themselves sight. The protest had wound down smoothly. It was dusk, that time in the demonstration when things can either turn more dangerous or more intimate, or they can dissipate entirely. A few people were still gathered near the treasured Palestinian cafes of Haifa's downtown.

How illuminating it can be to listen to what happens at the margins of events, off stage, as the crowd is half dispersing. In that twilight state, Walaa Sbeit, a locally loved musician and drama teacher, took to the center of the circle of protesters with a riff about Handala, a famous Palestinian character. Handala is a child refugee with a patched shirt, bare feet, and spiky hair created by Palestinian refugee Naji Al-Ali in 1969. Drawn in outline, he is usually depicted from behind. One explanation of this stance is that he is looking back to his homeland, longing for and looking to the land from which he was dispossessed in 1948 upon Israel's establishment. In this way he is a symbol of the right of millions of Palestinian refugees to return to their home villages and cities. Another interpretation of his turned back is that he is rejecting corrupt and ineffective Palestinian leadership. That night, Sbeit called out across time and geography and the very lines of imagination to exhort Handala to show his face, as Sbeit spun around with a dancer's grace:

> Handala, turn your back
> Handala, show your face.
> The time has come to say, Enough.[1]

As a child, Naji Al-Ali and his family had been pushed out of their Galilee village of Al-Shajara by Israeli forces in May 1948 and lived then in Ayn Al-Hilwe Refugee Camp in Lebanon, where 180,000 Palestinian refugees still live in some of the worst circumstances faced by Palestinian refugees.[2] We were a fifty- or sixty-kilometer drive from the ruins of Al-Shajara and perhaps a hundred kilometers from Ayn Al-Hilwe. Lebanon felt at once utterly inaccessible—the border has been entirely closed to legal civilian crossing since Israel's establishment—and just out of reach of the Galilee, like the breeze might really carry a message from this dancer in Haifa to a cartoon character dreamed up by an assassinated cartoonist in the last century. Like Handala could just maybe turn his head and answer Sbeit.

The prisons where the hungry prisoners waited were closer: Damoun, Al-Jalama, and Mejiddo were all within thirty-five kilometers, all former British Mandate detention facilities. They and the prisoners there, most of whom come from the militarily occupied West Bank, were out of reach in a different way. You could drive by them, but Israeli authorities tightly regulated visitors.

Sbeit soon turned to a meditation on the poetics of the name Handala itself. "Handala," he said, and let the word hang in the night air.

> Handala. Be kind to those who remained and those who did not remain.
> I'll remain here.
> Here I'll remain.
> We'll be kind to those who remained and those who did not remain.

> *Ḥanẓala. Ḥinn ʿalli ẓall wʿalli mā ẓall.*
> *Ḥanẓalni hōn.*
> *Hōn hanẓall.*
> *Ḥanhinn ʿalli ẓall wa ʿalli mā ẓall.*

And his words accelerated as he repeated them over and over until applause erupted around him and he settled again on the name Handala, suspended softly in the night.

All of the sounds of his riff came from the name Handala, and they are markedly Arabic sounds, like the hard ḥ that starts Handala, the hard ẓ sound in the middle, even the soft h sound of the end of his name. These sounds themselves signify Palestinian alterity, grace, and toughness for Palestinian citizens of Israel, especially because dominant forms of modern Hebrew tend to use fewer of the throat-based and "hard" sounds that make Arabic distinct. Indeed, Arabic is sometimes known as "the language of ḍād" evidence of how Arabic speakers can feel attached to the very distinctiveness of the sound of their language. To paraphrase the Palestinian poet Mahmoud Darwish's famous poem, Palestinians might have felt listening to Sbeit, we have in this word, Handala, what we need to express ourselves.[3] In its formal economy, the line of Sbeit's solo voice even bears some similarity to the Handala cartoon, that simple line drawing.

Sbeit articulates a determination to remain committed to this land. The reorientation of this Palestinian revolutionary symbol reveals its fertility. If Handala has been a symbol of refugees, here Handala helps Sbeit to articulate a message of tenderness for all Palestinians, those who were pushed out and those who remain. By using the sounds of Handala's name to talk about these different relationships, he suggests that these experiences are deeply related. This tender love is kinder than nationalism; it is a graceful challenge to the fragmentation, dispossession, and shame that trouble so many Palestinians at this long nadir of their liberation movement. With reggae style vocalizations, Sbeit gestures out to another geography of liberation.[4]

Palestinian nationalist political culture has tended to sideline Palestinian citizens of Israel, but they have found ways to engage, reframe, and stay connected to other Palestinians. Sbeit is a powerful messenger for this linking of refugee narratives and narratives of Palestinians in Haifa, since his family is internally displaced from the destroyed village of Iqrit in the far northern Galilee. He is like a refugee in his family's dispossession from land, but not defined as a refugee because his family did not cross international boundaries,[5] and he carries Israeli citizenship. In his performance, we see a symbol of Palestinian refugees' right to return (Handala) transposed, seamlessly, into an affirmation of the experience of staying. Handala is an iconic figure in Palestinian symbolism, evoked in everything from graffiti to jewelry, but that evening Sbeit added a new layer of significance to the little cartoon child.

It was moving for me as an ethnographer with experience living and working in a West Bank community with high rates of incarceration to witness the brave Haifa standouts for prisoners. While there were a few cherished political prisoners who were citizens of Israel, most were from the occupied territories of the West Bank and Gaza. During these same hunger strikes in the West Bank, mothers and fathers and sisters and brothers and friends of prisoners and many former prisoners would come to the marches and solidarity tents set up in each city. They would cradle photographs of people they wanted to hold in person. They sat in those tents for hours, mirroring the endurance of the striking prisoners, their presence an emblem of the stamina it indeed took family members to care for prisoners from afar, sometimes over many years. Being in these protest tents in the West Bank was intimate and painful, but it was also less politically (and perhaps physically) risky than to kneel in the street in Haifa. In the West Bank, Palestinians regarded prisoners as heroic men and women, or as vulnerable children, and they were beloved family members and friends. The Palestinian Authority (PA), an administering institution in the West Bank that operates within the Israeli occupation, paid prisoners small salaries, recognizing what they saw as their service to the nation and many of their families' dire need. Solidarity tents in Bethlehem would often be set up in the middle of town, where there were no Israeli soldiers. To stand with prisoners in the West Bank was not controversial. At these solemn events, there was rarely creative performance of song and dance. This is to say that the act of standing in solidarity with prisoners had a very different feel for Palestinian citizens of Israel than it did for Palestinians under occupation in the West Bank. The dangers and discomforts and the very weight of loss were distinct even if the photos of the prisoners they carried might have been the same.

This book is about the distinct environments for political expression and action of Palestinians who carry Israeli citizenship and Palestinians subject to Israeli military occupation in the West Bank, two Palestinian societies differently ostracized and endangered by Israeli settler colonialism and militarism and differently impacted by displacement and empire. It embarks from the idea that expression is always grounded in place and body, and that recognizing this is especially crucial under conditions of militarized settler colonialism.[6] Palestinians make up approximately one-fifth of Israeli citizens, while Palestinians in the West Bank are subjects of military occupation and make up about four-fifths

of the population of the West Bank, with the remainder being Jewish Israeli settlers. This is to say that Palestinians live with Jewish Israelis on either side of the
Green Line, the armistice line that separates Israel's 1948 territories from the
territory it occupied in 1967, albeit on very different terms.[7] Palestinian citizens
of Israel, who almost always live in the territory Israel claimed in 1948, can
vote and receive Israeli social services, though they are systematically discriminated against. Palestinians in the West Bank, some of whom were dispossessed
of their homes and lands in 1948, are subjects of Israel's military occupation
that began in 1967. They are unable to vote or access those social services. Yet
they are at the center of the dominant manifestation of the Palestinian national
project. That project is most obviously institutionalized in the PA, a state-like
assemblage that is itself over twenty-five years old and was meant to be a bridge
to Palestinian statehood, but lacks anything resembling full sovereignty as the
term is generally employed. These two Palestinian groups are separated from
each other by harsh Israeli movement restrictions and because they live under
different sets of laws. As a result, their forms of appeal and resistance have di-
verged, and subtle tensions have arisen between these groups. Nevertheless,
Palestinians in these two locations—which are of course themselves made up
of many other places with their own internal variations—manage to articulate
similar messages against Israeli oppression and for Palestinian liberation, and
recent years have seen a growing convergence in the forms of protest. Finally,
empire is a backdrop to this story both because of US support for Israel and
because US power tends to establish norms for various kinds of sovereignty
and forms of dissent.

Walaa Sbeit's performance exhibits a logic of juxtaposition, of resignification, and of bricolage that we will encounter throughout the book.[8] If the
ethnographer is one kind of bricoleur,[9] working in a science of the concrete
to make a collage of media, statements, and impressions that bring forward
a larger truth, I see not only myself but also many of those I write about as
bricoleurs, making politics out of the available lines of poetry, trees, stones,
paths, homes, etc.—working in a world not of their own making in a struggle
for liberation and life. Perhaps this is true of all political activism, in that activists inherit a set of symbols and a material world from those that came before
them, but it is especially true for Palestinians. Out of necessity and creativity,
Palestinians work with what they have, often lacking the power to pave roads or
protect archives. The concreteness of these processes is part of why it is difficult
to draw a clear line between speech and action for liberation, and why I look at

a wide variety of sites and practices related to expression as action in this book: not only media, but protests, commemorations, and more.

After a first chapter that contemplates the shifting and layered meanings of the placename Palestine for Palestinians, each chapter of this book addresses a different kind of political and expressive practice across at least two Palestinian places: protests against Israel's 2014 war on Gaza in Al-Lidd / Lod, Israel, and Bethlehem, the West Bank; commemorations of the Nakba in several locations on either side of the Green Line; a photographic exchange that I organized between Palestinian photographers in Jaffa, Israel, and Aida Refugee Camp, the West Bank; social media practices of offering condolences and memorials for Palestinians killed by Israeli soldiers or police; and practices surrounding Palestinian political prison. In each case the expressive is only one dimension of these practices: They also yield other results, such as drawing Palestinian communities together, physically challenging the Israeli army, enjoying the outdoors, or reckoning with the threat of state violence. Across the book, I trace three factors: First, I look at how Israeli laws, policies, and cultural norms restrict Palestinians differently within Israel's 1948 borders as opposed to in the West Bank. Second, I attend to how the Palestinians about whom I write are affected by these laws, policies, and norms, and how this shapes what I think of as their political habitus, or embodied sense of how to undertake political practice, as well as their structures of feelings, affective orientations to the political world that are in the process of taking shape.[10] Finally, I write about what these moments say about Palestinians' relationships to each other across settler colonial boundaries, whether the relationships are hinted at or imagined, whether they are comfortable or awkward, whether they are driven primarily by political ideology or they are rooted in chosen forms of kinship or love.

These chapters draw upon participant-observation in public spaces as well as in the photography exchange that I organized, media analysis, and interviews with activists, former prisoners, and others. They also draw on my own experiences in particular Palestinian places on either side of the Green Line and on the road between those places. This is emplaced knowledge, and it is also knowledge made in motion. I have not sought to find "equivalent" or "representative" places for comparison across the Green Line, as this would be impossible. Palestinian places are fractally "intra-connected, like in a kaleidoscope" with relationships "not external but integral to their parts."[11] So, I draw upon several locations on either side of the Green Line, recognizing their diversity and specificity. In the West Bank, I was based around Bethlehem, conducting research primarily in that city, in Aida Refugee Camp, and in Al-Walaja village, while inside Israel's 1948 territories, I spent time in Jaffa, the northern Galilee village of Tarshiha, and other places where relevant protests and commemorations occurred. Rather than a claim of comprehensiveness, I offer this volume as an invitation to others to continue to do research and activism that brings Palestinian places into relation in new ways.

Looking at commemorations, protests, comedy sketches, and cartoons, we can find elements of Palestinian political heritage that link practices across the Green Line. Ethnography also reveals what impedes these two groups of Palestinians from speaking to and acting with each other. Yet, this is not only a book about the conditions for speaking together. Just as important, I want to interrogate the model of political expression in which political speech should have one clear center. More than a century after the consolidation of modern Palestinian nationalism, and decades after the start of the Palestinian Revolution, Palestinians find themselves in a political crisis. The Oslo Accords of 1993 were meant to lead smoothly to a Palestinian state that many hoped would be the central instrument in resolving Palestinians' claims. In the decades since, Israeli occupation has continued, its violence only accelerating, while the PA has grown corrupt, autocratic, and complicit with Israeli occupation.[12] It has been unable to narrate Palestinian perspectives even in dire moments.[13] Other Palestinian political institutions have faded to the background. The Oslo agreements have entrenched a neoliberal politics that sidelines poor Palestinians more than ever. Israeli society has moved further to the right. Refugees outside of historic Palestine have suffered new displacements and another generation of dispossession.

In this context, as in others where nationalist projects have failed or faltered, or major collective ideological projects have fallen short, looking for other models of political expression and communication is an urgent task. Grassroots Palestinian action can enable speaking together on key Palestinian priorities like the right of return and the right to equality, but this does not necessitate speaking in unison. We can instead think about political expression that thrives in its multivocality, that aims to enable other Palestinian expression, and that is rooted in place and community experience even as it is connected to a broader Palestinian narrative of dispossession and struggle for liberation. I found that examples of this kind of expression often occurred on the periphery of well-organized political events. They more often came to the fore in Israel than in the West Bank since the West Bank is the troubled center of Palestinian politics today. Ethnography can attend to the political experiences and perspectives of poor people instead of only to the elite,[14] and looking at class and decoloniality can benefit from reflexivity.[15] Modeling how to look for political expression that helps to renew collectivities or create other kinds of collectivities—ones that recognize power differences, vulnerabilities, embodied experience, and wisdom gained over time, even or especially in less than ideal circumstances—is a contribution that I hope can inform democratic movements and practice well beyond the intra-Palestinian conversation: between Palestinians and Jewish allies, among Palestinians and other people of color in the United States, and well beyond.

Settler colonial fragmentation and knowledge production

The divide between Palestinians who carry Israeli citizenship and Palestinians under Israeli military occupation in the West Bank is only one part of a much larger and more complex story of Palestinian geopolitical fragmentation. Though there have long been religious, geographic, ethnic, and class diversities and hierarchies within Levantine society, as well as cultural differences and strong senses of regionalism,[16] the primary engine of Palestinian fragmentation over the last seventy plus years has been Israeli settler colonialism. The war and violent expulsions of 1947 and 1948—what Palestinians call the Nakba, or catastrophe[17] —immediately fragmented Palestinians, such that they were geographically dispersed, ruled by several different authorities, and assigned different legal statuses. Following the 1967 war, Israeli sovereignty expanded to the rest of historic Palestine, with its occupation of the West Bank and Gaza Strip. By 2010, roughly the start of my research on this topic, Palestinians held a number of different legal statuses under Israeli sovereignty: citizenship, Jerusalem temporary residency, a Gaza PA identity card, and a West Bank PA identity card. In Southwest Asia and North Africa but outside of historic Palestine, Palestinian refugees carry different statuses as either registered with the United Nations Relief and Works Agency (UNRWA) or unregistered, and they carry different travel documents or passports depending on their country of residence.[18] Each of these groups faces some legal and physical barriers to speaking with other groups.

One way to think of the causes and consequences of geopolitical fragmentation is to conceive of how settler colonialism operates by controlling mobility. It is certainly true that the Nabka of 1948 was a crisis of displacement, but today, as that displacement continues, immobility cements displacement.[19] As Julie

Peteet argues, the creation of camps and enclaves has defined many Palestinians' experiences of immobility.[20] If settler colonial states seek to eliminate Indigenous peoples through multiple tactics, including genocide, displacement, and assimilation,[21] we can think of geopolitical fragmentation and immobilization as other means of eliminating Indigenous collectives.[22] Such geographic and legal fragmentation makes it difficult for colonized peoples to constitute themselves as a collective. Fragmentation can even make it difficult to identify colonized spaces.[23] Hence, here I focus on the political consequences of ongoing displacement and various states of immobility across different polities.

While fragmentation is often noted as a key dynamic in contemporary Palestinian politics in scholarly work and in art, its political implications have rarely been studied in depth.[24] In some cases, fragmentation almost comes to the center of public policy discussions. In 2017, prominent legal scholars Richard Falk and Virginia Tilley co-authored a UN-commissioned report that asserted:

> [T]he strategic fragmentation of the Palestinian people is the principal method by which Israel imposes an apartheid regime . . . This fragmentation operates to stabilize the Israeli regime of racial domination over the Palestinians and to weaken the will and capacity of the Palestinian people to mount a unified and effective resistance. Different methods are deployed depending on where Palestinians live. This is the core means by which Israel enforces apartheid and at the same time impedes international recognition of how the system works as a complementary whole to comprise an apartheid regime.[25]

But shortly after being issued, this report was rescinded following pressure from the Trump administration, including accusations that the report was "anti-Israel" from then US ambassador to the United Nations Nikki Haley.[26] One key instrument of US empire is to regulate the bounds of acceptable discourse in diplomatic circles. Critique of Israel's occupation is limited in many ways, but criticism of Israeli policies inside its 1948 territories is rarely made at all in the domains of international politics. Here, the analysis of how the two systems are related perhaps constituted a red flag. The rescinding of the report exemplifies how scholars have faced obstacles in addressing more than one Palestinian location, even if those two locations are adjacent and under the same sovereign power, as are the West Bank and Israel. Data are fragmented just as are communities. Knowledge production in these two locations is uneven. For refugees and stateless people, issues of falling between or outside of categories, or into more than one of them, are common, as are issues around poor quality of data collection.[27]

Nevertheless, in recent years, Palestinian, Israeli, and international human rights organizations including Al-Haq, Badil, B'Tselem, and Human Rights Watch have begun to issue reports that analyze Israeli rule across the Green Line, often using a framework of apartheid.[28] Building on the precedents of Palestinian and Israeli human rights organizations, Human Rights Watch wrote in January 2021:

> About 6.8 million Jewish Israelis and 6.8 million Palestinians live today between the Mediterranean Sea and Jordan River, an area encompassing Israel and the Occupied Palestinian Territory (OPT), the latter made up of the West Bank, including East Jerusalem, and the Gaza Strip. Throughout most of this area, Israel is the sole governing power; in the remainder, it exercises primary authority alongside limited Palestinian self-rule. Across these areas and in most aspects of life, Israeli authorities methodically privilege Jewish Israelis and discriminate against Palestinians.[29]

It remains to be seen how journalists and researchers will incorporate this new framework for analyzing Israeli rule. Too often, we take for granted states' definitions of places and populations, often taking these definitions to be neutral and fact-based.

For fieldwork-based methods, the asymmetries and barriers to knowledge production across two Palestinian locations can be especially pronounced. Even in an era when multi-sited ethnography[30] is held in high esteem, most research about both Palestinian societies and Israeli rule tends to locate itself in one Palestinian location, in part because of the practical difficulties of doing otherwise. The ways in which ethnographic research, especially on Palestinians, is shaped and limited by state politics, even as it is critical of those states, has begun to be the subject of anthropological inquiry.[31] But even these works have focused less on experiences in the field and more on experiences writing and teaching. Working in Israel and the West Bank, as I have done here, is one of the easier options for a multi-sited Palestinian ethnography. This is perhaps paradoxically because, despite the dozens of checkpoints apparently dividing Israel's 1948 territories and the West Bank, they are so interconnected. The Green Line between them is permeable for someone with my passports. Still, Israelis (including Palestinian citizens of Israel) are generally not legally permitted to enter the Palestinian areas of the West Bank. All will encounter red and white warning signs as they enter Palestinian areas of the West Bank. Palestinians of the West Bank can be harshly punished for entering Israel's 1948 territories without a permit—and there are no research permits, out of the dozens of available permits.[32] Some visitors, upon entering Israel, have received visas that specify that they cannot go to Palestinian areas of the West Bank; other visitors have been permitted to only go to the West Bank and not to Israel.[33] The methodological constraints to conducting research in Israel and the West Bank in some regards mirror the obstacles that inhibit interaction between Palestinian citizens of Israel and Palestinians in the West Bank. Were one to attempt to extend this ethnographic project to Gaza, which has been under Israeli blockade since 2007 within the ongoing Israeli military occupation,[34] it would take inordinate amounts of logistical acrobatics, coordination with Israeli authorities, and good luck, given the constraints on entering and leaving Gaza. Adding a Lebanese field site would depend on one's passport, since Israel regards Lebanon as an enemy state and bans Israeli citizens from entering without a special permit.

There are conceptual barriers to working in more than one Palestinian location as well. Related to the predominance of what has been called "methodological nationalism" in which the "national framing of states and societies" is too often assumed, rather than examined,[35] scholars and others tend to take for granted states' own definitions of their territories and allow themselves to settle in one place for analysis of the domestic, rather than to interrogate the idea of the domestic itself. As I explore in Chapter 1, there is no Palestine existing as a sovereign state, and because of Palestinians' large refugee and diasporic populations, Palestinian places far exceed any definition of what such a state of Palestine might be. Studies of Palestinians should thus be especially well inclined toward challenging methodological nationalism. Similarly, Indigenous people, critical scholars of indigeneity, and scholars of borderlands have long challenged states' definitions of the domestic. Studying mobility—practices of mobility and the policing of it, especially at borders—is one way of challenging methodological nationalism.[36] One key task of settler colonial studies is to interrogate different forms of colonial sovereignties as they actually operate and sustain one another, and to explore the relationship between colonial and noncolonial (or apparently postcolonial) sovereignties.

In fact, the very frame of Israeli occupation promotes what Ilan Pappé calls "a false separation between Israel and the occupied areas . . . and produces the unacceptable dichotomy between 'democratic' Israel and the 'non-democratic'

Occupied Territories."[37] Even the name "Israel" as used to refer only to the territories Israel attained as a result of the 1948 war becomes part of the obfuscation, since Israeli sovereignty extends over the occupied territories and has for over a half century (and more than two-thirds of Israel's existence as a modern state). This is why, when I refer to that territory, I will often call it "Israel's 1948 territories," or refer to it as "inside the Green Line." To adapt an argument of political scientist Philip Abrams, "Israel" and other states are better regarded as ideas rather than as particular territories.[38] It is this conceptual division between Israel's 1948 territories and the occupied territories that often allows analysts to treat Palestinian citizens of Israel as a "minority"—whether ethnic or Indigenous—while treating Palestinians in the occupied territories as a people whose right to self-determination has been scuttled by foreign occupation, rather than conceiving their concerns as deeply connected, along with those of Palestinian refugees outside of these areas. As for the term "Palestine," one could say it takes a chapter (the first one) to unpack my decision to use it in the way that I have chosen here. In terms of other placenames, I use the English version of the placenames (that is, Jerusalem rather than Al-Quds or Yerushalayim) except when those placenames are not in wide use, and in those cases I use the Arabic placenames followed by the Hebrew ones, since my interlocutors in this book would be using the Arabic ones.

Discussing Palestinian fragmentation also requires a language to specify different Palestinian groups, yet many Palestinians reject most of the labels assigned to them. Palestinians who hold Israeli citizenship are sometimes called "Arab Israelis," referred to by their religious affiliations, or even called "non-Jews."[39] All of these negate Palestinian collectivity, as does the frequent designation of Bedouins as something other than Palestinian. A shrewd way of designating Palestinians is by the year they came under Israeli rule: Many Palestinians use the designations "'48 Palestinians" for Palestinians who hold Israeli citizenship and "'67 Palestinians" for those in the occupied territories. This designation is a shorthand Palestinian way of "historiz[ing] political identities" to show that it is colonialism that fundamentally divides Palestinians.[40] However, for the sake of this book, the fact that I am focusing on Palestinians in the West Bank rather than those in Gaza makes the "'67 Palestinians" label less transparent. The term "Palestinian citizen of Israel" is a legally apt descriptive phrase, but Palestinians in Israel sometimes bristle under this designation because they are systematically discriminated against and do not feel like citizens. It is an unfortunate fact that many citizens around the world lack legal equality.

A juridical lack of citizenship—statelessness or residency without citizenship—poses challenges distinct from what is sometimes informally called second- or third-class citizenship. For these reasons, "Palestinian citizens of Israel" is a phrase that I find useful. Still, in referring to Palestinians in Israel's 1948 territories as "Palestinian citizens of Israel," I'm aware that, while this is legally correct, it may be a misplacement of emphasis. I think of Yarimar Bonilla's tweet in the wake of Hurricane Maria, as US media commentators often referred to people in Puerto Rico as though they were foreigners and progressives reminded those commentators that people in Puerto Rico are US citizens. Bonilla wrote, "Dear allies: when feeling the need to assert that Puerto Ricans are 'fellow US citizens,' take a moment and ask yourself if what really needs to be asserted is that the US is an empire." Citizenship here too is a juridical quality, but we must recognize that there are severe gradations in citizenship, legally and culturally, including in countries that call themselves democracies.[41] The geographic designations "Palestinians inside the Green Line" and "Palestinians in the West Bank" sometimes seems apt, as many of the phenomena I describe are place specific. The fact that it takes multiple words to name a group (and paragraphs to explain what are, in the end, imperfect choices) should signal the tensions and discomforts around identity and naming, which are indeed a significant part of the story I am describing.

It should be obvious, then, that the difficulties of naming people and places are not only a practical challenge but also of analytical significance and even emotional resonance. In short, I have sought in my naming practices to be clear both from the perspective of description of actual territorial control and by following convention enough that those new to this topic will find the terminology accessible—though these goals are in tension. I have sought to be sensitive to interlocutors' preferences but not ideological in a way that would become a barrier to readers or that would negate other relationships to the places involved. My efforts here can also be seen as an attempt to balance what are sometimes called the "emic" (insider) and "etic" (outsider) perspectives, to put this in an anthropological language that shows that my conundrum is hardly unique—but it is also true that there are multiple insiders and outsiders with different stakes, and others in between.

Finally, I want to emphasize that in proposing a critique of fragmentation, I do not want to naturalize unity. To do so might be to presume or advocate for a nationalism that can also become a structure of oppression. Instead, I suggest thinking along the lines of partial connections.[42] The separation between

Palestinian groups is at once constitutive and integrative of them. Writing about a different set of relations constituted through colonialism, Marisol de la Cadena similarly explores how partial connection as a way of disrupting easy claims of unity or difference calls attention to relation and dislodges oversimplified comparison across difference: "emerging from the relation, entities are intra-related."[43] Importantly, while in this book I am thinking about Palestinians through a lens of partial connection, with this lens we can imagine other partially connected groups in Israel and the occupied territories: alongside Palestinians, Mizrahi Jews, non-Jewish migrants, Jewish refugees and their descendants, and, surely, others. I want to move beyond imaginings of political community through models of descent and sameness, as in those famous old arboreal metaphors.[44] Though they are both under Israeli sovereignty, Palestinians in Israel and the West Bank are not exactly part of the same polity—whether that polity is defined as the Israeli one or the Palestinian one—but their political projects are not separate either. We need only to think of the Palestinian political split between Gaza and the West Bank, of the fact that the majority of Palestinians today live outside of historic Palestine, and of the great diversity of Palestinian cultures and values within both Israel and the West Bank to recognize that to truly think about Palestinian fragmentation we must speak of much more than two Palestinian political formations. But to zoom in, as this book does, on the dynamic between Palestinian citizens of Israel and Palestinians in the West Bank—the vertiginous shifting of centers and peripheries, the different but related experiences of Israeli rule—the formulation of political worlds that are "partially connected" is illuminating.

"They kill you with bullets, but they kill us with the pen, with law."

In March 2014, I drove to the town of Qalansawe for a rally on the occasion of Land Day, a Palestinian national commemoration of protests against land confiscations in the Galilee (northern Israel) in 1976, during which Israeli police killed six Palestinians. One of the people featured at the rally, who I call Karam, was a Qalansawe native and Israeli citizen who lived with his family in a house with no glass in its window frames. He had owned land on the outskirts of town, but this land had not been zoned for residence. Israeli zoning plans in Palestinian towns like Qalansawe often make it impossible for towns to expand.[45] Lacking other options, he had built his home without permits. About a year earlier, Israeli authorities had delivered demolition orders to him and his family, and now they were threatened with homelessness.

I spoke to Karam at a dinner after the rally, and he introduced me to his twelve-year-old nephew, who lived with him. His nephew's teacher, he told me, had recently come to him with a complaint. His schoolwork was generally written in such good handwriting, but his homework was so difficult to read. The uncle explained to me, as he had to her, that this was because at home, his nephew wrote by lantern light. They had no networked electricity. They had neither long-term security nor short-term comfort. I imagined that my friends in the West Bank refugee camp where I was staying would be shocked to hear this story. Grownups there told their own stories of doing homework outdoors to escape crowded homes where there had not been electricity years ago. And many of their houses had been damaged in Israeli incursions during the second Intifada in the first years of the new century. But when this happened, they could ask UNRWA for assistance to rebuild. Now, everyone had windows and electricity in this camp.[46]

When I asked for directions back to Bethlehem, the response was vague, as though I were asking about going someplace far away indeed. But it did spark a conversation about the relationship between Palestinian citizens of Israel and Palestinians in the West Bank. "I told a friend of mine from the West Bank, 'You have it easier than us,'" Karam recalled.

My friend was surprised. But I said, "For you, you get shot and become a martyr. For us, it's the slow death of solitary confinement [al-zinzāna]. When you die a martyr, you go to heaven, but when your house is destroyed, they throw you to the street. They kill you with bullets, but they kill us with the pen, with law."

His words about the deadly quality of Israeli rule for both groups stayed with me.

I also wanted to complicate any dichotomy presented. If the paradigmatic image of the Palestinian child is of a stone-throwing youth, like Fares Odeh of Gaza who famously stood in front of a tank at the beginning of the first Intifada, a key image of a Palestinian child who is a citizen of Israel is perhaps from the poster from Elia Suleiman's 2009 fiction feature film *Time That Remains*, of a boy bowing his head while being reprimanded by the principal for a nationalist expression. (It is notable also that while there are truly famous images of Palestinian children under occupation, there are not equivalent images of Palestinian children holding Israeli citizenship, because they are less often regarded as political subjects and, for non-Palestinian audiences, less often seen as relevant to international politics.) This dichotomy between the stone thrower and the refusing student is an important starting point for analysis, but moving beyond a dichotomy is essential, as well. While Israel oppresses Palestinians in the occupied territories more uniformly with what Achille Mbembe calls necropolitical rule,[47] Israel uses a variety of mechanisms to govern Palestinian citizens of Israel that include the necropolitical but also encompass the disciplinary and governmentality.[48]

Karam's comment made me wonder: What is the relationship between bullets and law under Israeli rule? Israel presents itself as a beacon of regional democracy that would grant all citizens access to a liberal public sphere, but this formulation misses a few key points. Not only does it ignore that Israel also rules over Palestinians in the occupied territories who have no rights of citizenship, and has for over half a century, it also obscures that settler colonial conditions of militarism, imprisonment, walls, checkpoints, and spatial and legal fragmentation make conditions of expression and political participation difficult for Palestinian citizens, too.

This should also train our attention on the coloniality of borders themselves. A burgeoning scholarship on those who cross borders and on walls that enforce borders recognizes the violence borders promote and enable.[49] The Green Line—the 1949 armistice line that divides and delineates the West Bank and Israel's 1948 territories—is one element that upholds the appearance of Israeli democracy and allows for certain kinds of violence to proliferate in the occupied territories. But in fact, it has long been essential to acknowledge the "one state condition," the fact of one sovereign regime, that belies Israel's claim to democracy.[50] We too seldom question when borders delimit who should be allowed to participate in a public, even among people who are committed to remaining in conversation. What about state power, settler colonialism, and militarism is obscured by the apparent naturalness of state borders as we tend to see them in dominant political representations, such as mainstream news and international law?

The slippage between Israel as a set of institutions and concepts and Israel's 1948 territories (sometimes referred to as "Israel proper" by those who want to point out that Israel also controls the occupied Palestinian territories) is one element of what I call a "sleight of hand sovereignty,"[51] by which sovereignties are layered in such a way as to obfuscate who is responsible where. Various parties, ranging from the British Mandate and Egyptian rule[52] to the Israeli state and finally the Palestinian Authority administration, have with a shrewd sleight of hand at once asserted and denied their sovereignty over Palestinian populations. The appearance of Palestinian sovereignty in parts of the occupied territories not only shores up the corrupt oligopoly of the PA, it also defers Israeli responsibility for circumstances in the West Bank and Gaza and allows Israel to treat Palestinians—especially in Gaza—as an external enemy and thus to exercise more extreme forms of violence against them. Sleight of hand sovereignty serves to sustain Israel's occupation.

On the level of territory, the Green Line that divides Israel's 1948 territories from the West Bank is itself the product of sleight of hand. The Green Line was a military armistice line and has not been fully recognized as an international border.[53] The 709-kilometer separation wall ostensibly built to prevent Palestinians of the West Bank from entering Israel further fudges or smudges the Green Line because about 85 percent of the barrier is built within the West Bank,[54] such that many settlers living in the "seam zone" between the barrier and the Green Line do not feel that they are living in occupied territory.[55] Quite apart from the smudging of the Green Line, Israel is the sovereign over not only its 1948 territories but also the occupied territories of the West Bank and Gaza, since it controls who and what enters and leaves, and since it has the greatest control over the forms of violence exercised in those territories. As we will see, the PA has its own reasons for taking part in this "sleight of hand sovereignty." In short, without these games, its complicity with Israeli occupation would be impossible to mask. The phenomenon of sleight of hand sovereignty is not distinct to Israel and the PA, though—the US uses similar tricks of where it is and is not sovereign to carry out extraordinary rendition of prisoners, manage foreign military bases and prisons, and carry out drone attacks—practices of war that would not be acceptable against its domestic population.[56] Importantly, there are nevertheless connections between US domestic and international forms of violence; for the United States as well, one enables the other.[57]

In presenting an overview of the political status of Palestinian citizens of Israel and those subject to Israeli military occupation in the West Bank, I find myself moving back and forth across the Green Line. Comparison here is a provocation rather than a presumption that these two Palestinian groups constitute separate and homogenous units.[58] Those Palestinians who stayed within what became Israel in 1948 numbered about 160,000, or approximately 15 percent of the Palestinian population.[59] About 800,000 Palestinians became refugees in Gaza, the West Bank, Lebanon, Syria, Jordan, and Egypt,[60] where they have had various political statuses. Palestinians who stayed in their homes in the West Bank and refugees who fled there came under Jordanian rule and were given Jordanian citizenship; residents of Gaza and refugees who fled to Gaza fell under Egyptian administration. In 1951, UNRWA was established to address the needs of those displaced in 1948 and their descendants; most of these people were registered as refugees. The 1967 occupation of the West Bank and Gaza brought Palestinians in these two territories under Israeli military control. Especially since the Oslo Accords, Israel's bureaucratic and physical policies of closure and, since 2007, a military siege of Gaza have separated the West Bank, Gaza, and Israel from each other, and isolated East Jerusalem from the rest of the West Bank. In the West Bank, checkpoints, a discriminatory road system, and the separation wall also isolate villages, camps, and cities from each other.[61] From initial displacements, colonial and other state forms of violence and categorization have multiplied Palestinian statuses in a process we can think of through a fractal recursive logic, by which "the dichotomizing and partitioning process that was involved in some understood opposition . . . recurs at other levels" creating new subcategories.[62] The divisions themselves reveal how power operates in the prevailing system of nation-states.

After the establishment of Israel in 1948, Palestinians in Israel found themselves in what one Palestinian analyst called a state of "total defeat and shocking loss."[63] They dealt with a stunning depopulation of Arab urban spaces in places like Jaffa and Haifa. Zionist forces terrified or forcibly expelled people living in 531 Palestinian villages, and Israeli officials then prohibited them from returning.[64] About forty thousand Palestinians in the north and center parts of what became Israel were displaced from their homes but stayed within the boundaries of what became Israel.[65] The majority of Bedouin of the Naqab / Negev region in the south were also displaced from their family and tribal lands.[66] Palestinians in what became Israel were cut off from Palestinian cities and villages in Gaza and the West Bank, including Jerusalem, and they were isolated from relatives, friends, and associates who became refugees. Moreover, these Palestinians lived under Israeli military rule from 1948 through 1966— a similar legal structure as Palestinians in the West Bank and Gaza have been living under since 1967.[67]

Today, Palestinians make up 20 percent of the population of Israel's citizens. Palestinian citizens of Israel enjoy some of the basic privileges of Israeli citizenship such as voting, movement, and access to Israel's social service network. Despite such privileges relative to Palestinian subjects of military occupation in the West Bank, Palestinian citizens are nonetheless systematically discriminated against within Israel. The Palestinian human rights organization Adalah maintains a database of laws that discriminate against Palestinians; there are currently over sixty-five of them.[68] Since the turn of the new century a "new Zionist hegemony" has been established that constitutes what Nadim Rouhana and Nimer Sultany call a "consensus within Israeli society in support of new discriminatory policies and practices toward the Palestinian minority."[69]

Israel has also perpetuated policies of division among Palestinians. Israeli media policies and the inclusion of Druze in Israel's military draft have led to an ideology of "Druze particularism" in Israel.[70] Israel has also tried to recruit other Palestinian groups to join the military, such that, as Rhoda Kanaaneh has written, "the state has created a hierarchy within the Arab community: Druze are at the top followed by Bedouins, and then Christians. . . . By calling these groups Druze, Bedouins, Christians, and Arabs, the state tries to imply that the Druze, Bedouins, and Christians are other than Arab."[71] While Israel has tried to deny their collective national identity, a new generation of Palestinian citizens of Israel has increasingly demanded collective rights through creative expression, popular activism, and legal cases.[72] Over the last decades, and trending from the 1970s, they have been identifying more strongly as Palestinians in Israel or Palestinian citizens of Israel, rather than as Arab Israelis.[73]

While identification as Palestinian is on the rise, many politically active Palestinians in Israel and those in the West Bank have long asserted that they—along with other Palestinians in Gaza and outside of historic Palestine—share a single political struggle for national liberation. The founding declaration of the Al-Ard movement of Palestinian citizens of Israel in 1959 stated, "We are a part of the Palestinian people, who are in turn a part of the Arab nation,"[74] and this language was echoed in declarations of the early 2000s issued by Palestinian civil society institutions, as well. As the Haifa Declaration, crafted through the premier Palestinian research center in Israel within the Green Line, Mada Al-Carmel, proclaimed:

> Our national identity is grounded in human values and civilization, in the Arabic language and culture, and in a collective memory derived from our Palestinian and Arab history and Arab and Islamic civilization. It is an identity that grows ever more firm through active and continuous interaction with these values. It is continuously nourished by our uninterrupted relationship to our land and homeland, by the experience of our constant and mounting struggle

to affirm our right to remain in our land and homeland and to safeguard them, and by our continued connection to the other sons and daughters of the Palestinian people and the Arab nation.[75]

Related statements, made by and through the National Committee for the Heads of the Arab Local Authorities in Israel[76] and Adalah[77] offer remarkable unison on this stance.[78] In the spring of 2021, the Manifesto of Dignity and Hope, proclaimed on a historic day of general strike, declared, "The story of truth is a simple one in our land: the truth is that Palestinians are one people, one society." It described fragmentation through a metaphor of incarceration:

> This is how Israel imprisoned us in prisons of isolation; some of us caged in the "Oslo prison" in the West Bank, some in the "citizenship prison" in the part of Palestine occupied in 1948, some of us isolated by the monstrous siege and ongoing, devastating assault on the "Gaza prison," some of us isolated under the systematic Judaization campaigns on the "Jerusalem prison," and some isolated from Palestine altogether, dispersed across all corners of the globe.[79]

The statement did not have a clear authorship from a political party or civil society institution, but it sprung from Palestinians in historic Palestine and reached all of those Palestinian groups through its wide circulation on social media.

In terms of their place in Palestinian politics and cultural production, Palestinian citizens of Israel are prominent in Palestinian literary, music, and film cultures. Palestinian citizens of Israel have contributed to a culture of activism, as well. The response of Palestinian citizens of Israel to a massacre of people protesting land confiscations in 1976 led to the establishment of Land Day, a pivotal day of national commemoration that Palestinians everywhere now mark. Both in daily life and in their political writing and activism, most Palestinian citizens of Israel have maintained their use of the Arabic language, despite the Israeli state's attempts at stripping them of their cultural heritage. Today, many Palestinians recognize a resurgence in activism inside Israel's 1948 territories, such that while the official center of Palestinian politics continues to be in the occupied territories, a vibrant space of resistance thrives in places like Haifa and the Naqab / Negev.[80]

Legal scholar Nimer Sultany points out that Palestinian citizens of Israel are losing their political rights today, such that the distinctions between Palestinians in Israel and Palestinians in the occupied territories is becoming less clear.

As these twin processes of the ghettoization of the Palestinian citizens and the bantustanization of the Palestinian non-citizens unfold, the legal line between the citizen and the non-citizen will continue to blur. The Palestinians in Israel are occupied citizens, and the residents of the Occupied Territories are unrecognized citizens. Whether or not the legal line survives may be immaterial, however, as the effect is likely to be the same—the continuing subordination of the Palestinians.[81]

Integrative approaches to Israel's land policies, too, suggest that Israel has one overarching system of dispossessing Palestinians.[82] The passing of the Nation State Law of 2018 is another step in this process, because it applies to both sides of the Green Line. It declares that only Jewish people have the right to self-determination, not only in Israel's 1948 territories but also in the occupied territories, and affirms Jewish settlement as a foundational value in both Israel's 1948 territories and in the occupied territories.[83] The Israeli Supreme Court upheld the law following a court challenge in 2021.[84] The degradation of Palestinians' rights inside the Green Line is making clearer for all Israel's single system of rule over its 1948 territories and those it occupied in 1967.

Finally, Palestinian citizens of Israel are doubly marginalized. They are certainly excluded by the Zionist project of building a Jewish state, but they are also marginalized by hegemonic Palestinian nationalism, which has transformed from a liberation project that in some way addressed all Palestinians into (as PA officials would put it) a project for state-building in the occupied Palestinian territories of the West Bank and Gaza, or, as many critics correctly see the PA, a repressive institution complicit with the Israeli occupation.

For their part, Palestinians in the West Bank today number 2.8 million, with another 1.7 million Palestinians living under occupation in the Gaza Strip. After 1948, Palestinians in the West Bank lived under Jordanian control until 1967, when Israel occupied the West Bank, Gaza, Sinai, and the Golan Heights. They have lived under Israeli military occupation of various forms for over fifty years now. While the term "military occupation" is widely used, and carries a specific legal status, it has been contested because according to international law military occupations are supposed to be temporary. As United Nations Special Rapporteur Michael Lynk writes,

The prevailing approach of the international community has been to treat Israel as the lawful occupant of the Palestinian territory, albeit an occupant that has committed a number of grave breaches of international law in its conduct of the occupation, including the settlement enterprise, the construction of the wall, the annexation of East Jerusalem and the systematic violations of Palestinian human rights. In the view of the Special Rapporteur, while the lawful occupation approach may have been the appropriate diplomatic and legal portrayal of the occupation in its early years, it has since become wholly inadequate. . . . In the present report, the Special Rapporteur considers whether Israel's role as an entrenched and defiant occupant of the Palestinian territory has now reached the point of illegality under international law.[85]

Ilan Pappé argues Israel's occupation is more totalizing than other military occupations and conceives of the occupied territories as a "mega-prison."[86] As Sahar Francis writes, "Israel's military commander has issued thousands of military orders impinging on every aspect of Palestinian life and regulating its every detail."[87] Military occupation strips Palestinians in the occupied territories of basic rights to, for example, due process and movement, and systematically constrains and endangers their lives every day.

In 1994, the Palestinian Authority was established in accordance with the Oslo Accords between Israel and the Palestine Liberation Organization (PLO) to administer Gaza and parts of the West Bank. As Diana Buttu writes, the agreement had three main effects:

> First, it cemented Israel's apartheid regime. Second, it established a means by which Israel could separate itself from Palestinians while continuing to hold onto Palestinian land and demanding that Palestinians crush any resistance to Israel's colonial rule. And third, it established negotiations as the only legitimate means to end Israel's military rule with other options, whether resistance (armed or otherwise) and BDS [Boycott, Divestment, and Sanctions], criminalized or labeled as illegitimate. These effects will take decades to undo, particularly as the Palestinian economy is now heavily dependent on the existence of the Palestinian Authority, which is, in turn dependent upon donor funds.[88]

Indeed, Palestinians know the PA is much less than a state, since it is noncontiguous and unable to regulate the flow of goods and people. Israel's system of closure, which is made up of checkpoints, walls, fences, restricted roads, and a system of permits,[89]—what Diana Buttu calls "a process of containment sold as 'territorial jurisdiction' "[90]—is a product of the Oslo Accords. Moreover, the PA lacks full security control over the territory purportedly under its jurisdiction and is unable to guarantee even the basic functioning of the representative mechanisms of government, since many elected officials have been arrested by Israel. Even so, since its establishment, the PA has attacked opponents and endangered free expression.[91] Moreover, the PA operates in security coordination with the Israeli occupation,[92] effectively acting as a subcontractor for Israel. Israel has tried to force upon PA leaders the same kind of recognition of Israel as a Jewish state as is codified in the Nation State Law, but Palestinian leadership has thus far resisted at least this capitulation.[93]

These two groups of Palestinians—citizens of Israel and subjects of military occupation—share a great deal in terms of their public cultures. But they are separated by legal system and political geography within a single sovereign regime. Due to Israel's system of closure, few Palestinians in the West Bank can enter Israel's 1948 territories. Palestinian citizens of Israel can go to the West Bank, but they have to pass by a rather ominous street sign: "This Road leads to Area 'A' under the Palestinian Authority. The Entrance for Israeli citizens is Forbidden, dangerous to your lives and is against the Israeli law." This is one of many official Israeli state messages that will be read quite differently by most Jewish Israelis than by most Palestinian citizens of Israel. For the former it is a pragmatic marker of space, a warning about safety. For most Palestinians in Israel, it is another level of threat and surveillance of the sort to which they are quite accustomed.[94]

However, as I conducted this research, I was somewhat surprised to realize that even the contemporary differences between Israel's rule over Palestinian citizens of Israel and its rule over Palestinians in the West Bank are less different than they may first appear to be. While in some regards Israel holds these two groups apart from one another, it is also true that the modes of violence deployed against one Palestinian population depend on the modes of violence deployed against other Palestinian populations: These spaces are by no means the same, but they are interrelated.

If, as we will see, Palestinian citizens of Israel and Palestinians in the West Bank are profoundly hindered in their ability to speak together, they have some ability to connect in the economic realm. Despite those warning signs posted at the entrance to PA areas, many Palestinian citizens of Israel do go to the West Bank for shopping and recreation. Palestinians from the West Bank enter Israel to work, especially in construction and as domestic workers, and they encounter Palestinian citizens of Israel in this work.[95] Palestinian citizens of Israel also go to the West Bank, especially Bethlehem and Jericho, for tourism and even, in 2006, to escape Hizballah rocket fire that pummeled the Galilee.

Some Palestinian Muslims who hold Israeli citizenship have committed to a devotional practice that protects holy sites in Israeli-occupied East Jerusalem.[96] Palestinian citizens of Israel and those in the West Bank are also involved in musical,[97] poetic,[98] artistic, academic,[99] and other realms together. Yet, there are limits to these shared spaces.

The dispossession of discourse

As lawyer and scholar Suhad Bishara writes in an article about the criminalization of Palestinian politics for Palestinian citizens of Israel, "The Nakba dispossesses Palestinians: not only of land and territory, but also at the level of political discourse."[100] Palestinians in these two locations experience different limitations on expression. Palestinian citizens of Israel face obstacles to expression because Israel is increasingly using laws and policy to constitute and enforce a Zionist environment for expression—or a Zionist public—in Israel, thus marginalizing Palestinians as a collective within a state that, from a Zionist perspective, is meant to be Jewish. In the West Bank, Israel does not so much restrict what Palestinians can say, as it does for citizens of Israel; instead, it places barriers to forms of expression that can be heard or registered in Israel at all. It makes sure they are not allowed to participate in an Israeli public. It also physically endangers journalists and others especially in times of heightened conflict. While these differences are undoubtedly important, it is also true that legally and socio-politically, a hard line cannot be drawn between limitations on expression in Israel and the West Bank. Legally, this blurring occurs because many of the relevant laws come from British Mandate Emergency Regulations.[101] They were the foundation for occupation law for Palestinians in Israel from 1948 to 1966 and for Palestinians in the occupied territories after 1967. These laws are also a foundation for Israel's state of emergency, which has been in effect since Israel's establishment.[102] Culturally and politically, this blurring surely occurs because forms of violence, repression, and racism tend to expand beyond their formal bounds.

In Israel, since its earliest days, the state-supported press addressed Palestinians through Arabic language media as an attempt to create a quiescent minority population.[103] In this atmosphere, as Maha Nassar describes in a crucial recent history, Palestinian intellectuals took several steps to sustain resistance, including engaging with state media to the extent they were able, creating new Arabic-language local media, smuggling in Arab press from outside Israel, and creating a vibrant local press, even under circumstances of censorship.[104] A long history of restricting Palestinian journalists produced a situation in which editors and journalists were constantly negotiating a dynamic between confrontation and accommodation in order to maintain space for political expression.[105] When Palestinian critiques became too threatening to the state, Israel used arrests and denials of permits to shut down Palestinian media.[106] Israeli television broadcasting—which was, in its early decades, fully state-run, as was the case in many countries—was structured around a Jewish sense of the public, promoting Jewish Israeli culture while seeking only to meet the "needs" of Arab populations.[107] This is an example of the way in which, in its early years, Israel treated Jews as part of a national group while it treated Palestinians, at best, as individual citizens.[108] In the 1990s, these patterns continued in new ways as new televisual technologies, like satellite television, emerged.[109] Amit Schejter writes about this as the "muting of democracy."[110]

Under military occupation, constraints on the press have taken on a somewhat different form. From 1967 until the establishment of the PA in 1994, Israel imposed a system of prior censorship over Palestinian publications, such that an Israeli military censor reviewed all Palestinian newspapers before their publication and demanded removal of whatever material they found to be objectionable.[111] This system disappeared under the PA. Tellingly, not only are the rules behind this system of censorship (which date from the British Mandatory Emergency Regulations) still formally on the books, but they were never actually limited to the occupied territories. Hebrew-language Israeli publications also legally operated and continue to operate under the watch of military censors, but they are only censored on very limited occasions. Palestinian media were thus under a spectrum of forms of control. Under the tightest constraints were media in the West Bank and Gaza, followed by Palestinian media based in Jerusalem. English-language Palestinian publications had somewhat more leeway, followed by the Arabic-language Israeli Communist Party paper, and then the non-Arab press inside Israel's 1948 territories.[112]

Since 1994, the PA has also repressed journalists in a number of ways. From the early years of the Oslo Accords, demands for unity in support for the nationalist movement were employed as modes of repressing criticism of the PA.[113] As Amal Jamal wrote in 2005, "The PA's lack of sovereignty puts it in a position where it must violate the democratic right of freedom of expression and move against the opposition movements in the hope that it will thereby advance the chances for progress in the peace process."[114] After Fatah's loss in the 2006 elections and its consolidation of power in the West Bank in 2007, the

PA became still more repressive of dissenting voices.[115] A recent internet press freedoms law is especially dangerous for journalists and activists.[116] Today, the PA in the West Bank operates in close coordination with Israeli authorities to repress dissent.[117]

In the 2000s and 2010s, laws have increasingly limited the space for Palestinian expression inside Israel's 1948 territories. A 2002 amendment to the Basic Law of Israel prohibits political party platforms that "deny the existence of the State of Israel as a Jewish and democratic state."[118] In 2011, Israel passed an amendment that authorizes a reduction in state funding to institutions that hold activities rejecting Israel's existence as a "Jewish and democratic state" or that commemorate "Israel's Independence Day or the day on which the state was established as a day of mourning."[119] Even without any prosecutions under the law, Palestinian lawyer Sawsan Zaher asserts the law "has been used as an excuse to limit freedom of expression. It has a chilling effect."[120] Nevertheless, the Israeli Supreme Court, once regarded as a potential source for advancing civil liberties claims for Palestinians, declined to hear a case on this issue.[121]

Such laws have made it especially difficult to organize across the Green Line. For example, in the occupied territories, the Boycott, Divestment, and Sanctions (BDS) campaign is one of the most visible and vibrant grassroots Palestinian campaigns. The BDS call renewed by Palestinian civil society within the West Bank in 2005 builds on over a century of Palestinian history.[122] The current call for BDS, moreover, integrates a call for equality for Palestinians in Israel, a right to return for Palestinian refugees, and an end to the military occupation of the West Bank and Gaza, and thereby addresses the claims of Palestinians in multiple places. Yet, support for this campaign is dangerous in Israel. In 2011, the Israeli Knesset passed a law prohibiting public promotion of boycotts against Israeli institutions or settlements. The law allows for civil lawsuits against proponents of a boycott to be filed by those purporting to have been harmed.

Israel has systematically marginalized and criminalized Palestinian political participation within Israel, repressing both movements (like Al-Ard, the Land movement of the 1960s) and individuals of a variety of ideological backgrounds.[123] A 2016 law allows a supermajority of Knesset members to expel other elected members of the Knesset for: (1) denial of the existence of Israel as a Jewish and democratic state; (2) incitement to racism (charges that are deployed disproportionately against Palestinians); or (3) support for armed struggle of an enemy state or a terrorist organization against Israel. Court cases have threatened leading Palestinian politicians with the revocation of their citizenship.[124] In 2015, Israel illegalized the Northern Branch of the Islamic Party, and it has periodically imprisoned its leader, Sheikh Raed Salah.[125]

Military law in the occupied territories also criminalizes Palestinian politics there. Since 2006, Israel has arrested many Palestinian parliamentary members. In 2009, almost one in three of all legislators were held in Israeli prisons,[126] many under administrative detention, a way of imprisoning people indefinitely without charge. As a report by the Palestinian NGO Addameer states, "The continued targeting of Palestinian legislative council members must be viewed in a broader context of systematic attempts by the Israeli occupation to suppress Palestinian political processes."[127] Moreover, Palestinians in Israel have increasingly been arrested for social media posts deemed to be incitement.

One consequence of this (different) criminalization of politics for each Palestinian group is that, crucially, not only do Palestinian citizens in Israel and Palestinians in the West Bank never vote in the same elections, they do not vote for the same parties. Instead, elite Palestinian elected officials in Israel's 1948 territories and in the West Bank are in touch with each other behind the scenes—an arrangement that further undermines Palestinians' confidence in their leaders. After all, if Palestinian parties in Israel must reject armed struggle, this is a point of discussion among Palestinians in the occupied territories. For Palestinians of either group to accept Israel's status as a Jewish and democratic state is to deny certain basic facts of their experience and their own right to self-determination. While Palestinian citizens of Israel may make pragmatic decisions for the sake of political participation despite the limitations imposed by Israeli law (though they debate participation hotly),[128] many Palestinians in the West Bank entirely refuse such rhetoric. The two groups have separate leadership structures. While the PLO and the Palestine National Council (PNC) had once attempted to represent all Palestinians, the place of Palestinian citizens of Israel was always precarious because membership in the PLO was for decades illegal under Israeli law. When the PNC, by lapsing in activity, more or less ceded its place to the Palestinian Legislative Council of the PA, this further marginalized Palestinian citizens of Israel as well as all refugees outside of historic Palestine.

In the West Bank, Palestinians have been arrested for incitement by both Israeli and Palestinian authorities. However, in the West Bank, Israel also represses Palestinian political expression by suppressing protests through arrests and shootings. Israeli forces killed fourteen Palestinians at protests in the year before violence intensified in the 2014 Gaza War.[129] In addition to this, Israel arrests and detains many people in the West Bank with no charges at all under its policy of administrative detention, which allows authorities to hold people without charge for renewable terms of three to six months.[130] Many of these cases revolve around acts of expression. That is, under military law in the West Bank, Israel does not need to go to the trouble of charges of incitement which, in Israel, can involve serious exegesis of everything from poems to Facebook posts and profile pictures. Instead, in the West Bank, Israel can hold people without any charges at all.

Meanwhile, the tactics that Israel uses under military occupation are not unheard of in Israel's 1948 territories: In the fall of 2000, as the second Intifada began, Israeli forces killed thirteen protesters in the Galilee, in northern Israel. In the spring of 2021, Israel also used administrative detention against Palestinian citizens of Israel.[131] Such moments can be watersheds for the identities and aspirations of Palestinian citizens of Israel.[132] Thus, while there are important differences between the legal landscape in Israel's 1948 territories as opposed to the West Bank, and while these differences yield distinct prevailing Palestinian ways of doing politics, it is also the case that the systems and struggles are more interrelated and less well-defined than some would expect.

Permission to converse?

In his seminal essay, "Permission to Narrate,"[133] Edward Said addressed how Palestinians lacked the institutional and political authority to narrate their history on the world stage, a common problem of colonized and subaltern people.[134] Scholars, activists, and diplomats, including Palestinians and others, have been deeply concerned with how Palestinians represent themselves to powerful outsiders through journalism, law, and the arts, among other means.[135] Yet, I contend here that it is at least as urgent to examine the conditions of political communication among Palestinians. Relatedly, rather than examining only the content of expression, we should attend to the elements of communicative practice that have to do with establishing connection or expressing feeling. This is especially important because often the content of messages—a priority, say, of an independent state with Jerusalem as its capital, the right of refugees to return, or the release of prisoners—remains consistent. Focusing on these connective and expressive elements gives flesh to the bones of political experience by shedding light on everyday lives, aspirations, and fears. More than just being deliberative, these conversations are also transformative in and of themselves because they help to constitute and shape Palestinian collectivities.

Thus, I argue that we must recognize the role of colonialism, empire, capitalism, and outright military violence in shaping what Palestinians and other colonized and dispossessed people can say to each other as much as their role in what they can say to outsiders. When dispossessed people insist upon or struggle for expression and communication despite all the obstacles they face, this is itself a mode of challenging oppressive structures. Sovereignty "at the level of method and representation" is crucial.[136] My use of the term sovereignty here draws upon critical indigeneity and Palestinian scholarship that thinks beyond and against repressive settler colonial sovereignty to approaches that draw on other histories and imaginings of political community.[137]

In investigating the dynamics of communication, it is essential to address holistically the obstacles to Palestinians' capacities to speak to each other and as a collective by looking at the physical barriers of checkpoints, laws that differently limit Palestinians' ability to speak, forms of state and non-state violence that differently threaten them, and other broader cultural distinctions also related to residency. Israel's settler colonial sovereignties present an especially complex situation from which to examine how sovereign power shapes what is often called "the public." This is a situation that illuminates a necessary critique of classic liberal ideas of the concept of the public.

For Jürgen Habermas and others in a liberal tradition, the public was meant to be a space for rational discussion of issues of public importance that sits apart from the state.[138] Yet, what publics can do—especially creating collectivities—has long been a topic of consideration.[139] Analyzing the violence at the center of what is called the liberal state project and how that violence shapes publics is also crucial. Publics as they exist today are organized by states, in ways tacit or overt, and they are also shaped by other histories, forces, and norms. The concept of the public is most useful when we think of the public not only as a space for speaking but also as a space for action on a continuum with other kinds of spaces for action. Using the metaphor of "environments of expression," I want to recognize that expression is always in relation to a place, that places present specific conditions for expression based upon many complex and interacting variables, and that these places (with their conditions) are not isolated entirely from each other, but rather that, like related physical environments, they are connected and influence each other, based both on proximity and across different scales.

Thinking about sovereignty and representation together leads to a critical vantage on the concept of the public. As Alejandro Paz observes, "models of communication lie at the heart of debates about citizenship."[140] The people authorize the sovereignty of the state in a liberal model, a concept as familiar as the phrase "we the people."[141] But there are at least two problems with this liberal model of rational deliberation to discuss here. First, it presumes a certain relationship between the people and the state, that of citizenship defined in terms of equality and rights. When this is not the case, expectations of how expression and action interact must shift. Second, it privileges a certain kind of expression over other expressions and action. As James Slotta has argued, building on Roman Jakobson's concept of six dimensions of communicative acts,[142] we must pay greater attention to the phatic, or connective, dimensions of speech.[143] Thinking about the phatic dimensions of speech is crucial on the many occasions when the collective is itself a matter of great contestation, in contrast to when the public, the national group, and a body of citizens may seem to easily coincide. Moreover, the conventional placing of great analytic focus on what is said—the referential dimension—presumes that authorities or those in power care about what is said, another assumption that is quite troubled for Palestinians on both sides of the Green Line. Thus, I want to examine how limits on the ability to speak to each other shape—and even help the analyst describe—the Palestinian collective. Moreover, it is often in marginalized publics that the ideal of the individual speaker is compromised or complicated,[144] and so through this ethnography we may find emergent practices of expression that operate in important ways in these less-than-ideal circumstances.

Attending to the emotive and affective dimensions of expression is critical because Palestinian experiences of geopolitical fragmentation are indeed so fraught. Fragmentation is not only geographic or legal; it does not only shape the media one watches or how non-governmental organizations operate[145]— geopolitical fragmentation impacts intimate details of Palestinians' lives. Palestinian approaches to fragmentation are rooted in longstanding Palestinian ways of being and relating: in modes of mourning, hosting, and attending to kin. And they are not static. Because Israeli rule, like other colonial rules, operates in part by reinforcing patriarchy, and because it operates by severing ties and immobilizing, Palestinians in this volume respond by drawing new relations, or "emergent intimacies," to draw upon Lisa Lowe's conceptualization of the intimacies that bridge subject positions formed in response to colonialism.[146] They are akin also to Svetlana Boym's conception of a diasporic intimacy that "is not opposed to uprootedness and defamiliarization but constituted by it."[147] These emergent intimacies can challenge both Israeli rule and forms of patriarchy. They extend love and care where, for different reasons, neither Israeli authorities nor Palestinian hierarchies would have them grow.

We can think beyond the nation-state by noticing different kinds of collectivities that political expression creates, imagines, and announces, by keeping an eye out for publics that are hardly spherical but rather may have uneven or undefined edges. What purports to be a liberal public sphere—which is actually a racialized colonial public—could never contain the liberatory dreams of many of the Palestinians in this book. The dynamic of Israel's fluid tactics of repressing political expression and action for these two Palestinian groups is key to what I wish to explore in this book. But I'm also interested in how hierarchies and competing desires within Palestinian society shape expectations of what a Palestinian conversation might be, or where Palestine is at all. This is the topic for the next chapter. Before we turn to that momentous placename, Palestine, though, and think how it signifies for Palestinians their own collectivity, we will explore a smaller space, a bus in motion, and the smaller collective it produced one day many years ago as its passengers crossed the Green Line together.

Passage. Aida Refugee Camp to the Haifa Beach

It was spring 2005, years before I began conceptualizing this research project, and a day that I had not planned as "fieldwork." No, in fabulous contrast, I was going to the beach with a large bunch of some of my closest Palestinian friends. That spring, after the death of former PA President Arafat and the PA elections, Israel had been easing off on the closure a bit and issuing more permits, so leaders of the youth center where I had been volunteering in Aida Refugee Camp, the West Bank, decided to apply for permits to take children on the daytrip of their young lives.

Dozens of kids arrived at the youth center at six in the morning on their only day off from school. The lights of the mosque were still glowing green above us, and the sky was pink behind the military encampment. Many lived so close to the youth center that they practically rolled out of bed. We greeted each other with sleepy "good mornings" and incipient smiles that were a comment on the bigness of the day ahead. The grownups held their small coffee cups and children wrapped their arms around themselves sleepily in the chill. No one knew how that day would go. The buses quickly filled, minus a few spots saved for those of our group who had been refused permits and who had thus decided to chance it: They would hike through the hills to evade the checkpoint and meet us on the other side. The bus listed its way out of the camp. We did not go straight out the old Jerusalem Road because the direct course had been, by then, blocked for a year or two by cement blocks and barbed wire: We were essentially on the edge of a construction site for the separation wall. So the bus wrapped around a graveyard, up past a school to the main road, and then looped again past a completed section of the wall, and finally up to the checkpoint. In my fieldnotes at the time, I wrote that it reminded me of a quote from The Simpsons spoken by an alien dressed up as Bill

Clinton on the campaign trail: "We must move forward, not backward; upward, not forward; and always twirling, twirling, twirling towards freedom!" [1]

The checkpoints were ridiculous.

We cheered when the first bus made it through the checkpoint, but then soldiers pulled the second bus aside. What was the problem? We had permits for those on the bus, but not for the bus itself, I heard. The soldier on duty spoke neither English nor Arabic adequately, I heard. A few of the men negotiated for a while, found someone among them who spoke Hebrew, negotiated some more. Eventually the soldiers came on board to check identity cards and permits. Then the bus backed up so that it could return to the middle lane and pass through. The landscape then felt utterly familiar to me. This was territory I often walked alone from a minibus toward the checkpoint to go from Jerusalem, where I was living, to Aida. I realized that this was the first time my seatmate, a woman my age, had been here in perhaps five years, since what is known as the second Intifada, or uprising, had begun in 2000.

We were about 300 meters from her home, as the crow flies.

We turned left onto a bypass road built for Israeli settlers and suddenly this bus full of mostly children was looking back at their refugee camp, across a field behind the nearly completed eight-meter wall: their homes, the mosque, the monastery on a hill. We drove by a green military jeep next to which a bunch of Palestinian men were being detained. I whipped around to check that they were not the friends who were supposed to join us. We surged ahead through the first of two tunnels, and the kids cried out with the thrill of suddenly being in the dark together. This was another place they had never been, but in fact, we were underneath the ground of their community. These tunnels had been built about ten years earlier, as part of the US President Clinton–funded bypass road program, to help settlers more easily navigate the West Bank without having to take the older roads through Palestinian cities. Months earlier, I had been a few stories above where we were now, with many of these same children, to a protest against the section of the separation wall that was now being built to protect these roads.

But the roads gave us little time to contemplate any of this. We sped through the tunnels, and we picked up our friends who had walked through the hills. Soon we were driving past the villages of Al-Khader and Wadi Fukeen, both in the West Bank, and moments later, Al-Qabu, Ras Abu 'Ammar, 'Ajjur, and Beit Jibreen, villages that had been depopulated in 1948 where many of these children's grandparents had been born, before they became refugees. One of the leaders of the youth center was on the bus microphone, calling out the village names, pointing out Israeli street signs that now signaled the places that had replaced those villages: Begin Park, Agur, and Beit Govrin. I had not realized the profound closeness of these villages to the camp: We had not been on the road twenty minutes when we passed the first of them.

The road was smooth and black, newly painted, and when the bus swerved it felt fun, because we were going fast. It was like we were driving through something but weren't part of it. But then the man on the microphone directed the kids to open the bus windows, so that the kids could breathe the air of their family villages. When that air came in, and it was as fresh and green and alive as the land around us, the man on the microphone said, "We are finally on our lands." A small return. A fleet of seed fluff came twirling through the windows of the bus like magic drifting through fifty-seven years of exile and loss, the sparkly stuff of childhood in a movie, floating over the heads of little boys and girls.

We made it to the beach that day, and it was as sweet as we could have expected, but that is a story for another time. We came home that night much later than the permits would have allowed. The bus drivers debated what to do as midnight approached and the children slept in the rows of seats behind them. Israeli soldiers stop people going into Israel much more than they stop people going back to the West Bank, they knew. In the end, the drivers took a risk, and just drove right through the checkpoint, without stopping, without saying anything. Then, much more slowly, they spiraled back into the refugee camp. A few minutes later the children were home safe in their beds.

1

The Shifting Ground of Palestine

IS PALESTINE A PLACE OR A PROMISE? Is it a state in the making? Is it a compromise or is it a revolutionary proclamation? Is it a threat or is it even, as some seem to think, violence in and of itself? Sometimes it is a memory, and sometimes a marketing tool. The name "Palestine" is itself a site of struggle, both between those who would embrace Palestine and those who would, in various ways, deny it and among Palestinians vested in the concept of Palestine. Such contests around a placename are not distinct to Palestine—certainly "America" and "USA" are contested, too. While there is a robust literature about mapping and coloniality, including in Palestinian and Israeli places, scholars have attended less to placenames: their stakes in colonial struggles and their feel in people's mouths as bold or quaint. When, for Palestinians, does invoking Palestine affirm existing arrangements of power, when does it name dreams of statehood, and when does it evoke dreams of freedom? When can dreams of freedom can move beyond nationalist aspirations for a state?[1]

The geographical, political, and emotional meanings of Palestine differ whether one is in Israel's 1948 territories or the West Bank, though certainly, as is the case with many phenomena that bridge the Green Line throughout this book, the meanings are not dichotomous, but rather interrelated and overlapping. The meaning, as we will see, can differ whether one is at a protest or reading a news article. Sometimes Palestine refers to historical Palestine (Israel's 1948 territories, the West Bank, and Gaza today, as comprised the British Mandate), and sometimes it refers to the occupied territories or the even smaller areas controlled by the Palestinian Authority (PA) within the occupied territories. Sometimes, people use the term "historic Palestine" to refer to the whole, to dignify this place with its sense of unity. Yet to avoid negating Israel's existence, they also relegate Palestine to the past. Sometimes, the shape of historic Palestine wordlessly alludes to a vision of liberation, and sometimes the minute details of Palestinian fragmentation are themselves the theme of jokes or artwork. The shifting meaning of Palestine over time is a topic taken up by Haifa-based writer Majd Kayyal:

> What is the geography of Palestine? Who is the Palestinian? What is the Palestinian cause? What is the world in relation to Palestine? The geography of Palestine has come to consider Hebron (and not Bir Al-Sabʿa) in the south, Jenin (and not Safad) in the north. The centrality of the refugee in the formation of the "Palestinian" identity has been exchanged for the centrality of those who are submissive to the military government in the West Bank and Gaza, and the "Palestinian" has become the person who is present in Palestine rather than the person expelled from it, so his cause has become independence on his land rather than return to it, the issue of the state rather than the issue of the homeland, the matter of a political entity rather than the matter of a human presence. [My translation.][2]

Kayyal suggests both how the territoriality of Palestine has changed—in his opinion especially because of the Oslo Accords—and also how crucial extraterritoriality is for Palestinian identity: that a core element of Palestinianness had once been lack of presence in Palestine. Beshara Doumani writes of a temporal "tension between Palestine and the Palestinians, as if one could exist only at the expense of the other."[3]

Paradoxically, one fundamental way in which Palestinian citizens of Israel and Palestinians in the West Bank are separated and are urged to think of themselves as separate is through the word "Palestine" itself: When Palestine is defined as the PA, as Kayyal suggests, it excludes Palestinians in Israel and refugees beyond the boundaries of historic Palestine—and while refugees have a claim of a right to return, Palestinian citizens of Israel are simply ignored in this formulation. And yet, the word Palestine can still point to liberation: For many, it is not just a place, whatever that place might be, but a longstanding dream for liberation, a means by which Palestinians can assert collectivity. More modestly, more intimately, for many of the people in this chapter, it is what they might call their home.

This is to say more than simply that Palestine has more than one meaning. I want to emphasize that the meaning of this placename is context specific, related to how a body in a specific location articulates it. In this sense, a placename can be regarded as a "shifter," such that its significance is contextually specific.[4] Reference "is a kind of communicative action," and "a social practice,"[5] and it is rooted in embodied presence. Placenames are referential terms, but like other terms of reference, their referential quality cannot be divorced from other functions, such as poetic and performative elements of language.[6] This is perhaps especially clear with regards to Palestine, because it does not exist as a nation-state: Its invocation can be part of a performance of statehood or a process of statecraft.[7] Becky Schulthies writes about the Arabic language itself as a shifter as a way of exploring a crucial "tension between unity and diversity" in how Arabic is used and named as a language.[8] For Palestinians, a similar tension abides: Can one word hold together and bring in people who have been so utterly fragmented? Do the meanings of Palestine shift or do they layer and accumulate?

The production of place, including large and abstract places, happens through linguistic, embodied, and everyday practice.[9] Invoking the name of a country is to state a claim, certainly, even to assign jurisdiction, but it is also, often, an emotional expression. A placename can have a chronotopic character,[10] linking a place to a temporality—a history or a future, or both—as in the slogan, "Make America Great Again," which glorifies a white supremacist past to assert these values for the future. The evocation of highly politicized placenames can be provisionally mapped using Raymond Williams' characterization of the dominant, residual, and emergent, and his concept of structures of feeling.[11] I argue here that dominant meanings of the word "Palestine" today tend to be associated with the PA and its neoliberal state project. Even though obviously many powerful institutions (like the United States) deny this state project, it still has a role for many of those powerful institutions as a kind of placeholder; moreover, Palestinians living in the PA experience the cultural force of the PA's definition of "Palestine." Usages of the word "Palestine" that are residual and emergent—associated with the Revolution of the past or with other possibilities for freedom—require even more explication. Placenames can be both tools and shelters of struggle. Even the emotions associated with a placename have trenchant temporalities—nostalgia or hope. It is not only that placenames can be associated with the past or the future, but that placenames have momentum, that place itself is affectively complex.[12]

Palestine has been denied in so many different ways, ranging from Golda Meir's statement, "It was not as though there was a Palestinian people in Palestine considering itself as a Palestinian people and we came and threw them out and took their country away from them,"[13] to quite recently when an Israeli

Knesset member from the party of the prime minister declared that there could be no such thing as a Palestinian people because the Arabic language does not have a letter P.[14] Well before I knew of the Meir quote, as a child, I knew there were some contexts in which I should not use the word Palestine at all. When I was a little girl and traveling every few years to my father's village in the Galilee in northern Israel, always via Tel Aviv, we were strangely specific in naming where we were going. We would not tell acquaintances or airport officers we were visiting family in Israel, first because it would mislead those to whom we were speaking, who might assume that we were Jewish Israelis, and second because the name felt dissonant with where we were going for our *zayt wa za'tar* breakfasts. Although we were always outspoken about being Palestinian, I understood that we could not always say Palestine. Some people would not understand us, hearing Palestine as Pakistan, for example. I was aware that for most people—especially those checking tickets and passports at the airport—Palestine did not quite exist. So we said we were going to Tarshiha, or "the village"—making it sound strangely like we were going to Lower Manhattan.

Even today when I say "Palestine" to some people in Israel, I am aware that it sounds mythical or maybe even silly—pointing to the loss of historic Palestine or to the failure of the PA. In the film *Wajib*, such skepticism emerges when a father who has lived his entire life in Nazareth, inside the Green Line, argues with his son, who has been living abroad: "I don't want to live anywhere else. I don't want to go to Europe and wear fancy shirts and sit in the parlor with [the son's girlfriend] Ms. Nada and her [PLO affiliated] daddy talking about the liberation of Palestine." His voice rises: "What's this Palestine you keep talking about? Where is it?" More quietly, and emphasizing each syllable, he declares, "I'm living it here."[15] For him, the word Palestine seems a little unreal, until it is grounded in place and the everyday.

The meaning of Palestine has shifted since the 1980s at least in the United States—that arbiter of recognition. A few years ago, I found a puzzle of the world for my daughter in my local (non-radical) toy store that included Palestine right next to Israel, on the same tiny piece of wood. And her public school hung a Palestinian flag in its hallway of flags, without us even asking them to do so. What, I wondered, did it mean that the Palestinian flag hangs around the corner not only from the Israeli and the Greek and the Egyptian flags, but also from a rainbow LGBTQI pride flag? While the school sees the world mostly in terms of countries, whoever decided to hang the flags seems to want us to recognize other kinds of affiliations, too.

I relay these anecdotes because the names of countries and an unchanging map of sovereign states can seem a matter of inevitability from the time of our childhoods: sovereignty as something unchanging and unquestioned. But it is worth posing an ethnographic question about when and how can we get beyond the "national order of things"[16] by conceiving or remembering other kinds of places: places made around borders rather than by them, places that hold on over time as the political seas change.[17] We can look at places that are made and remade outside of the usual order of sovereignty.[18] J. Kēhaulani Kauanui analyzes Kanaka Maoli (Native Hawaiian) movements historically and today, demonstrating how models of state sovereignty have shaped the politics and aspirations of some Hawaiian leaders and activists, and how other activists have resisted these frameworks.[19] Her research demonstrates the difficulty of escaping the strictures of state sovereignty as a norm for politics. Still, Kauanui presents parallels between Hawai'i and Palestine and explores possibilities for "no-state" solutions in Palestine. She writes:

> With regard to these two current nationalist movements, asserting sovereignty and self-determination by citing international law is a necessary *tactic* by which to challenge U.S. and Israeli domination, respectively. This, then, calls for accountability to indigenous peoples and the development of meaningful modes of solidarity that promote decolonial practices of relationships not premised on state recognition or other forms of (non-consensual) domination.[20]

Today's analyses of anticolonial liberation that cannot end in statehood build on those of other activists and scholars who recognized that earlier anticolonial movements were not leading to full liberation.[21] The Palestinians' struggle, with their political project invigorated at the time of the 20th-century anticolonial movements and continuing to a contemporary age when many are disillusioned by the possibilities of sovereignty, spans different eras of liberation, even as the vision of statehood remains the dominant vision. Other visions coexist in many places. By bringing together the literature and approaches related to the concept of place with a consideration of sovereignty, I hope to sharpen our view of what Palestine is today and open possibilities for what it might become.

Declaring Palestine

The idea of Palestine as a nation-state has been forged in relation to three different colonial regimes, Ottoman, British, and Israeli—exemplary of the way in which the international order of states is itself a product of colonialism.[22] Some anticolonialists at the end of the Ottoman era and the beginning of the British Mandate preferred to rally around the idea of "Southern Syria," not wanting to divide interconnected territory.[23] Many were reluctant to identify as Palestinians because they did not want to give up a claim to being part of Greater Syria. Still, as the British Mandate over Palestine emerged and Zionism became a threat specific to Palestine, political thinkers and activists began to regard themselves as Palestinians.[24] The British civil administration imposed Palestinian citizenship upon Palestinians in 1918, a status Palestinians were wary of because it was a colonial citizenship that did not bestow political rights or recognize Palestinian nationhood. Still, this citizenship was recognized internationally by the Treaty of Lausanne.[25] This is an interesting moment because it reminds us that Palestinians have long been aware of the possibility that citizenship itself can be a ruse or a means of confinement as well as a tool for attaining rights.

The UN Partition plan of 1947 articulated in General Assembly Resolution 181 called for a Palestinian state next to a Jewish state. Palestinians and surrounding Arab states rejected the partition, arguing that too much land was designated for the Jewish state given their smaller numbers and that the Jewish state was a settler colony facilitated through British support for Zionist settlement. Zionists accepted the plan but wanted to extend the territory of the Jewish state. In the ensuing war, Israel indeed gained territory. The Palestinians who remained in what became Israel were regarded in Israel as "non-Jews" or "Arab Israelis" and considered in much of the rest of the world as just refugees. Palestine certainly seemed to cease to exist, with 78 percent of the territory becoming part of the Israeli state, with the remainder falling under Jordanian control as its "West Bank" and under Egyptian rule as the Gaza Strip. To invoke the name of Palestine was, in the 1960s and 1970s, revolutionary. The Palestine National Charter of 1964, the founding document of the PLO, embarks from an assertion about Palestine's territorial unity:

> Article 1. Palestine is an Arab homeland bound by strong Arab national ties to the rest of the Arab Countries and which together form the great Arab homeland.
> Article 2: Palestine, with its boundaries at the time of the British Mandate, is an indivisible territorial unit.[26]

One of the successes of the 1970s was to place Palestinians—and thus, in a way, Palestine—back into international diplomatic conversations.[27]

Statehood has appeared to Palestinian leaders to be a way of recovering Palestine—but it has also been a way of consolidating personal power. Its declaration has been nothing if not iterative. In 1988, PLO Chairman Yasser Arafat declared a Palestinian state in a speech to the Palestinian National Council, Palestinians' legislature in exile. He did not declare the borders for this state, but he did assert that it would have "holy Jerusalem as its capital."[28] After the speech, a band played the Palestinian national anthem, and men in uniform raised the Palestinian flag, a familiar tactic for making a play for legitimate sovereignty for multiple audiences.[29] This was also the moment of the emergence of the Palestinian acceptance of a two-state framework: The decision to make the declaration was linked to a movement toward PLO recognition of Israel. This was the period when "a distinctly nation-statist project became the hegemonic articulation of Palestinian nationalism."[30] The PLO recognized Israel in 1993. It also led to the Palestine National Council declaring Arafat the president of Palestine in 1989.

According to public proclamations and Palestinian expectations, the Oslo Accords of 1993 were supposed to lead to a Palestinian state, but they did not. Still, new political initiatives referenced and reiterated older declarations of statehood. In 2009, then PA Prime Minister Salam Fayyad's plan for statehood referenced Arafat's 1988 declaration several times.[31] In 2011, PA President and PLO Chairman Mahmoud Abbas went to the United Nations to ask for the recognition of the establishment of the State of Palestine and its admission into the United Nations as a full member. This time, the boundaries were more clearly defined. As Abbas said in 2011, "The goal of the Palestinian people is the realization of their inalienable national rights in their independent State of Palestine, with East Jerusalem as its capital, on all the land of the West Bank, including East Jerusalem, and the Gaza Strip."[32] In 2012, Palestinians declared statehood unilaterally, and the United Nations General Assembly voted to upgrade Palestine's status to a "non-member observer state." As of June 2021, 139 countries recognized the State of Palestine.[33]

But sovereignty is also related to people's sensed experience of place. This sense emerges not only because of state violence that asserts power,[34] but also from services that demonstrate—or attempt to demonstrate—to residents that a state exists[35] and through the "branding" of a state across a variety of forms of public communication.[36] Palestinians' experiences of their own territory belies the sense of Palestinian statehood in the occupied territories, and yet the PA has taken many steps on the ground to appear as though it is a state. Billboards in Ramallah declare the "birth certificate of the Palestinian state" with the UN logo behind it, even as roads and schools—basic state services—are built with international donor funds, and these international donors are advertised publicly.[37] The websites of the Palestinian ministries bear the seal of "the state of Palestine," declared in Arabic and English, with a gold, graphically simple eagle looking skywards, with the Palestinian flag in red, green, black, and white on its chest. Underneath the eagle is the word Palestine in Arabic once again. This seal bears some resemblance to the seal of the United States. Palestine is hardly unique in its mode of nationalism as mimicry.[38] The URL addresses themselves assert a kind of digital statehood, with the endings ".gov.ps."

The Palestinian case confirms what has been shown elsewhere: that sovereignty is a matter of mutual recognition,[39] a fundamental kind of interdependence among sovereigns.[40] Some would say that there is a particularly dyadic structure of relationality in sovereignty for Israel and Palestine, since the United Nations played such a role in Israel's creation through a partition plan that was to create a Palestinian state alongside it. The Palestinian case, like others, also suggests that statehood is often a ruse, a means of performing sovereignty that does not provide most states with anything like a classic understanding of sovereignty as "the unification of power and the basic concept of political organization."[41] Instead, we see a "sleight of hand sovereignty,"[42] a performance of sovereignty in which both Israel and the Palestinian leadership are vested.

Where is "Palestine" in the news?

Perhaps all Palestinian journalism is border journalism—but it is also quite often complicit with the PA state project. It has long been recognized that our daily engagements with news are a practice through which we establish and confirm national identities.[43] Here I want to explore how Palestinian journalism in both the West Bank and inside the Green Line is often a site for the circulation of a certain dominant Palestinian nationalism that is constituted by and reconstitutive of the international system of nation-states. In what are termed "liberal democracies," as in a wide variety of other locations, mainstream political news tends to uphold dominant visions of this nation-state system, because these outlets report within established spaces of politics and are dependent on them.[44] Even when local journalists have interests and perspectives that differ from journalists working in the capital or those at the geographic center of a nationalist project, they often work within the expected norms of the nation-state or reiterate nationalist norms of how diversity should be managed rather than exposing the fictions and fissures of the nation-state.[45] Writing about Tijuana, Mexico, Rihan Yeh argues that the "the border radicalizes the basic split in the public sphere" in that area,[46] making even more harsh the dichotomy between the legally mobile middle class who can be represented by mainstream media and the poorer, less mobile, more Indigenous parts of Tijuana society. Various local or regional journalisms may write the nation in their own distinct ways, but they often refract dominant themes and modalities around class, ethnicity, and mobility.

Meanwhile, those threatened or failed by liberal models of citizenship, and by this nation-state system as a whole, commonly find less voice in news media, and so may establish their own journalistic outlets,[47] as Palestinians inside the Green Line do, turning to media in Arabic. Perhaps surprisingly, Palestinian journalism operates on similar assumptions across the Green Line, such that "Palestinian news" happens primarily in the occupied territories, even if there are Palestinians in both Israel and the West Bank. Here, I examine how news websites determine what counts as "local" and "Palestinian" according to the headings and organization of news websites. Analyzing this categorization of news considers the infrastructure of news—rather than its content—as constitutive of locality and nation. The basic organization of Palestinian news sites upholds the existence of the Green Line and defines Palestinian news as news occurring in the occupied Palestinian territories of the West Bank and Gaza— and this is true even of the most prominent and Palestinian-identified news organization inside the Green Line.[48] In this way, mainstream news reinforces hegemonic geographies of the nation-state. Having surveyed a larger number of media organizations, I focus here on how two popular media organizations on each side of the Green Line present their news.

Donya Al-Watan (AlWatanVoice.com, literally "The World of the Nation/ Homeland") is a top-rated Palestinian news site.[49] Its Facebook page declares itself as "the top news website in Palestine."[50] The name "Palestine" defines its mission and markets the website. How, then, does the site define Palestine? Under "local," this site has listed the districts of the occupied Palestinian territories, plus the category of prisoners, such that the only people inside Israel's 1948 territories covered by the term "Local" are those in Israeli prisons, who are mostly holders of PA identity cards.[51] At the very bottom of the website, under sections about sports, crime, and society, there is a set of subheadings that includes "Refugees," primarily addressing refugees outside of Israel and the occupied territories. Just below this, and at the absolute bottom of the website, is another set of four headings including "'48 Palestinians," a term used to refer to Palestinian citizens of Israel. This layout demonstrates that refugees outside of the occupied territories and Palestinians in Israel are as far as possible from being headline news.

The organization of news on other West Bank news sites similarly reflects a focus on the occupied territory as the locus of Palestinian news. Another popular news site, Maʿan, follows a subtly different format that ultimately proposes the same hierarchy of places.[52] Under a heading of "Local" we find the subheadings organized by district.[53] We see a nationalist hierarchy of places, as the list starts with Jerusalem, Palestinians' desired future capital of a Palestinian state, then Ramallah, the de facto capital of the Palestinian Authority, and then other districts in the occupied territory. The list ends with "'48 Palestine" as one unit somewhat set apart from the West Bank districts—part of the local but not, for example, distinguished by its own districts and divisions. Scrolling down the website, the homepage has separate sections for topics like main news, local, prisoners, Israeli news, etc. Only after many of these sections is there a heading for "'48 Palestine."[54]

Inside the Green Line, Palestinian news sites—which are also in Arabic—also suggest that "Palestinian news" is in the occupied territories, but on these sites, the "local news" revolves around communities of Palestinians inside the Green Line. There is, then, a split between "local" and "Palestinian." Moreover, the "local" is especially important because Palestinians in Israel are neglected by Hebrew language Israeli news (or depicted as a problem community) and marginalized by Palestinian papers in the West Bank.[55] Panet, launched in 2002 as a business enterprise, has been for many years the most popular Arabic news website in Israel. Its stated market is "Arab Palestinians in Israel ('48 Arab)."[56] Its website prioritizes local news: Panet's breakdown of localities lists twenty-four towns and areas, all inside the Green Line.[57] Rather than being geographical districts that cover all of the territory of Israel today, the localities are areas where most Palestinians live in Israel: a territory of islands, some small and some large, suggesting how different Palestinian space is from the geography of a nation-state.[58] The second topic listed on the Panet sidebar is "Palestine news."[59] This category deals primarily with the PA. On Panet, the local—everything from crime in Palestinian towns in Israel to car accidents, from preparations for Israeli elections to preparations for Ramadan—is prioritized. Still, it is interesting that while according to Panet there are Palestinians (and not just

Arabs) inside the Green Line—as indicated by their naming of their audience, the "Arab Palestinians in Israel"—Palestine itself is elsewhere.

The news website Arab48, established in 1996, is associated with the political party National Democratic Assembly (also known by the acronym Balad).[60] Even the outlet's name hints at its political orientation, since referring to Palestinians in Israel as "'48 Arabs" recognizes that Palestinian identities today were constituted through acts of dispossession and war in 1948. However, it is not only the political nature of the site that distinguishes it from outlets like Panet. Arab48 offers more in-depth reporting and rich editorials, and it foregrounds hard news. As its Facebook banner declares, it provides "speed of news, precision of information, and depth of analysis." Nevertheless, its website's basic organization is similar to that of the other Palestinian news sites discussed here. It has a bar across the top of the page that lists, first, Local News, which features news from Palestinian citizens of Israel, and then Palestinian News which features news from the occupied territories. Following this across the top bar is the category of Israeli News and then Arab and International News. What interested me most was the identification of Palestinian news as news from the PA. Balad, the party with which Arab48 is associated, has as its first statement of principle that Palestinians in Israel are "part of the Palestinian people and the Arab *umma*,"[61] and leaders have declared, "Balad is part of the Palestinian national movement. We are not the Israeli left."[62] On a practical level, Balad operates as a political party fully and exclusively inside the Green Line. The use of "Palestinian" to denote news coming from the PA diminishes the Palestinianness of Palestinians in Israel. Perhaps to use a different categorization than any of the other outlets would be confusing for readers. Perhaps a full redefinition of Palestinian news would even be seen as politically risky.

The infrastructure of news websites—how they geographically organize news—offers insight into basic assumptions about space, politics, and the boundaries of a community's concern. The prevailing structure that we see across these sites implicitly locates Palestine in the occupied territories. This placement of Palestine in the occupied territories becomes more a matter of supposition than outright argument—and this is what makes it so powerful.[63] This survey of the organization and style of these four important Palestinian news organizations demonstrates several things. Across these various outlets, Palestinian citizens of Israel are indeed recognized as being Palestinians, rather than as being "Arabs" or "Israeli Arabs." While Palestinian people are on both sides of the Green Line, according to news websites and their interfaces, "Israel" and "Palestine" are two separate geographic entities, and "Palestine" corresponds to the PA. This helps to secure the PA's state-building project.

Brand Palestine

Complementing the PA's state-building project, sometimes "Palestine" is invoked to sell goods—another dominant instance of the deployment of Palestine. In advertising, the word Palestine can be powerful in invoking a version of the present and a vision for the future that is consistent with capitalist dreams of mobility and pleasure, tropes that are similar in advertising elsewhere.[64] Buying Palestinian goods has a long history in the Palestinian struggle as a complement to boycotting Israeli products.[65] Local businesses, international companies (with their local middlemen), and international organizations all use nationalist appeals in their marketing. Everyday products like Palestinian dairies use red and green, colors of the Palestinian flag, in their marketing. Yet in the Oslo age, brand Palestine can also support a state-building project that is decidedly neoliberal in character and aimed at creating a certain class-based vision of Palestinian success.[66]

What struck me most one day as I drove along some of the compromised roads of the West Bank were the car ads. The speed of cars and their association with normative concepts of masculinity mean that they are frequently associated with ideas of the nation and freedom, and it turned out that the West Bank was no exception. The US car company Chrysler opened a franchise in the West Bank in 2014, consistent with Palestinian Prime Minister Salam Fayyad's efforts of neoliberalization of 2007-2013. More loans became available, too. Soon, shining Jeeps sped down Palestinian roads. Advertisements on billboards or on the Jeep Palestine Facebook page showcased each new model, with the iconic grill of the Jeep and the tagline: "Now in Palestine."

What does Palestine mean here, geographically and affectively? Geographically, when the new franchise announces that Jeeps have arrived in "Palestine," they are obviously using the term to refer to the PA areas. After all, Jeeps have been available in Israel for many years. Thus, this advertising uses nationalist language in a way that equates the national project to that of the PA. Facebook posts celebrated this vision of Palestine. One post from November 15, 2017, even celebrated Palestinian "Independence Day" with an image of a huge Palestinian flag towering over three large flags that flew over three Jeep SUVs. Enjoying the dream of mobility and prosperity may mean accepting a political project that is limited to the PA statelet, with its limited territory and sovereignty—"Palestine Ltd.," indeed.[67]

The Jeep signifies in several ways. It is an American SUV, a status symbol because it is expensive both to purchase and to maintain due to high gas prices in the occupied territories and Israel. It is part of a culture and economy of consumerism and loans that has discouraged resistance, forcing Palestinians to pay more attention to their monthly paychecks than their national struggle. It represents a reductive, consumerist version of masculinity, one that is familiar in car cultures the world over. As billboards in the Bethlehem area, alongside ads for Coke and for Palestinian food companies, the giant Jeep ads that first attracted my attention played it straight: They sold their big beasts of fuel combustion framed by nothing by sky. This left any reading of dissonance between the cars' evocation of a dream of speed and the closure all around us, or the Americanness of the car and the repressiveness of US in the region, to the viewer. Did drivers, stuck in traffic due to poor infrastructure, or stuck in rundown cars because of the poverty imposed by neoliberalism and occupation, enjoy these images, or resent them?

On Facebook, though, the same or similar images were framed by cheeky little comments from whoever managed the accounts. One Facebook post by Jeep from May 13, 2015, shows a Jeep at the edge of a cliff on a semi-arid terrain that could be in the West Bank, but almost surely is not. The bottom reads, in English, "Jeep. Roads? Where we are going, we don't need roads." This is a common meme for Jeep that quotes the 1985 American film Back to the Future. But posted here it just might have another meaning. The accompanying text of the post was a single winking emoticon—subtle enough to be an ordinary enticement of advertising, or, perhaps, a nod to the local context, where Palestinians indeed need to escape their road system.

Another Jeep ad posted on Facebook on December 28, 2016, shows a white Jeep speeding down a green hill with what looks like a Palestinian village behind it. The text of the graphic reads, in Arabic: "Cross all of the borders at full strength." The Facebook post accompanying the image reads, "a new understanding of freedom." Here we see Palestine imagined as a borderless place of great hilly roads that one can enjoy best in a Jeep. The ad indeed offers a new meaning for the word freedom. Linked as it has customarily been for Palestinians to political freedom, here it is about both the freedom associated with consumption and the sensual quality of mobility as freedom: as one experiences when one speeds down the road or even moves beyond roads altogether.[68] Is

this an off-roading geared toward evading checkpoints? In a West Bank fragmented by so many obstacles to movement, it is impossible to disentangle the
capitalist dimension of the Jeep from the feeling of mobility-as-freedom with
which the Jeep is associated—and from the nationalist hopes for freedom from
occupation-imposed fragmentation and confinement. If using "Palestine" as a
marketing tool is generally associated with a dominant concept of Palestine as
neoliberal and limited to the occupied territories, there is clearly an excess of
meaning that escapes these bounds.

Palestine as unwieldy fruit

On January 8, 2011, Palestinian President Mahmoud Abbas had a front row seat
for a Ramallah celebration in commemoration of the forty-sixth anniversary of
the establishment of the Fatah movement. The rest of us watched on Palestine
TV (or, later, on YouTube). The show was to feature performers from the show
Watan 'a Watar (A Homeland on A String, e.g., a country strung out in tension, or on the edge). *Watan 'a Watar* was known as the premiere Palestinian
satire program, a means by which the PA tried to demonstrate its liberal attitude toward the media until, soon after this broadcast, it shut down the show
entirely.[69] For this program, at least, a logo in the top right corner of the screen
read "Palestine," which turned the curved top of the shape of the central ṭ into
a mosque like Jerusalem's Dome of the Rock. Never mind that Palestine TV
broadcasts from Ramallah because Jerusalem was profoundly off limits, under
Israeli control.

A woman and two men assembled on stage, with one man acting as a
teacher in the middle and the other two as students. They were receiving a
lesson in the geography of Palestine. While the students acted childishly during the skit, their oversized adultness and the lack of any difference between
the teacher and the students itself undermined the sense of authority of the
teacher, perhaps a metaphor for the lack of authority of the political leaders
assembled in front of them. The teacher held a large map. First, the teacher
told them, "Palestine is a beautiful country!" Palestine has many beaches, many
rivers, and many religions, he explained, drawing on familiar Palestinian nationalist tropes. One of the students interrupted to ask where these beaches
and rivers were. The teacher gestured in the area of the Galilee and explained
they were "up there" without being specific, and then admitted quickly that he
had not seen the beach himself. The teacher then announced that Jerusalem
is the capital of Palestine, explaining that it is in the middle of the country.

A student asked what was in Jerusalem, and the teacher responded that the *"Ḥaram"* was there—the golden Dome of the Rock and Al-Aqsa Mosque. The student seemed unfamiliar with the term—though this is the single most important religious site for Muslim Palestinians, an iconic landmark for all—so the teacher explained, "something round, with something yellow on top. You think I've ever seen it?" When one student indicated that he had been to Jerusalem, the other two became suspicious that he was a spy or a collaborator. How else would one attain such a permit?[70] If, in this skit, the presumed definition of Palestine was of all of historic Palestine, it was just as deeply engrained that much of this area was off limits. Palestinian wholeness was nationalist rhetoric, but in fact Palestinians were alienated from these crucial Palestinian sites.

The sketch then centered on a large and homely fruit that the teacher referred to as a watermelon. "Let's say," the teacher intoned, "that Palestine is a watermelon. They divided it into two parts." His student said a blessing as though for a slaughter of a lamb, and the teacher sliced it into two unequal parts. They would return to the larger side—presumably Israel—later, he said, setting it aside in a sly reference to the right of return. The woman student pointed toward the smaller piece, which was presumably the occupied territory. "You call that a slice [*shakḥa*]? That's just a little chunk [*fal ʿūṣa*]." "That's a chunk? Saʾeb Erekat took eighteen years to negotiate over that chunk!" The word *fal ʿūṣa* itself adds to the absurdity: It is neither a term of geography nor of politics, nor even of watermelon slicing. *Fal ʿūṣa* was just a funky word. Here, as elsewhere during the skit, the live broadcast cut away to Mahmoud Abbas sitting with his hands clasped and an amused look on his face. On either side of him, other Fatah leaders were more animated in their laughter. The teacher again, by now speaking in a very colloquial Arabic, divided this smaller piece into two, one larger than the other as though they were the West Bank and Gaza, and he explained, "This slice, they sliced into two slices" (*Hadha al-shakḥa shakaḥūhā l-shakḥatain*). The silliness of the language was continuing to flourish. Again, the teacher set aside one piece, this time naming it Gaza. The teacher explained that the West Bank was divided into two parts, Jerusalem and the West Bank. Setting Jerusalem aside, he continued with another blessing on another swift slice:

TEACHER: In the name of God, the merciful and beneficent. The West Bank slice, children, they sliced it into several slivers [*shukayḥāt*].
STUDENT: Yes, yes.

TEACHER: The sliver of Ramallah.

STUDENT: Yes, that one is important…

He went on to name other slices. Again, the blessing before the act of slicing gave the division of "Palestine" an ironic veneer of legitimacy, as did the student's interjected expressions of support. This was in contrast to the introduction of the new word, *shukayha*, which I have translated as "sliver." In the Arabic, it is a made-up diminutive of *shakha* (slice), itself an informal word. The fragmentation of Palestine was so far along that a new word was needed to describe it—and this word was especially ridiculous. He went on to explain that in order to travel between these parts, you needed to make a long overnight journey. The absurdity continued: "For each sliver, they sliced its cracks [*shukūku*] up. The Anata crack. The Beit Jala crack." Here, as in the Panet listings of twenty-four small islands as distinct news areas, we hear a list of small towns rather than regional centers. The teacher jabbed at the slice of the squash, and the student again egged him on with her small exclamations: the student as yes-man or pro-authority stooge. Perhaps all Palestinians were complicit in the fragmentation we all witnessed. The word for "cracks" pronounced in colloquial Arabic (*shukūk*) sounded similar to "slice" (*shakha*) and "sliver" (*shukayha*). Further, between the cracks were fences (*shīk*).

By this time, the student had to express her confusion. "I don't get it anymore. Slices and cracks and slivers—do you get it?" The teacher responded, "I understand that the situation is all watermelon"—in other words, nonsense. Finally, the teacher turned to the audience, the very members of Fatah who had signed off on decades of divisions: "If anyone understands better, come on up. Really, anyone." Though perhaps this was the dramatic climax of the skit, it continued a while longer, as indeed it seemed fragmentation itself continued long after one might have expected.

A student went on to describe the president's itinerary to travel between Ramallah and Bethlehem, which involved a course along "the Ramallah slice, the sliver of Hizma [a village], the slice of Jab'a [a village], the slice of the Container [a checkpoint], and a piece of the Ta'mara near the sheep." She recited this in the breakneck pace with which so many Palestinian drivers course down the hills and curves of those roadways. In fact, the most direct route between these two cities goes through Jerusalem, but that route has been off limits to Palestinians for a generation, relegating them to the swerves and congestion of the route the student described, even as Israel has built for its citizens faster and smoother highways through the region. This was not the smooth open road of the Jeep ads, enjoyed in a luxury car, but rather a route that had a few too many swerves in it, that felt uncertain and harried. It was a route imposed by colonialism, and Palestinians knew it. If the Galilee could hardly be named, the Naqab / Negev was not even alluded to. While it was nearly suspicious to know about or have access to Jerusalem—though it was supposed to be the national capital—the itinerary between Ramallah and Bethlehem could be recited in the most intricate detail. This route gave us a homely view of Palestine, where the landmarks were not the Dome of the Rock but the sheep and the checkpoints. It was one in which Israeli occupation could never be obscured. This pointed to a structure of feeling around Palestine as not just embattled but rundown—a sense only too familiar in the West Bank.[71]

The feeling of the sketch is uncomfortable, contradictory, ridiculous, fragile, but still grounded. And the fragmentation of Palestine required a whole new vocabulary, in the Palestinian vernacular, of slices, slivers, chunks, and cracks. Here, also, was the leadership of the PA being confronted with the absurd situation to which they had acquiesced, on an occasion meant to celebrate the inception of their movement. Or perhaps the situation had been imposed upon them and was actually the fault of the Israeli authorities—the skit left this possibility open, as critical cultural production performed for and in official spaces often does.[72] The skit toggled between a sense of Palestine as a conceptually unified whole and lived experiences in a fragmented Palestine. In this acknowledgement of those lived experiences, the sense of Palestine in this skit challenged the dominant one of a state under construction.

Furtive Palestine, talismanic Palestine

In contrast to the official meanings of Palestine that we find in news media and diplomacy—those meanings that were mocked in the above skit—"Palestine" is often in trouble with the law, an outlaw country, though it is lacking in standing and institutions to fully qualify it as a "rogue state." So it is that Palestine is intimated and asserted in circumstances of struggle, even if the name is not spoken outright. One way of not saying Palestine but wordlessly referring to it is through a simple outline of historic Palestine, an icon that is instantly recognizable to Palestinians.[73] The simple shape of historic Palestine crops up not only in graffiti but also in jewelry, embroidery, posters, t-shirts, and Facebook profiles and frames. The benefit of this shape is that it can seem to be beyond negotiation or debate: just there, whole, unlabeled, out of historical time. While some might read it as a negation of Israel's territorial claims, it does not necessarily make any such specific an argument: This is Palestine evoked without being declared. Some Palestinians enjoy spotting the shape in natural forms: in rocks or tree bark or leaves, as though Palestine exists as a unit, uncontested, cropping up in unexpected times without being bidden.

A 2018 Nakba Day t-shirt created at the refugee rights organization Badil in the West Bank features this shape of historic Palestine, along with the verse in Arabic:

> I revive,
> I love,
> I challenge,
> And I return
> To exist[74]

The shape of Palestine is linked to this existential series. In these cases, the shape of Palestine, full and complete, is not accompanied by an overt explanation of what it means or claims, or even by the word "Palestine." It asserts nothing so specific as a belief in a one-state solution. Nor it is only a sketch or a history lesson in what Palestine was. Perhaps it is best understood as related to a structure of feeling, "against the terms of reduction,"[75] an evocation, a reminder, a dream that stands in its own temporality, neither past nor future tense. It is a way of saying something without articulating it fully because to do so might be too dangerous or too complicated, in that way that squaring desires, demands, and practical concerns often is. Or perhaps it suggests that a fuller articulation of what this shape means is unnecessary, so engrained is the significance of Palestine to Palestinians.

Another example of this shape outlined especially caught my attention because it seemed destined not to catch my attention. Damascus Gate in East Jerusalem is iconic in tourist imagery of Jerusalem and an actual passage for people into the Old City. It is physically imposing when one sees it from afar, like the history for which it stands, but it is also a structure that envelops you as you approach. Descending smooth stone stairs, worn with millions of footsteps, you are ensconced amidst massive blocks of limestone that index their age. A Palestinian's sense of belonging is often interrupted by an Israeli soldier posted above the main entrance. Just inside Damascus Gate is the Muslim Quarter of the Old City, where storied shops sell everything you can think of: fresh squeezed juice, spices, shoes, cell phone covers, curtains, toys, underwear, tourist goods. In just a few minutes, one can walk to the Old City's most famous holy sites. To be in Damascus Gate is to be a walker, squeezing by tourists, workers, and children, encountering passersby with a glance or a dodge "like a series of hellos."[76] Damascus Gate is also a site of intense policing: of those who sell vegetables without licenses, of prayers that occur outside of Jerusalem's gate when people cannot get to Al-Aqsa, and it is a stage for all kinds of confrontations between Palestinians and Israeli police and army.[77]

As signaled by the presence of that Israeli soldier so often stationed above the entrance, Damascus Gate is also important to a Zionist imaginary of the city as "united," undermining the distinction in international law between Israeli-occupied, Palestinian East Jerusalem (of which Damascus Gate is a part) and West Jerusalem, which has been under Israeli control since 1948 (though it was also designated as an international zone under the UN partition plan). One is also more and more likely to encounter Jewish settlers—sometimes those carrying semi-automatic weapons—who live either in the Old City or in the area outside of it.

The Jerusalem Lights Festival runs just after Jerusalem Day, an Israeli holiday in late May celebrating what was, from the Zionist perspective, the "unification" of Jerusalem in 1967. The light show attracts people of many different backgrounds, including Palestinians and religious Jews, who may have planned to be there or who had just happened by. So it was that I stumbled upon the Lights Festival in Jerusalem in early June 2014. It presented various styles of architecture projected on Damascus Gate, including Arab architecture, each replaced with a new style, sometimes by curtains falling or by pieces of a new style flying into place, and sometimes through images of fire and of fracture projected onto the Damascus Gate. The show proposed that Jerusalem had been through many stages throughout its history and that Israel was certainly in control of its narrative now: able to project anything onto the face of one of the most iconic Arab places in the city.

After the show, I went into the Old City for my planned meeting. On my way out, the area was much quieter. Something caught my eye. Facing the gate, and below the main entrance to the Old City was the spray-painted outline of the shape of historic Palestine (Figure 1). The location of the graffito was striking: This would never be featured or even visible in the tourist photography of Damascus Gate, which always shows the walls from above and outside— more the spectator's view.[78] The modest scale of the spray-painted shape here suggested how little control Palestinians have over space and representation in

Figure 1 Spray-painted line drawing of Palestine at Damascus Gate, Jerusalem. Photo by author.

Jerusalem. Unlike the light show, and indeed unlike the Jeep ad, this was low-tech, a single color and a single line, but more permanent. It was cheap and illegal. Here, at the very heart of Jerusalem, which is itself at the heart of the Palestinian national project, the simplicity of the graffito at once underscored Palestinians' powerlessness and their determination. Jerusalem is meant to be the national capital of Palestinians' state-in-formation, and yet most Palestinians cannot come there. PLO representatives have long been kicked out of the city, and residents cannot vote in PA elections. Though the PA mobilizes imagery of Arab Jerusalem such as the Dome of the Rock as part of its branding for statehood, the PA can do nothing for this city in need. Here, instead, was an unofficial representation of Palestine in Jerusalem, a message to the walkers through the city, to those who operate by "tactics" that forge paths through a space that they cannot control.[79] The graffito suggested that the place, Damascus Gate, stood for the whole, Palestine. Graffiti is an eminently tactical mode of expression, poaching on the spaces created or managed by those in power to say something different. Once again there was a subtle contrast between the abstract whole of Palestine and its component parts. There was the graffito, in this iconic place, and there was also this place as walked and experienced: not the Damascus Gate of postcards, but the Damascus Gate as a place we might sit and rest despite trash strewn nearby or pungent smells, the crannies we might not notice if not for a graffito.

The dispossession of Palestine in 1948 is not only about the depopulation of those hundreds of villages and the destruction of those beloved cities, it is also about the making of home inevitably into places of exile, where one never feels as secure as one should: As Mahmoud Darwish writes, "Now in exile, yes at home."[80] So it is that an everyday landmark like Damascus Gate—a place treasured, revered, and inhabited—can be quietly reclaimed from an ostentatious light show by a line drawing of Palestine. Palestine is at once exile and home, a place of displacement and the only place left. These are some of the unofficial meanings of Palestine that exist out of range of the PA.

If the graffito above existed in an everyday space, sometimes Palestine was evoked in spaces of protest. In rage and grief at witnessing another brutal Israeli assault on Gaza, hundreds of us marched down Haifa's great hillside on July 18, 2014. We rounded a curve onto Ben Gurion Street, with the cherished Arab cafes in front of us that are the heart of Haifa as the "cultural capital" of Palestinians inside the Green Line,[81] and the shining Bahai temple above us. Then, we turned around to see a line of police and border control forces closing the road

Figure 2 Arrest at a Haifa demonstration against the war on Gaza, 2014. Photo by author.

behind us, heavily armed, and some on horses. They corralled the protesters into the area around the traffic circle, in a familiar police tactic of crowd control. Arrests quickly ensued (Figure 2). A young man in handcuffs shouted the famous slogan "*Filasṭīn ʿArabiyya!*"—"Palestine is Arab!"—his hands cuffed behind his back and Israeli police seizing both of his elbows.

To declare that Palestine is Arab while on the way to an Israeli jail makes one's arrest on the street a continuation of protest, a rejection of the batons and the shields, the rifles and the pistols, the making of horses into enemies, the naming of this street after a man who would dispossess all Palestinians, a rejection of Israeli authority itself. Those moments of arrest are times of shock. For this man, perhaps, the talisman was the word, always inside him, made public. The Palestine in his chant as voiced here—in Haifa—references all of historic Palestine, and the slogan (or is it a mantra?) hearkens back to earlier eras of Arab nationalism, an assertion that Palestine belongs to a larger Arab whole.

Maybe the word had a similar talismanic quality for another Palestinian under arrest. A widely circulated image of an incident in Haifa, Israel, shows Israeli police arresting a girl wearing a sweatshirt that declares "Palestinian" across it in fluid Arabic script (Figure 3).[82] She is aglow, smiling and brightly

Figure 3 This photograph of a Haifa arrest became part of a campaign to protect the right to protest. Photo by Zaher Abu Elnaser. Reprinted with permission.

illuminated despite the arrest having happened at night. The sweatshirt is iconic for Palestinians inside the Green Line, where wearing it is an expression of pride in identity. (In the West Bank, in contrast, the shirt is cool, but it is by no means revolutionary: Nearly everyone in Palestinian areas is Palestinian, after all.) Though her hands are cuffed behind her, it is as though the arrest is an achievement, or even a fulfillment of her declared identity as Palestinian. The Haifa-based civil rights organization Adalah used the image to promote its "Protect the Protest" campaign, to support its advocacy for those arrested for participation in protests. In this sense, Palestine and Palestinian identity are located at the nexus of the outlaw and the claims to rights.

Palestine can be invoked by a chant made in handcuffs. There are such counter-hegemonic[83] meanings of Palestine that coexist alongside the dominant ones that support the PA and the neoliberal economy. Their temporality mixes past and present: The chant "Palestine is Arab" and the outline of historic Palestine as symbols of Palestinian unity harken to a previous era of nationalism, and thus can be categorized as "residual" as Raymond Williams might regard it: a part of the past that is also an active part of the present.[84] Yet, they are also, in Williams' terms, emergent, signaling a new politics in formation that foregrounds Palestinian unity and the strengthening identification of Palestinian citizens of Israel with Palestine. Political trends are not always moving in one direction or another, but instead are fluid and open-ended. This is one factor that can make emergent cultural elements especially difficult to identify.[85] As we will see in the next chapters, Palestinian politics are often drawing from earlier moments or the politics of other Palestinian places. Through it all, this sense of Palestine as renegade—whether in relation to Zionist attempts to eliminate Palestine or PA attempts to hem it in—remains enticing: a part of Palestinians' past that remains in process and contested and that, it increasingly seems, is shaping Palestinians' views of the future.

Conclusions

As I was working on this manuscript in the late months of US President Trump's term, I was startled receive in my inbox an email with the subject heading, "Palestine could end in 6 days" from Avaaz, a U.S.-based non-profit that promotes activism on a variety of progressive issues. Then, I was irritated. On their homepage was a countdown of the days, hours, and minutes to July 1, 2020, the time "until Israel plans to annex Palestine." It is true that at the time analysts were talking about the looming threat of Israeli annexation of parts of the West Bank. But Palestine was not going anywhere.

Equating the West Bank and Gaza or PA administered areas thereof to Palestine is complicit with the PA project. When the PA is called Palestine, this erases the legal reality—and injustice—of Israel's ongoing occupation, and it undermines larger projects for Palestinian liberation. At least as importantly, for Palestinians, Palestine is at once deeply territorial and also exceeding of any legal territorial definition. Thus, for many Palestinians it cannot be "ended" by any Israeli action nor defined by any state project (even a Palestinian one). This open-endedness of the significance of national space is not unique to Palestinians, but it is perhaps especially complex. In many postcolonial states, nationalism has both anticolonial and authoritarian force—and the former can mask the latter. For Indigenous people living in settler colonies, concepts of "nation" can be qualitatively distinct from those of the colonial state—or they can overlap in unsettling ways. For Palestinians in the West Bank, living under military occupation and within a state-like institution, the placename can carry many resonances at once. On seals and billboards, the PA's version of Palestine threatens to overcome the Indigenous and anticolonial notion of Palestine—but contestation continues.

Thinking with placenames and place icons is one way of deciphering the possibilities offered by anticolonial sovereignties. They can stand in opposition to securitized, expanding colonial sovereignties, as when the protester under arrest calls out to the rest of the crowd that Palestine is Arab. Placenames and their evocations can become markers for hegemonic statist projects of their own, or they can hold out a vision of liberation that may feel nostalgic, like the Palestine outlined on a t-shirt or a graffito. Today there are emergent discussions about what Palestine could be if not a state. Some would see thinking of Palestine as anything other than a state as diminishing Palestine's prospects. Still, sometimes the word "Palestine" may suggest different horizons of liberation. Sometimes Palestine does refer to a place with which people have a collective relationship of care and connection. It seems that when Palestinians, among themselves, invoke Palestine they are sometimes thinking beyond the state to another kind of connection to land or even to each other: One that forthrightly denies handcuffs; one that is just an outline of a place, whole; one that describes where one is or where one is going that is impervious to the security staff at any airport.

Perhaps one way to read the rest of this book is to look out for where else Palestine comes up as a term or an icon, just as many Palestinians have their eyes attuned to the word or the shape. But Palestine is not the only place or placename to which Palestinians are devoted. There are the regions, like Gaza, that in being the location of the most intense Israeli violence, demand that people go out to their own streets, as I discuss in the next chapter. And each of the cities and streets where people gather in protest have their own smaller landmarks that shape protests. So perhaps another way to read this book is to read for how Palestinians regard cities, villages, camps, and even street names and landmarks in their specificity. Just as Palestine as a placename itself has multiple meanings for Palestinians, some aligned with state nationalism and capitalism and others aligned with more creative modalities of liberation, a reader might keep an eye out for how various Palestinian political practices suggest different Palestinian geographies and different Palestinian futures. But as all of us who live in place know (and that, I believe, is indeed all of us), place is never only about signification, it is also about the very everyday ways of being in and moving through territory. I found those places that signify, that comfort or disturb, can be as small as a (small) parking space.

Passage. Aida Refugee Camp
to the Northern Galilee

I had parked my car just feet from the beloved patio of dear friends in Aida Refugee Camp. There was a measure of comfort here: They had fragrant rosebushes to welcome their guests and a grapevine to shade them. But as the family expanded and expanded and more family members bought cars, parking had become more and more of a puzzle. I often marveled at how they packed cars into a small space, crosshatched at different angles. In the evenings the sitting space felt a bit more hemmed in. The alternative—parking on the street—presented its own problems: The main street through the refugee camp was narrow enough that one had to know the area well to gauge whether a car could be stowed away in an uneven nook or cranny. And one should never block active garages. And a few of the spaces were informally reserved. And there were often construction materials, trash barrels, or other miscellaneous things on either of the street, unpredictably narrowing it further. Both the social knowledge and the physical maneuvering required to park on that street felt overwhelming. Indeed, I tried not to drive on it at all, because it was so narrow that just driving down it felt like a minor social and physical feat: Not only did one have to not hit anything and manage tight turns, but one had to keep pedestrians safe, all the while greeting acquaintances and hoping (against hope) that a car would not appear wanting to go in the other direction, requiring one or the other cars to back up. This was one of the few streets left through which one could drive a car at all in the camp, because people had closed in all open spaces to build more housing as new generations sought to find housing in the camp. To my eye, it should have been a one-way street, but this was not the usual purview of the local committees or UNRWA; there were no street signs within the camp as there were out in the rest of the city. The car situation was so crowded that I had once brought my friends the puzzle game Rush Hour, in which one moves trucks and cars around a grid in order to free one small red car out the only path available to it. It was best, I usually determined, to park on the periphery of the camp and enjoy a bit of walking instead.

Just that once, I had parked in my friends' driveway for a few minutes before traveling north to the Galilee—and now I had to back up. I was parked facing down their steeply sloped driveway, so close to the house that I could smell their honeysuckle. But backing out, I knew, would be a hassle. The driveway was narrow, the street was narrow, and there was, indeed, a car parked immediately across the street from the driveway. My friends chuckled as they watched me reluctantly press on the gas. A few moments later after bumping down the uneven pavement and adjusting through the narrow street, I exhaled and loosened my grip on the steering wheel: I was out.

A few minutes after that, I pulled onto the main road out of town, swerving around a traffic circle that had been built on the occasion of the visit of one dignitary or other. I noticed that the flowers in the circle had wilted, neglected in the summer heat. And my fingers tightened on the steering wheel once more. This was another improbable main road, made up of two narrow lanes that had been rerouted into one-way passages at its narrowest, full of swift swerves, and very steep. People enjoyed speeding down it, but I did not appreciate their fun. A few minutes later, I passed by the Israeli military base that was, at this point, almost imperceptible at the top of the mountain. During the second Intifada, it had been a closed checkpoint: either impassable or a place where one would scramble by foot over dirt mounds and around concrete blocks to transfer from one car to the next. Turning left, the road was straight and fast. I had a moment to enjoy the view of those mountains, rolling out westward, to notice the stone remains of the old summer homes of those who would tend the olive trees. I thought too of the boy about whom my friend had made a documentary who had been arrested here, not realizing that it was Area B, under Israeli military control, and that Israeli soldiers patrolled regularly. Then I curved down and around to the Tunnel Checkpoint. As I wrote in my fieldnotes in 2011, "when you're leaving, the Tunnel Checkpoint is, in its laxity, a demonstration of Israeli racism. I've never been stopped," in my whiteness, secular appearance, and Americanness.

And then I was on the highways, encountering only the usual kinds of traffic and disruption for the next two and a half hours or so, until I found myself driving along another high ridge, another beautiful set of mountains, a few kilometers from my father's village in the Galilee and more cherished and fragrant patios. In the distance on the left, I could see the faded skyline of pastel-colored buildings of Ma'alot, and closer by were the Palestinian villages of Tarshiha and Me'lia. The road descended, and I pulled off the main road onto the entrance to Tarshiha, passing by signs pointing to the police station, and then I was on an incline again, slowing down to go around a well-manicured traffic circle, and another, until I was on my family's street. I felt welcomed by the street names: Al-Mutanabbi Street, named after a famous Abassid era poet, and Jibran Khalil Jibran Street, after the early 20th century writer and artist. I knew these had been the result of local political organizing. Here, too, I felt that there were more passersby who rec-ognized me than whom I recognized, presenting another small social feat of slow driving. A brick gutter ran down the middle of the paved road, constructed in the last decades as a reminder of how the village used to manage water.

As I approached my aunt and uncle's house, I started to look for parking. Some spaces were marked, but others were not. I worried (again) about taking spots that were informally reserved, or that would make it difficult or impossible for people to pass or back up. (There's even a song that mentions these parking difficulties, voiced by someone who left the country, asking a friend back home: "Does Hasan still punch holes in the tires of the car parked in his spot?").[1] One of the "best" spots near my uncle's house was up against a heavy iron fence on the edge of the moun-tain, just in back of a dumpster. It was sometimes hard to get out of the car on the passenger side from this spot—but it was close to my family's home. As I scanned the side of the street I thought about the bigger picture: Some of my relatives were adamant that parking was a political matter. Since Israel's establishment, much of Tarshiha's agricultural land had been expropriated for new Jewish towns, includ-ing Ma'alot, Kfar Avredim, and Me'ona, some of which restrict Palestinian resi-dence.[2] Other land around Tarshiha had been zoned for non-residential purposes. As a result, many of Tarshiha's residents who marry and want to establish a new household must build on top of their parents' homes—much as they do in Aida. The result is severe overcrowding. One relative who had lived in Tarshiha all his life told me that in his estimation Tarshiha would soon become something like a poor neighborhood in relation to the larger Jewish Israeli areas nearby, because it would be so overcrowded that it would be unlivable.[3] Parking was one of the most tangible elements of this overcrowding on an everyday basis: People were often double parked or occupying spaces that made the roads so narrow that the garbage collector could not pass through. Talk about parking was at once about

urgent everyday matters and about their village's long-term fate—and on an ex-
periential level, parking in Tarshiha was not so different than parking in Aida
Refugee Camp, despite the profound differences between the two communities.
With relief, I noticed that my uncle had left a space for me to squeeze in at an
angle, the fourth car packed into a driveway designed for two. And so gratefully I
disembarked, feeling welcomed again in another beloved Palestinian home.

2 Protesting the War on Gaza Together, Apart

THE PALESTINIAN VILLAGE OF TARSHIHA is so far north that you can see Lebanon from the porches, and just far enough west that the sea shimmers in the distance from the higher locations of town. During the periodic military hostilities, Gaza may seem far away, but war is never so distant. Generations of Palestinians in Tarshiha have grown up there hearing the searing snarls of Israeli warplanes overhead, breaking the sound barrier, flying north toward the border. Whatever other purpose they have, they also remind residents of Tarshiha that they are under the rule of a country that is fighting their brethren. In the summer of 2014, Brazilian, Italian, and German flags flew from the houses of Tarshiha as residents marked their loyalties for the World Cup. You could read these as a sidelong recognition that no state truly represented them. But that summer about fifty people came out for a protest against Israel's war on Gaza just outside of town. The location drew residents outside of a quiet zone of consensus inside the village itself. In 1963, Tarshiha had been incorporated into a single municipality with the much larger neighboring town Ma'alot, which had been established in 1957 as a "development town" for Jewish immigrants arriving from Romania, Iran, and Morocco.[1] Though Ma'alot-Tarshiha has a shared governing structure, and though Palestinians have moved from Tarshiha to some neighborhoods of Ma'alot, the areas are physically separate. Many people know each other by face in Tarshiha, and up on the mountain, away from the commercial areas, one rarely sees Jewish Israelis, but Jewish people come to shop in Tarshiha's stores downtown, and Palestinians from Tarshiha work in establishments around the area. Both the economic health of many people in Tarshiha and the prevailing atmosphere of relative tranquility have depended on a certain kind of coexistence.

On this day, though, protesters had gathered right on the main road despite the unpopularity of their stance in Israeli society. They waved the Palestinian flag and held small signs with the names and ages of Palestinians killed in Gaza. They held banners with the word Palestine on them. Most of the signs were in Arabic, and many emphasized Palestinian unity: "Raise your hands for our Palestinian people." Another quoted a line of Arabic poetry from the Tunisian anticolonial poet Abu Qasim Al-Shaabi that had recirculated widely during the Arab Revolts of 2011, "If, one day, the people wills to live."[2] Others said simply in English: "Free Gaza." We chanted against the war and held our signs toward the passing cars. On an opposite corner, a group of pro-war demonstrators waved a bevy of Israeli flags. Police officers stood at a certain remove, but much, much closer was a heavyset man with a thick stubble wearing t-shirt emblazoned with an American flag-like pattern (a funny knock off, as though the t-shirt makers were not licensed to reproduce the real thing) and both "USA" and "United States of America," lest anyone miss the references. This man walked the length of our protest taking video of us with his smart phone (Figure 4). It was easy for me to return his shot with photos of my own: I had no job in Israel to protect and two passports with which to maneuver. But surely what made me especially

Figure 4 A man photographed all of the attendees in a standout against the war in Gaza in the Galilee village of Tarshiha, 2014. Photo by author.

bold in my photography was that t-shirt. It laid bare the racialized settler co-lonial logics and imperial flow of weapons and political support that connect Israel and the United States. It reminded me of my own strange position as a Palestinian-American woman in Israel: undeniably privileged but vulnerable in certain circumstances—and paying (through my taxes) for so many of the crimes around me. But then I stepped back into the line of protesters.

This was one of many Palestinian protests against Israel's 2014 war in Gaza that I attended that summer.[3] (Note that the term "war" is applicable because it captures the scale of violence, but it problematically suggests that there were two states engaged in it, though there were not.) During this fifty-one-day war, Israeli bombs and bullets killed 2,251 Palestinians, including 1,462 civilians; Hamas rockets and fighters killed six civilians in Israel's 1948 territories and 67 Israeli soldiers; Israeli bombings and incursions damaged 73 medical facilities and destroyed 18,000 homes.[4] Protests against the war occurred in Israel (led by both Palestinians and Jewish Israelis), in the West Bank, and beyond.[5] Here, I focus on Palestinian protests in Israel, where the predominant Palestinian forms of protest were vigils and marches, and the West Bank, where the most visible form was stone-throwing clashes with the Israeli army. These are what Charles Tilly would regard as different "repertoires of contention."[6] The form of these protests echoes the modalities of Israeli rule in each location, even though the rigidity of a polarized division both in forms of Israeli rule and in terms of Palestinian protest should be complicated. Protests were a practice through which Palestinians in each location grappled with the appropriate and effective modes of asserting themselves as a community and confronting Israel. Protests were not only a means of articulating a rejection of Israeli policy. They were also, in some cases, a way of directly confronting the Israeli state.

A history of shared protest among Palestinians in Israel and the West Bank includes the way in which Land Day originated with a day of protests inside the Green Line and became a significant day of protest and commemoration for Palestinians everywhere, and also the October 2000 protests that took place on both sides of the Green Line at the start of the second Intifada. Nevertheless, there is a significant difference in the political contexts within which Palestin-ian activists operate in Israel's 1948 territories as opposed to the West Bank. Perhaps because Israel within its 1948 territories holds regular elections and purports to be a democracy in which people can participate in changing public policies, Palestinian citizens of Israel often hold protests that fit expectations of contentious politics in what are often called liberal democracies. This is true even though Palestinians holding Israeli passports have been systematically marginalized within this system. Even these "nonviolent" forms of protest are often treated by Israeli authorities as though they are a kind of violence, and authorities respond to them accordingly.

Palestinians in the occupied territories use tactics common to what are called liberal democracies, too, but they also regularly employ what they call "popular resistance" (*muqāwima sha'biyya*), protests that mix marches and slogans with confrontation through stone throwing, spiraling slingshots, and other similar handmade weapons used against well-armed Israeli soldiers. Organizers are usually careful to limit the scale of protester violence because they know that any escalation could elicit a much more deadly response from Israeli forces. Popular protest is a kind of political action that blurs symbolic contention and outright confrontation. This difference in Palestinian approaches to protesting in these two locations becomes another subtle barrier to collective political action because each kind of protest looks somewhat inadequate from the perspective of the other. The difference in Israel's modality of rule leads to distinct approaches to protest, and this difference, in turn, tacitly comes to be read as a cultural difference, even by other Palestinians.

Indeed, a reading of practices of resistance in an essentializing way—in which cultures are seen as unchanging and culture is isolated from power[7]—is even more pronounced for non-Palestinians looking at Palestinian protest. Palestinian forms of popular resistance are iconic and very polarizing. The stance of the protester wielding a stone or a slingshot is revered by many supporters of Palestinians and reviled by supporters of Israel. For Israel's supporters, the Palestinian with a stone is repugnant: a violent rioter. This image becomes evidence for Palestinians' illiberalism and ill-preparedness for democracy and thereby for self-determination. While popular resistance does have deep Palestinian cultural roots,[8] it is also a recognizable and familiar response to colonial violence and colonial rule the world over, a way of confronting authorities when there is little or no consultation of the governed, when appeals for change without (a threat of) force often seem as ineffectual as whistling into the wind.

Protest—gathering in and often processing through the street with signs and chanting—is also a recognizable form of action around the globe with a long history, but it is important not to universalize protest as a form of contention.[9] In the vocabulary of democracy, it is a means to participate in public actions in between elections, a way of voicing a collective perspective simply by appearing. We find in mainstream US news, for example, that there are similar expectations about protests whether they are happening in Tiananmen Square, Tahrir Square, Gezi Park, Civic Square in Hong Kong, or Zuccotti Park—even though political structures and cultures of resistance differ quite a bit across those locations. Pushing back against those expectations of similarity and pointing out the damage that such expectations can do is a crucial way of protecting dissent.

Commemoration and protest are two related ways of appearing in public as a means of embodied political expression. Commemorations tend to be focused inward, practices that Palestinians engage in to build collective memory and collectivity itself, while protests tend to be focused outward, sending a message to or actively confronting Israeli and other authorities. In this sense they are more performative. However, I do not want to paint too bright a line between commemorations and protests. Some commemorations can become protests. And while Palestinian reactions to the war generally were motivated by a sense of outrage, they also struck a tone of grief, or tried to provide ways to support Palestinians in Gaza; in this sense the protests were also inward facing. While Israeli and Palestinian authorities shape commemorations to a certain degree, Israel's mode of rule in each place structures the forms of protest even more directly, in part because protest can be quite risky for both groups of Palestinians. Still, as we think of embodiment at these protests, the prevailing mode of presentation of the Palestinian body in both places is not one of vulnerability, but rather one of defiance.

Bodies marching in the street

We tend to underestimate the essential embodiment of expression. Protests are one form of expression that make the importance of embodiment especially clear: Protests are judged—by authorities and the news media—by how many bodies comprise them, and how those bodies behave. Representation of protests through photographs often features protesters' embodied bravery, grief, pride, or defiance, their ability to stand out or their ability to present themselves as a collective. This embodied quality of protests also makes them crucial sites at which we can explore the relationship of the state to expression. The concept of the public remains our dominant mode of thinking about how expression creates collectives and how expression shapes political action. Publics and crowds have too often been held apart in analysis, but there are many good reasons to hold them closer together to understand how acts of expression can shape political processes (and vice versa).[10]

A public, according to the liberal model as articulated by Michael Warner, is meant to be "a space of discourse organized by nothing other than discourse itself."[11] Publics are thought of as being independent of the state, defining themselves "against the public authorities themselves."[12] Yet, as Nancy Fraser has pointed out, this concept of the public is implicitly Westphalian, presuming that the state coincides with the nation-state.[13] When we think of publics as made up of practices, it is generally difficult if not impossible to imagine forms of expression that exist outside of a relationship to a state, whether that relationship is enabling or constraining, prominent or hidden. In liberal contexts, the apparent independence of the public is a product of the state's willingness to allow public speech to take place. This is why publics are ultimately undergirded by state power, shaped by how the state defines threat through law. The apparent independence of the public sphere idealized in the classic liberal public sphere literature can be seen as the product of another version of what Tim Mitchell might call the "state effect," in which the state is reified as an entity separate and apart from society.[14] The public seems to be independent of the state, but this apparent separation is a product of liberal ideologies and conceptions of freedom that are more tenuous than they might seem to be even in what are termed liberal democracies. The line of independence may seem especially bright when one looks at, for example, newspapers as sites of expression in a liberal model of the press,[15] but it fades quickly away when we consider protests—and both are vital forms of political expression.

To understand this dimension of the "state effect"—and a distinctively colonial version of it, where the definition of the state's boundaries themselves are part of the effect—we can analyze how Israel shapes public expression in the West Bank and in Israel's 1948 territories. I want to think alongside Charles Tilly's book, *Regimes and Repertoires*. The central assertion of Tilly's book is that forms of protest vary in relationship to forms of regimes, and that each may change the other. Tilly's concept of repertoires of contention suggests that people select forms of contention based on a history of previous actions and authorities' reactions to them: "Performances clump into *repertoires* of claim-making," he writes, and they "vary from place to place, time to time;"[16] moreover, "when people make collective claims they innovate within limits set by the repertoire already established" in their context,[17] and the characteristics of the regime play a role in establishing the context. Tilly argues that regimes vary according to two major axes: governmental capacity and degree of democracy, "the extent to which persons subject to the government's authority have broad equal rights to influence governmental affairs and to receive protection from arbitrary governmental action."[18]

Tilly's approach appeals to me because it pushes against racist assumptions that Palestinian protests are violent because Palestinians are violent, and instead helps us see protest forms as responses to forms of rule and cultural and historical factors. But instead of Tilly's global comparative approach, I want to interrogate the work done by the very appearance of a division between two different regimes that is accomplished by the "sleight of hand sovereignty" of Israel and the PA: Their political performances make it look (at least some of the time) as though they are sovereign and separate.[19] How should we think of the degree of democracy in Israel and the occupied territories? This is a complicated question. Israel is regarded in dominant US discourses and by institutions like Freedom House that create indices of democracy as being quite democratic. Freedom House reports, for example, that "Israel is a multiparty democracy with strong and independent institutions that guarantee political rights and civil liberties for most of the population," and gives it a green sticker indicating Israel is "free."[20] However, limits on democracy in Israel's 1948 territories disproportionately affect the 20 percent of the citizens who are Palestinian.[21] The "broad, equal rights"[22] part of Tilly's definition of democracy is seriously compromised. This inequality, we will see, naturally extends to how Israeli authorities deal with protest. But limitations on democracy in Israel's 1948 territories pale in comparison to the utter lack of political participation that Palestinians in the occupied territories are afforded into the government of Israel, despite the fact that they have lived under Israeli rule for over fifty years. It is no coincidence that the map that Freedom House places on its website is of Israel's 1948 territories, cutting out the occupied territories. Thus—and this is the key point—it is the appearance of a division between Israel and the occupied territories as perpetuated by most news media, diplomatic structures, and much scholarly work as well that tends to address Israel as though it can be analyzed separately from the occupied territories that allows Israel to claim to be anything like a healthy democracy. Avoiding these kinds of blind spots is the benefit of a study of global relations that consistently accounts for structures of colonialism and empire and the disparate forms of sovereignty and nonsovereignty that they produce.

Finally, though Tilly is interested in contention that can include practices like popular protest, Palestinians do not always regard these forms of protest as contention, but rather as confrontation. As Abdel Razzaq Takriti argues, "Contention becomes a replacement word for a range of expressions—resistance, revolutionary action, popular mobilization, and so on—that are laden with political and normative meaning."[23] This is why the Palestinian term of popular resistance is essential as an analytic here, as is an ethnography of protest that accounts for how people think about what they are doing.

Protests as citizens and subjects

In Israel's 1948 territories, which are under civil law, a permit for protest is required only when more than fifty people are expected to participate in a demonstration and when speeches will be made with amplification. Police can refuse to grant a permit only if they can prove there is "near certainty" of harm to public safety or an infringement on the rights of others (e.g., the right to movement).[24] Even so, a recent Israeli High Court decision suggested that the rules regarding permits should be loosened: "The demand for a permit to hold protests is nothing but a [British] Mandatory remnant [and] it seems the time has come to examine its removal from Israeli law."[25] Indeed, in practice, many protests are held without permits, and as long as protesters stay on the sidewalk and do not use amplification, police do not become involved. Deciding whether or not to get a permit can be a matter of convenience, since if people do apply for permits they sometimes face other obstacles or conditions, like the police asking for a change in location or expensive marshals. For some Palestinians, it can also be a matter of a political stance, a refusal to deal with Israeli authorities. As one young woman activist told me in discussing protests related to the Gaza War and related demonstrations, "In the end it becomes something political. If you work with permits, it has to be calm. If you want a permit so families can come and thousands can attend, ok, but you need to be careful. This is a protest against Israeli laws, and so you can't work with those laws." On the other hand, an older Palestinian activist I spoke to who was involved in both electoral and street politics said that he had worked hard to cultivate decent relationships with the authorities in order to get permits, and he resented that what he described as some younger activists' rejection of this approach. In short, organizers thought carefully both about the legality of what they were doing and the political strategies behind their decisions, and especially the younger generation did not mind occasionally breaking the law in order to make a stronger political statement.[26]

Palestinian protest is dealt with more harshly than Jewish Israeli protest. As a human rights lawyer stated in an interview in 2016 in talking about Israeli approaches to protest,

There are two legal systems. One applies to Arabs, and one applies to Jews. If you are Jewish, you can go to Tel Aviv and block the highways in Tel Aviv. And they will give you the right to stay there for one hour, two hours, and they will not use excessive force. But when it comes to Arabs, even if you protest here in Ben Gurion Street, which is not the highway or the main road in Haifa, they will be more violent.[27]

He continued by describing the many ways in which Israel represses Palestinian protests:

There are several stages in how Israel can ban you from expressing your ideas. First, they will ban you, or they won't give you a license for a demonstration. Second, they will call you if you are the organizer a day before or a couple of hours before and will tell you, don't do that, don't go, don't protest, if you do, if you organize the protest there, we are going to arrest you. Of course, this is illegal, according to the law. Pre-arrest? You haven't committed a crime yet. Third, if you get a permit or even if you didn't, they are going to limit your area in the street. …Fourth, they will try to disperse the demonstration using violence. Fifth, they will arrest you if you defend yourself physically or if you don't accept or don't listen to them, if you don't go to the sidewalk, if you stay where you are, if you keep blocking the road. Sixth—now you are in detention in arrest—they will ask to extend your arrest. Even though you don't pose a threat to the public safety. You're not a criminal and they know that. Seventh, the court will accept the police request and the judge will keep you in jail for a couple of days. Usually, they justify that by saying you pose a threat. And the police need time to investigate. More time. And eighth, of course, the indictment, if they can. Now usually they don't indict, because they don't have evidence. [But if they do] you argue in front of a judge that you didn't do anything, and usually they don't accept your arguments.

In 2014 and 2015, lawyers and activists alike had been caught by surprise by Israel's increasingly repressive approaches to protest, in particular the pre-protest arrests. While such arrests did not always hold up in court, they meant that the planning for the demonstration was significantly disrupted.

In the occupied territory of the West Bank, Israel grants Palestinians no democratic rights at all, and it has undermined the very limited self-rule processes of the PA. Palestinian protest in the occupied territories is generally regarded by Israel to be rioting that needs to be repressed with military force.

Palestinians in the occupied territories very rarely seek permits for demonstrations, both because to do so would implicitly recognize the legitimacy of the occupation and also because attaining permits entails interactions with Israeli military authorities, which are both unpleasant and compromising, as they can lead to requests to collaborate with Israeli authorities.[28]

Before the establishment of the PA in 1994, even waving a Palestinian flag or displaying its colors could lead to arrest by Israeli authorities. But today, Israeli arrests more often revolve around such actions as throwing stones at protests.[29] Crucially, though, activists can also be arrested and held without charges under the policy of administrative detention. This policy has been used against parliament members, human rights researchers, elementary school teachers, and construction workers.[30] So Palestinians know well that they can be arrested for anything or nothing. In the occupied territories, the regular risk of demonstrating is not only of arrest, but also of military violence. In the measured language of an Amnesty International Report entitled "Trigger Happy: Israel's Use of Excessive Force in the West Bank,"

> Groups of Palestinians, usually comprising mostly children and young adults, gather to protest against Israeli occupation, as well as the policies and practices that underpin it, including the creation and expansion of illegal settlements, land seizures, closures, arrests and detentions and other violations of the rights of Palestinians. Often, these groups resort to low-level violence, throwing stones and rocks at Israeli soldiers but without posing any serious risk to them due to the distance and the heavily protected nature of their positions. In return, Israeli soldiers use a wide variety of measures against the protesters; these include less-lethal means such as various chemical irritants (commonly called tear gas), pepper spray, stun grenades (sound bombs), malodorants (foul-smelling "skunk water") and hand-held batons, but on frequent occasions Israeli forces have also resorted to lethal means and have fired rubber-coated metal bullets and live firearms ammunition at protesters, causing deaths and injuries. In some cases, they have also killed or injured demonstrators by firing tear gas directly at them from close range or by using tear gas in enclosed spaces causing asphyxiation. Often, the force used by Israeli forces against protesters seems to be unnecessary, arbitrary and abusive.[31]

While Israeli officials may claim that they are only repressing violence, it is clear from the "orders" of the system of Israeli occupation that this is not the case: It is political expression that is being thwarted. As stated in a B'Tselem report:

Commenting on the demonstrations against the building of the Separation Barrier, a senior military official recently claimed that "there is no problem with people coming to the place with signs, with songs, but they must not commit any act of violence." However, the claim that the military only restricts the demonstrations in the West Bank because of the violence that occurs during them is inaccurate. The assumption underlying Order No. 101, signed some two months after the Territories were occupied, is that the residents have no vested right to demonstrate or right to freedom of expression. Even non-violent resistance and civil protest, including a peaceful gathering, are prohibited.[32]

This order was used frequently during the first Intifada to prohibit gatherings, but its use waned in the years following the establishment of the Oslo Accords. Since 2010 it has been used more often.[33] To put it succinctly, there are frequent pleas to Palestinians from some of those who claim to support Palestinian rights to be "nonviolent" in their protests, but these pleas miss the fact that in the occupied territories, Israeli military violence is the fundamental condition of politics, and has been for half a century. Palestinians who gather to throw stones are collectively rejecting Israeli rule in a situation where Israeli authorities refuse to hear their words.

While Palestinian citizens of Israel can participate in Israeli elections and Palestinian parties have long been represented in the Israeli Knesset, Palestinian protests inside the Green Line should not be regarded as a means of influencing the decisions of the ruling party—especially regarding a war in which Palestinians are being defined as the enemy. In Israel's parliamentary system, Palestinian parties had never been part of a ruling coalition until spring of 2021, when one Palestinian party became part of a multiparty coalition led by Naftali Bennett, a right-wing figure unable to make a coalition without some power-sharing. Indeed until 2021, Palestinians' participation has been regarded as toxic, as in 2020 when, after much discussion that they would finally be part of a ruling coalition, the more moderate Israeli party refused to invite Palestinian parties to join them.[34]

The other crucial caveat in this outline of the logics of protest in Israel's civil territory and the territory under its military rule is that on several key occasions, Israel security forces have shot and killed Palestinian protesters inside the Green Line, as in 1976, when six unarmed protesters were killed and hundreds others injured as they protested land expropriations. This protest is commemorated each year in many Palestinian locations as Land Day.[35] In 2000, at the start of the Al-Aqsa Intifada, Israeli security forces killed thirteen Palestinians living in Israel's civil territory as they protested.[36] Thus, while the shooting of protesters is relatively rare in Israel's civil territory, it happens, and memories of these kinds of violence shape current Palestinian politics inside the Green Line. Indeed, I saw people wearing t-shirts commemorating one of the young people killed in 2000 at one of the 2014 protests.

Now I turn to the protests themselves. The protests in Al-Lidd / Lod and Bethlehem exhibit key similarities as well as important differences. In both places, Palestinians ground their resistance "morally and historically in the traditions of past insurrections,"[37] as in other traditions of resistance, yet they articulate or enact this connection to traditions of resistance differently. Importantly, what seems like a worthwhile mode of protest in each location is somewhat different: There are different "repertoires of contention"[38] in each location. Both are battles for a creation of a collectivity, won or lost by the hour, yet these battles are carried out in different terms. Though protest chants are prominent in one location while direct confrontations with security forces are prominent in another, we must recognize the ways in which speech and collective presence on territory—the semantic and the bodily—are interconnected in both sites.

Al-Lidd

On August 3, 2014, I joined a protest in solidarity with Palestinians in Gaza in the city known in Arabic as Al-Lidd and in Hebrew as Lod, a "mixed city" in Israel of about seventy thousand. As used in the context of Israel the term "mixed" itself is fraught: In these cities, Israeli Jewish populations are always dominant over the Palestinian ones, and the term "mixed" often elides a history of mass dispossession of Palestinians in 1948 and after.[39] Silvia Pasquetti, whose ethnographic work focuses on Al-Lidd / Lod, suggests that "segregated"[40] might be a better term. Al-Lidd / Lod, a city with a prominent history in the Roman era now known as (for one thing) the birthplace of Palestinian hip hop, is afflicted by high rates of poverty and crime, and is located less than ten miles southeast of Tel Aviv. In 1948, the vast majority of the inhabitants—who were Palestinians—became refugees. Today about a quarter of the population is Palestinian, many of them having come to Al-Lidd / Lod after being pushed off lands in other areas, and they are concentrated primarily in a single district.

Of the hundreds of people who gathered for the protest, almost all were Palestinian, with just a few Jewish Israelis or internationals. While young men made up a plurality, there were also women, children, and people of all ages. This demographic makeup was typical of the Palestinian protests I attended in Israel throughout the summer; predominantly Jewish Israeli protests against the war were held separately from these Palestinian ones, and many Palestinian activists felt that their leadership of these protests was important. A few Palestinian activists I interviewed commented that Israeli Jews were welcome to organize their own protests or to come to the Palestinian ones as long as they did not dictate or dominate Palestinians' messages. As one put it: "I think it's important that Jewish Israelis carry out demonstrations in Tel Aviv, in Herzliya. I think Israeli society has a lot of problems they need to solve. Let them solve their problems. We have our own problems. But if anybody comes [to the protests we have organized], they are welcome as long as they don't think they have privilege in joining and can tell me what to do."

Indeed, the implicit goal of the protest was not only to oppose the war, but also to build and assert the strength of the Palestinian community inside the Green Line and its unity with other Palestinians. Jewish Israelis who attended this protest were thus far to the left of the mainstream. The protest was part of a wave of youth-organized protests that situated itself outside of the realm of formal politics. As one woman arrested for being involved with organizing such a protest in 2015 said, "We as youth see that the street is the only legitimate place for struggle." She continued,

> The struggle in the street has many outcomes, for example to unify the people. It brings forward the young generation. It has come time for us to take control, not the [political] leadership. When you are in a street, an open space, and you are in control of it and you have chosen it, with the idea that young men and women are going to the same place, where there is unity in what will be said: This is one of the most important things for any people that wants to be liberated.

As another activist put it, these demonstrations "can give this daily anger a language." These statements suggest how these protests contribute to a re-enlivening of a structure of feeling surrounding Arab people's protest that occurred in 2011 with the Arab Revolts.[41]

The Facebook invitation for the event declared this Palestinian unity in a number of ways. The name of the event was "A day of cohesion [al-talāḥum] with Gaza." Cohesion sounds unusual in both English and Arabic in this context; it substituted for the anticipated word, solidarity (al-taḍāmun). On both sides of the Green Line, Palestinians discuss the politics of the word solidarity, pointing out that while it is supposed to signal a bringing together, in the very act of doing so it also signals a current state of being apart. At a demonstration in solidarity with hunger striking political prisoners in Haifa earlier in 2014, a speaker from Jerusalem explained to the audience, "We should not use the word solidarity to talk about prisoners from the West Bank because we are one people." In a similar vein of asserting unity rather than solidarity, the banner at the top of the Facebook invitation included the statement "We are all Gaza," and a key slogan from the protest was, "An injury to you, Gaza, is an injury to us."

The textual format and contents of the Facebook invitation underscored that this was a Palestinian protest. The first line of the description read, in Hebrew, "Hebrew follows Arabic;" after this came Arabic, Hebrew, and then English invitations to the demonstration. Such an announcement to scroll down for other languages, common in such invitations, was a means of establishing a hierarchy of languages and voices that reverses the dominant order in Israel. The Arabic invitation decried the extreme violence of Israel's occupation and war and proclaimed Palestinian unity:

> We direct our call to you, our dear people in our beloved cities and villages, and we call for you to come out in a mass demonstration of anger in uprising against this savage aggression. . . . To reaffirm . . . that there is no difference between Gaza and Al-Lidd, or between Haifa and Khuzaʻa, or between Nazareth and Shujaʻiyya. The aggression is an aggression against any Palestinian Arab, wherever he is.[42]

The word "reaffirm" again presumes that Palestinian unity has already been established. It is a kind of Bakhtinian "authoritative discourse" from below, because it does not explain unity but rather declares it.[43] It is made even more authoritative by the text's unspecific authorship.

The invitation also reconstituted Palestinian space within the mixed city of Al-Lidd / Lod, a formidable task given the way in which Israel has criminalized Palestinian space in the city.[44] The Arabic text invited people to meet "on Salah Ad-Din Street," using the pre-1948 name for the main street. Salah Ad-Din liberated Jerusalem from the Crusaders in 1187, so this name has extremely strong Arab nationalist and anticolonial resonances. Only between parentheses did the invitation introduce the corresponding official—and deeply Zionist—Israeli name, Herzl Street. The invitation also listed that the demonstration would end in Martyr's Circle, in front of the Dahmash Mosque, a reference to the site of the massacre of hundreds of Palestinians in July 1948 by the Palmach, a Zionist militia.[45] Again, this Palestinian name stood in stark contrast with the Israeli placename: In Hebrew, this space is referred to as Palmach Square.[46] While there is not now a robust movement in Israel for permanent name changes at sites like this similar to the campaigns for the removal of Confederate monuments in the United States, even temporary renamings as in the Facebook invitation contribute to a Palestinian remaking of place and memory.[47]

On a pragmatic level, Palestinian unity contained gaps and absences by necessity. The invitation ended with a list of numbers to call to find a shuttle to the demonstration from twelve different locations: universities, cities, and villages. All of these shuttles were coming from inside the Green Line. Organizers would not have even considered having shuttles come from the West Bank, because almost no Palestinians would be able to enter—and no ordinary bus would be able to break the siege to move from Gaza to Israel. Israel's permit system, in operation in the West Bank, is very restrictive,[48] and certainly does not give permits for people to protest. Entering illegally is difficult and risky.[49] These restrictions on movement are one factor that naturalizes the Green Line.

When I arrived at the protest, the demonstrators were gathering in a park in an area cordoned off by a plastic police line, a physical indication of how our collective speech was both permitted and contained. Dozens of counterdemonstrators waved Israeli flags perhaps fifty meters away. Israeli police stood in the shade. As in Tarshiha, a person in street clothes stood immediately next to the demonstrators pointing a video camera at the demonstrators. I almost always found such a figure at demonstrations taking pictures, and I always photographed him in return. I had never faced problems for doing this, but I was aware that as a light-skinned, apparently secular woman who was often identified as being an American, I had more leeway in doing so than others. In contrast, I certainly kept my distance from the counterdemonstrators. At first, as the protesters left the park, several police officers in regular uniforms (i.e., wearing sunglasses rather than helmets and wielding handguns rather than machine guns) blocked our path onto the street, but then one appeared to receive a call. They let the protesters into the street. The momentary delay was a reminder that the authorities were allowing this protest to take place.

For the next hour, the street rang out with the protesters' call-and-response chants, all in Arabic. One of the longest chants riffed upon a poem by the prominent Palestinian poet Said Al Muzayin, "I'm Steadfast" (*Ana Ṣāmed*), written in the 1970s. Like the Facebook invitation, the adapted version of the poem—unlike the original—included a long list of Palestinian placenames:

I'm steadfast, steadfast
If they kill my brother
Steadfast

If they kill my father
Steadfast
If they bomb my neighborhood
Steadfast
My people in Gaza
Steadfast
In Al-Lidd and Ramla
Steadfast
In Jaffa and Acre
Steadfast[50]

After naming these historically Palestinian cities inside the Green Line, this chant called out names of Palestinian villages in Israel's 1948 territories and the West Bank and refugee camps in the West Bank and Lebanon: Ayn Al-Hilwe, Kafr Bir'im, Balata Camp, Arraba. This chant established that all of those places—large, small, all but destroyed, inside historic Palestine and beyond—were Palestinian, and linked these places to Al-Lidd, where the placenames rang out into the summer evening air.

Elliott Colla, writing of the 2011 Egyptian uprisings, reminds us that slogans and chants "are not merely linguistic texts" but "public performance . . . shouted and sung by embodied people moving, often in coordinated ways, in and through public spaces" and that "these movements and actions are not mere context for the production of slogan meaning,"[51] but rather part of the meaning of the protests themselves. Similarly, the embodied performance of the Al-Lidd / Lod chant, in the context of a protest march, provided a crucial aspect of its meaning. This chant was steeped in the locality of the protesters' region, their town, and their streets. As protesters called out the rhymes together, it created a collectivity. Moreover, it was just as fiercely asserting connection with other Palestinians with whom they could never join in protest. Through words spoken together, they did what they could not do in actuality; they created a cohesive Palestinian geography, based this time in the small, struggling city of Al-Lidd / Lod, where Palestinians usually felt marginalized and fragmented by multiple forms of dispossession. This imaginative geography exceeded the outlines of the Palestinian state-in-making in the occupied territories, and indeed any territorial conception of Palestine, also incorporating Palestinian places elsewhere in the Arab world. Here, building on themes suggested in chapter 1, was another instance in which a vision of Palestine beyond that of a state was called into being.

Other chants took up questions of how resistance should operate. One chant concerned chanting itself:

> Raise your voice, raise your voice
> From Al-Lid to Beirut
> You who chant will not perish[52]

For Colla, "ambiguity is key to the study of slogans and slogan performance."[53] The ambiguity here is in the need to point out that those who speak will not die, indicating the level of tension that exists around political speech. Everyone knew that in the current atmosphere, speaking out could cost one a job or precipitate a trip to the police station. Israeli police arrested and detained about 1,500 people, almost all Palestinians, for protests during the war.[54] Through their chant, these protesters reclaimed the innocence—so valued on the liberal democratic political stage[55]—of the act of speaking.

Another chant concerned a tactic that these protesters would not engage in that day, and was instead a rejection of a performance of innocence:

> Light it, light it, light it, light it up
> Today we will shut the streets[56]

Burning tires and road closures are tactics for disrupting business as usual recognized around the world. They are particularly poetic in the Palestinian case, as in a variety of Indigenous struggles,[57] since Israeli authorities have fragmented Palestinian spaces with a great variety of road closures of their own. Yet this chant as voiced in Al-Lidd / Lod that day contains a contradiction: These protesters did close the streets, but they did so with the acquiescence of the police, and they did not light anything on fire. Still, to articulate this chant in a protest in the streets of Al-Lidd / Lod is not just to reference a history of Palestinian popular resistance. It is to take part in that history and hold open a potentiality for future action. In fact, some smaller protests in Palestinian towns in Israel that summer did involve closing down streets with burning tires. These, one activist who was a Palestinian citizen of Israel whom I consulted concluded, were likely spontaneous actions by groups of local activists who knew each other well. Chanting about resistance suspended protesters between language and embodied action corresponding to that language. This collective movement through the streets suggested a momentum to something bigger.

Another chant that briefly rang out explicitly supported the bombing of Tel Aviv: "You fighter, my dear / Hit, hit Tel Aviv."[58] This chant referenced a 2012 song by the Palestinian singer Qassem Al-Najjar. It was a dangerous kind

Figure 5 A pro-war demonstration awaited the end of the anti-war demonstration in Al-Lidd / Lod. Photo by author.

of solidarity on multiple levels. First, even roundabout support for violence against Israel has led to legal action against Palestinians in Israel.[59] Second, this kind of expression of solidarity could be understood as an incitement to these Palestinians' own physical endangerment, given our proximity to Tel Aviv. Still, the risk of arrest or recriminations likely felt more intense than the threat of rockets. Even in the risks they took, protesters were foregrounding a collectivity with other Palestinians, rather than with Jewish Israelis.

Soon, we arrived at Martyrs' Circle / Palmach Square, where another pro-war counterdemonstration awaited us (Figure 5). Again, dozens of people waved Israeli flags as they chanted anti-Arab slogans. I did not write down these slogans in precision, but in recent years, slogans have included "death to Arabs," "May your village burn," and "A second Nakba is coming."[60] This was a more energetic demonstration than the first one, and I was glad for the space between us, and even for the several police that stood in a loose line in the road between the two gatherings. This moment underscored for me that police both enabled and restrained the protest as an act of collective expression. The police were, this time, at once protecting us from the right-wingers and surveilling us. The presence of border police—armed with both handguns and M-16s—was also a tacit threat to the protesters. They and their guns were

Figure 6 A young man climbed a light pole to raise the Palestinian flag as the protest wound down. Photo by author.

familiar eruptions of military occupation inside Israel's 1948 territories, part of a global phenomenon in which the violence of the "border" is brought well inside the apparent edges of the state.[61] They were a reminder of how, in Israel and elsewhere, militarized violence that is or seems to be outside the officially recognized geographic boundaries of the state enables and perpetuates the possibility of such violence within the state, both because of the availability of equipment and personnel and also, in this case, because of Israel's simultaneous cultivation of an enemy at home and abroad. Yet, the police and border patrol were not visible in very large numbers or in full riot gear, as I had seen them at other demonstrations in Israel's 1948 territories that summer at which arrests ensued. Israeli authorities' decisions about how to police such protests, with a wide variety of forces at their disposal, demonstrates how the state—through its policing—shapes the forms of public speech that are possible, and thereby shapes what Tilly calls repertoires of contention.[62]

Even as the protest ended, the chanting continued. One young man climbed a streetlight to raise a Palestinian flag (Figure 6), enacting another chant I heard more than once at protests in Israel that summer: "The Palestinian flag is our flag / It's our duty to raise it high."[63] He wore a kaffiyeh as a face covering, in an embodied re-articulation of Palestinian histories of resistance. Wearing the kaffiyeh in this way also signaled that he was aware that it might be dangerous for him to take this action. Indeed, Palestinian flags flew in multiples at the protest. As one activist commented, the flags encapsulated the fundamental significance of these gatherings:

> First, it's the only thing that is supposed to unite people, as opposed to the flag of the Islamic movement, or the Communist party flag, or the flag of x or y. It's the only thing that everybody has agreed upon. Second, it's the clearest possible political message: We are here not because we are against war, but because we are Palestinians; we are not here because we are against the housing crisis, we are here because we are Palestinians; we are not here because of the violation of international human rights, but because we are Palestinians.

Climbing the streetlight was a powerful act that Palestinians anywhere would recognize as brave.

Protest organizers urged caution as we went into the night and as we went home to post pictures on Facebook. Walking back to the car, I thought of the counterdemonstrators behind us and of the kidnapping and lynching of Palestinian teenager Mohammed Abu Khdeir just a few weeks earlier. I felt sure that this was the most dangerous time of the night. But then I was reminded of ways in which I, at least, felt fairly safe. When I approached my car, I saw a police officer leaning against it. I snapped a picture as I approached. Then I asked him in English to move. My ability to speak to him in this way underscored the presumption of "normal" relations between security forces and protesters, enhanced in this interaction by my Americanness—a sudden unhinged sense that I paid their salaries, due to the amount of US aid to Israel—and femininity. The officers moved, uneventfully, and I drove home.

Protests, like other performances, are "dialogic . . . between and among performers and audience."[64] How do we conceive of audiences for protests like this? Is audience even the best term for thinking about the parties upon whom this protest should act? Some audiences the protesters assumed would be supportive and others would be critical or even threatening. Some were immediate, like people taking photographs of the protest from their window, or observing from a shisha water pipe and coffeeshop (a group of whom apparently went inside as the protest approached) (Figure 7). Some were mediated. The protest was covered in Arab48.[65] The article focused on the text of the call to protest and attendance at the protest and counterprotest. It also included a lengthy quote from the right-wing mayor of Al-Lidd / Lod, who had tried to prevent the protest from

Figure 7 Customers of a shisha shop stepped away as the protesters approached.
Photo by author.

happening at all. The article repeated some of the key place- and collectivity-making tactics of the protest, referring to the streets and squares of Al-Lidd / Lod by their Palestinian names. However, the article was conventional in that it did not seek to in any way attend to the actions and chants of the protest itself. In this way, the article maintained the norm of mainstream news of marginalizing voices from the street.

Especially because, in the midst of this war, Palestinians knew that the Israeli government was not consulting its Palestinian population and because of the Arabic language focus of the chants, one primary "audience" of the protesters was themselves: They made themselves visible as a collective for each other. But even the language of "audience" suggests passive onlookers, when the key dynamic here is that protesting was transformative of the protesters. Protesters were moved by hearing each other speaking these chants, in Arabic, together. Here, in a segregated city in a time of war and intense enmity against Palestinians, these protesters not only took over space; they renamed it, and connected it with a Palestinian geography of cities, villages, and refugee camps that completely countered Israeli organization of space. Jewish Israelis who participated in the protest acquiesced to and participated in this radical reordering. Others who heard the protest or read the handful of protest signs that were written in Hebrew—whether from their balconies, from the street, or as police—surely would have been struck by this public assertion of Palestinian collective voice and space. Indeed, Palestinian citizens of Israel know that language choice itself signifies. Protesters would be aware that the ringing out of a language that many could not understand might be as profound as any specific message sent.

For some activists inside the Green Line, the idea of media coverage or even sending a message was not the main point. One activist told me that protests like those during the Gaza War and against the Prawer Plan should be about direct confrontation, but that this is difficult to carry out inside the Green Line:

> In '48, there is the idea that the goal of the demonstration is to make your voice heard to show or express solidarity, to send a message . . . One of the crucial differences that happened was that the goal of the big [anti-war] demonstration in Haifa was not only to send a message, but also to try to exhaust the biggest number of Israeli forces to contribute to the pressure on Israel. Try to imagine in a situation, like the one during the Gaza War, that in addition to dealing with Gaza, Israeli authorities need to deal with four big demonstrations where they need to bring helicopters and reservists to open a main road at Wadi 'Ara, or the road between Acre and Safed. Part of the conflict is how much pressure you

can apply on the "Institution" to the point of explosion or driving it crazy. So our goal was not only to send a message. Our goal was to create a clash to pressure the security system. We want this to extend and ignite similar situations in Umm-el Fahem, Nazareth, and other places, and this would reduce some of the pressure on Gaza. As in a war operation, we could start a new front to reduce the pressure on the main front. In the West Bank, this was the approach.

For him, the West Bank was a model. One woman compared the weekly demonstrations against the wall in the West Bank with those she organized: "In Bil'in you get the sense that it is more like a media event than a demonstration. It is working directly with the European and American media. We need to be careful. I am against our struggle becoming a media event. And yet at the same time we need to recognize that this is part of the subject." The goal of "sending a message" was a stubborn one in the minds of protesters. The first man suggested: "psychologically, they [activists] keep telling themselves that our message was heard, and the media filmed us, and we spread our message to the whole world, we can go home now." This suggests how a liberal ideal of protest as a form of democratic expression was engrained in the approaches many Palestinian citizens of Israel held to political action, even as many felt disillusioned and isolated from Israeli electoral politics. Our senses of political efficacy are often hard to explain and contradictory given the gaps in democratic processes; in Israel, with its deep and harsh inconsistencies, this is even more pronounced. One of the central assumptions of this book is that it is important to see street actions and media events as interrelated, and indeed sometimes part of the same events.[66] Yet, these activists make the important point that Israel may need to feel pressure in more ways than through the media.

In sum, the protest was a way of creating a "large-scale political subject"[67]—a kind of a public—through a face-to-face event that was a gripping embodied experience and that participants knew would be mediated. The call-and-response chants allowed people to speak together as they moved together, transforming space. Protesters also implicitly grappled with the question of how to legitimately resist Israeli rule. While they chose the path of a protest that authorities allowed to occur, they took risks by aligning themselves with other kinds of Palestinian resistance. The gathering was remarkable in the Israeli context because it was simultaneously an assertion of Palestinian presence in Al-Lidd / Lod and, through the chants, an assertion of a Palestinian collectivity across political boundaries. It was as though a new Palestine could be summoned into existence by hands cupped around mouths and feet moving through the street.

Bethlehem

That night I returned to Bethlehem, located on the southern border of Jeru-salem in the Israeli-occupied West Bank. My returns always felt extremely fraught, since I—with my US and Israeli passports—was virtually the only one in my circle there who could enter Israel legally. Still, I told them that I had been at a demonstration that consisted of nearly an hour of chants—poetry in the streets, I exclaimed! I told them that the chants had been old and new, that they had called out to Gaza, to the West Bank, to Beirut, to all Palestinians, ev-erywhere. I told them also about the police officer leaning against our car. Once I was in Bethlehem, conjuring the sheer proximity of police and protesters in Al-Lidd / Lod was dizzying.

In Bethlehem, a metropolitan area made up of about four municipalities and three refugee camps totaling a population of just fewer than eighty thou-sand people, protests of various types took place nearly every day during the Gaza War. One evening, children gathered with their parents and other com-munity members in front of the Church of Nativity in the middle of town—and thus away from Israeli soldiers—to commemorate the loss of children's lives in Gaza. Children held posters, lit candles, and spoke in English and Arabic about the injustice of the war. Early on the morning of 'Eid al-Fitr, the celebration after a month of fasting for Ramadan, residents of Aida Refugee Camp painted a mural of names of the children who had been killed by Israel during the war. On another occasion, camp residents gathered water and raised money for do-nation to Palestinians in Gaza.

However, the dominant form of protest—both in terms of frequency and in terms of perceived seriousness—was certainly clashes with the Israeli army. These occurred on a nightly basis, because of Ramadan (and sometimes during the day). Because they were so frequent, I was less aware about the call for them being made on social media, though one of the organizers assured me that such calls were being made. Facebook groups spread calls for protests among a net-work of camp, city, and village-based groups; group text messages also spread the word.

On most days, young men and boys over the age of about fifteen—including many of the same people who went to the Church of the Nativity or took part in the events in Aida—would gather near Rachel's Tomb, an Israeli military base embedded in the eight-meter concrete separation wall that had for almost a decade closed and re-routed the main road in Bethlehem. There protesters would confront the army after the late evening Ramadan prayers concluded.

Sometimes an organized procession would start off from a location in the city and process toward Rachel's Tomb. In this case, the participation was wider, with people of all ages and genders participating, though there would still be a prevalence of young men. Here too, chants concerned unity:

> Unity, national unity
> All the power is revolutionary power[68]

Yet, this was a narrower conception of Palestinian unity than I heard articulated in Israel, alluding mostly to the split between Fatah and Hamas, the two main PA parties, in the West Bank and Gaza. Their political identity did not rely on embracing Palestinians in other locations.

Again, protest chants encouraged a range of modes of resistance. Protesters saw speech as a means of recovering lost dignity.

> Raise your fist and your voice
> Death is better than humiliation.[69]

As in the "Raise your voice" chant in Al-Lidd / Lod, this chant addresses the power of protest itself, but this chant's tone is grimmer, suggesting that death may be the price of speaking out. Death hung over other chants, as well:

> To Jerusalem we depart
> A million martyrs[70]

Protesters were indeed marching in the direction of Jerusalem, on the very road that used to lead from Bethlehem to Jerusalem. Yet rather than entering this treasured city, they would be stopped by the separation wall that Israel built to enclose Palestinian populations of the West Bank.[71] This chant asserts that Palestinians were willing to risk death to reach Jerusalem. Though they were not trying to enter Jerusalem, these were dangerous protests. During the 2014 war alone, thirteen Palestinians were killed in the West Bank, mostly at protests.[72]

Just as in Al-Lidd / Lod, there was a protest chant supporting the bombing of Tel Aviv that echoed the song by Qassem Al-Najjar:

> Gaza is irreplaceable
> Hit, bomb Israel[73]

The voicing of this chant in Bethlehem was quite different than in Al-Lidd / Lod. It referenced a more prominent and proximal history of armed resistance in the West Bank, as during the second Intifada. Also, it flirted with

Figure 8 The Israeli army used large amounts of tear gas to suppress Bethlehem protests against the war in 2014. Photo by Mohammad Al-Azza. Reprinted with permission.

self-endangerment from rockets somewhat less than the Al-Lidd / Lod protesters did. Clearly Hamas was not targeting the West Bank in the same way it was targeting Israeli cities. Yet, in Bethlehem, we, too, occasionally saw Hamas rockets flying through the air, perhaps targeting the settlements we could see nearby.

For me, though, the key point was that soldiers would never have heard the chants at this Bethlehem protest, because long, long before protesters reached the separation wall, Israeli soldiers would disperse the crowds with stun grenades and tear gas (Figure 8). My field recordings are almost comical in this regard. Just as I would start recording a particular chant, the staccato of tear gas canisters fired in the air would interrupt the recording and scatter the protesters and me down into side streets. Exactly what made the protests so moving to me in Al-Lidd / Lod was curtailed by military violence in Bethlehem. My recordings demonstrate that these weapons affect not only the movement of people, but, of course, their abilities to express themselves. These Palestinian protesters rarely sense that they have an Israeli Jewish audience. Here, the "repertoire of contention"[74] takes the form it does because state violence and restriction take a different form than they do inside the Green Line.

This point helps me to analyze one chant that I was initially surprised to hear, because it included a curse—something which stood out given many West Bank Palestinians' adherence to a certain standard of respectability and modesty related to religious mores.[75] I knew from watching other protests that during stone throwing clashes, individual protesters also may hurl obscenities at the army.[76] What did it mean that the individual callout had become a chant? It spoke, to me, to the prevailingly youthful and masculine atmosphere at these late-night protests, since cursing is associated with masculinity in this context. Certainly some experienced activists with whom I spoke about the curse said it seemed to speak to the degradation of a proud and dignified political culture. From another angle, though, we can see the obscenity as itself a statement about the communicative circumstances in which these Palestinians find themselves. The Israeli army allows no way for Palestinian protesters to be heard. More broadly, Palestinians in the occupied territories lack any effective way to be heard in the Israeli public sphere. These protesters sensed that the Israeli army deals with all attempts at speech with force, and this may make rational deliberation or even poetry in the street seem less meaningful. Colla notes that invective "strikes at the legitimacy and rectitude of the power . . . by way of familiarly regressive categories of masculinity and femininity, sexual activity and passivity, moral purity and filth."[77] For Hamid Dabashi, the word obscenity itself has to do with "incomprehensibility . . . a vast discrepancy between what one sees and what one reasons."[78] "Now suppose, for the sake of argument," Dabashi writes, "that the obscenity in question is the very idea of 'Israel,'" due to its combination of state violence and its parading of its own righteousness.[79] For Palestinians at this wartime protest, curses were a rejection of Israel's claim to righteousness in the face of what many Palestinians see as the obscenity of Israeli violence, and of the very representational lopsidedness of the conflict.

But again, the main characteristic of these protests was not chanting. After the first volley of tear gas, the crowd would separate into those who were engaging in direct confrontation with the army and those who stood back, watching. Those in the front threw stones and Molotov cocktails and lit firecrackers in the direction of Israeli positions. They used their arms and slingshots. Protesters rarely threw pipe bombs in protests because this, they knew, would escalate danger to Palestinians dramatically. The main street would be closed by the protesters who moved such items as dumpsters and the skeletons of cars to block the path (Figure 9). Soldiers mostly stayed in jeeps, but they sometimes were on foot, shooting tear gas, rubber bullets, rubber-coated metal bullets, and

Figure 9 Protests closed down the main road through Bethlehem each night during the war on Gaza in 2014. Photo by Mohammad Al-Azza. Reprinted with permission.

live ammunition. These clashes would go on for hours and hours, often starting around ten at night and continuing until two in the morning. The Israeli army injured dozens of people at these Bethlehem protests. Notably, though, few if any people were arrested at these demonstrations because protesters prevented soldiers from drawing close enough to arrest them. Instead, arrests would come in the following weeks and months. Soldiers would come to young men's houses to take them away in the middle of the night.

The near impossibility of Israeli arrests during these protests is a hint to the way in which, differently than in Al-Lidd / Lod, these protests rearranged space. Protesters closed down the main road to all car traffic for hours—but this was, of course, a Palestinian street, used only by Palestinian traffic. They transformed the street into a battleground, moving old car frames, dumpsters, and large planters into the streets to be used as shields against the soldiers. They lit fires in dumpsters and tires. Protests transformed space in another way, too. When no protest was going on, the location to which they were walking seemed to be just another bend in the eight-meter, concrete separation wall. However, when demonstrators approached, the gray gate in the gray wall would open, revealing soldiers and the full violence of the occupation. The protest made visible the omnipresence of the soldiers meters away from everyday city life. Night after night, the protesters re-animated the street as a space of struggle. Importantly, just as protesters in Al-Lidd / Lod began their chanting with some limited forms of freedom of expression in place alongside awareness of a set of restrictions on Palestinian expression, Palestinians in Bethlehem began the struggle for space with limited control over space alongside the awareness that Israel is ultimately sovereign over their streets and their city.

The army presence transformed space, as well. Worse even than the tear gas, the Israeli army used skunk water, a chemically engineered substance that smells like a mixture of sewer water and rotting flesh, to repel the protesters. Tear gas residue settled into the street and the sidewalk and could be smelled faintly for days; the putrid skunk water stained space for weeks. The business of nearby tourist hotels was badly damaged. These weapons are very different than those used to repress protests in Israel. As one of my interviewees from Haifa pointed out, skunk water would never be used in Haifa or in Al-Lidd / Lod, because in these mixed cities such a killing of public space would be unimaginable. As Kristen Simmons writes about the use of skunk at Standing Rock and the Mni Sose river where water protectors stood for land and water resources, "with substances like these, the atmosphere becomes not only a medium for violence and control but also one through which affects to demean are engineered."[80] Indeed, soon after this, the Intercontinental Hotel disassociated itself from the Jacir Palace where it had housed one of its two hotels in the West Bank. The fires, the smoke, the stench—eventually it was clear that this was not just a matter of a few days of inaccessibility, but a constant threat to the comfort of guests. If the Jacir Palace Intercontinental Hotel had been a sign of the success of the neoliberal Palestine project, its end suggested that revolutionary Palestine and neoliberal Palestine could not easily coexist.

These protests were difficult for journalists to cover in that they occurred with basically the same pattern night after night. One might say that the messages of the protests were hardly breaking news: Palestinians in the West Bank have been vocally and collectively opposing Israeli military violence since 1967. So Palestinian news media coverage of these protests tended to focus on Palestinian injuries and on Israeli weapons of counterinsurgency. As with the community-based media in Al-Lidd / Lod, YouTube posts by local videographers captured the feel of the protests: the risks taken by young people, the density of Israeli violence.

At least some of the activists involved with the protests saw their importance not as saying something but as opening a second front against the army so that Israel would have to fight not only in Gaza but also in the West Bank—something hinted at in the discussion of protests in Israel, but rarely achieved. According to this perspective the protests were performative, but differently so than in other kinds of Palestinian protest, in that protesters' own personal risk was integral to the performance. Similar to the way in which Judith Butler characterizes the experiences of protesters who slept in Tahrir Square in Cairo, Palestinians' protest was "not only a way to lay claim to the public, to contest the legitimacy of the state, but also quite clearly, a way to put the body on the line in its insistence, obduracy and precarity."[81] However, the point here was not about a performance of precarity—it was about outright confrontation. To make another comparison, many have commented on the theatricality of protest in the West Bank, especially in villages like Bilʿin, where protests against the separation wall have thrived. As Rania Jawad points out, "the performance of Bilʿin's demonstrations defies the distinct separation between theater and resistance action."[82] Yet, in Bilʿin, the performative dimension is seen as being linked to the village's claim to nonviolent resistance.[83] Here, in contrast, we saw direct confrontation as performance, a perilous clash that was simultaneously an assertion that confrontation is necessary. In this sense, protests in Bethlehem exceeded a logic of contention as Tilly characterizes it.[84]

In this light, the chants of Al-Lidd / Lod seem almost luxurious. The Bethlehem protests were a complete rejection of the norms of the liberal public sphere by oppressed people who "have no necessarily unmediated access to 'correct' resistance."[85] Rational discourse—or even poetry—is replaced in this angry moment with a curse and a stone. Rather than constituting themselves as a collective—something which is already well established for Palestinians in the West Bank, who are at the center of the state-building project—they saw what they were doing as a struggle over territory. On one occasion I showed a friend in the West Bank pictures of a Palestinian vigil against the war inside the Green Line. He read the signs the Palestinians held, and I noted that there were few if any signs at the nightly protests. How, then, I asked, did they send a message to the Israelis? He replied, "Just in that we go out and do a demonstration against them. That is the message."[86] If the chants in Al-Lidd / Lod were strategically ambiguous on what the appropriate means of resistance were, here protesters were clear that resistance should entail direct and dangerous confrontation with the army.

Conclusions

There is not necessarily anything essential dividing Israel's forms of rule in the West Bank, Israel, and, we must add, Gaza; in fact, they are constantly shifting, and they change in relation to each other. The "cohesion" (*talāḥum*) of Palestinians in the West Bank and Israel with Palestinians in Gaza is an acknowledgement of this. Recalling the killing of thirteen Palestinian protesters in Israel at the start of the second Intifada, Hassan Jabareen, general director of the Haifa-based Palestinian human rights organization Adalah, commented:

> The problem isn't Arab protesters. The problem is that the Israeli public sees them as an enemy against which force must be used. The police use lethal force against Arab protesters not by chance, but because the police are part of the Jewish public and internalize its racism. Of course there are members of the Israeli public who oppose this sort of hostility toward Arabs, to the use of violence, and who support equality, but these are a minority. The majority does not distinguish between legitimate solidarity and violence—the only question being if you are Jewish or Palestinian.[87]

He suggests that the majority of Israelis do not distinguish between protests of the state and violent acts taken to undermine it, and that Israel responds similarly to both. Jabareen was speaking in October 2015 with the events of the 2014 Gaza War and the fall 2015 upsurge in violence in mind. The silencing logic of elimination in the settler colony inside Israel's 1948 territories calls forth a different kind of violence than the more violent eliminatory logics in the West Bank[88]—but, again, with Israel's obfuscation of its own borders, overt violence can crop up seemingly arbitrarily. And Israeli military violence in Gaza does not stand outside of this dynamic. Israel's attacks on Gaza are a warning to Palestinians in the West Bank about what could be on the horizon. Increasingly, Palestinians recognize the similarities between Israeli rule in the occupied territories and inside the Green Line, similarities that disrupt dominant Israeli and Palestinian statist performances of a hard separation between Israel and the PA. Yet, for a variety of reasons, for now, Palestinians in Israel and those in the West Bank still are not protesting together.

Palestinians in Israel and the West Bank resist Israeli rule with what Tilly would call different "repertoires of contention"[89] even as they draw on a shared heritage of resistance. In Israel, the primary forms of public opposition to the 2014 Gaza War were vigils and processions, with a few demonstrations involving confrontation with Israeli police. In contrast, while people in the West Bank held vigils, they poured most of their energy into direct confrontation with the Israeli army. When one larger protest in Nazareth, inside the Green Line, erupted into stone throwing, I heard different explanations among Palestinians in the West Bank than among Palestinian citizens of Israel. The former praised the step. The latter said that it had been Israeli undercover officers (*must 'arabīn*, literally those pretending to be Arabs) who instigated the violence to make the protest more dangerous. However, on other occasions, Palestinian citizens of Israel argued that Palestinians there should also open lines of direct confrontation, and that when they did, this would be even more effective than similar protests in the West Bank.

Tilly's concept of the "repertoire of contention" is helpful because it does not reduce modes of resistance to culture and disrupts arguments that suggest that Palestinians "just tend to riot." But beyond looking at how modes of contention relate to forms of state governance, we need to interrogate the geographic boundaries that the state system offers to us to delineate its own power, and examine how those lines themselves shape and limit forms of resistance. We need to look at the work that the Green Line itself does to legitimize some political actions and delegitimize others. Moreover, we must be careful that we do not limit our horizons of analysis of resistance to contention alone, and instead that we recognize that symbolic forms of protest are continuous with confrontational forms of struggle. Repertoires of contention cannot be easily separated from repertoires of confrontation. It might be tempting to say that outright confrontation happened only in the West Bank, but the protest chants that foreground confrontation happened in both places. Just as Israeli forms of rule are less bound to geography than they might seem to be, so are Palestinian modes of protest.

What, then, do we learn about geopolitical fragmentation by studying Palestinian protest across the Green Line? Palestinians' inability to protest in the same place across these two communities is partially due to Israel's closure policies, which limit actual co-presence, but it is also due to Israel's different communicative restrictions on these communities, which yield different modes of protest. What looks and feels like a successful protest in each place is quite different. Fragmentation—in political geography *and* political habitus— compounds the obstacles to expression that come from either being a colonized group of citizens excluded from the national project, as are Palestinian citizens of Israel, or being colonized subjects of military occupation, as are Palestinians in the West Bank. The more general point, then, is that state-produced divisions between related polities affect conditions for group expression. It is not only that states set limits for political expression in a variety of ways. It is also that the naturalized sense of separation between people into different polities—in this case Israel and the West Bank—acts as another limit on expression. The differences between two Israeli legal and cultural modes of colonial repression multiply their effectiveness. This is one key dimension by which the state produces publics and their norms; it is also one way in which colonial and imperial logics circumscribe global politics.

It may seem that chanting and stone throwing are quite different forms of resistance. However, both groups of Palestinians saw protesting for Palestinians in Gaza during the 2014 war to be of crucial importance, worth significant risks. Though they never protested together, when they did chant, they used similar words. Each of these protests constituted a collective subject serially and intertextually with other protests and commemorations that year and across decades of Palestinian resistance. The forms their resistance took differed somewhat, but each form of resistance was a means by which Palestinians worked through ideas about Palestinian collectivity and Israeli violence. Protests dominated by embodied talk and those dominated by physical action are intimately related. Indeed, we need to insist on recognizing the embodied in speech and the semantic in action, and the ways they blend, augment, or contradict each other in single performances. When we look at speech as embodied and emplaced and recognize the performative in a wide variety of protests, the relationships among practices of resistance can become clearer.

If these two kinds of protest are cousins to each other, we might think of Palestinian protests and commemorations, the topic of the next chapter, as bearing a similar family resemblance as prominent forms of Palestinian political practice. In their performativity, protests are a mostly outward looking form of political expression—though as we have seen, protests have audiences internal to the crowd as well. Commemorations might be conceived more as spaces for communities to mark time and injury—though they, too, can be pointedly visible to outsiders. Protests address present and urgent injustice, while commemorations concern histories and circumstances of hurt that come around year after year. I saw many of the same people at the commemorations and the protests. For many of them, we laced up our shoes, got out our flags or kaffiyehs, put on our t-shirts, designed our posters, and headed out to be together. As always, though, before I was on my feet, these events had me out on the road, and the circumstances we were commemorating were hardly divorced from the roads that took us to the events themselves.

Passage. Bethlehem to Lubya

We set out for the annual Nakba commemoration together, just my friend, who held Israeli citizenship, and me in her yellow-plated (and thus Israeli licensed) car. The clever option, we knew, was to take a bus—more fun and a better way to avoid inevitable traffic—but there was no bus departing from Bethlehem. Almost no one living there could go to an event in Lubya, inside the Green Line. If Israel is trying to sanction Palestinian citizens of Israel for marking the day of Israel's independence as a commemoration of dispossession, they surely will not issue permits to Palestinians from the West Bank to attend such a commemoration! We left Bethlehem from the Al-Walaja Checkpoint, where the soldiers guarding the checkpoint were, my friend said, speaking Arabic in an accent that indicated they were Druze from her region of the Galilee. This did not prompt a friendly exchange, even though Druze are drafted into the Israeli army.[1] While the soldier sought recognition, my friend saw betrayal.

Soon we pulled onto what is called Begin Parkway—which inevitably elicited a caustic remark from my friend. Menachem Begin was the leader of the Irgun, a Zionist militia that participated in the attack and massacre at the Palestinian village of Deir Yassin in December 1947, as well as a Likud prime minister of Israel in the 1970s. As she drove, I just struggled to keep track of where we were: Early in each visit to the field, I had to catch up with the latest road work. This parkway was constantly extending southward, further into the West Bank. The shifting exchange from one road to the next kept me disoriented.

Moving north, the road was smooth. We passed through Jerusalem, slid onto Road 443, passed by the prison of Ofer, where we thought for a moment of the young men we knew inside. Then we passed easily through another checkpoint, came upon some of those olive-covered hills that I have always regarded as espe-cially beautiful, and passed through yet another checkpoint. These checkpoints generally operate to strictly regulate green-plated PA cars, which are allowed to move only in particular directions on various segments of this road, and to pre-vent them from crossing the Green Line. They divide and regulate this area of the West Bank where Palestinian villages and Israeli settlements neighbor each other. They also allow soldiers to police people they regard as suspicious on a more occasional basis. Usually, soldiers just waved yellow-plated Israeli cars like ours through as we slowed down. Sometimes they asked a question of the driver, occa-sionally they checked an identity card, but I regarded a stop here for us as unlikely: We were two secular-looking women. The Green Line was just after the third of these checkpoints, and we crossed it uneventfully.

Then we surged toward Highway 6, the main north-south tolled highway in Is-rael. If, a while earlier, I had felt ensconced in the hills of the West Bank, comforted by the sight of mosque after mosque in Palestinian villages that were nevertheless not easily accessible from Road 443,[2] on Highway 6, two Palestinian cities were almost entirely hidden by high embankments. These strange artificial green hills—half hills, actually, since they seemed to be abruptly bisected—had been built to disguise the separation wall around the cities of Tulkarem and Qalqilya. We sped by—this was old news and hardly elicited a remark from either of us.

Soon, we were nearing the site of the village of Lubya, near Tiberias, where the commemoration was to be held. I snapped a picture of the first Palestinian flag I saw flying from outside of a car, knowing its passengers were headed to the March of Return. For weeks, we had seen more and more Israeli flags flying from car windows and light poles as Independence Day approached. Now this flag and oth-ers were making another story visible. As we drew closer to Lubya, though, we hit fierce back-to-back traffic. Drivers sized each other up as either Israeli Jewish or Palestinian (sometimes using the same social tools the soldiers used at the check-points to determine whom to stop) and allowed each other to merge accordingly. People on the buses disembarked to walk ahead on foot because traffic was so bad. Along the way, we encountered an Israeli Independence Day celebration appar-ently populated by many religious nationalists. Shouting confrontations ensued, with a highway barrier and Israeli police acting as buffers between the two groups. People unfurled their Palestinian flags to pose in front of the Zionist demonstra-tion, hands held high in a V-for-victory, or they just walked by in their kaffiyehs. Eventually journalists snapped photos as a police officer stood by. Our car moved (slowly) on toward the actual commemoration.

Figure 10 Near the March of Return in Lubya in 2014, one officer recorded the author as another, it seemed, posed relaxedly for the camera. Photo by author.

Finally, we were there. We passed by soldiers carrying multiple weapons: po-lice batons, handguns, large, rubber-tipped bullets slung around their waists and accompanying rifles for shooting these bullets. They looked European rather than Arab. They photographed us, and they also, it seemed, posed for pictures (Fig-ure 10). To find the parking area, we had to follow the official signs toward the Jewish town of Lavi, the town that had been built on top of the Palestinian village of Lubya. We encountered a rustic wooden sign from the Jewish National Fund inviting people to plant a tree, and I knew that these tree planting projects had been used to erase depopulated Palestinian villages and were still in action in other parts of the country as a means of dispossessing Palestinians.[3] Finally, I spot-ted a small hand-drawn cardboard sign pointing to the March of Lubya. Again, quite literally written into the infrastructure were signs of Palestinian erasure and exclusion, and Palestinian acts of rewriting presence were handmade.

As at other marches, the parking area was quite crowded, and not situated in an actual parking lot. Managing logistics of these marches of return—find-ing large parking areas near destroyed villages—was often a challenge. This time, there were police officers there to direct traffic. My friend spoke with one in Ara-bic, and this Palestinian officer of the Israeli police directed us to park along the side of a wheat field, as cars squeezed by on this dirt road. I noticed how she spoke with some familiarity to these officers, even as I had watched her barely be able to stand interacting with the Arab Border Patrol officer she encountered at checkpoints. I pointed this out, and she remarked that she did not like it, but they were doing a job. I spotted another police officer overseeing the jumpstarting of a car. At the start of our journey, we had encountered the Border Patrol at the first checkpoint, then barely noticed the soldiers waving us through the checkpoints on the northern outskirts of Jerusalem. For a few hours, we had had no interaction with police or soldiers, and then we arrived here, where within moments we had been surveilled by heavily armed officers and provided an ordinary service by police. Moving through space as Palestinian citizens of Israel, we on this occasion did not experience a great separation or dichotomy between the West Bank and Israel, but rather a strange coexistence of the threat of state violence and identity-based control of movement on the one hand and a veneer of normalcy on the other— and Palestinians were thoroughly part of this system as both soldiers and police.

3

The Momentum of Commemoration

ON NAKBA DAY, MAY 15, 2011, we piled into the buses waiting on the main street on the edge of Aida Refugee Camp. There were community leaders, a smattering of people in middle age, many men in their twenties, and a host of teenagers and kids: boys and girls who were committed to commemorating this occasion, or at least to enjoying a short trip together. They were all refugees, and in that sense their lives had been preconditioned by the events of 1948: Their parents and grandparents had lost their homes and their agricultural lands, and they had come to this refugee camp. This was the "catastrophe" to which the Palestinian historical term Al-Nakba refers. The youngest of them knew the camp only as surrounded by the separation wall, as it had been since 2005. Most of their families' home villages were an hour's drive away or less, but they were forbidden from visiting them by Israel's closure policies. Many of the same people had participated in a Nakba Day commemoration a few days earlier in Aida Camp itself, an annual kite making (and flying!) contest that celebrated children's ingenuity and dreams of mobility. But on this day, they would recognize the struggles of another nearby community, in the village of Al-Walaja, near Bethlehem, at one of several demonstrations planned in different locations.

Al-Walaja has a long and complex history of displacement. It is located right on the Green Line near Jerusalem and at the site of the Tel Aviv-Jerusalem railway. As villagers often tell visitors, whether they are delegations of internationals for a tour or Palestinian youth for a protest, villagers were expelled from their stone homes in the armistice agreement of 1948. They lost about 75 percent of their agricultural land and much of their water resources, as well.[1] However, they only moved to the next mountain over, staying on agricultural land owned by the villagers and building new houses there. Even Palestinians who did not lose their lands entirely in 1948 sometimes suffered these partial removals. I heard this history and thought of ʿAyn Hawd, one of the first village stories I learned about as one of my relatives took me on a tour of the Galilee as a youth.[2] Village stories like these resonate across geography, and can become the foundations of Palestinians' understandings of history. In 1967, Israel incorporated more of Al-Walaja's land into the municipal boundaries of Jerusalem, an act of annexation regarded as illegal under international law. More village lands were expropriated for the Israeli settlements Gilo and Har Gilo. Under the Oslo Accords, over 97 percent of the land of Al-Walaja was under full Israeli military control, and all structures were vulnerable to demolition.[3] While Al-Walaja won a 2004 Israeli High Court case that stipulated that the separation wall would not pass through residential areas of their village, in 2006 Israeli authorities announced plans to build the wall around the town. Villagers would be cut off from one-third of the remaining 4,400 dunums of agricultural land, and their access points to the village would be limited.[4] For all of these reasons, Al-Walaja was a front line of ongoing colonialization, a place where people were suffering every day because of the military occupation. But it was also a beautiful area. Indeed, in a familiar stinging irony, Israel has since turned much of the land into a national park.[5] Our group, coming from the concrete jungle of Aida Refugee Camp, felt happy for the change in scenery, even as we recognized the grave threats with which people in Al-Walaja lived.

This small Nakba Day commemoration exemplified other larger commemorations in that it occurred in a specific Palestinian place under threat, and it involved people gathering to learn about that location on threatened ground. Such commemorations—many of them—occur in Israel's 1948 territories, the occupied territories, and refugee communities on a shared annual calendar. They play a crucial role because, with a few exceptions,[6] Palestinians have long lacked national institutions of history-making that are standard in nation-states, and because Israel has so systematically denied Palestinian history through such practices as its placenames, archeological institutions, and educational systems.[7] Annual commemorations offer a "form of control over time [that is] an especially valuable asset when control over public space is extremely limited."[8] Commemorations take place under Israeli civil law and Israeli military occupation, and in Palestinian refugee and diasporic communities where Palestinians face various political pressures and restrictions. There is also a growing movement of Jewish Israelis to learn about and remember

Palestinian perspectives on the Nakba, especially through the organization Zo-chrot,[9] which works with Palestinian organizations in both Israel's 1948 territo-ries and the West Bank.

A rich literature on Palestinian commemorative practices focuses on in-formal practices of historical narration, books of commemoration, honoring martyrs, monumental sites, and commemorative events.[10] This literature estab-lishes how Palestinian national identity and memorializations have a tendency to emphasize geographic specificity, for example by focusing on particular vil-lages of origin.[11] The commemorations about which I write follow this pattern. Building these and on foundational literature on the social, emplaced, and em-bodied quality of memory and rituals of commemoration,[12] I have found that even as much is similar about these commemorations across the Green Line, place refracts Palestinian history differently depending on the political context. Commemorations are a practice through which Palestinians and others explore and expand the meaning of Nakba and of Al- 'Awda or "return." The right of re-turn is legally established by UN General Assembly Resolution 194 of 1948, and "return"—with multiple possible meanings—has also become central to the way in which Palestinians envision justice and their future, alongside the idea of statehood. While a largescale return of Palestinians to historic Palestine and granting them rights would certainly transform Israel, it would not negate Jew-ish presence or rights, and could invite a vitalization of democracy, new ways of coexistence, and community renewal for Jewish, Palestinian, and other Israelis.

As people gather to mark historic and ongoing forms of dispossession on each side of the Green Line, commemorations are often a means through which Palestinians can learn about different communities, as was the case for the youth from Aida Refugee Camp who went to the village of Al-Walaja for Nakba Day. However, never was there one primary occasion that all Palestinians—or even all Palestinians in Israel and the West Bank—could attend. Indeed, com-memoration is doubly shaped by the politics of fragmentation. First, people cannot all gather in one location, whether across all of historic Palestine or even separately in Israel's 1948 territories, the West Bank, or Gaza. Second, people experience Israeli settler colonialism differently both across those three areas and within them. Through many small acts of commemoration, Palestinians obtain a glimpse of various histories and present processes of dispossession, and they stand with other Palestinians despite and across difference. Com-memorations create knowledge through and in motion across multiple scales, including transportation to the event and motion within the event—even as that mobility is ultimately limited by Israeli closure.[13] As a researcher, I was also constantly aware of how my own process of making knowledge in motion was made possible through my privileged mobility as a US and Israeli passport holder.

Still, for both Palestinians in Israel's 1948 territories and Palestinians in the West Bank, these annual commemorations are not only a mode of learning by being in a place with others; they are also a way of sustaining collectivity. Especially for Indigenous, displaced, and other marginalized people, places can be sites of power and wisdom in knowledge and memory.[14] The commemorations I study here are akin to the historical walks Yarimar Bonilla analyzes in Guadalupe that connect Guadalupans to their ancestors' histories and struggles, walks that are practices of knowledge production and embodied ways to connect emotionally with the past, ways of "feeling history."[15] As in Guadalupe, these commemorations are, at least sometimes, the somewhat less confrontational edge of a larger politics, and they are integrally connected to other practices like protest. As Julie Peteet writes, "Palestinians have a conscious and profoundly political sense of place."[16] I would add that Palestinians are especially aware of the politics of small places that are not national capitals or landmarks. When Palestinians honor these many small places, they also open the possibility of multivocality that can speak toward a common vision, like that of return.

One way in which Palestinian commemoration under Israeli control in historic Palestine differs from commemoration in Palestinian refugee communities outside of historic Palestine and in the diaspora is that under Israeli control commemorations resonate with everyday experiences, especially as historical commemorations have been reframed around the theme of ongoing dispossession (*al-nakba al-mustamirra*).[17] These Palestinian commemorations foreground how recognition of one atrocity reiterates or recalls others.[18] Given the multiple ways in which dispossession and fragmentation operate, even regional commemorations are occasions for an important kind of mobility and change in perspective. At these commemorations, participants also think of Palestinians in other political entities from whom they are more profoundly isolated. Commemorations can be occasions for exploring questions of voice, place, and shared political action among different Palestinian groups.

Palestinians commemorate a large number of political holidays, from Prisoners Day to Land Day to Jerusalem Day. These occasions have indeed historically been seeds of shared political work across the Green Line and beyond. For example, Land Day became a day of commemoration for all Palestinians in the years after Israeli forces killed six Palestinians during protests against land expropriations in the Galilee in 1976. That this day could take on such significance well beyond communities of Palestinians who hold Israeli citizenship demonstrates that while Palestinians who hold Israeli citizenship have long been marginalized by the national movement, there is a shared national culture to which they have long contributed.

Today, Nakba Day is the most prominent occasion for commemoration. Nakba Day commemorates Palestinian dispossession that was a result of the establishment of Israel. *Nakba* is the Arabic word for catastrophe that has crystalized Palestinian popular historical thought about Israel's establishment in 1948.[19] Crucially, in both Israel's 1948 territories and the West Bank, commemorations—especially of Nakba Day—are constrained by authorities. Israeli authorities have proscribed and even threatened Palestinian commemoration since the first years of its existence.[20] Basic forms of political expression were illegal under the period of direct military occupation from 1967 to 1994. Under civil law in Israel today, certain commemorations of the Nakba are threatened by law.[21] Under PA rule and Israeli military occupation in the West Bank, commemorations are at once co-opted by the PA and—through distinct spatial logics—hemmed in and repressed by both the PA and Israel.[22] As with other kinds of political practices, in the occupied territories, Palestinians are threatened by outright military violence that is not tied to a particular law, while Palestinians are constrained in Israel's 1948 territories by law and threat of government sanction—even as the threat of physical violence looms.[23] Palestinians' awareness of these constraints is one reason that the category of commemorations blurs into the category of protest as a kind of political practice.

Despite Israeli restrictions and PA repression and co-optation, these commemorations offer a space to do something, each round a new opportunity. Attending closely to place, I show that when people are speaking together, but are geographically apart, the meanings of shared occasions and chants can shift across space, as people invoke (or overlook) other Palestinians who cannot gather with them. I have been attending these events for many years whenever I am able, but in 2011 and 2014 I went to them more intentionally as fieldwork.[24] I generally went to commemorations with other people who were already going because these are fundamentally social gatherings. People go to these events not primarily to sit and listen to the speeches, but rather to catch up with friends, to introduce children to these issues, and to mark history and contemporary struggles with others. The prosaic quality of these events mirrors the prosaic quality of other political gatherings. While Lori Allen emphasizes the quality of being bored and frustrated (*zahaq*), as she writes about Palestinians' experiences of marches and funerals of the second Intifada,[25] I found that people embraced these events as times to do something that had some political significance. If the speeches grew dull, there was much else going on. Along these lines, a friend in Haifa once told me—as I scrambled to go to as many events in a few days' time as possible—that one hardly needs to attend these events to write about them because they are so predictable. It perhaps goes without saying that this person was not an anthropologist. It is certainly true that these events are repetitive, but this is part of a dynamic I am exploring in this book: the repetitiveness of settler colonial violence and Palestinians' iterative response. Moreover, as has been observed by musicians, anthropologists of performance, and musicians who are anthropologists of performance, no repetition is just repetition.[26] Instead, repetition of the same slogan in a different context can mean something new. Still, I see these gatherings as sites not primarily for discourse but rather for practice. To the extent that I analyze speech at these events, I see speech as one of many forms of embodied, emplaced practices that occurs at these annual gatherings.

Writing of memories of the much more temporally distant and immensely violent slave trade, Rosalind Shaw observes that memory need not always be about continuity, but instead can take in rupture. She writes, "Far from being lost through experiences of disruption, dislocation, destruction, and even apocalypse, the habitus feeds on these and takes them into itself. Instead of being inimical to reproduction, then, rupture becomes part of what is reproduced."[27] Here we find that the iterative quality of the annual commemorations can invite Palestinians to reflect on fragmentation itself. Similar to the shifting meaning of the placename Palestine discussed in chapter 1, we find here that slogans and lines of poetry change in their significance slightly as they are evoked in different places, becoming more layered and richer. Those involved with the commemorations evoke a common history, but they do not try to erase difference. These events allow for an annual reassertion or reevaluation of collective experience and aspiration.

Wearing catastrophe on our chests

In 2014, my family was in Bethlehem having dinner with a visitor from the United States when my three-year-old leaned over and whispered, "Tell her about the Nakba!" I was struck that my daughter had learned about the Nakba in just a few short weeks. For days before Nakba Day and weeks after, Nakba remembrance transformed the cities of Bethlehem and Ramallah. The Bethlehem-based refugee rights organization Badil ran a contest for the best Nakba Day poster, and it was plastered around town. It even became the basis for a graphic of a t-shirt that many people—especially in our community in Aida Refugee Camp—wore.[28] Each year, the t-shirt had the winning graphic on the front and the number 1948 on the back, with the numbers 194 in black, and the 8 in red. In this way, the t-shirt both memorialized both the year of dispossession (1948) and called out the United Nations Security Resolution 194 that established refugees' rights to return. UN resolutions themselves held popular cultural significance. The posters and t-shirts are evidence that historical memory and international law are highly visible for many Palestinians in the West Bank—so much so that even a young child can hardly help but recognize this. The tent in that year's graphic was a remarkably visual way for a child to grasp (or a parent to explain) the concept of the Nakba, since so many people actually did live in tents when they lost their homes and lands. In the West Bank, especially in refugee camps, the Nakba as a historical event is not abstract or academic—it is prominently displayed in public spaces and made personal and domestic.

Perhaps because the idea of the Nakba has become so prominent, thinking about the Nakba has advanced such that many people now point out that the Nakba is an ongoing phenomenon rather than a past event. This, too, is visible all around Palestinians. The day was long called a "commemoration / remembrance of the Nakba" (*dhikrat al-nakba*), but in recent years people have pointed out that the Nabka is not past, but rather that "the Nakba continues" (*al-nakba mustamirra*). Like other days of national commemoration, this day is commemorated by Palestinians in many locations within historic Palestine and beyond. Nakba Day embraces refugees in diaspora and allows Palestinians to focus on the right of return as the central demand of Palestinians.

Commemorations of the Nakba emerged in the early years after Israel's establishment. In the West Bank, then under Jordanian control, Palestinians began marking May 15 with general strikes in 1949. In the 1950s, May 15 was known as Palestine Day in the Arab world.[29] Inside the Green Line during this time, Palestinians were under military rule and subject to strict control over movement. Israeli authorities would lift movement restrictions on Independence Day due to Israeli leaders' early hope that Palestinians in Israel would also adopt Independence Day as a holiday because it was purportedly anticolonial in opposition to the British Mandate and, unlike other state holidays, secular.[30] On this day, many internally displaced Palestinians would go to their villages.[31] As journalist Najwan Simri Diab writes of these occasions:

> In my youth, Al-Birwa was the site of a small annual ritual for our family. We would enter it only on "The Independence Day of the Jews," with a heavy silence. We did not at all enjoy these visits in a place where silence was imposed upon us, without the young among us understanding why, without understanding why my father would sit far away from us on a rock near some graves, to return to us after a while with two glistening and red eyes. It was my mother who would forbid us from speech or questions with a look, so we would just be silent in the sanctuary of sadness.
>
> After gathering wild plants, we would return to our house in our village a few minutes away from Al-Birwa to breathe a sigh of relief.[32]

It was a strange holiday, she notes, that yielded no new clothes, as other holidays did for children. Nor were these visits quite political events, as she describes, since her family did not tell her the story of Al-Birwa. Indeed, they called the territory Ahihud, the name of the town built on Al-Birwa, or "the Yemenis' land." But years later such visits to home villages became a collective political practice after the Association for the Defense of the Rights of the Internally Displaced (ADRID) began planning marches of return. Nakba Day was slowly institutionalized in the occupied territories, as well. In the West Bank, the 40th anniversary of the Nakba in 1988 was commemorated during the first Intifada as "a day of national mourning and a general strike,"[33] and PLO Chairman Yasser Arafat declared it a national holiday in 1998.

Palestinians in the occupied territories and in Israel commemorate the Nakba on different days. Palestinians in the occupied territories mark it on May 15, the day on the Gregorian calendar after the declaration of the Israeli state. Palestinians in Israel have debated whether Nakba Day should be commemorated on May 15, with the rest of Palestinians, or on Israel's Independence Day, which follows the Jewish calendar and thus shifts throughout late April and early May. While the former option has the value of being in unity with other Palestinians, the latter places Palestinians in Israel in direct opposition to the Zionist holiday. Palestinians in Israel have rallied with the refrain, "Your day of independence is our day of catastrophe,"[34] a pointed rejection of Israel's attempt to incorporate them as individuals and strip them of cultural identity. It sets forth a Palestinian collective set apart from the Zionist public and asserts that Palestinians have a fundamental critique of Zionist narratives of history. This approach to commemoration that sets one historical narrative in direct contrast with another occurs in other settler colonial contexts, as with the National Day of Mourning, which takes place on US Thanksgiving in Plymouth, Massachusetts, as a remembrance of the dispossession and genocide of Native Americans.[35]

Unlike in the West Bank and well trafficked camps in Lebanon,[36] commemorations in Israel attract little attention of internationals and instead have become a central event around which local Palestinians organize. In the West Bank, commemorations have been a site of struggle between the PA and grassroots organizations. Still, they have allowed for grassroots organizations to make their messages about the right of return resonant to Palestinian community members.

West Bank commemorations

In the West Bank today, there are a great variety of commemorations of Nakba Day. The PA organizes rallies in Ramallah, often including a march through town that features youth in scouting uniforms or in marching bands and concluding in speeches by PA officials on a stage. Other marches through regional cities like Nablus and Hebron feature Palestinian flags flown alongside the flags of the dominant political party, Fatah. For years, the Badil contest, mentioned above, culminated in an event in a Ramallah theatre, the Cultural Palace. One year, I heard the beloved Palestinian singer Reem Banna, a Palestinian citizen of Israel. We watched Palestinian *dabka*, or popular dance. Winners of various elements of the Badil contest—for photography, posters, children's books, art, etc.—would be announced in front of an audience that generally included many young people who travelled there on buses as well as a significant representation of elders who had lived through the Nakba. Badil leaders regarded this as an important event for building a Palestinian culture of return, and for celebrating talented Palestinians' contributions to this culture.

Other West Bank commemorations of the Nakba are sit-down rallies like one I attended in Manger Square in Bethlehem where school children and activists gathered to watch *dabka* and listen to speeches as they hold placards with the names of destroyed villages on them. There are, as mentioned above, kite-flying contests and even (also in Aida Refugee Camp) a "train of return," large enough that children can get on board. Here I focus on a popular form of Nakba commemoration that mixes speeches and marches in places that are deemed to be vulnerable to ongoing processes of Israeli dispossession, starting with a return to the Nakba commemoration with which I began this chapter.

Al-Walaja, the West Bank, 2011: Minding the Green Line

When the bus from Aida Refugee Camp arrived in Al-Walaja, attendees listened to local activists—the kinds of brave and persistent women and men who are at nearly every demonstration and who often serve as guides and hosts for international visitors—delivering speeches in English and Arabic that presented the history of Al-Walaja and articulated core themes of Nakba Day, about the right of return and the ongoing Nakba. Then the procession began. As we started moving, we passed by homemade placards for the right of return. One that incorporated much of the imagery of the day consisted of a simple map of historic Palestine made of rope and paper on burlap, emblazoned with the Palestinian flag and a single word, "return" ('awda), and a large key, a symbol of the right of return because so many Palestinians left their homes during the Nakba carrying their keys expecting to return home, only to become refugees. I wondered whether these placards, hung on a chain link fence, were part of the Nakba Day commemoration or whether they were always there.

Then we embarked from the center of the village toward the original village of Al-Walaja, the one that had been depopulated in 1948. To arrive at the original village would involve walking across the small valley and across the Green Line. Young men in tight clusters led chants and clapped their hands. School children still in their blue striped uniforms joined in. As we descended the mountainside, we passed by the rubble of homes that had been destroyed in recent years: slabs of concrete smashed flat that showed the violence of this ongoing Nakba. We arrived at the edge of the village's houses. First, we were on a paved road, then a dirt road, then a smaller path. We passed the future track of the wall: a swath of packed earth shaved bare, with huge round concrete pipes lying there to become part of some future wall infrastructure. Some of the youth began to maneuver one so it might roll down the mountain, but they appeared to think better of it: This was an extremely dangerous move, given the road below. Some began to go down the hill toward army jeeps and police cars that had suddenly appeared to block the road. The army vehicles sat next to a beloved spring, where many of us—even those coming from Aida—have happy memories of barbeques, donkey rides, youth trips with drumming circles, and slow afternoons admiring the red poppies or how the water flows from the stone well. If they had these memories, as people who lived in a neighboring community, how did Al-Walaja residents relate to these places? I remember thinking how each place of loss is a site to be cherished, a site loved by residents and visitors, each in their own way. I remember looking across at the train tracks on the opposite hill that trace the path of the Green Line and recalling how during one of those picnics with friends from Aida Camp, a young boy had asked his father where the train went. His father had replied that the train went to Tel Aviv. Everyone knew the child would go there no time soon. For Palestinians in the West Bank, Israel's closure policies are one of the most obviously discriminatory elements of life under occupation,[37] and they are also central to Palestinians' feelings of restriction. Palestinians in Al-Walaja were protesting dispossession, but in protesting the construction of the wall and looking toward the Green Line, they were also protesting closure and the larger systems of discrimination that enable closure. These closure policies also essentially prohibit return: If Palestinians of the West Bank could live and work in all the territories under Israeli control, this would in fact fulfill one element of the right of return, as people often told me. Toward the end of the protest, dozens of protesters ventured down to the spring. They stood on the skeleton of an old house there and raised a flag. But nobody confronted the army on that day (Figure 11).

When we returned to Aida Refugee Camp, we were alarmed to find PA security officials armed with AK-47s stationed outside our house. They had been positioned there to prevent a protest from emerging near the separation wall that was, in places, a mere ten meters from the houses of the camp (Figure 12). A scuffle ensued between residents of the camp and the PA soldiers, in their green uniforms and black berets, over the soldiers' presence and a perceived affront to one of the soldiers. As I watched from my window, it felt like I was seeing the curtain of PA complicity with the occupation pulled back. I snapped my photographs furtively as one of the soldiers glared back up at me.

It would not be the last time PA soldiers played such a role in Aida or elsewhere, but the affront—on Nakba Day, in a refugee camp surrounded by Israel's apartheid wall—vexed our sense of home. My husband and I had left our young daughter in the care of someone else while we went to the place that we worried could become dangerous only to find armed security forces below our balcony. Moreover, that it was the PA on guard underscored how the PA wanted

Figure 11 At a Nakba Day commemoration in Al-Walaja in 2011, people looked down toward a cherished spring, as others descended the mountain toward it. Photo by author.

Figure 12 After we came home from the Nakba commemoration, I found PA officers breaking up a gathering under our veranda in Aida Refugee Camp. Photo by author.

to limit commemorations to the least confrontational of territories: the center of Ramallah or the center of Bethlehem, as I had seen happen on Land Day that same year.

We had come home to other news, too. Protesters in Lebanon and Syria had actively challenged the border of Israel, and some had managed to cross into Israel. An article in *Haaretz* made a striking observation:

> Nakba Day events passed relatively quietly in the West Bank, but caught Israel unawares on its northern borders. Thousands of Palestinian refugees stormed the fences on the Lebanese and Syrian borders, some managing to cross into Israel. The IDF and the Lebanese army fired at the protesters, killing at least 14 people altogether.[38]

Haaretz reported that 137 people crossed from Syria into the Israeli-annexed Golan Heights.[39] The article stated that Israeli soldiers stationed there had quickly used up their supply of riot control weapons. Meanwhile, at the Qalandia Checkpoint, where there had also been talk of crossing into Israel, only a few hundred youth clashed with Israeli soldiers in a larger and more extended version of popular protests that routinely occur. Some of the thousands of people gathered in the center of Ramallah to commemorate the Nakba had tried to join the protests at Qalandia, but there too PA forces had turned them back. As the *Haaretz* article reported, "Israel's tight-knit cooperation with the Palestinian Authority's security apparatus, which was maintained over the last three days in preparation for yesterday, was evident in Qalandiyah."[40] Likewise, in Gaza no protesters managed to cross into Israel. The next day we were astonished to hear on the news that Hassan Hijazi, a 28-year-old Palestinian refugee living in Syria, had arrived in Jaffa to visit his family's former home.[41] In an interview on Israeli television, conducted in Arabic, he said that a Jewish solidarity activist had taken him part of the way and that he had taken a public bus, riding next to an Israeli soldier part of the way. He showed his Syrian identity card to the camera.

In short, during the tumultuous time of the Arab Revolts, it was possible to cross what was usually one of the most highly fortified borders in the Middle East, because leaders were more concerned about preserving their power in the center of their territories, and, for that moment, less about not provoking Israel's ire. But Palestinians, policed by both Israeli and PA forces, did not cross from Israel's militarily occupied West Bank or Gaza into Israel's territory that is under civil control. Palestinians of the occupied territories had deeply internalized the fact that crossing the Green Line would trigger grave Israeli violence. They had been steeped in the stasis of decades of constraint and pervasive threat. It did not help that the PA was doing all it could to secure these lines, as well.

Al-Walaja, the West Bank, 2014: "The barrier broke"

Three years later, in 2014, a group from Aida Camp and others from the Bethlehem region were back at Al-Walaja for another Nakba Day protest. The construction of the wall and the settlement near Al-Walaja had continued. In Aida, sustained protests against the wall had transformed daily life;[42] Berkeley researchers had recently declared Aida one of the most tear-gassed places on earth.[43] Trust in the PA had further decayed, both in Aida and in the West Bank as a whole. This time, on our way into Al-Walaja, an Israeli military jeep briefly detained our bus, heightening tensions and giving us a sense of the intensifying Israeli presence. But the soldiers let us pass. When we arrived, an activist from Al-Walaja explained to the assembled marchers, "It's not necessary to do more than to take a walk in Al-Walaja to see the situation, all of the violations from the wall, the settlers, the settler road, all of the methods of the program of expulsion of the occupation against the Palestinians, the ethnic cleansing, from 1948 until today." A young girl in a scouting uniform and a leader of Badil were among those who spoke passionately to the assembled marchers. We again embarked on the road out of town, toward the pre-1948 location of Al-Walaja, carrying Palestinian flags and black flags that declared "Return is a right and the will of the people." Again, participants wielded giant keys. A tent housed photographs and information about some of the hundreds of villages whose residents had become refugees, thus linking the ongoing dispossession of Al-Walaja and its residents to the erasure of so many other villages.

When the procession set out, we passed the same rubble of destroyed houses, with flat roofs and protruding iron rods, that we had seen in 2011. I wondered if any had been destroyed recently, and I thought about the ways in which new rubble and old rubble can look the same, and how this makes visible and material how this catastrophe is not an event but a situation.[44] Again, when we arrived at the top of the mountain, we saw that several Israeli police jeeps awaited us on the street below. The street was an area that was, if not completely off limits to Palestinians, certainly a place that Palestinians were not expected to be—as signaled by the coils of barbed wire in triplicate rolled in parallel to the street. The beloved spring was less welcoming to Palestinians now; settlers were often there, and construction on the Israeli Refa'im Stream National Park was underway.[45]

Once again at the crest of the mountain, people decided whether or not to descend toward the road. Because so many had become accustomed to popular protest since 2011, they were emboldened that day, too. As in Aida Camp, when they took action, they were met with tear gas. It was a different terrain for confrontation: greener and more spacious than the camp, certainly, but the steep mountainside trapped those who descended the hillside. Aida Camp residents were accustomed to protests, yes, but not as much to mountain climbing. Nevertheless, a small crowd—young and middle-aged men and young women— had soon gathered at the bottom of the hill, and they had found a way across the barbed wire. A few protesters threw stones in the direction of the fortified army jeeps, and soldiers emerged in helmets and face shields, carrying M-16s, shooting tear gas toward the protesters. They retreated as Palestinian protesters took the street, and their tear gas arched across the blue sky. Protesters sat down in the middle of the street, and another stood on the railing of the highway holding a Palestinian flag against the backdrop of the train tracks above. Some of the men and women in the street dismantled a piece of the highway guard and put it in the middle of the road, along with some rocks, to act as a barrier to the jeeps. The road was a site of struggle because constraints on mobility inhibited Palestinian rights and even Palestinian return (Figures 13 and 14). The road was familiar to me as my favored fast road out of town. I knew its flowers and its curves, but I had never walked out on it before. Standing on the road, I felt small next to the mountains. The soldiers shot more tear gas, and finally there was a retreat. When at last we staggered up the hill, we were out of breath, and many were overwhelmed by the tear gas and the exertion. I found my friend, a man in his late thirties, sprawled out on the ground gasping for air. A while later, soldiers met us at the top of the hill at the protest tent where photographs of dispossessed villages had been hung. Soldiers tore down the tent and upturned the chairs. Several of the protesters confronted soldiers, and yelling and shoving ensued. These dramatic and dangerous skirmishes are a recognizable "repertoire of contention"[46]—or perhaps repertoire of confrontation—in the West Bank, exchanges through which Palestinians challenge the relations of occupation in a one-on-one dynamic. The confrontation between an unarmed Palestinian civilian and an armed Israeli soldier still (somehow) feels less like it has a forgone conclusion than the oppressive structures of the occupation writ large.[47]

Figure 13 In a Nakba Day event in Al-Walaja in 2014, protesters crossed coils of barbed wire to occupy the street that was increasingly off limits as Israel expanded its control of the valley. Photo by author.

Figure 14 Israeli soldiers shot tear gas to disperse those who had descended the mountain at a Nakba Day event in Al-Walaja in 2014. Photo by author.

So it was that at this Nakba Day commemoration, confrontation was the point. Something had changed in people's attitudes since 2011; as some of my activist friends might say, "the barrier broke." People were no longer so afraid of tear gas or shouting matches with soldiers. Yet, in staying on the road, well beneath the railroad tracks, they still did not quite cross the Green Line, and even if they had crossed the Green Line on this rural mountain, they would not have truly challenged the politics of fragmentation that Israel has imposed, given that the mountain on the other side of the valley was uninhabited.

Here was a crucial blurring of categories between commemoration and protest, built on a locally cultivated commitment that because the Nakba continues, resistance must also continue. Protest was a reassertion of place and belonging as well as identity. Despite the scorched throats and cheeks wet with snot and tears, despite the barbed wire in new and disorienting places, the protesters knew where they were: on green Palestinian land, where even the rocks would serve those in struggle. Here, as in the protests against the war on Gaza, some Palestinians under occupation felt that symbolic practice should be joined to certain kinds of action, especially confrontation of Israeli forces. Viewing the "ongoing Nakba" as violent, they believe in an active and challenging commemoration of the Nakba.

On Nakba Day, it seems, there is always a coda, because there are always so many events going on elsewhere. One comes home from the event to learn of more events. Only as we were getting back on the bus did we learn that two teenagers had been killed at a protest near Ofer Prison, an hour or so away near Ramallah. A relative of many of the attendees at this protest had been injured, shot by live ammunition in his stomach. Many of us rushed to the Ramallah hospital. It reminded us that those confrontations with soldiers could have had a different outcome.

Commemorations inside Israel's 1948 borders

Each year since 1998, the Association for the Defense of the Rights of the Internally Displaced has organized a March of Return in a destroyed village. As an activist with ADRID Rula Nasr-Mazzawi described it to me, "the place they choose becomes symbolic of all of Palestine, a little Palestine." ADRID founder Mohammad Kaial explained to me that they generally ask people from the village to be involved with the planning and hosting of the marches. The marches are a one-day revival of villages, and they require a great deal of work. Kaial detailed, "You're talking about 20,000 to 30,000 people that we want to bring together for two hours in a town of the displaced—a place that doesn't have anything. No water, no electricity." They must obtain permits from the Israeli authorities for the event. Then in the space of a day, they must set up a stage, chairs, and exhibitions.

The marches carry more than one political message around return. They are an opportunity to highlight the experiences of internally displaced people within Israel's 1948 territories who have no official leadership advocating on their behalf and whose stories are not well known even by Palestinian citizens of Israel. The marches are ADRID's largest single event of the year. And the marches are also an opportunity to voice a commitment to the right of return for all refugees from inside the Green Line—a relative space of privilege. If refugees in Lebanon hold a march calling for the right of return, Israeli authorities can completely overlook it. When internally displaced people in Israel lead a similar march—and thousands of others join in—then Israeli society must take note, if even in perfunctory ways. Its police officers must regulate it, reporters must cover it, and neighboring towns will necessarily notice it happening.

Israeli leaders have responded to this growing Palestinian movement with legal restrictions. What is often called the 2011 Nakba Law sanctions Nakba Day commemorations by allowing for the cutting of state funds to institutions that mark Israel's Independence Day as a day of mourning.[48] While to date no one has been sanctioned under the law, it has created an atmosphere of threat for Palestinians.[49] Because commemoration of the Nakba is so central to Palestinian political identity in Israel, this law is one of many legal mechanisms that declare Palestinians' exclusion from the Israeli mainstream. As Nadera Shalhoub-Kevorkian writes, "the settler colonial regime uses the Nakba Law to legally portray the colonized as the Other that endangers and threatens the 'democratic nature' of the Israeli state."[50] But the Nakba Law has not stopped these commemorations from happening.

Al-Ruways and Al-Damoun, Israel: "Return is individual and collective"

On May 10, 2011, Israel's Independence Day that year, the March of Return was held in Al-Ruways and Al-Damoun, two depopulated villages near Acre. The plan for the day was that the families of Al-Damoun would welcome participants in a march of return near a village spring in Al-Damoun that, the invitation noted, was opposite the western cemetery of the village. As with the protests analyzed in the previous chapter, invitations revitalized Palestinian senses of place. Then the cars and buses would process from Al-Damoun's land through the still-existing Palestinian village of Kabul, where many internally displaced people from Al-Damoun and Al-Ruways had resettled, and from there people would park and then walk by foot to the village of Al-Ruways.

The traffic was difficult, as it often was on these occasions. But as my friends and I began the walk to the lands of Al-Ruways, we could enjoy being in the land. We smelled the wild rue, that, as my friend pointed out, his father picks to season black olives. I saw others picking sage used in tea.[51] Arriving at the site of the commemoration, we were surrounded by the kinds of pine trees that Israeli authorities had planted to erase the presence of Palestinian refugees.[52] Many Palestinians would be able to read this landscape, because many of us came from similar ones. My own family's village of Tarshiha a half-hour drive away had been famous for its fig orchards, but Israeli authorities uprooted many of these fig trees and replanted the mountains with pine trees so that refugees would not be tempted to return to that rich agricultural land in the years after 1948. The trees were a reminder of how very commonplace dispossession was. This doubled sense of loss and everydayness is intrinsic to many Palestinians' experiences of dispossession in Israel: They were always reading invisible texts of loss and placing their own identities and histories within them. But on this day, the intelligibility of loss was heightened. As in the West Bank, these marches deepened local knowledge among attendees. People from the area may have known of the location of a depopulated village, or the march might be the occasion to learn of it. They would also learn about what is on the village lands now as they plan their arrival. That year, we learned that there are no post-1948 towns on the land of either village, but the kibbutz of Yas'ur, established in 1949, uses their lands for agriculture.[53]

In the formal event, the rhetoric and symbols both articulated a common Palestinian approach to the right of return and also amplified arguments specific to Palestinians in Israel. People carried Palestinian flags and cards with the names of hundreds of villages depopulated in 1948. The display of placenames is a common means of commemorating the multiplicity of experiences of loss. I remembered doing the same at a Nakba Day commemoration in 1998 in Boston. Here a friend joked that it would be easier for her to take me to the site of her family's depopulated village than for us to find a sign for the right village, because there were so many. A speaker expressed the unity of the Palestinian people as well as the idea that the Nakba is ongoing, and that the right of return is "both individual and collective"—both political catchphrases that I had heard before in the West Bank. The music—including songs by Julia Butros, Ahmad

Qaʿbur, Fairuz, and Marcel Khalifa—likewise reflected a shared Palestinian and Arab cultural politics, spanning several generations.

Yet, some elements of the event were specifically oriented around a Palestinian politics inside the Green Line. Speeches reiterated the message that "their Independence Day is our day of catastrophe," a clear and direct confrontation of Israeli nationalist rhetoric. They emphasized that they had the right to commemorate the Nakba despite Israel's new law. One made the comparison that the denial of the Nakba was akin to the denial of the Holocaust, implicitly a way of engaging and acknowledging Jewish history while asserting Palestinian history as well. The insistence on the right of return was also phrased in part in relation to Jewish history: If Jews maintained a connection to land over thousands of years in exile, one speaker said, certainly Palestinians also maintained their right to return over a much shorter time period. This was the kind of argument one would not hear in the West Bank, where human rights and nationalist rhetoric were central, rather than Jewish historical narratives.

Even as the gathering centered around a rhetoric of Palestinian unity, there was a mostly unspoken material exclusion at the center of it: that of Palestinians from outside the Green Line. I saw few police officers and no soldiers or border patrol at the march, but as it happened, a police officer did stop us right after we got out of the car. For some reason, he immediately asked a Canadian friend who had come with me from the West Bank where he was coming from. There was a tense pause until he replied that he was from Canada. As the officer moved on, my friend from the Galilee said to him with a sharp smile, "You can tell him you are from Canada, from Haifa, from Jerusalem—anything but Bethlehem or the West Bank." Gathering in support of refugee rights was undoubtedly important, but the notion of connecting with Palestinians from the occupied territories was risky. Even with Israel's Nakba Law in place, holding a commemoration felt like free expression that could not be prohibited in Israel. But breaking the movement laws—challenging fragmentation with one's body—was risky for all, as it had been for Palestinians in Al-Walaja and Ramallah. Gathering like this was an important practice of memory for Palestinians on this specific land, and it also allowed Palestinians who were usually marginalized from the national movement to articulate political messages that resonated with Palestinian activism in other places.

Jaffa, Israel: "Where are my house's owners?"

A few days later, on Saturday, May 14, 2011, I joined a group of about 2,000 people to gather in a Jaffa city square and then process to a park. In some press coverage, the message of the procession was reduced to the standard political narrative of two states:

> Gabi Abad, head of the Arab Jaffa organization, told *Haaretz* that the purpose of the protest is first and foremost to return and talk about the Palestinian Nakba and about the expulsion of an entire nation out of its land.
>
> "The message of our protest is to aim for a just, sustainable peace, with two states for two people and a divided Jerusalem," he added. "We are stressing the need for the right of return and an end to the occupation."[54]

However, in the moment, the protest voiced a more radical politics. Jaffa is a historically Palestinian city, but most of its population became refugees in 1948 after a wave of Zionist paramilitary attacks. Still, the city remained Palestinian, in part because of internally displaced Palestinians arriving in Jaffa from other parts of the country. In recent decades, it has gentrified and seen a major shift in population from Palestinian to Jewish as the city has been absorbed both legally and increasingly practically into the much larger, much more populous, and prevailingly Jewish Tel Aviv, such that the population of the Tel Aviv–Yafo municipality is only 5 percent Palestinian.[55] The area of Jaffa, meanwhile, is about one-third Palestinian.[56] If the Zionist success in places like Jaffa is to erase Palestinian collective presence, this Nakba Day procession dramatically reversed this, reclaiming public space both visually and audibly, even if just for a few hours.

This transformation started well before the procession itself. The cityscape was transformed by posters splashed in multiples on billboards announcing the event, as though to counter the intense proliferation of Israeli flags hoisted on light poles and cars that one saw each year around this season. The poster was a deft integration of national symbols recognizable to Palestinians anywhere and images and phrases specific to Jaffa, and it was in Arabic. The background of the poster was mostly the blue of the Jaffa sky, above the vista of Jaffa's old city and port, as seen from the water. The use of the blue was refreshing and slightly unconventional because it was not the traditional red, black, green, and white of the Palestinian flag. Indeed, it was a few shades away from the blue of the Israeli flag, as though to recuperate blue from Israeli nationalism and reclaim the sea and the sky themselves as Palestinian. This felt more like a celebration of Palestinian local culture than a reiteration of Palestinian nationalism. The poster incorporated other recognizable elements of Palestinian political culture, though. The main graphic integrated the phrase "Returning to Jaffa" (*ʿĀʾid ilā Yāfā*) into a key and a tag. The key is a classic symbol of Palestinian return, while the tag was a symbol often used in a campaign against a proposal for Palestinians to do civil service rather than being drafted into the army.[57] The phrase was a variation on the title of a famous Palestinian novella by Ghassan Kanafani, *Returning to Haifa*.[58] The title evokes the wealth of Palestinian literary culture and Kanafani's literary and political commitment. Haifa and Jaffa occupy similar places in the Palestinian national imaginary as coastal cities. The concept of "return" here carries both the standard reference to a concept of "return" as the fulfillment of refugees' rights, and it also resonates with the idea, becoming popular at that time, that return can be an everyday contemporary practice, even if the larger political act of return is deferred. The procession itself, the poster suggested, is a gathering of people to retake public space, a Palestinian return to a beloved city.

Moreover, the poster—all in Arabic—announced the locations of the procession with reference to pre-1948 placenames, stating that the march would embark from the historic municipality building of Jaffa, and relegating a current street name to a parenthetical. The main goals of the march as stated on the poster were to mark Nakba Day and to "Challenge the racist Nakba Law!" The poster also articulated the goals of ending the occupation, ending racism and apartheid, and the return of the refugees to their lands—the same core goals of the Boycott, Divestment, and Sanctions movement that deftly addresses the three main Palestinian populations, those living under occupation, those inside Israel, and refugees.[59]

On the day of the protest, people of all ages, including many children, gathered in a plaza in front of the pre-1948 municipal building—now a hotel— whose old stones seemed another testament to Palestinians' enduring presence. Our arrival transformed the cityscape: Palestinian flags flew by the dozens through a main commercial area of the city. One flag had Intifada (the Arabic word for "uprising") written on it, aligning with the idea of popular resistance as it has been made famous in the occupied territories of the West Bank and Gaza. Notably, this was not a situation in which people flew two flags side by side to demonstrate the value of coexistence, as one sometimes sees with certain peace activism, or to indicate their continued loyalty to the juridical state alongside another kind of affiliation with another state, as one sometimes sees in the United States when an immigrant might wave the flag of a home nation alongside a US flag. I saw no Israeli flags as part of the demonstration (or any other Nakba Day event that I attended, ever). If the Palestinian flag can sometimes stand for the PA's state project and thus for a two-state solution, this fluttering throng of Palestinian flags in the middle of Jaffa suggested a more expansive concept of liberation.

Language from the protest was sensitive to what it meant to mark the Nakba from Jaffa. A hand-written sign read in Arabic, "We are remaining like the *za 'tar* and the olive trees," a popular political phrase that draws from poetry by Tawfiq Zayyad, the Palestinian leader and poet (1929–1994) from Nazareth. The phrase is voiced from the perspective of someone who is living under Israeli rule, rather than someone in exile.[60] A sign in English read, "Where are my House's Owners?" This is a question that recognizes the layers of dispossession that have shaped Palestinian society in Israel since its establishment: In Jaffa immediately after Israel was established, Israeli officials moved the few thousand Palestinians who managed to remain into a single neighborhood, Ajami, meaning that even those who stayed were displaced. Israeli authorities also pushed about forty thousand Palestinians in the north and center of the country out of their original homes,[61] and many more Bedouins from the south of the country were also displaced.[62] Some of the houses of Jaffa came to be filled by these other internally displaced people, such that they were living in the homes of Palestinian refugees, their own brethren. These dynamics have shaped Jaffa until today.[63] By evoking this layered history of dispossession, the procession was not only an occasion for the voicing of well-known national priorities, it also created a time for contemplation and commemoration, grounded in this specific place.

Here, as on other occasions, Palestinian citizens of Israel used their place in Israeli society to articulate a message of return audible—if not necessarily comprehensible, because they were in Arabic—in an Israeli public space. In one chant, a leader called out a series of villages and cities from which Palestinians had been dispossessed in 1948 and the crowd responded, "returning":

Al-Lidd
Returning
Haifa and Jaffa
Returning.[64]

Palestinian citizens of Israel on the streets of Jaffa were speaking as though they were refugees, inviting and imagining their compatriots' return.

The march ended with a concert—what was called in the poster an "oppositional festival." This, like the concert in Ramallah, underscored another tension in Nakba commemorations: Many reject the idea that these occasions should be celebratory, and yet there was doubtlessly an element of pride and pleasure in listening to these musicians in an outdoor concert. It featured Palestinian popular musicians Amal Murqus, DAM, and Saz, again highlighting the local richness of Palestinian popular cultures, since not only are all three of these performers from inside the Green Line, but two are from the Jaffa region. As they performed, giant Palestinian flags framed the stage. An urban commemoration like this challenged Zionist public space in Jaffa, celebrated Palestinian presence, and opposed a Palestinian view of history to the Israeli one. It addressed local political priorities, but it also drew evocative connections to Palestinians who could not be present.

Lubya, Israel: Invoking those who are absent

The 2014 the March of Return was held on May 6 in Lubya, a depopulated village in the district of Tiberias, located ten kilometers west of that city. With its residents entirely evacuated in 1948, its homes were demolished in the 1960s. While most of Lubya's refugees are in Lebanon, Syria, and Jordan, a few remained nearby, primarily in the village of Dayr Hanna, less than an hour's drive away,[65] and are thus internally displaced people. Here, too, the march was an opportunity to get to know more about Lubya, even before the event. An article, "On the Occasion of the March of Return: Learning about the Depopulated Village of Lubya,"[66] described how the village had been liberated by Salah Ad-Din Al-Ayoubi and that its villagers had played a role in the Great Revolt of 1936. Religious immigrants from the United Kingdom had established a kibbutz named Lavi on the land in 1949, and the Jewish National Fund established a forest by the same name (once again tall pines) on Lubya's land.

After our long journey from Bethlehem on the day of the commemoration, it felt like a major act of arrival when my friend and I finally stepped out of our car and were greeted by the sign: "The Depopulated Lubya Welcomes the returnees." Walking to the main event through another pine forest, the towering legacy of erasure, we again saw people holding Palestinian flags and placards of village names. Up at the speaking stage were the same posters of destroyed villages I had seen before in Al-Ruways and Al-Damoun, and the speeches were similar, too.

What stayed with me most were giant portraits of people who had been displaced from their villages. Often, they paired an older refugee who might have been born in the original village with a younger person. Sometimes the portraits were taken outdoors, such that the green background of the photo faded seamlessly into the forest around them. The warmth of the affection between

Figure 15 These banners hung at a March of Return in Lubya in 2014 were a reminder of all those not in attendance. Photo by author.

the figures shone through the photograph. A sign next to each of them in Arabic read, "We are from Lubya," "We are from Jaffa," "We are from Iqrit," or "We are from Hadatha," written in a colloquial accent. This was followed by their names and the refrain, "Return is a right. Return is coming" (Figure 15). The photographs were a way of bringing those who might not have been physically present into the demonstration itself—and perhaps even more significantly to suggest all those millions of refugees in the wings.

Once again, Palestinian citizens of Israel—in this case Palestinians who had been internally displaced—were voicing a message of refugee rights on behalf of refugees who could not be there. Indeed, they were almost standing in for these dispossessed, exiled Palestinians on this territory of loss. Once again, the sensed pleasures for the Palestinian participating in the walk was undeniable: walking through the land with friends, with a flag flying from a pole or tied around one's back, taking in the feeling of being together, sheltered by that sense of collectivity.

Gaza, Haifa, Ramallah, Bethlehem

Years later, I was back in Boston when the most prominent commemoration in a generation occurred. While most of the commemorations of the Nakba are not covered by international media, the Great March of Return of 2018—which occurred not in Israel's 1948 territories or the West Bank but in Gaza—did attract such attention. This bold march demonstrated that each annual commemoration opens up the possibility of more commemorations, that smaller, more routine commemorations can be seeds for larger ones.

On Land Day, Friday, March 30, 2018, thirty thousand Palestinians in Gaza stood up to those decades of dispossession and fragmentation, to more than fifty years of military occupation, and twelve years of all out siege. They gathered for the right to return, for the end of that siege, and for their right to movement: three issues that are integrally connected for Palestinians in Gaza, about two-thirds of whom are refugees. The right of return was central. As co-founder Ahmed Abu Artema wrote in Arabic in a May 2018 message sent to US-based Palestinian activists:

> The Right of Return is the heart of the struggle for Palestinians. The first generation of refugees has been passing down the right of return and love of their villages and towns that they were forced to leave 70 years ago to their children and grandchildren. This is one of the main reasons behind the massive response to the March of Return, which brought together all political and social groups. The March of Return represents a rebirth in the face of the many attempts to kill the Palestinians and their cause. The March of Return is a proof of the will of the people and their determination and belief in their rights. It proves that the people are stronger than the arsenal of weapons owned by the occupiers. It also sends a strong message to the world that Zionism, which relied on the factor of time to legitimize the reality of occupation and end the Palestinian presence, has failed.

The movement also decried the flying of any flag but the Palestinian one. It rejected the divisions of the political parties that had become so fractious. Organizers planned a six-week encampment, culminating on Nakba Day with an actual march into Israel so Palestinians could return to their villages.

Like other kinds of Palestinian political practice, this march again envisioned the Palestinian struggle through a capacious political geography. As stated in a widely circulated document entitled the General Principles of the March of Return, while Gaza is "a central arena of the movement," "[the March] includes the various locations of Palestinian refugees in the Gaza Strip, the West Bank, Jerusalem, the areas occupied in 1948, Lebanon, Syria, Jordan and other countries around the world. It aims to peacefully protest at the nearest points to their homes which they were forcibly displaced from." Ahmed Abu Artema published an op-ed in the *New York Times*, where he explained: "My hatred of borders is both universal—in the sense that all Palestinians suffer from them—and very personal . . . I wondered on Facebook what would happen if a man acted like a bird and crossed that fence. 'Why would Israeli soldiers shoot at him as if he is committing a crime?' "[67] In these moments, the Palestinian movement went beyond the dream of statehood.

On that first day of protest, thousands lined up to pray together at the protest. They set up tents so they could stay for the long-term. There was free wireless internet access and free food. That day, Israeli forces killed fifteen people, and injured over a thousand. Over the next several weeks, the protest would attract as many as two hundred thousand people on Fridays.[68] Groups of tents mapped out familial groups and villages of origin, marking people's connection to lands they lost in 1948. Girls wore traditional Palestinian dresses. Youth played soccer. Couples got married. People continued to pray together. Closer to the line of confrontation, they burned tires to obscure Israeli fire. Protesters flew burning kites in the air and over the border, taking a traditional Gaza pastime and a popular means of commemorating the Nakba and transforming it into a weapon of the weak. Palestinians from the refugee rights organization Badil in the West Bank sent the design of their annual t-shirt to march organizers and paid for them to be printed in Gaza, and they were pleased to spot the t-shirt in photographs of the protests, with its refrain, "I revive, I love, I challenge, And I return, To exist," written near the shape of historic Palestine.

It was another one of those seasons when Palestinians learned the names of people killed by the Israeli military, over and over again. Palestinians mourned a journalist, Yasser Murtaja, age thirty, whose photo circulated on social media as he cradled a kitten and posed with children, and then they mourned another journalist killed, Ahmed Abu Hussein.[69] They mourned one medic, Musa Jaber Abu Hassanein, and then another, a woman, Razan Al-Najjar. They mourned 8-month-old Leila Anwar Ghandoor, who had been brought to a protest tent by her young uncle, only to have his tent, far from the front lines of the protest, overcome with tear gas. On May 14, in the same hours as US President Trump's daughter and son-in-law attended a ceremony to open the US Embassy in Jerusalem, breaking decades of international global consensus that rejected Israel's illegal annexation of East Jerusalem, Israeli forces killed more than sixty Palestinians, shocking Palestinians and the whole world.[70]

Palestinians in Haifa gathered on May 18 to stand in solidarity with the fallen. In front of the demonstration were four red letters: GAZA. They expressed their commitment to the right of return in a version of a chant I had heard years earlier in Jaffa. It went, "I'm returning, returning / To Acre / Returning / To Kufr Kanna / Returning." Again, this chant positioned these activists—with the relative privilege of access to Haifa—as sharing the voice of refugees, similarly to how the large posters in Lubya allowed Palestinian internally displaced people to stand in for refugees.

But also in Haifa, Israeli authorities' response was harsh. Police cordoned protesters into a tight space and arrested twenty-one people, in many cases using batons and fists to assault those detained. Police swore and spit at the detainees. A video circulated on Facebook, and human rights organizations like Adalah mobilized to circulate it. The most seriously injured in the protest was Jafar Farah, the director of the Mossawa Center, The Advocacy Center for Palestinian Arab citizens of Israel, who had a fractured knee from being hit by police. He received only cursory treatment in the hospital while in shackles.[71] Two nights later, protesters gathered in front of the courthouse again in solidarity with the people of Gaza and to insist on the release of the prisoners, even as the prosecutors demanded the extension of their detention for another five days.

Were these renewed protests a significant development? Were they another in a series of actions that would not have a clear outcome? Or were they perhaps both? A pair of writers, Rula Nasr-Mazzawi, from a family of internally displaced people inside the Green Line, and Nidal Al-Azza, a refugee born and raised in Aida Camp in Bethlehem, saw in the Haifa demonstration an important shift, calling the march in Haifa "not less important than the march in Gaza, because revolution is measured not in the number of sacrifices but by its effects." "Gaza," they wrote, "brought back the idea of return. Haifa stresses the importance of Palestinian unity. . . . The march shakes Israel's sense that [the politics of the Oslo Accords] won. It demonstrates the failure of Israel to divide Palestinians."[72]

Meanwhile in the West Bank, the situation was untenably quiet, with only a few small demonstrations. This silence—imposed by the PA, which was not at the time in the mood for reconciliation with the Gaza-based Hamas or for street protests that could turn against it—persisted until finally a series of protests was organized in early June. This time, they were not only (or even primarily) against the Israeli authorities but against the PA itself. They called for the "lifting of the punishments" against Gaza—specifically that the PA pay the salaries of employees, which were being paid at only 50 percent normal rates, and that the PA return its services to Gaza. These services had been cut to punish Hamas and force it into an agreement with Fatah. They chanted, "Why do we besiege Gaza? Isn't the siege of the [Israeli] army enough?"[73] and called for national unity.[74]

In response, the PA issued an order forbidding demonstrations altogether. In Nablus, demonstrations occurred despite leadership disavowing the calls for such demonstrations saying that they came at an inappropriate time, right before Ramadan Eid.[75] When people nevertheless gathered in Ramallah's main square, security forces told journalists not to cover the protests, threatening those who continued to work with arrest. Still, people held signs that said in Arabic, "Gaza unites us #lift_the_obstacles."[76] PA police threw tear gas and stun grenades to disperse the crowd.[77] Security forces with rifles and covered faces shoved protesters. Video of the PA repression of the protests went viral. Then the videos on YouTube and as embedded in both Ma'an and Arab48 articles were apparently removed. A few days later, the authorities allowed a protest in Bethlehem. A news article noted that police officers distributed cold water to the protesters on the hot day, and that only traffic police stayed near the protest. Still, the protesters' chant boldly recognized the multiplicity of threats to their rights: "Once the PA, Once the Army."[78] For the protesters, each was an obvious enemy to Palestinians' right to protest.

The March of Return in Gaza demonstrated the interconnectedness between commemoration and protest and of Palestinian political practice among Palestinians in Gaza, the West Bank, Israel, and beyond. The march, after all, carried nearly the same name as the series of marches held inside the Green Line. And it began on Land Day, a day which started out as a commemoration of deaths in the Galilee, but which has become a Palestinian day of commemoration across many Palestinian communities. Around the world, as Palestinians and their supporters marked seventy years of dispossession, the massacre motivated even larger gatherings and more media coverage. Indeed, I joined Boston-area Palestine activists gathered in a great empty church on Park Street, escaping one of those fierce spring thunderstorms. We read Ahmed Abu Artema's speech and took in what it meant that he addressed the audience of solidarity activists as "brothers and sisters." Practices of commemoration over many years had laid the ground for the Great March of Return, and it had in turn inspired commemorations and protests around the world.

Conclusions

The 2018 March of Return did not end the siege of Gaza or lead to mass "return," just as the storming of the border by Palestinians from Syria and Lebanon in 2011 did not signal return, either. But crucially these practices hold open the possibility for the next round of actions to occur. As Nidal Al-Azza, the executive director of the Bethlehem-based refugee rights organization Badil, wrote in an article published on the ADRID website for internally displaced people, "It is incumbent upon all Palestinian citizens . . . to be innovative in approaches to return. We still need more preparation and organization to arrive at the 'Great' march of return, but this does not mean we should sit on our hands and wait for that day to come."[79] Among the approaches he suggests are gatherings of Palestinian citizens of Israel and Palestinians in the West Bank on both sides of the Green Line, or raising the Palestinian flag on the wall or facing the settlements, or replacing a road sign and putting up the Arab name for a street or village. This, he suggests, can "lead to a deepening of the movement of return."[80] Al-Azza and other organizers understand that resistance is a practice that has unfolded and will unfold over many years. Many Nakba Day commemorations are part of this process.

Indeed, political gatherings like these—where people commemorate the past and call for land rights and the right of return today—matter even when they do not seem to accomplish their immediate goal, or even if, as some tired of commemorations and protests would say, the speeches become formulaic. Not only do they create collective memory and allow for a discursive practice in which new things can be stated alongside the reiteration of longstanding messages, but they maintain the possibility for future action. Repetition is never just repetition. Palestinians—like so many other Indigenous people and oppressed people around the world—are playing a long game.[81] We can see each of these acts of gathering as acts of sustenance, of exercising that collective.

These embodied practices also help to develop political concepts. As we have seen in this chapter, the term 'awda, or return, has many resonant meanings that shift slightly according to where the call for return is voiced. The term focuses on the return of refugees to historic Palestine, and in this sense the right of return focuses on refugees outside of that territory, and secondarily perhaps on the two out of three people in Gaza[82] and about 30 percent[83] of Palestinians in the West Bank who are refugees and whose families lost land and homes inside what is now Israel. But "return" as voiced from the Gaza March of Return is also a call for the end of the siege. From the West Bank it can be about freedom of movement and about the ending of the closure laws that treat Palestinians there so differently than people living under Israel's civil law just across the Green Line. This was the meaning as Palestinians from the West Bank at the protest in Al-Walaja eyed the train tracks that run along the Green Line to Tel Aviv. Return is a strong concept because it is a flexible one, a "shifter"[84] that has slightly different meanings depending on who is articulating it and from where, and even more importantly, one where meanings can layer. Nakba Day commemorations and the language of "return" also invite Palestinians to speak on each other's behalf and to call out to each other, as the portraits of internally displaced people did in Lubya.

Historical commemorations like Nakba Day demonstrate a fundamental shared quality of Palestinian political practices that happen inside the Green Line, in the West Bank, and in many other Palestinian places—Gaza, refugee camps in Lebanon, and beyond—that I have not been able to address ethnographically here. This shared quality is important even though commemorations may also be organized with local priorities in mind, and despite the fact that Israeli authorities restrict these commemorations inside the Green Line, and both Israeli and Palestinian authorities repress them in the West Bank. These commemorations not only maintain Palestinian knowledge of the past. They also are a practice through which people become accustomed to gathering despite the risks of doing so. They transform public space by recalling Palestinian placenames and by returning Arabic to streets and open spaces. They help people learn about new Palestinian places, a revelatory practice even within the limits of Israeli closure. These practices of commemoration sustain communities and maintain the possibility for oppositional street politics by bringing Palestinians out into the cities and onto Palestinian lands to make political statements on a regular basis.

Importantly, through their serial quality, they allow Palestinian political practices and conversations to grow and change. Land Day, once the most prominent day on the Palestinian political calendar, receded in importance in favor of Nakba Day because refugees were recognized as being at the center of Palestinian claims in the Oslo period when many feared that statehood would not accommodate most refugees. Then the idea of commemorating the Nakba year after year led people to reflect on the ways in which "the Nakba is ongoing" for all Palestinians, and not just for refugees (though refugees are still held to be at the center of conversations about the Nakba). Looking especially at practices of commemoration in the occupied territories, we see that these practices of gathering and speaking together are continuous with protests. A commemoration that grows confrontational is not a failed commemoration, or a breakdown of civic discourse, but proof of this important point.

What do we gain from looking at commemoration across several different Palestinian places? Other studies have focused on how commemorations in Israel are attempts to be in dialogue with the Israeli state and Jewish Israeli citizens.[85] My approach shows that commemorations in Israel's 1948 territories are in many respects similar to those that happen in the West Bank, pointing to shared elements of political aspirations and practices of each location. Diana Allan is highly critical of the politics of voice that she found in Nakba commemorations in Lebanon in the first decade of the 21st century. She observes that an "ambivalent relation of the 'I' to the 'we' was a feature" of some of her fieldwork regarding commemorations, and she continues, "The Palestinian saying 'my story is the story of my people' is subtly undermined by more intimate and circumscribed forms of cultural retrieval."[86] But we see here that commemorations can also bridge geographic and political divides in their imagery and conception, as they bring people living in the city into rural areas, or as they invite people to march toward the Green Line. They make Palestinian history a felt, acknowledged part of people's regular experiences. Still, in thinking about how Palestinians can commemorate the same historical occasions, we should not expect them to say the same thing. Here we found Palestinians acknowledging that they cannot substitute for each other, but that they can invoke loss and absence, as with the person in Jaffa who held a placard that asked, "Where are my house's owners?" Multi-sited, politically engaged anthropological practice and research can open up space to recognize and explore what people can say in conversation with each other, rather than only looking for people to say the same thing due to the oppressive nature of nationalism that Allan aptly recognizes. We can identify how one March of Return can inspire another, in another place. Congregating to remember shared histories and mark ongoing struggles not only remakes space and helps to strengthen the sense of a collective, it is a practice that makes the next gathering possible.

Some kinds of gathering, though, are not possible under Israeli rule. Sometimes conversations do not happen as easily as we might wish they could. How can Palestinians—and committed writers and researchers—cultivate exchanges across difficult boundaries? Might these exchanges also push beyond a striving for unity in favor of a Palestinian polyphony? In the next chapter, I address an exchange in photography undertaken in a time of war between Jaffa, under Israel's civil control, and Aida Refugee Camp, Bethlehem, under Israel's military control. These are two Palestinian communities that are, on the surface, different not only because of the legal form of Israeli rule extant there, but because of the disparity between the big city and a smaller town refugee camp, a place of hip local haunts and a global site of pilgrimage, the sea and the edge of the desert. Can a spirit of creativity open new visions of Palestinian places? As I undertook this project, traveling between them each week, I had a lot to think about on that open road between them.

Passage. Jaffa to Aida Refugee Camp

I was leaving Jaffa for home in Bethlehem during the Gaza War in 2014 after an afternoon of fieldwork in a photography workshop I was conducting in the two locations. This was always a good part of my week: I wasn't worried about arriving on time or getting lost or getting the next part of the day right. I was reflecting on this or that from my fieldwork, and relieved to be alone in that singular way that mothers of young children appreciate time. I'd turned on my music, one of a few CDs I had brought with me that was on heavy rotation at the time. Nina Simone sang, "I wish I knew how it would feel to be free." For me, the song always resonated with her line in "Blues for Mama": "Ain't nobody perfect, cus ain't nobody free." Wasn't that the same song? All of a sudden, I saw all of the cars on the highway pull over. Many people got out of their vehicles and huddled next to the concrete barriers at the side the road. I was, at that moment, more or less off the grid: lacking cellular data service on my smartphone and listening to my own music rather than the radio. Or perhaps my music had just been too loud to hear an ambient siren. So it took me a few minutes to register that this must be the prescribed response to an air raid siren, and that the warning must have come through some medium from which I was (blissfully) disconnected. I looked at the people huddled next to the roadside, and I looked at the road ahead. I decided I might as well continue, that I was safe enough on my own.

If the Tel Aviv-Jaffa area always felt a bit like foreign terrain to me, I was soon speeding on Highway 1 on the hilly parts that lead to Jerusalem, remembering this road from my youth. I thought of the aging tanks that had sat there for decades as a celebration of the Zionist victories that led to the establishment of the Israeli state.[1] I remembered how as a child this stretch of road always felt dangerous and exciting to me: because of the hills and the speed at which my family members navigated them and because I knew that we were approaching Jerusalem, where we would have fun visiting family for a few days. Even for me, these hills had seemed associated with a certain kind of Zionism: closely tied to the 1948 military victory because of those old tanks, slightly underdeveloped (or that road would be "better," my young American sensibilities reasoned—and within a few years, the road had indeed been re-graded). By 2014, the road was in the midst of a long process of improvement. It seemed like each year I came back, new parts of it were re-graded and widened. Still, it had its hills and its curves, and I marveled that I was grown up enough to be zipping down these streets alone. The feeling of speed-as-freedom was undeniable in this summer night air. I rolled down my windows as if to compel everyone else to listen to Nina too.

But it was not all speed and pleasure on these roads: I thought also of how close I was to Gaza, how a few weeks earlier on the same drive home I had taken a wrong turn as I chatted with my mother in the car. Suddenly we seemed to be approaching Sderot, the Israeli town on which Hamas rockets periodically fell and a place where I would have felt surely out of place. I had turned around and followed my nose until I was back on the roads I recognized.

I snapped back to my driving as I approached Jerusalem neighborhoods and highway driving became city driving. I arrived at an intersection where religious Jews always stood waiting to cross the street. This intersection always reminded me of the tensions between religious Jews and others in certain neighborhoods when they felt the sabbath had been broken in their areas. I worried about my wrong turns and tried to stay on well-worn roads. You could slip from one place to another and end up somewhere unexpected, in this small place, even though it was beleaguered with barriers. I passed through Jerusalem and headed toward the small Al-Walaja Checkpoint and up more of those hills, this time without the Jerusalem traffic that could make driving seem like a wild video game. It was just me and another car or two, coursing up toward Bethlehem. I passed the entrance to the Har Gilo settlement and the streetlights ended, and then the street narrowed, all-too-predictable indicators that I had moved from an area used by Israelis to one used by Palestinians. I slowed down. Soon I passed the store on the edge of town where one could buy arak and beer and Israeli cell phone cards: items that were harder to find in some other parts of town that I frequented more regularly on foot. I knew this store well, since I had both an Israeli and a Palestinian cell phone and had to maintain money on both accounts. Passing by, I exhaled. The drive was over, I was back in known territory where friends could easily drive to meet me if, say, my car broke down. But I also remembered how this was an area that had been quite tense, just a few years ago. During the second Intifada, cars could not drive through this area, and Israeli soldiers sat in jeeps on the ridge of the mountain. One time of war, one kind of violence, can bleed into the next, and driving through these territories, it was not hard to anticipate the next round of violence.

4 A Juxtaposition of Palestinian Places

THIS WAS SUPPOSED TO BE THE fun part of the day. The Palestinians coming from Jaffa on the coast in Israel's 1948 territories had crossed the checkpoint into Bethlehem, the hills of the West Bank. They had entered Aida Refugee Camp and parked their cars despite the sudden appearance of the Israeli army. We had introduced ourselves to each other and spoken about the differences and similarities between our experiences of Israeli rule despite the sounds of Israeli soldiers shooting tear gas and stun grenades outside (more on all that later). Finally, it was time for lunch. We were to share the signature dish of this community center, as prepared by our neighborhood celebrity chef, a woman who often cooked for the youth center for extra family income: She had made *maqlouba*, a rice casserole whose name literally means "upside down" because in order to serve it, one turns the large pot over, so that the chicken and vegetables cooked on the bottom appear on top. Everyone in the community of the youth center looked forward to its fried vegetables, garlicky flavor, and bright turmeric-colored rice. We were proud to share it, too. We were milling about, mouths watering, when suddenly—BOOM—a sound louder than any we had heard that day exploded in our ears and rattled our nerves. Everyone flinched. Was it a gunshot? A stun grenade?

Then the glimmer of a pot upturned caught my attention, and I realized that the clamor had come from the pot of *maqlouba* hitting the tray as it was being turned over—with somewhat less than the usual grace with which this is supposed to happen. This was metal on metal echoing off the bare floor and walls. We all burst out laughing and lined up to fill our plates. The young man with the pot in his hands looked just a little delighted at the bedlam he had caused.

It was an accident that brought to the fore the tensions we had been feeling all day—and a delicious meal was right ahead. The moment suggested the way in which even the simple and deeply Palestinian act of hosting felt dangerous as these two groups of Palestinians came together for the first time.

The meal was part of a summer 2014 photography exchange that I organized between two groups of amateur photographers from different sides of the Green Line that separates Israel's 1948 territories and the West Bank. I worked closely with two photography teachers, one in each location, who led workshops and eventually curated a joint exhibition in Jaffa and Bethlehem. Though I had hoped that we would meet regularly during the summer, after this day, the next time the two groups would gather would be for that exhibition in Bethlehem. I conceived of this project as an opportunity to analyze the politics of space and representation in two Palestinian areas, to think about the political habitus in each place, and to start a conversation between two groups of Palestinians about their relationships to each other. I wanted to learn about how each saw their respective environments in relation to the other group, based on the idea that concepts of politics—like documentary photography—are tied to place and the body. In a kind of bricolage, photographers worked with the material world around them to create messages that they wanted to explore, and they juxtaposed different locations and vantages off each other. This was the politics of the concrete turned digital. But I was at least as interested in process as in the product of the photographs. Here, I describe the journeys we took together and apart as photographers and as Palestinians in a summer that turned out to be more fraught than I would have first imagined.

This project happened not with the usual international funders' support, but with research money for which I applied. In my grant for this project, I described my goal from this research. "Conducting research in two Palestinian communities, one in the West Bank and one in Israel, I will examine (1) how the built environment shapes Palestinian political experiences and knowledge in these two locations and (2) the factors that enable and constrain solidarity or collaboration between these communities." I sought to examine submerged forms of political knowledge, but I also sought to feel out the barriers to exchange: "This research seeks to analyze how the local orientation and groundedness of this kind of political knowledge may impede solidarity or collaboration across disparate political environments." While in other contexts, photography has been used as a means for disempowered communities to reach policymakers,[1] here we recognized that the very definition of community was complex, and that instrumental communication could not be a transparent goal in a situation where the state systematically overlooks Palestinians' wills.

This photography project was a part of a recognizable cultural practice within Palestinian society. Many Palestinian community organizations carry out youth media projects with external funding.[2] These projects often promise that they will teach "youth" practical skills for media production, provide them with an outlet for empowerment and expression, or present a means for them to represent their stories to outside audiences.[3] These projects are often seen as part of a larger field of human rights education programs in the West Bank.[4] Even in a situation where it is widely recognized that NGOs have contributed to depoliticization and demobilization,[5] youth media production can be transformative for those involved.[6] Such media projects usually take place in the West Bank, rather than inside the Green Line. Projects usually result from a confluence between donor priorities and the interests and capacities of local organizations.

However, it has been difficult or even impossible to fund projects that take place on both sides of the Green Line, as organizers in both communities told me. Indeed, the leadership of Lajee Center, the organization I worked with in Aida, told me that when they applied for a grant through which Lajee would have worked with a number of different sites, including at least one inside the Green Line, funders responded that this proposal would not work because it fell under the jurisdiction of two different branches of the same large funding agency. The Yaffa Youth Movement had tentatively undertaken programming that crossed the Green Line, for example by running daytrips to different parts of the West Bank, but they had found scaling up to be difficult. It is difficult to overstate the importance of this problem: NGOs have taken the place of public institutions in different ways for Palestinians in Israel's 1948 territories and especially in the West Bank. In Israel's 1948 territories, the Israeli state systematically underfunds Palestinian communities, while in the West Bank NGOs played an outsized role in the purported "state-building" processes of the 1990s, then stayed on to support Palestinians during humanitarian crises of the 21st century. Large donors tend to be affiliated with state development agencies or the United Nations, and both tend to define populations along statist terms that presume Palestinians in the occupied territories to be the primary population in need of aid. To span across the Green Line is to do work that is overtly disruptive of the political order, both of Israel's own public definitions of its sovereignty and of the purported division between humanitarian work and political work.[7]

Place and the affective politics of connection

As we have seen, Palestinians in Israel's 1948 territories and the West Bank are governed by different laws; they also tend to see different media outlets, though certain videos will go viral on both sides of the Green Line. But since embarking on this project, I have hypothesized that there is something that is at least as important as all of this. The everyday experiences of politics of these two groups are different despite many activists' common ideological orientations. The way in which history and the politics of place have played out on their bodies shape a different kind of political habitus[8] despite—or precisely as a side effect of—their both being shaped by settler colonialism. The mechanism of settler colonialism has often operated through trying to erase the identities of Palestinian citizens of Israel, while under military occupation, Palestinians are treated as enemies. The concept of political habitus is useful because it helps us to move beyond ideas as expressed in more formal and explicit ways and instead to think of how our senses of the political are formed through history and in the body. It helps us to attend to how our different social positions lend themselves to the cultivation of specific embodied orientations toward politics. This history and these experiences inform in very basic ways how people approach public life as citizens or subjects. Everyday politics are built into the environment for Palestinians: into where people feel safe or unsafe, into the risks that people wish to take, or those that they avoid. The concepts of affect and structure of feeling[9] help us recognize that while so much of political life builds upon habit and structure, sensations and happenings erupt out of these structures, not necessarily to utterly upend them but to complicate them, to reveal other possibilities. The ways in which fear, pride, and excitement flare up differently attune us to distinct sets of affect in ways that are nevertheless difficult to account for in formal representations. In the case of the events discussed in this chapter, both the shock of the war and the circumstances of the encounter between these two groups of photographers made for surprising outcomes.

Moreover, across many different contexts, photography itself is an embodied practice. Photography involves an emplaced perspective on the world, and it entails particular risks and thrills depending on one's location and presentation of self. A photographer in Aida Refugee Camp is often an "affected and

affecting embodied subject who may stake his or her life for testimony"[10] covering Israeli military presence in Aida. But photography is also an embodied
practice in in Jaffa. Deployed in public, the camera creates "unconventional and
unanticipated registers for politics."[11] Palestinian appearance in public[12] itself
can make a bold statement in Israel's 1948 territories.

This project is also inspired by the "shared anthropology" of Jean Rouch,
who saw media production as a means of creating and documenting episte-
mological leaps from one place to another. "Ethnography," wrote Rouch, "is a
permanent crossing point from one conceptual universe to another; acrobatic
gymnastics, where losing one's footing is the least of the risks."[13] As in Rouch's
films, the camera can be a means of provocation or a tool for play, even in dire
circumstances of colonialism, racism, and the side theatres of war. The shared
element here happened on multiple levels: between my interlocutors and me,
among interlocutors in each location, and between the two groups, with our
many and cross cutting differences and similarities. Perhaps more clearly than
observing protests or commemorations, here we can see that this relationship
between Palestinian citizens of Israel and those under military occupation in
the West Bank was not only of one declared unity but also of longing, frustration, and anxiety.

Places in relation

I selected the sites of Jaffa and Aida both based on practical considerations and
out of a sense that we could productively set these places in relation through
difference and practice. No community would be representative of all of the
West Bank or of Palestinian society in Israel, since each are diverse in terms of
class, rural-urban divides, and many other factors. Rather than choosing communities that were in some senses "representative," I chose to work with two
strong, community-based organizations with a history of work in photography
in locations that would allow me to commute at least once a week between
them. Participants were generally middle or working class and the community
around them with which they identified was poor or working class. Though
these two locations are quite different, they have each been constituted and
continue to be shaped through processes of Israeli dispossession.

The events of 1948 and the establishment of Israel were constitutive for both
communities. The Arab city of Jaffa, one of the oldest ports in the world and a
flourishing and cosmopolitan town under the Ottoman Empire, became neighbor to Tel Aviv, after Tel Aviv was established to be the quintessentially modern

city and centerpiece of the Zionist project.[14] By the time Israel was established, Tel Aviv had annexed Jaffa and nearby villages. In the war of 1948, Jaffa was almost entirely depopulated: 95 percent of the Palestinian population of Jaffa was forced to leave. The 3,500 Palestinians who remained were concentrated in one neighborhood.[15] While in 1947, 70 percent of Jaffa's population of 110,000 was Palestinian, in 2012 it was 30 percent Palestinian, out of a population of 45,000.[16] Aida Refugee Camp was created because of that same act of ethnic cleansing. Established in 1951 by UNRWA, it houses refugees from 27 different villages, many of them a short drive away from the camp, and perhaps an hour's drive from Jaffa. Today there are about 3,150 refugees living in Aida.[17]

Both are small areas with a fraught relationship to a larger city, though in quite different ways. Aida is on the outskirts of the Palestinian city of Bethlehem, a historically Christian town known as the birthplace of Jesus. Its Christian history and identity have been materially and symbolically important: pivotal to the economy because of tourism as well as to Palestinians' imagination of themselves as embracing religious diversity. Bethlehem was transformed by the influx of mostly Muslim refugees in 1948, and social and spatial divides remain among long-time residents, refugees, and other newcomers. Tel Aviv-Yafo, as it is officially named in Hebrew, is much larger than the Bethlehem metropolitan area, just as Jaffa is larger than Aida. Tel Aviv-Yafo is regarded in Israel as one of the "mixed cities" or towns, a label that attests to the prevailing logic of separation in Israel as well as to the ambivalent valuation of "integration."[18] In most or all of these mixed towns, political and economic power remains in the hands of Jewish Israelis. Indeed, the official name of the city—Tel Aviv-Yafo—as well as the proportion of Palestinians in the city as a whole (only 5 percent in 2003) suggests how Jaffa has been subsumed by the much larger city of Tel Aviv.[19] In Jaffa, as in other coastal cities, gentrification has pushed out Palestinians over the last decades and has become a major concern.[20]

In both Aida and Jaffa, Palestinians live with Jewish Israelis, though on very different terms. In Aida, people above the age of forty will remember the years before the second Intifada when they could more easily cross the Green Line to work and when Jewish Israelis frequented a strip of restaurants just a few hundred meters from their own houses. Israelis are present as soldiers who are based at Rachel's Tomb, a small formerly syncretic but now Jewish shrine and an Israeli military base embedded in the separation wall around Aida. Civilian Jewish Israelis are present—though generally not visible—as religious Jews who come to pray at Rachel's Tomb.[21] Some of the soldiers are in fact Palestinian citizens of Israel, a point that causes particular consternation in Aida.[22] The looming military base instigates frequent and direct confrontation. Here, Palestinians almost never speak to Jewish Israelis other than soldiers, and these conversations are almost never cordial.

In Jaffa, Palestinians live with Jewish Israelis quite differently. Anthropologist Daniel Monterescu sees Jaffa and other "mixed cities" in Israel as "polysemic," and he holds that ethnic logics of separation are untenable in cities like these. He argues that although Jaffa has been shaped by settler colonialism and continues to be a tense place due to ethnic conflict and class tensions that together drive gentrification, and "[e]ven if the immediate future of Israeli-Palestinian relations is premised on a logic of purification, the very survival and enduring vitality of mixed towns persistently reminds us that nationalistic attempts at effacing diversity and rewriting history in an effort to create a cityscape which is ethnically cleansed are bound to fail."[23] In Jaffa, Jewish and Palestinian Israelis share streets and even (occasionally) cafes. Palestinian storeowners—especially restaurateurs—rely on Jewish customers. Even some of the most prominent popular cultural references to Jaffa are about the workings of ethnic mixing, such as the film *Ajami*, itself a co-production between a Jewish Israeli and a Palestinian Israeli.[24] Many Palestinians study or work with Jewish Israelis. This co-presence colors politics. When I was introducing my project to a leader at Yaffa Youth Movement, I told him that I was interested in the relationship between what one can say and where one is, and he responded with an enthusiastic, "Yes!" He continued that in his opinion, in Jaffa they had to be very careful about the chants they chose at protests. Violent chants that spoke about revenge, he said, would not fly, because "we are here, after all." As a political activist, he had worked hard to develop relationships with authorities that, he said, made it easier for him to organize protests. This was, then, a necessary compromise, in his opinion, though some younger activists disagreed.

The institutions with which I worked in each place were also similar but different in a way that reflected larger dynamics for Palestinians in each of the two societies. Lajee Center in Aida Camp is a youth organization established by people who, by 2000, saw the political system under the Oslo Accords failing and who thus turned to civil society as a way to form a new generation of activists. It has held rounds of human rights education for youth in Aida as well as other refugee camps throughout the West Bank, with funding from the European Union. The Yaffa Youth Movement is younger and has a less well-established history of funding; in 2014, it had an active Facebook page, but not a website. However, it, too, functions as a grassroots organization through which young people have organized school festivals, trips, and other events. Each space felt like a refuge from the surrounding areas, and each felt proudly Palestinian. Lajee, located just outside of Aida Refugee Camp, is close to a military outpost. Were it not for Lajee, very few Palestinians would venture onto this street at all, and so its presence effectively reclaims space for this community. Upon entering Lajee Center in 2014, one was greeted by a life-size painting of the Palestinian poet Mahmoud Darwish. The Yaffa Youth Movement is located on a street in a mixed Jewish and Palestinian neighborhood. Upon entering Yaffa Youth Movement, one entered a courtyard painted with a giant Palestinian flag, adorned with plants and trees.

In Aida, I worked closely with the director of the existing Media Unit, who had been born and raised there. He had not been trained as a photographer or teacher except through Lajee Center, but he regularly documented army incursions into Aida as well as community activities, and he had already taught a number of the participants photography. In Jaffa, the photography teacher was a professional photographer, as well as an art teacher in a school. His presence was an important validating one for the group. With regards to the equipment, too, the organizations had asymmetrical resources. In Aida, the two cameras I brought replenished and upgraded an existing small cache of digital single-lens reflex cameras (DSLRs) that had been used in previous projects. In workshops for younger children, participants tended to use point-and-shoot cameras; the DSLRs were used in advanced workshops, but still by early learners. Autofocus tools had been worn down by misuse. In our workshops, photographers used both older cameras and our new ones. In Jaffa, photographers tended to use their own DSLR cameras out of convenience. In short, institutionally, Lajee Center was more established than the Yafa Youth Movement, but the individual participants in Jaffa were somewhat better off. This was not necessarily because Palestinians in Jaffa were living more comfortably over all; instead, it was because those who participated in the workshop included professionals and college students living in Jaffa for their studies rather than members of the local community, who, the director of Yaffa Youth Movement explained, were difficult to pull into such a project because they were busy with everyday commitments like work and school. All this is to say two things: The participants should not be regarded as representative of their communities, and they were not in any way equivalent to each other. This is also a reminder to be wary of claims to easy balance or comparison.

When, in setting up the project, its leaders and I tried to conceptualize a name and framework, I noticed that they thought connectively rather than through a logic of sameness or comparison. When we attempted to formulate a name for our group, they floated two ideas. "Aida to Jaffa" (ʿĀida ilā Yāfā), a suggestion of someone from Aida, is a reference to Ghassan Kanafani's famous novella, "Returning to Haifa"—and coincidentally drew on theme from a Nakba Day protest years earlier. It also means "Returning to Jaffa," expressing the refugee desire to return. The second proposed name, "Camp Jaffa," (Yāfā al-Mukhayyam, literally Jaffa the Camp) suggested that Jaffa was itself a kind of refugee camp. This idea that Palestinian areas inside the Green Line that had been depopulated or whose populations had been denied fundamental rights were like camps was also a theme for Palestinian citizens of Israel.

The two proposed names for our group posited an expression of something shared that was not based on sameness, historicity, or futurity, but on the sense that each could contribute to the significance of the other. I noticed also how each name also decenters the place of the person who proposed it: The person from Aida suggested "Returning to Jaffa," positing Jaffa as the center of the story, while "Camp Jaffa" posits the camp as the quintessential Palestinian place and poses the comparison of Jaffa to it. I would see this sense emerge again and again: that putting these two places together might yield something new. Notably, these proposed names were not so much fully thought-out theories of place or nationalism,[25] but rather participants' poetic ways of working with what they had at hand: a bricolage of the placenames themselves that was wise to the riches of Palestinian literature and politics, akin to the word play around the name Handala with which this book began.

The politics of appearance, the appearance of politics

Doing photography and, especially in Israel's 1948 territories, being in a public Palestinian group was a political act because public space is, in Jaffa, contested, and in Aida, militarized.[26] Residents in each site are acclimated to this reality, though, so this was often a backgrounded element of meetings that focused on photography skills or the fun of being together. Each group met approximately once a week. During those meetings, we would receive an introductory lecture on photography and discuss the photographs each group had taken in the previous week. Most meetings also involved a walking tour of a different part of town. In Jaffa, the photography teacher was an experienced teacher, artist, and photographer as well as a Jaffa native. He took special initiative to plan excursions to different neighborhoods: Jabaliya, Manshiyya, the touristy and gentrified old city, and Ajami. These tours took on special importance for the participants because many were still learning about Jaffa. The participants there included some who worked in Jaffa, especially as teachers, or who studied at Tel Aviv University, but were from the Galilee. In Aida, the structure was similar, though the participants were already more familiar with Aida and Bethlehem, so tours were somewhat less formal.

From the beginning, the logic of the project as it unfolded, for both the participants and me, was less about representation than about process.[27] Depicting a community or issue from a "Palestinian perspective"—often via a human rights lens—is so often the stated central purpose of Palestinian NGO media interventions, but here, the interests were more varied. Participants wanted to spend time together and wanted to learn, and they also were not necessarily primarily interested in creating representations of their own community.

When, at the first meeting in Aida Camp, we discussed what our hopes were from the project, people presented various reasons for wanting to participate in the project. Some wanted to tell the story of their community, but from the start it seemed that certain of the most obvious stories were off limits. Would they avoid or tackle head-on the questions of occupation violence that cropped up regularly in Aida? We advised people to think of their safety, but we did not make a clear policy regarding photographing the army. In everyone's memory was that just a few years ago the leader of our workshop had been standing on the balcony of the youth center taking photographs when he was shot in the face by an Israeli soldier from short distance. What one could say about the army, then, was implicitly limited by concerns about safety through these practices of appearance. So instead of output-based goals, participants remarked that they hoped it would allow them to visit Jaffa. One participant commented that he had only seen his home village of Abu Ghosh as a prisoner being moved from place to place. Abu Ghosh, he knew, was located on the main road between Jerusalem and Tel Aviv. I passed by it each time I went to Jaffa. As it turned out, this participant was not able to take part in the program because he was arrested and detained a few weeks after it started. Closure prevented him from photographing his village of origin, and prison took away his ability to express himself through photography at all that year. Finally, these participants also wanted to build relationships: to learn how Palestinian citizens of Israel see the world. One person commented, "We assume they are happy and living well, but they may be suffering more than we are, in some ways." "We are one people," said one participant, but, he acknowledged, there are stereotypes about Palestinians in Israel.

In the first meeting in Jaffa, people articulated slightly different reasons for taking part in the program. While in Aida, participants were mostly college students who knew each other well through work with Lajee Center, in Jaffa, they were looking forward to getting to know each other (as the summer went on, they would take a lot of group photos), and were glad to be participating in an activity in Arabic. They were interested in learning more about photography. They were also interested in learning more about Jaffa itself.

In Jaffa, our photography excursions were often a practice of seeing and being seen as Palestinians in a territory remade by Zionism. We witnessed a history of violence and continued Palestinian presence that would be mostly invisible to Jewish Israeli or non-Palestinian visitors. We walked through what was once the neighborhood of Manshiyya, which had been evacuated and demolished in the years after Israel's establishment, only to be redeveloped with little trace of its history.[28] On this walk, we went to a tall high-rise building where many of us experimented with depth of field, pointing our cameras skyward. We encountered beautiful old olive trees planted in the courtyard. Our photographs of the trees and the skyscrapers juxtaposed old and new, but even more than that, they were a testament to an enduring Palestinian presence, as well as to Israeli theft of Palestinian heritage that participants knew to be pervasive. This was another site where the Nakba could be commemorated not just once a year but any day one happened by this courtyard.

This was one occasion when I experienced Palestinian citizens of Israel in a kind of a symbolic relay of narratives of dispossession with Palestinians in the West Bank. Photographers that day wondered aloud from where this tree had been stolen and displaced. Palestinians in the West Bank were also concerned with the pattern of stolen trees; on many rides between Bethlehem and Ramallah, friends had pointed out to me the immense olive tree in the middle of a traffic circle near Ma'ale Adumim, the huge settlement that effectively divides the north and the south of the West Bank for Palestinians. The tree, they would tell me, had been stolen from a Palestinian grove.

In some cases, our mere presence in Jaffa was disruptive of a presumed Jewish Israeli hegemony of space. We moved through the city as a group with cameras, speaking Arabic, with one of us who wore hijab. This performative act of appearance in predominantly Jewish neighborhoods during the Gaza War when some Palestinians, I knew, were refraining from speaking Arabic in public was what Judith Butler might regard as an "embodied political claim to equality" or "the ability to move with and within this social category in public space."[29] Our photography teacher took us to the Andromeda development, a site that has become, for Palestinians, an orientalist symbol of a gentrification that takes elements of Arab architecture familiar in Jaffa and rebrands them as "Mediterranean" using new materials and a domineering scale.[30] Our photography teacher explained to us that a court case had won people the right to walk through Andromeda's public space from the street toward the shore.[31] We took photographs and lingered as residents eyed us with caution. Our photography practice was akin to its own small protest of the exclusions embedded in Jaffa today.

On another day, when I showed up proudly wearing a t-shirt in Arabic and English calling for a revitalized Palestinian political structure—"One vote for every Palestinian everywhere"—one of the leaders of the group in Jaffa cautioned me that he would not feel comfortable wearing such a shirt in the city, especially not during the Gaza War. T-shirts were one common way of appearing as Palestinian in Israel. But for an afternoon of walking through the city during the Gaza War, this was too much for my friend.

As we continued past Andromeda, we went on to a swiftly gentrifying neighborhood, where mostly Jewish hipsters were replacing many Palestinian families. Photographers from our group were taking pictures of guys with long hair on the balconies of old buildings. A group of Palestinian boys—perhaps ten or twelve years old—looked on, and one insisted we stop taking pictures. The photography teacher tried to explain who we were. He told them (in Arabic of course) that we were all Palestinian, and he was from Jaffa, giving them his family name. The boy retorted that he doubted we were all Palestinian and looked pointedly in my direction. I told him I was Palestinian from the United States, and held up the necklace that I was wearing, with its iconic pendant of Handala. Handala, a cartoon character of a child with patched clothing usually shown from behind, is a common symbol of Palestinian refugees. The boy seemed not to recognize him, though. "What," he asked, "You have a child?" "He doesn't know Handala," one of the participants whispered to me with some astonishment. Perhaps he thought that Handala was one of those charm necklaces that women sometimes wear to show how many children they have, which I had also seen in Israel. This suggests he could easily recognize that I was not a (local) Palestinian—perhaps by the way I moved or the way I dressed—and that this difference was important to him, but he that did not quickly recognize this fundamental symbol of Palestinian identity. For him, in this moment, identity was about familiarity more than it was about cultural history. My everyday habitus signified for national politics. Or perhaps he would have recognized Handala had he been closer to me. In any case the participant's slight anxiety that he would not know Handala was itself revealing: The question of whether young Palestinians will learn about Palestinians' political heritage is a source of concern. Moments later, with a few more words from the photography teacher, the energy of the moment somehow changed. With the same vigor that they had demanded that we stop taking pictures, the children exhorted us to photograph them, throwing their arms around each other's shoulders. Both the demand for us not to take pictures and the demand for us to photograph them were these boys' assertions that these streets were their territory, not only Palestinian despite it all, but indisputably local. While we were taking photographs, our embodied presence in public spaces demonstrated the risks of making an appearance as a Palestinian photographer in each space: In Aida, photographing the army, which itself could appear at nearly any time, invited army violence; in Jaffa, appearing as Palestinian felt like a claiming of space.

Obstacles and encounters: Sensing politics

On that same tour of the orientalist Andromeda complex in Jaffa, I told one of the participants that the site reminded me of one of the most beautiful hotels in Bethlehem, then known as the Intercontinental Hotel, and later as the Jacir Palace. Centered around an old family mansion, this hotel, too, commodifies Arab architecture, but it is old—a real example of a Palestinian *qasr* or "castle"—and still carries a Palestinian name. Andromeda excludes all but the wealthiest; the hotel—with its swanky restaurant and its catering to tourists—similarly excludes most people who lived nearby. In the Bethlehem hotel, unlike in Jaffa, there was not even a "walk through." If you were a young man from the neighborhood, you would be stopped at the elevator if you tried to go upstairs and you did not have a key. I thought there could be an interesting photographic connection between the Andromeda complex and the Bethlehem hotel. When I suggested this possibility, the participant in Jaffa wisely commented, "See, you can make these connections, because you go back and forth. But we wouldn't see this in a million years." Here, the symbolic relay—the traffic in meanings across the Green Line—was just not working. Throughout the summer, she had repeatedly emphasized that it was a challenge to imagine how to take photographs in dialogue with photographs from Aida, and this moment underscored her point. Indeed, in these two sites politics was deeply sensual and affectively rich, and differences in affective experience could impede connections between Palestinians in these two sites.

Participants' inability to move across spaces in fact limited the possibility of political analysis and connection of the everyday politics of exclusion and dispossession in each location. Palestinians on either side of the Green Line might share a set of concepts and chants, but they did not share a habitus, an embodied way of being in the physical world immediately around them that grounds political knowledge and sparks sentiments. If I had imagined this photo exchange as a kind of a game, Israeli closure made it quite difficult to play. When I pointed out the same comparison between Andromeda and the Jacir Palace in Aida, the photographers were not eager to follow me toward the analogy, and no one photographed the hotel. Palestinians in Aida rarely commented on the hotel as an exclusive space, perhaps because they are so focused on the much more overtly violent Israeli military base that also overlooks the camp. Unlike in Jaffa, for these young people, capitalism and class difference often felt like a separate problem from Zionism, though recent scholarship shows the importance of a political economic approach that links neoliberalism and Zionism, including in Bethlehem.[32]

There were other, even larger obstacles to our exchange. Our initial plan called for each group to visit the other at least once during the summer, and then to meet up again during the exhibitions. Both I and the Aida coordinators knew that it would be difficult to orchestrate these visits due to Israel's restrictions on movement, and yet we thought that at the very least it was worth a try. I imagined that the process itself would be revealing for people in Jaffa. But in this, too, there were gaps in how Palestinians from either side of the Green Line understood each other's positions. In other experiences trying to obtain permits for people from the West Bank to enter Israel, I had found that Palestinians inside the Green Line were surprised at Israel's seemingly arbitrary (or at least widespread) denials of permits. For example, when I would report that someone had not received a permit, Palestinians inside the Green Line would ask, "Why not?" Among Palestinians in the West Bank, it was perhaps more common to ask, with some sense of dark humor, why a particular person had received a permit than why they had not. After all, in 2006, nearly a quarter of a million residents of the West Bank (and about 20 percent of the men in 2007 between the ages of sixteen and fifty-five) were blacklisted from entering Israel, and this is a list from which, as Israeli officials have said "you can go in but not come out."[33]

As it turned out, we did not even apply for the permits that summer. On June 12, Palestinian militants kidnapped and killed two young Israeli settlers near Hebron, just a short drive away from Bethlehem. Much of the Hebron area was locked down as the Israeli army conducted searches and arrest raids. Aida coordinators told me that no permits were being issued. Israel often extends closure in response to what it deems to be heightened threats. I knew it was always a distasteful process for Palestinians in the West Bank to ask permission from Israeli authorities to go somewhere they felt they had a natural right to be. Now, dealing with authorities was even harder to stomach. It was also an extremely dangerous time to try to enter illegally.

Meanwhile, though they did not need permits to come to the West Bank, some of the participants in Jaffa were anxious about coming to Aida given the tense situation. Members of the Jaffa group had arranged to come together in the SUV of one of the participants. In Aida, they planned a meal, a meeting, and a tour of Aida. But the day before the trip was to take place, one of the key people in Jaffa called me with concerns. Aware of the frequent incursions of the army into Aida, she was worried about the safety of the group. It was true that the road situation had worsened severely during the crisis. During my own trips to Jaffa, I had encountered waves of bumper-to-bumper traffic, often ending with a "flying" checkpoint, or an inspection point in an unexpected place. As a person coming from the West Bank, I always felt slightly anxious. I understood the worries of those in Jaffa, but I also really wanted the trip to happen—not only because of my research project but because I knew that the group in Aida was eager to host.

When I conveyed to coordinators in Aida that the trip might not happen, they were indeed vexed. They were accustomed to hosting delegations—mostly from European and North American visitors. For those in Aida, mere presence can be a small act of solidarity, demonstrating a willingness to be in the space of conflict and to listen to them directly. Here, too, there was a politics of appearance, wherein those who came to Aida and submitted themselves to the discomforts and potential violence of this intense military occupation were perceived to be acting in solidarity. Moreover, for many Palestinians, hosting is a means of demonstrating one's generosity and honor. For the visit to fall apart at this late date could truly undermine trust. In the end, I put the two coordinators in direct contact with each other. As I expected, the Aida coordinator reassured person from Jaffa: Even if the army entered the camp while they were there, he told her, they would not be harmed. They agreed to come. This was when the meal with which I started this chapter took place.

The day of the visit, I drove out to meet the group from Jaffa on the outskirts of Jerusalem so they could follow me into Bethlehem. That they wanted me to come out was another small signal of their discomfort and lack of familiarity with the city. The situation in Aida was calm when I drove out to meet them just beyond the checkpoint. But by the time we were nearing Aida, a friend called with an alert I had heard all too many times: "There's army in the camp." We parked the late-model, Israeli-plated car in a safe courtyard to prevent it from attracting attention from children and to keep it relatively far from where the soldiers were, near the youth center—but we knew that it could still be damaged if tear gas canisters hit it from above. It was a little alarming, and it showed that concerns from the Jaffa group had been warranted. Such was life in Aida: The army could truly appear at any moment, even on a calm afternoon.

As they were accustomed to doing, the participants at Lajee worked around the army presence, switching the schedule to do indoor activities before the tour. The participants introduced themselves, their organizations, and their communities. As someone from Aida was presenting a narrative I had heard many times about where residents of the camp came from, we heard the sound of a big explosion. He hardly paused, continuing on about the camp's high unemployment. Everyone started laughing, and this became its own nervous interruption. Someone from Jaffa said, "We need some explanation of what is going on outside." One of the Aida leaders explained, "It's just the kids being provoked by the army. It's not serious. It happens a lot. It's just the little kids and the army. The older ones have already been arrested. You are safe here." Note the many ways the routineness of the violence is built into the statement: "it's just that . . . ," "it's not serious," and the grim (and just slightly tongue in cheek) comment that the older activists were already in prison. The sound, he said, had been a stun grenade, a weapon that is designed to scare people. The explanation would have to do. In Aida, people had become inured to a certain level of military violence.[34] The noise raised people's tension, but they were used to going on with their days. We closed the windows to prevent tear gas from entering. The leaders of the Aida group regulated how we looked at the soldiers from the window, and in doing so protected us from the remote but real possibility of being injured while inside the building. But we could do nothing about the sound.[35]

If our sensoriums were somewhat out of tune, the vocabulary of the two groups was largely shared. During the introduction of Jaffa, one of that group's leaders used the common expression, "the catastrophe is ongoing " (*al-nakba mustamirra*). Nakba is the Palestinian term for the dispossession of Palestinian society in 1948. The idea that the Nakba was ongoing suggested that Israeli repression continued—akin to Patrick Wolfe's idea that settler colonialism is a structure rather than an event (see chapter 3).[36] Here Palestinians from Jaffa used the phrase to refer to displacement caused by gentrification, home demolition, and other means of threatening Palestinians' abilities to hold onto their homes.[37] Photographers from Aida were curious to hear a familiar expression being used in this novel way, especially since they were less accustomed to linking class and occupation politics in this way.

After our eventful (and then delicious) *maqlouba* lunch, described at the start of this chapter, the rest of the visit went as planned. Photographers from Jaffa checked out the books and publications of Lajee. They took photographs of children standing on their front stoops and of a giant fig tree that towered green over a courtyard wall. As people did on other of our photography tours, they took photos of each other: smiling standing in front of a mural declaring the rights of a child, walking and talking with style and assurance, standing and explaining with a smile, holding a camera to their faces poised to shoot. They took photographs that required careful tricks, as of a shadow reflecting on a piece of paper held in front of the army watchtower, as though to playfully assert: Our representations can transform reality! They took more pictures of soldiers. One was wearing a gas mask and carrying so much equipment that he looked like a warring robotic elephant. We took a group photograph in front of the separation wall itself, one of the most iconic markers of place in Aida— even though some from Aida would have preferred a backdrop other than the architecture of occupation. In general, on this tour as on others, photography was a way of witnessing the everyday violence that surrounded us, of noticing each other's strength and poise, of recognizing the steadfastness of Palestinian communities, and of making connections among people.

Raymond Williams observes, "Practical consciousness is almost always different from official consciousness . . . practical consciousness is what is actually being lived, and not only what it is thought is being lived."[38] Affective shifts can take shape in unlikely moments, all at once. A commitment to collective Palestinian liberation was hardly enough to make our collaboration run smoothly. Even when Palestinians wished to do something simple together, well-founded fears nearly overtook us. It was through the sensing body that we had our most visceral lessons: of the pervasiveness of military threat, yes, but also of the possibility for connection and release in the simple gestures of Palestinian tradition, as in the hilariously loud and alarming clamor of the pot of delicious *maqlouba*. Still, it is important also to remember that Israeli closure had almost prevented this visit from happening. While decades of Palestinian activism across all parts of society mean that many Palestinians are in agreement about the terms of discussion for Palestinian liberation, closure is effective at preventing them from sharing sensed space and experience. In that summer of 2014, Palestinians in each location even listened to the war differently—though both were quite apart from the way that Palestinians in Gaza themselves listened to the direct bombardment of Israeli weapons.

Listening to war, separately

One day, as class in Jaffa was coming to a close, we started to hear sirens. A few of us made cautious eye contact around the circle. The sirens are supposed to be signals to move to a shelter or take a protective stance due to the Hamas or other rockets being fired from Gaza, but none of us moved. A few minutes later we heard a distant thud. Later at our iftar meal, one of the group members checked her smart phone and reported that a rocket had indeed hit Al-Lidd / Lod, a city about twenty-five kilometers away. Our attitude was a kind of "apprehension"—"a sensuous means of understanding" that pairs fear and understanding,[39] possible when the news can be heard—and felt—even before the alert arrives on the phone.

During the Gaza War, Palestinians in Jaffa, like other Israelis in the center of the country, lived with the threat of Hamas rockets. What did they do, someone from Aida asked the group from Jaffa when we met, when they heard sirens signaling an incoming Hamas missile? Someone from Jaffa responded that people reacted differently. Some were more cautious or more frightened than others. And many simply ignored them. For Israeli civilians during the extremely asymmetrical Gaza wars, the primary sensory mode of experience of the recent wars in Gaza has been through sound. Moreover, Israelis more often hear warning sirens than actual explosions. Even the warning sirens were a second level of defense because the Iron Dome system was designed to intercept and destroy missiles even before they hit the ground. As in other places where the thanatosonic sphere is intense, people's structural position in relation to a war can orient them very differently to the sounds of weapons. In Israel, as Danny Kaplan has argued, Israeli public culture "produces a parallel between times of emergency and sacred time,"[40] in particular for Jewish residents. Just as Palestinians are differently oriented to Israeli memorializations, they are also differently oriented toward the warning sirens of war. Being a citizen meant that one was supposed to internalize that the state is trying to protect, and that one should heed its warnings. Doing so may have been second nature for many Jewish Israelis, but many Palestinians thought twice before reacting.

The week after hearing sirens in class, we heard them as we were walking in an Arab neighborhood taking pictures. We looked over our shoulders and glanced at each other with disquiet, but we did not interrupt our tour. A Palestinian man smoking his shisha water pipe on an outdoor couch did not move inside, either, and nor did the children playing on the street. Publicly refusing to heed the warnings of the sirens to take cover was a way of refusing the prevailing security logic in Israel.[41] Instead, we concluded our walking tour and headed for the pier where we planned to have dinner. Someone commented that it was likely to be less busy than usual because people would avoid the open space of the pier. They were right. The pier, usually bustling on a summer evening, was nearly deserted. We headed toward a popular Arab-owned restaurant. As we got settled, we noticed that most of the other people at the restaurant also seemed to be having an iftar meal. They too watched the sun set over the water and listened for the call to prayer before beginning to eat. Watching the sun set where the sky met the Mediterranean Sea was a particularly lovely way to mark the end of the fast. And it was a momentary recovery of Palestinian public space in Jaffa. Yet, we knew that it came not only because of those eternal annual and daily rituals of Ramadan, but also because of the horror of a war just sixty-five kilometers away.

Another time that summer, I was at Lajee Center when we heard sirens in Aida, likely coming from Gilo settlement just a few hundred meters away. People at Lajee immediately sprung to the window and then to the rooftop to see a rocket and its contrails in the air. In both places, Palestinians staked out a position in relation to the Hamas rockets that set them in contrast to Jewish Israelis. In both places this involved small physical risks. In Jaffa it entailed social and political risk as well. Here, too, we can see a distinction between the political habitus of Palestinians in the West Bank as opposed to citizens of Israel. Inside the Green Line, just quietly being outside in these moments was a kind of refusal of Israeli hegemony, a rejection of a security logic that permeates the society in which they live. In contrast, in the West Bank, a momentary celebration of the missiles was an ecstatic instant of reversing the military logic under which they lived—finally, they were not the group being targeted by weapons—even though that moment neither made them safer nor led to concrete gains for their community.

From practice to exhibition

By the end of the summer, we faced the challenge of putting on exhibitions. I remember my surprise and disappointment when a member of the Jaffa group asked whether the Jaffa work would be exhibited with the Aida work, since this was the whole point of our summer's work. The project had not (yet) succeeded in generating a strong sense of connection between the groups. But we decided that we would indeed exhibit all of the same photographs in each place. We designed an invitation and banner that featured the skylines of Jaffa and Aida. The angle of the photo of Jaffa's old city taken from the port and the angle of the photo of Aida taken from the main street made the two places look like mirror images of each other, crowded towns on a hill, each with a prominent mosque. As with the names brainstormed at the beginning of the summer, this image put these two places in relation and even suggested a parallel between them.

The locations of the exhibitions themselves reflected something about the place of Palestinian cultural resistance for Palestinians in Israel's 1948 territories and in the West Bank. In Jaffa, where space is at a premium, organizers arranged to hold our exhibition in an upstairs room of the Yafa Café. This centrally located café was first jointly owned by a Jewish woman from Nahariyya, a town in the far north of Israel, and a Palestinian resident of Ramle, a city just outside of Tel Aviv; however, the woman had passed away and the restaurant was, in 2014, owned solely by the Palestinian man. It is enough of a cultural institution to have had an article written about it in *Haaretz*,[42] as well as other articles that mention it prominently.[43] These articles focus on the café as a center of Jewish-Palestinian coexistence or of Arab cultural revival in Jaffa, a space where Jewish and Palestinian Israelis "met in peace, as equals, and as representative of two identities and culture."[44] Painted in turquoise and warmly lit, the café sells Arabic, Hebrew, and English language books and presents small plates of Palestinian food. While the less political Arab restaurants in Jaffa had apparently taken a business hit during the 2014 war—as they always did when tensions increased—Yafa Café had not, according to its owner.[45] The owner's boast that his business was doing fine suggested that his customers consisted of Palestinians and Jewish Israelis who were critical of state discourses on war and security.

Long before group members had figured out the venue for the exhibition, I had noticed the café's outdoor signage as I passed through town. A mural outside showed an iconic cartoon by the assassinated Palestinian cartoonist Naji Al-Ali, in which a grim man in a suit with dark eyes asks of an emaciated old man sitting on a barrel, "Are you Muslim or Christian, Sunni or Shi'i, Druze or 'Alawi, Orthodox or Catholic?" The old man responds, "I am Arab, you ass." Standing by is Handala, the iconic figure of the refugee child also created by Al-Ali. Handala was a silent witness to the crimes and betrayals of officials. The cartoon suggested that the very act of categorizing by religion within the Arab identity was regarded as odious by Naji Al-Ali, because it created and perpetuated divisions. In Jaffa, as in Israel as a whole, Israel has indeed fostered sectarian divides among Palestinians.[46] But the significance of the cartoon here could be read in another way, too. Here, there was a subtle transposition to the logics of Jaffa, where in addition to the politics of religion, Israel's official state designations and its dominant culture frequently misrecognize Palestinians. Even if the terminological debates here were different, the message was the same: Despite those who wrongly categorize us, we know who we are. As in other cases, the transposition of a political message from one part of Palestinian political culture to Palestinians inside Israel's 1948 territories required an awareness of subtext.

The sign for the café had another subtly subversive message. The sign complicated norms of language and naming in Israel. The name "*Yāfā*"—Arabic for Jaffa—is written in three alphabets, Arabic, Hebrew, and English, importantly using the Arabic pronunciation in each case, rather than *Yafo* (Hebrew) or Jaffa (English)—the more conventional way in which Palestinians did trilingual signage. This was the inverse of the logic one sometimes finds on Israeli street signs in which one finds the Hebrew name written in an Arabic alphabet (e.g., *Yerushalayim*, the Hebrew name for Jerusalem, written in Arabic script, rather than *Al-Quds*, the Arabic name for Jerusalem). With this sign, whatever language one reads one would have to acknowledge Jaffa's Arabness. Under each of the names is the description, "Book Store & Coffee Shop," written in three languages. However, disrupting convention, the sign matches the Arabic scripted name with the Hebrew description, the Hebrew scripted name with the Arabic phrase, and the English scripted name with the Arabic phrase. The result is an assumption of mixing, of juxtaposing languages with each other. We can read this as an example of something close to what Daniel Monterescu regards as Jaffa's "cultural indeterminacy," by which in Jaffa there is a "failure of national mediation in forming a hegemonic narrative sequence of identity and locality."[47]

In Bethlehem, organizers arranged to hold the exhibition at the Peace Center on Nativity Square, very near the Nativity Church that marks the heart of tourism in Bethlehem. The Peace Center was built as part of the Bethlehem 2000 project supported by the World Bank, the United Nations, and the Israeli and PA governments.[48] This Bethlehem 2000 initiative was dramatically curtailed by the start of the second Intifada in September 2000. Its own signage signals its orientation to tourists, declaring in English and Arabic, "Bethlehem Peace Center." The Arabic script is on top, but the English is larger. Below them, it specifies in English only, "Galleries | Tourist Information | Auditorium | Archaeological Museum | Library | Bookstore | Tourist Police." It is an underutilized space, but one that has been a backdrop or host to major international visitors, such as Pope Benedict in 2009, and to a plethora of local Palestinian events. Its logo, hung outside the building, is of a dove with an olive branch and a star—globally recognizable symbols of peace. Like so many larger Palestinian institutions in the West Bank, it anticipates North American and European audiences. The main floor consists of a wide-open hall and a small gift store. In a sense, the Peace Center's availability to a small community organization like Lajee is the result of the failure of the initial mission of the center to promote tourism under the general banner of development and state building. It permits such a small community exhibition, it seems, because such projects are the only business in town, even if the space was designed with a different logic. The Yafa Café and the Peace Center, then, were each positioned carefully in relation to their surrounding contexts: The Yafa Café intervened in Zionist space with pointedly Palestinian cultural symbolism, and it made money as a small place in a busy city. There was a market for quirky in Jaffa. In contrast, the Peace Center was part of an NGO-development model driven by international funds and foreign tourism. It traded on an element of Bethlehem's cultural significance on the world stage as the birthplace of Christianity and, in that sense, a "city of peace." These differences—between Palestinian cultural life positioned in relation to markets and Israeli dominant culture in Israel's 1948 territories and Palestinians positioned in relation to an international donor community and amorphous global conceptions of Christian history in the West Bank—were indicative of broader dynamics for these two Palestinian communities.

Pairs resignifying place

In addition to selecting the location, project leaders in each place had to select the images for the exhibition. Curating, here, can be seen as an act of intersubjective care across communities.[49] It was also an act of bricolage, of making do and making meaning with what we had after a summer punctuated by war and heatwaves, when it seemed nothing had gone exactly as expected. To create the exhibition itself, the two photography instructors curated the exhibition by selecting one image from each photographer. Additionally, they made five collages of images, loosely organized around themes of the built environment and landscapes, portraits, protests of the Gaza War in each place, the idea of home (this one also heavily featured cats, dogs, and plants), and the visits between the two groups. In a few cases of the paired images for the main exhibition, one image inspired another to be taken, but in most cases, the instructors selected from existing photographs by the participants. Juxtaposed with each other, photographs of Aida and Jaffa each refracted pieces of the other to reconstitute something new. No one suggested posting text with the images.[50] This was a practice of photography among people who knew themselves to be profoundly politically marginalized. Instead, photographers and curators alike seemed to appreciate the open-ended sense of the images' meanings, the sense that the significance of the images was in their relationship to each other and to the project as a whole. As I was preparing this manuscript, though, I did return to the photographers and photography teachers and request a comment from them about their images. Thus the analysis I present of these photographs is through the curators' selection of them, the comments the photographers offered me, their own visual qualities, and the relationship between each pair of images. This process helps to value the open-ended significance of the images and the multiplicity of our perspectives on them.

Pairing 1: *The writing on the walls of dispossession.* The photograph from Jaffa, Israel, shows a red fairy stenciled onto a rusted red door, poised above an old lock (Figure 16). What kind of a contrast is this of playful and serious, lightness and heft, sweetness and violence? The photographer, Shams Abu Ajweh, commented to me about the image in an email:

> You see that little cute Fairy? That's Light, Love and Freedom. And then right beneath it, pay attention to 'beneath' ;) there's the lock, and it's rusty, but still can lock things/people/thoughts/voices and most importantly, souls in or out. I just could feel that whoever airbrushed that Fairy there had the same exact feelings and thoughts and it was there waiting for me to notice it and take a picture of it . . . I would like to emphasize the fact that I strongly and deeply believe that locks can be opened by little cute fairies, using the Love and Light from which they emanated. Locks emanated from that exact Love and Light, it's just that they have forgotten where they came from, and so they must go through their life experience as locks. So yes, I know that only love can bring love, only compassion can bring compassion.

Figure 16 Jaffa. "You see that little cute Fairy? That's Light, Love and Freedom." Photo by Shams Abu Ajweh. Reprinted with permission.

The photographer saw herself in a dynamic of friendly co-creativity with the stencil artist without knowing anything for certain about the artist. And she embraced a sense of play and magic.

In exhibition in Jaffa, this open-ended photograph of a juxtaposition was juxtaposed again, paired with an image from Aida Refugee Camp, the West Bank. That photograph showed a child looking through the broken glass of a dark window, in front of two doors that are locked shut. Next to him is spray-painted, "Your memory lives" (Figure 17). But the graffito ends in a blur, rather than in a name as is conventional. The photographer, Shurouq Asad, explained her photograph entirely through a quote from a song sung by the Lebanese singer Julia Butrous, a favorite of many nationalist Palestinians: "My home is here. My land is here. The sea, the valley, the river are ours. So how can I make peace in the face of fire? I will resist!" It seemed that for her, a nationalist frame validated her photograph, gave it meaning and poetry.

For me, the enticing puzzle of the photograph was that the graffito writer must have been interrupted—by what, we cannot say. By a soldier? By the approach of a collaborator? By a phone call? By needing to look up the name? Or had the paint run out? Still, the notion of an interrupted memorial seems, in its

Figure 17 Aida Refugee Camp. A different pairing of graffiti and lock. Photo Shurouq M. Asad. Reprinted with permission.

way, profoundly Palestinian. The phrase "Your memory lives" is familiar from the Palestinian nationalist canon that hails martyrs and their sacrifices. But the institutions that usually produce official history are weak and fragmented for Palestinians because they lack strong public institutions. Their lack of control over territory means that they have fewer resources with which to produce popular memory. The PA, with its compounding roles of entrenching its own undemocratic leadership and being complicit with Israeli occupation, has not yielded strong institutions of memory. Nevertheless, in Aida, Palestinians generally control what is written on the walls in these furtive memorials, even if they have no way of preventing Israeli soldiers from entering their streets day and night to arrest or threaten community members.

How does this photograph intersect with the photograph of the fairy, stenciled on a street in a historic Palestinian city? The photographs both contain a lock and graffito, but both the content of the photograph and the apparent intent of the photographers are quite different. While politics dominate graffiti and murals in Aida Refugee Camp, we can guess that the fairy was stenciled without political intent—by whom, Jewish Israeli, Palestinian, or neither, we do not know. It is only the exhibition space itself that might reframe this image as

Figure 18 Aida Refugee Camp. Youth use a dumpster as shield in confrontations with the army. Photo by Meras AlAzza. Reprinted with permission.

having a political context. As with the resignification of the Naji Al-Ali text on the Yafa Café sign and other instances throughout this book, inside the Green Line, acts of resignifying are a key Palestinian semiotic practice, because Palestinians lack control over space and media where they are and are marginalized by Palestinian nationalism. This, indeed, is what makes the act of curation itself so fertile. The fairy floated over the heavy stability of violence. Had the fairy become a kind of angel for the memorialized person in the Aida photograph? Does the photograph of the fairy floating over the lock become a quirky vision of liberation just as the graffiti stands in contrast to the lock in the Aida photo? Should Palestinian liberation indeed become more welcoming to quirky stencils? When the Palestinian curators put this next to the photograph of the graffiti from Aida and other photographs from this exhibition, new significances became available.

Pairing two: Resignifying infrastructure of waste. From Aida Camp, a photograph showed an overturned dumpster being used by youth as a shield during a protest against the army (Figure 18). Meras AlAzza explained his photograph in Arabic:

The people of Aida Camp inhale tear gas instead of oxygen, and it appears in the photograph that they have become accustomed to it to the degree that they are no longer affected by it. As appears in the left side of the photograph, there are two youths demonstrating who are being sheltered by the dumpster so the army's sniper cannot manage to injure them directly. [My translation.]

Despite the many protests in Aida that summer, this was the only featured photograph of confrontations in the exhibition. Taken from a distance, it shows that the Israeli army is effectively held at bay by the dumpster and by the stones of the youth. The everyday infrastructure of disposal becomes a system of defense. Here the repurposing is not of symbols but of the lived environment.

In Jaffa, a photograph showed a green plastic dumpster from a public housing neighborhood (Figure 19). The photographer Amal Salem reflected on this photograph under the title "Jaffa's alleyways" in Arabic that half personified Jaffa as a woman, with the feminine pronoun that is used to refer to cities:

The beautiful Jaffa, past and present, and her alleyways overcrowded with tales of this place. The "Arab neighborhood," overcrowded with residents' cramped apartments. The worn-out laundry line becomes part of the character of the place, and the green dumpster becomes the face of this building and every other

Figure 19 Jaffa. Garbage and laundry adorn the threshold of a building. Photo by Amal Salem. Reprinted with permission.

building around the neighborhood. Jaffa in all of her components is "the Mother of the Stranger," the beach, poverty, hope, suffering, steadfastness, and confrontation. Jaffa is us, and we will not turn away from this place. [My translation.]

She wrote of how this photograph captures the heart of Palestinian presence and everyday struggle in Jaffa. She imagined how it must feel to walk into one's home each day past a dumpster.

A photographer from Jaffa, Sami Bukhari, offered a commentary on the two photos together, once again tying themes of class with Palestinian dispossession:

In Israel, the big garbage containers are made of iron and their color is green, which is perhaps why they are called "Frogs." They are usually used to collect garbage in industrial areas, but also in distressed neighborhoods, which are mainly Arab neighborhoods. In contrast, the little plastic trash container is used for serving a single housing unit and is located in the wealthier neighborhoods. The photo taken in Jaffa depicts in the front such a trash container, flooded with garbage, against a building, in a neglected slum, in southeast Jaffa. Needless to say, it is a stolen trash container, a kind of protest against the policy of systematic discrimination and neglect against Palestinian citizens within Israel. The same policy, but in a more pronounced and violent way, is practiced in the Occupied Territories. In times of protest, demonstrations, and clashes, those garbage containers—symbols of status, State systematic discrimination, and oppression—are burned or used as a shield against the Israeli occupation.

Bukhari's remarks suggest that there are two kinds of politicized lawbreaking here depicted, one more subtle than the other, and he ties dispossession and discrimination to impoverishment. Paired together, the two photographs also showed how the very materials of everyday life under Israeli colonialism had different use values in the two settings.

Pairing three: The dead, in context. Two photographs of cemeteries in the exhibition showed that not even the dead escape the policies of exclusion and segmentation that are engaged against Palestinians in each location. A photographer in Aida photographed the cemetery that is on the edge of the camp with a watchtower and the Israeli separation wall in the background (Figure 20). This is the view many Aida residents have from their homes. On any given day, they may witness soldiers clambering through the cemetery, fully armed, antennae from their radios waving high above their heads. They are often there pursuing a child who they suspect of throwing stones or a Molotov cocktail or a pipe bomb. Even in death, Aida residents know, they will not escape these

Figure 20 Aida Refugee Camp. Hundreds of residents of Aida Camp would see something like this view of the cemetery and the Israeli military watchtower from their windows. Photo by Mahmood Al-Araj. Reprinted with permission.

intrusions. The photograph shows how the Israeli army encloses, threatens, and steals any sense of peace that the trees might otherwise provide.

In the photograph from Jaffa (Figure 21), we see an institution that would seem to represent the very opposite of the separation wall, the Peres Peace House. Its architect Massimiliano Fuksas says that the building "is the representation of an emergency," made of concrete and glass materials that, for him, represent places that have suffered and with layers that refer to the "stratification of the history of two peoples."[51] The building is well reviewed within architectural circles. Yet, this too is a contested site, built on confiscated refugee property.[52] In the photo, the building itself is mostly cropped out. Once again, we see that being Palestinian in Israel often means looking away from the thing that is supposed to be the thing. Instead of the building, we see two women strolling in the gardens, with a giant concrete wall behind them. Beyond this wall, up on a bluff, is a Palestinian cemetery. The background is the focal point from this Palestinian perspective. Of course, there is no architectural review for the graves that lie just beyond its concrete containing wall, but this, for Palestinians, is certainly monumental space.

Figure 21 Jaffa. This cemetery by the sea holds the family members of many Jaffa residents. Photo by Sami Bukhari. Reprinted with permission.

The photographer, Sami Bukhari, hardly had to do research (as I did) to situate the photograph. As he wrote,

> The photo depicts in the background, the "Kazakhana" cemetery that served before the Nakba until the late seventies and where my two grandfathers are buried.
>
> It symbolizes for me the first generation of the Nakba, my childhood and my personal and collective memory. In the past I've made a series of photos from this cemetery because of its connection with the natural landscape and my interest in issues related to the traditional way of building in the Palestinian society regarding the Israeli society that is also evident in the planning of cemeteries. In contrast, the foreground of the photo depicts the yard with the artificially over planned gardens of the "(Shimon) Peres Center for Peace," another washing tool and fundraising machine for the continuity of the Israeli occupation and ethnic cleansing, from the river to the sea. Under statements calling for peace and coexistence between Arabs and Jews lies a policy of systematic racism and discrimination against Palestinians. Meanwhile, we have history, beliefs and words and they have killing machines and propaganda . . .

The personal and the national are never distant from each other, and history always rests nearby.

Paired with the photograph of the cemetery and wall in Aida, the clean gray wall at the edge of the Peace Center's garden, lined with young trees that might someday grow in to hide the wall, seems less an architect's statement structure than one that references a military one, the separation wall that is only an hour's drive away. The gray containing wall is another wall of separation, perhaps blocking the two women inside the gardens from confronting Palestinian history, preserving their sense of spaciousness-with-enclosure from the surrounding area of Jaffa, which can feel cramped and neglected. Bukhari noted a connection between the photographs:

> The two photos reveal the true face of the Israeli occupation policy. In one, it is expressed and clear as sunlight, a military rule of systematic oppression and apartheid. In the second it is disguised under seemingly democratic but actually racist laws, and under false slogans of a desire for peace and coexistence between Arabs and Jews. In both cases, those who pay the price are the Palestinians, either as citizens under Israeli rule or as occupied and persecuted by the Israeli army.

The photography teacher from Aida, who preferred not to be named, also saw connections as he looked at the two photographs:

> In the photo from Aida, we see the cemetery of Aida Camp and behind it the military watchtower of the Israeli military forces. We are killed twice in our lives: in life and in death. From this watchtower, a sniper has killed more than one refugee while they are in their homes. The army follows them when they are dead, in one way or another: Exhuming graves, firing bullets, shooting tear gas canisters, and so forth. If this indicates anything, it indicates the systematic Israeli occupation policies against the Palestinian people and their lack of acceptance of us on this land, alive or dead.
>
> As we see in photo of the graveyard in Jaffa, it is distinguished by being in '48 territory and next to the beach, but despite the fact that Palestinians [in Israel's '48 territory] carry Israeli identity cards, what happens here does not differ much from what happens in Aida. It is one occupation, with the goal of getting rid of all Arabs alive or dead. Jaffa graveyards face confiscation from the occupier due to the Absentee Property Law. [My translation.]

Indeed, the Aida watchtower above the graveyard was especially dangerous during the second Intifada, and Jaffa's Palestinian cemeteries have faced a variety of threats of destruction since 1948, especially due to the Absentee Property Law, which allowed the state to expropriate refugees' properties and much Muslim public property.[53] For each of the photographers, treatment of the dead reflects a continuity to Israeli policies on either side of the Green Line.

The more I looked at the photograph from Jaffa, another significance seeped through, one mentioned in passing in the Aida photography teacher's statement. To a Palestinian in Aida, focus might fall not on the cemetery but on the edge of the photo, to the deep blue of the sea below the pale sunset sky. Palestinians of the West Bank had been mostly forbidden from visiting the sea for almost two decades, and it was naturally a site of great desire. From the perspective of someone who could never go to the beach, the presence of the sea in the background might overpower anything in the foreground in another displacement of focus. The availability of certain interpretations—and the prevalence of certain longings—was structured by the different physical and political worlds in which Palestinian citizens of Israel and Palestinian subjects of military occupation in the West Bank lived.

The openings

The room in the Yafa Café was warm and crowded. Some of the luminaries of Palestinian culture and arts attended, including a member of the Palestinian hip hop group DAM and leaders of the Yaffa Youth Movement who had not been involved in the project. The photographers brought their children and other relatives. Notably absent were any participants from Aida, who again had not applied for permits because the permits system was both stalled and regarded as illegitimate. Instead, we tried to connect via Skype. This involved a clumsy rigging of a computer and projector and yielded an uneven image appearing on a wall.

The project coordinator of the Jaffa group spoke about our shared endeavor, declaring, "If you ask what ties these two places together, I would say one sentence: There is one thing that brings us together, and it is something that separates us also. It is the occupation." In this sentence, she summed up the politics of division, the contradictions of similarities that led to distance. Both places were created through Israeli violence, even as they were created quite differently. Still, she continued, "We did not try to highlight the occupation here. We tried to showcase our cities and villages, the things we love about them." Notably, she uses the word "occupation" (al-iḥtilāl) here to refer not only to Israeli occupation in the West Bank but to refer to Israeli presence in all of historic

Palestine. Again, language choice suggested the occupied territories of the West Bank and Gaza were the presumed center of Palestinian politics—and also that Israeli rule in Jaffa was as illegitimate as that in the West Bank and Gaza. She also expressed regret that the Aida group had been unable to attend.

Following this, the photography teacher spoke about the project, reading prepared remarks in formal Arabic:

> While the Israeli "revenge" army [*jaysh al-intiqām*, a contrast with the official name of the Israeli Defense Forces] has looked with enthusiasm to take pictures of wartime, we have paid the price in innocent martyrs, including women and children. Meanwhile, two groups from Aida Camp in Bethlehem and Jaffa have undertaken to take pictures of the process of brotherhood, bringing these two groups together and shortening the distance between them. These groups have realized a victory over the politics of marginalization through a communication between Palestinians wherever they are. So this exhibition is a first station in a long journey.

His statement was eloquent and kind, and it indicated a recognition that this modest project might speak to much larger collective goals that exceed the specificity of these two Palestinian groups in these two locations. The use of formal Arabic not only dignified the event, but it also emphasized that this project throughout was an exercise in strengthening Palestinian culture.

Finally, over a weak Skype connection that left the faces of the photography teacher and Lajee's director heavily pixilated, the director of Lajee spoke about the unity of the Palestinian people and Palestinians' will to work together despite the checkpoints and the walls. His message was intensified by distance and mediation. Despite their absence, the opening was festive, with the photographers having their pictures taken in front of their own photographs, sometimes with friends or family members.

In Bethlehem a few days later, we hung the same pictures, albeit in a slightly different order. Again, the exhibition was attended by prominent community members—this time including recently released Palestinian long-term prisoners from the Bethlehem area who were regarded as local dignitaries. We were welcomed by the director of Lajee, declaring, "We are very proud to have Palestinians from the inside [*min al-dākhil*] here together." He then introduced a special guest, the Archbishop of Sebastia of the Greek Orthodox Patriarchate of Jerusalem, Atallah Hanna, who, he said, "represents all Palestinians, whether they are in Jerusalem or Aida or Jaffa or Gaza." Atallah Hanna represented a nationalist vision of liberation and spoke in a different register than we had heard in Jaffa. He emphasized how he was coming that day from "Jerusalem the capital, and in its name, I thank you." His message was of the ongoing need for unity, despite the dreadful crisis of the Gaza War. "We will not relinquish Palestine. We will not relinquish Acre or Nazareth or Jerusalem. It is natural that we would go to Jaffa and Jaffa would come to us."

The photography teacher from Jaffa then read the same statement he had read a few days earlier. This time, he began with a comment on the place of Arabic in his life and the lives of other people from Jaffa. He explained that as a student in a private, church-affiliated school in Jaffa, he had received just one hour of Arabic education per week as a child, and that he had learned Arabic over time by reading and listening to the news in Arabic. This was a glimpse into the practical, everyday challenges of being Palestinian in Israel, though this school does, he told me later, require more Arabic classes today. When he announced that this was the first time he had written and publicly read something in formal Arabic, a Palestinian from Aida called out in praise and appreciation. Arabic itself took on a new significance. In the West Bank it was the language of all everyday interactions, while in Jaffa its use was marked as an achievement. The shout-out recognized this. Once again, the opening was an opportunity for people to take pictures next to the photographs they had on exhibition, to show off this work to friends and relatives, and for some celebratory group photos. As the opening wound down, the Jaffa group took the opportunity of being in Bethlehem to also see some of the tourist sites there.

All summer long, the connection between the two groups had been tenuous, fleeting, strained by their differences in circumstance as well as by closure itself. Our one visit had almost been called off and had required closing windows to keep out the tear gas. But the afternoon suggested the possibility of real connection, a connection that was Palestinian, but not nationalist in the confines of the West Bank and Ramallah-centric, state-building version of nationalism.

Conclusions

Palestinian citizens of Israel and Palestinians in the West Bank inhabit different worlds, both created through Israeli settler colonialism. As these curators and photographers showed, these worlds can be productively seen in relationship with one another, as images and sentiments ricochet off each other to produce new sentiments and meanings. The cemeteries, the walls, the dumpsters, the graffiti, and the Arabic language itself: As these objects and ideas moved across the Green Line, their political significance shifted or became amplified, sometimes in surprising ways. They opened up questions more often than they provided conclusions. We find here a logic different than that of solidarity or sameness, which we saw motivating the political action I address in other chapters, and distinct from a logic of comparison, too. Letting places reverberate off each other produces new understandings, for example about the link between capitalism and Zionism, an insight familiar in Jaffa that is important and illuminating in Aida, too. The Jaffa facilitator's insight that occupation both brings together and separates Aida and Jaffa is a core insight for this book. And again and again, we saw that Palestinians in Israel were always resignifying material around them to express or reflect something specific to their experience, whether by taking pictures of things which would not be regarded as political by most Jewish Israelis or by reframing a canonical element of Palestinian political culture just a little bit so that it could be seen in a new way.

Finally, we see in this chapter that even in fraught political circumstances, we should look to modes of research that happen alongside or through creative processes. Play gives space for a wider range of affects and multiple, non-idealized vantage points on our communities. It opens the door to a kind of multiplication of norms of communication. Nationalist communication is often made to be about a single unitary speaker, a leader with a singular brilliance or authority on display, or it is about a national unison of "we" with its hegemonic views of the past. Here we have explored a decentering approach to Palestinian societies that makes peripheries visible. This project is not about what one person can say alone but rather about what is tentatively expressed together. And even this expression together is not unanimous; rather it is expression through juxtaposition, contrast, exchange. If democratic futures are to be established, these tools and approaches are valuable resources. This exchange also constituted a Palestinian space. While creating this exchange was difficult due to closure, especially during wartime, it became clear by the time of the exhibitions that creating this space was valuable to all involved.

This was also, I hope the reader can see, a fun process. We took pictures of each other and of cats and of pretty sunsets. Maybe this kind of play with images was all the more delicious because we knew that public images of Palestinians are rarely so lighthearted. We were watching other images in those days, too: not only the bombings of Gaza that can kill dozens in a moment, but also those very 21st-century videos of killings of individuals that happen right before our very eyes. It has long seemed like danger looms everywhere for

Palestinians, especially under occupation: at a "flying" checkpoint when people drive between cities, with a nighttime knock on a door by a group of soldiers. But surveillance cameras and camera phones open killings up for deeper analysis, harder grief. How do Palestinians mourn these very public deaths? How do they tackle the divide between different experiences of Israeli threat when it comes to these kinds of online images? This is the topic of the next chapter. But there may be one of those flying checkpoints between here and there.

Passage. Jerusalem to Nablus

Between 2003 and 2005, I made several trips to Nablus, one of the two largest cities in the West Bank, but only sometimes did I make it into the city. These were especially tense times in Nablus,[1] a city known for its mountains, its meat, its gorgeous old city, its olive oil soap factories, and its sweets. A joke I jotted down in my fieldnotes from February 2004 reflects how Nablus was regarded as a special target of Israeli forces: "An [Israeli] soldier stopped two Palestinians. He asked the first where he was from, and the first said, 'I'm from Nablus.' He asked the second one where he was from, and he said, 'I'm from Ramallah,' and so the soldier says to the second one, 'Good, will you hold my rifle while I search the guy from Nablus?'" (The joke also needled suspicions about Ramallah and the Ramallah-based PA's complicity with Israeli rule.) Soldiers stopping people was the quintessential experience of Palestinian travel in the West Bank during those days, the beginning of a thousand interactions and stories. As a result of all those checkpoints, the West Bank bus system had broken down during the Intifada, and Israeli regulations often prohibited private Palestinian cars from travelling particular routes. Travel was accomplished by a more agile system of shared cabs that seated roughly between four and ten passengers. There were at that period four checkpoints along the way, in what was a less than seventy-kilometer (about forty-mile) trip, and this was fewer than there had been earlier in the Intifada. Arriving late in the Intifada, I had mostly missed the Surda Checkpoint, which had restricted traffic moving north immediately outside of Ramallah. Still, I often did not know how far the next leg of public transportation would take me, because Israeli soldiers only sometimes let the shared cabs through; sometimes the drivers deemed that it would be faster for passengers to just walk across the checkpoints.

In 2003 and 2004, I lived in East Jerusalem—east of the Green Line but an-nexed by Israel—on the main road that goes from Shu'fat through Beit Hanina to Al-Ram. My journeys started easily: I would walk barely twenty steps to the street and could hail one of the white Ford minivans that were the main form of Arab public transportation through Jerusalem in those years of the second In-tifada. These vehicles were celebrated in Hani Abu Assad's film Ford Transit,[55] which focused on the heroic and imaginative possibilities of these vehicles. More often, these vehicles would take me just ten minutes down the road to the Al-Ram Checkpoint, where, if required on that particular day, I would flash my passport to the Israeli soldiers and then walk across to approach another Ford Transit or perhaps an old Mercedes eight-seater for the next leg of the trip. I'd eye the next car and check my watch to guess how long my journey would take: How many seats were still empty? How many passengers would need to arrive before the car departed? This car would take me sometimes to the Qalandia Checkpoint just down the road and sometimes, if I was lucky, all the way to Ramallah. There, I would disembark, scope out the next car, and wait again for the next shared taxi to fill up to go toward Nablus. This was the pretty part. I loved being surrounded by the mountains of olive trees. But it was on this leg that, during one trip, our old Mercedes taxi was stopped by Israeli soldiers at a "flying" checkpoint—where a jeep or two stopped traffic unpredictably. The soldier told us all to get out of the car and hand over our identification documents. One examined our papers while the other had us standing at gunpoint, and so I found myself for a few moments in a scene I had driven by over and over, and seen in dozens of news photographs: Palestinians, usually men, standing near the side of the road or the side of a check-point. This stop was quick. When the soldier handed back our papers, we were on our way, a little rattled.

Usually, we would have to stop but not change cars at Za'tara/Tapuah Checkpoint, a place that felt surrounded by settlements. And then the tension would heighten, for me, as we approached the Hawara Checkpoint, just outside of Nablus, as I wondered whether or not I would get in to the city at all: whether I'd make my appointment, or call the person I was to meet with an apology, with a bouquet of shame—for my failure, for my privilege, for the way in which this great city had become a space of confinement. When Hawara was open, it usually meant a change in cars once again, and then a bumpy ride into the city. When Hawara was closed or closed to "foreigners" or nonresidents of Nablus, a whole other set of options emerged. Once I was offered a donkey (with a young boy to guide it) to ride through the hills to evade the main checkpoint. Other times,

Palestinians advised I go to the Israeli military's District Control Office (DCO), to see if that route was open. Other times, I simply had to go home. I would think of friends, college students from surrounding villages, who were not being allowed to enter the city to reach Al-Najah University. This was a major disruption for their education.

If I was lucky enough to get in through the main checkpoint or the DCO, I would do my interview or go to my meeting, and then the education on mobility and occupation would continue on the way back. On one occasion in fall 2003, I returned to Hawara to find that the soldiers were not allowing anyone to pass. I wrote in my fieldnotes at the time:

I knew this not because there were announcements to this effect; it was simply that taller people among us could see that no one was getting through, and we all could tell that no one was moving forward. It was about two o'clock in the afternoon, during Ramadan, and the crowd was mostly students wanting to get home from the university to their own villages for the iftar. It was a sex-segregated checkpoint, shaped like a funnel, with a more organized line of men and women at the front becoming a large crowd contained by concrete barriers after the line got too long for the structures that were meant to confine it.

A young American activist approached me, identifying me by my clothes as American, and told me she had just come from the front of the crowd. She said the soldiers were pushing and insulting Palestinians, letting people by only sporadically. And then she said the soldiers complained to another international activist that the Palestinians were like animals, because they were behaving in a disorderly manner. Soon, the soldiers decided to open up the checkpoint, but not from the front. Instead, they opened a barrier on the side, quite near where I was standing. The soldiers stood a few meters from the opening and asked that the women approach them one by one. However, as there was no line in this part of the crowd, and as the opening in the concrete barriers was itself at least four people wide, it was difficult to tell who would go next. We pressed forward until some women were slightly in front of the barriers. The soldiers told us that we had come too far forward and asked us why we were so disorderly. Then they physically pushed us backwards, until we were all squeezed very uncomfortably—even, I felt, dangerously—into a tight space.

It took about forty-five minutes to get through that checkpoint. Then twenty minutes down the road we were back at the Za'tara / Tapuah checkpoint, at which much the same thing happened: We were waiting, first as the soldiers refused to let anyone pass and then as they took people one by one, checking IDs and opening bags. Then, it began to rain. There was no shelter, and so people pressed forward. The soldiers first regarded us as though we were willful children, as though it were unimaginable to them why we would not simply stay in queue, and then they physically pressed us back, their shoulders against our chests, and their machine guns inches from our thighs. At another point, they threatened us with either a sound bomb [stun grenade] or a tear gas canister, and women scattered back. Eventually, we were on our way again toward Jerusalem.

Reading those notes again, seventeen years later, I reckoned with how much things had changed, though they had not actually changed. Palestinians are now accustomed to driving their own cars between the cities, and some of these checkpoints have disappeared or receded into the background, even as others of them have been built up so they feel like international boundaries. People are less often dramatically delayed or refused entry into a city than they were in those days. But soldiers still shoot and kill at checkpoints that divide not Palestinian areas from Israeli ones but Palestinian areas from each other. And Palestinians know that no political development has occurred to protect them from the repeat of those days of dire closure.

5 Territory and Mourning on Social Media

WE WATCH THE VIDEOS, and we are still haunted by the grainy details. How the young man stumbles on a train track tiled in that iconic Jerusalem limestone. How a youth walks toward his friends standing at a storefront and slumps to the ground in the sun. How a woman bleeds amidst a checkpoint's fences and turnstiles until the soldiers pull her away. How the officers drag the man they have just shot into the van and drive off. Some of the videos have no sound because they were captured by surveillance cameras. Some have bone-chilling soundtracks, as the person holding a camera-phone or someone near that person incites violence against the person on camera. We have watched these young Palestinians die, thousands of us, and some Palestinians have returned to walk on those same streets or have seen an identical police van in front of their houses. Sometimes the surveillance video's angle looks just like surveillance footage that they see at their own office or hovering behind the grocer from whom they buy ice cream or bread or nuts. We all know what comes next: those days of weeping, of receiving crowds of condolences, of a house full, full, full, until is it empty, empty in a new way with a ferocious kind of loss, with only a story of how a loved one was just going to work, or just coming home from school, or just afraid of the checkpoint, or just looking out the window, or just growing up, or just participating in protests like he always did.

Social media and videos taken from cell phones and surveillance cameras have made Israeli military and police violence against Palestinians visible in new ways and with new temporalities, as these technologies have done in the United States for racist police and extrajudicial violence.[1] In contrast to annual memorializations or occasional protests, the everyday, always renewing quality of Facebook, which has been the most popular social media platform for Palestinians, including youth,[2] mirrors the everyday and iterative quality of Israeli settler colonial violence. Social media constitute emergent spaces of mourning where Palestinians work through loss with each other. Social media can be a respite for people so often viewed only as perpetrators.

How is Palestinian collectivity mediated in mourning? State violence structures sentiment for people living in a variety of colonial settings and with a variety of relationships to the racialized structures of violence, neglect, and exclusion. Poet and author Claudia Rankine observed at one of the peaks of police violence against Black people in the United States that mourning is a condition of Black life in the United States.[3] For Indigenous people in North America, who, as Jodi Byrd put it, "exist liminally in the ungrievable spaces of suspicion and unintelligibility,"[4] invisibility or forced disappearance is often a part of structures of violence and loss. In Kashmir, while women's mourning is usually a private practice, for women whose husbands have been disappeared, the "half-widow's" role turns public and performative.[5] For many Palestinians, too, mourning is a backdrop to everything else because of state violence. The spaces of mourning described here are public but not necessarily mobilized as modes of appealing to leaders, spaces for deliberation, or even approaches to political organizing. Instead they are oriented toward expression and maintenance of connection. Circulation of videos and photographs of the dead on Facebook convenes and extends spaces for Palestinian grief and anger despite the fragmented quality of Palestinian expression both on and off social media. This dynamic is at the heart of Palestinians' lack of a place to speak to each other as a result of the Green Line and other lines of division. Through watching these videos, Palestinians take in the varieties of Israeli state violence against Palestinians in different places and cultivate emergent Palestinian intimacies of loss. As Palestinians grieve, they also take in the deep vulnerability of their own bodies.

State violence against Indigenous and Black people in North America, Kashmiris in Kashmir, and Palestinians under Israeli rule have different histories, but these contexts are connected through systems and ideologies of global racism and militarism that have been formed through settler colonialism.[6] While racial divisions in Israel and the occupied territories are quite different than in the US or other Atlantic contexts, racism is a crucial analytic here. As settler colonial studies scholar Patrick Wolfe observed, "race is colonialism speaking."[7] Geographer and prison abolition scholar Ruth Wilson Gilmore's definition of racism as "the state-sanctioned or extralegal production and exploitation of group-differentiated vulnerability to premature death" certainly frames Israeli military, police, and civilian violence against Palestinians.[8]

What we can learn from taking in Palestinian rituals of digital mourning is, first, their terrifying sense of the inseparability of military and police violence. The lack of a strong distinction between these both for Palestinians and beyond is a result of the longstanding imbrication of policing, settler colonialism, and empire, as well as the ongoing militarization of police.[9] It is also a result of Israel's blurring of its own borders, a frontier logic that means that the "foreign enemy" in the West Bank is actually a subject of occupation, and the "domestic threat" to public order of a Palestinian inside the Green Line is always implicitly connected to that purported foreign enemy. In looking at Palestinians' encounters with these videos, we are also asked to take in what it means when death becomes less a spectacle than an ordinary occurrence caught on camera, like so many others, and how Palestinians grieve with an embodied intimacy despite their grief being expressed online.

Importantly, Palestinians watch these videos of killings in the shadow of another kind of threat: their ability to express themselves safely and freely online, as I examine in more depth in the next chapter. Facebook can seem like another arm of the Israeli occupation, as suggested in a graphic by Sami Bukhari (Figure 22). Was Facebook, as many hoped social media would be, a bridge to communication across geographic distance, or was it like the wall in Bukhari's graphic, another divider between Palestinians in the West Bank and in Israel? If there are dangers to posting, why do people share or post such remarks on Facebook at all, given the sense of risk they might feel, and given that for a time an app like WhatsApp—also popular among Palestinians—felt somewhat more secure? First, people's sense of the risk of posting on Facebook—their own understanding of the "age of surveillance capitalism"[10]—has accelerated dramatically since these months in 2014 and 2015 on which I focus, and it is possible that people would be more prudent if there were another wave of killings. Palestinians, like others, do seem to be pulling away from Facebook somewhat as other apps like Snapchat and Instagram become more popular and as they evaluate political risks.[11] However, in 2014-2015, Facebook felt like a kind of a general space for posting. It was a platform on which one would have a large network. It many ways, it seemed to mirror public space as a whole, and thus it is not surprising that the general comments of grief and sometimes anger were the kinds of things one would hear in offline public spaces of mourning.

Figure 22 Is Facebook complicit with Israeli military occupation? Is it part of a structure of separation between different groups of Palestinians? Created by Sami Bukhari. Reprinted with permission.

Also, while people might think of WhatsApp and now Signal as slightly more closed or secure, they likely had little faith that Israeli authorities could be truly evaded anywhere. Indeed, on many occasions people shared posts about Palestinians who had been killed not because they had something new to say about a particular killing, but in a similar vein that the NAACP would, in the early- and mid-20th century, fly a flag at its New York headquarters that declared "A Man Was Lynched Yesterday": flying a flag for all passersby to read. In that case, one priority was to make sure that New Yorkers knew what was going on in their country but mostly at some geographic remove, in the South. In this instance, the geography involved is more intricate: People posted from their multiple locations about killings that occurred under different Israeli legal regimes and with different kinds of visibility.

Interrelated geographies of death

I saw the video of the shooting for the first time on YouTube, directed from a Facebook link from a friend's post. This version of it had been distributed by Defense for Children International, Palestine, a children's rights organization based in Ramallah, with narration from a shopkeeper who had been nearby.[12] Earlier that day, youth had been throwing stones and Israeli soldiers had been shooting tear gas, a shopkeeper describes, but when the teens were shot, the youth were just standing around. The high angle of the shots that follow his introduction indicate that we are watching security camera footage. We see youth milling around next to a building. At 13:45, according to the time code, a figure walks calmly toward the building on the right side of the frame. Suddenly he stumbles. By the time his body hits the ground he is limp, and then still. People crowd around him and carry him away. Then there is a cut. According to the timecode stamp, just over an hour has passed. As black smoke clouds the left corner of the video, a boy walks slowly away from the building. He, too, suddenly crumples to the ground. By the time the time code reads 14:58, an hour and thirteen minutes later, it is all over—and on YouTube, the deaths of these two children are compressed to the few minutes we can be expected to watch such a social media post. This is the video of how, on Nakba Day 2014—May 15, a day on which Palestinians commemorate the mass dispossession caused by the formation of the state of Israel—Israeli army snipers shot and killed teenagers Nadeem Siam Nawara and Mohammad Mahmoud Odeh Abu Daher during a protest outside of Ofer Prison near Ramallah, where Palestinian political prisoners are detained, in the Israeli occupied West Bank.

A few days later, I saw the video again with a friend, a Palestinian man in his twenties, at youth center where we both worked in Aida Refugee Camp, also in the West Bank. When my friend opened the link, I was about to turn away, to tell him that I had already seen it, and I did not need to see it again, but it was clear from his introduction that he had also seen it before. Did he want to see it again to get some new insight about what had happened? Had he clicked so we could see this together, some kind of a test of what my reaction would be? Or had he opened the video almost inadvertently, as we so often do these days? While in the United States people discuss what it means that so many watch videos of the killings of Black people by police, I did not hear these conversations frequently in Aida. Not only were more explicit videos of bloody political death more visible on television, and thus somewhat omnipresent as many households left their televisions on liberally, but also under occupation the overt violence of Israeli military seemed to be all around us anyway. Indeed, my friend and I knew all too well about the incident in the video. He and I had been part of another demonstration on Nakba Day in the Bethlehem area, at which soldiers fired tear gas, stun grenades, and rubber bullets at the protesters (see chapter 3). When we had returned to the bus, we had heard about the shooting in Ramallah, reacting with special alarm because we knew a third boy who was also shot that afternoon. Soon, we were at the Ramallah hospital where our fifteen-year-old friend was receiving care. The hospital teemed with medics' exertion and families' grief. I remember how strange it felt to know that our friend had been lucky, though live ammunition had pierced his lung.

The formal qualities of the video we watched—the angle of surveillance camera footage—might seem to put distance between the viewer and the subject. Yet, watching the video with my friend and thinking back on the demonstration we had attended together and then about our injured friend, who was recovering slowly at home, I hardly felt distant. My friend was right in that demographic of young men who could be shot by Israeli soldiers and immediately dismissed as being a perpetrator deserving of death rather than a victim of excessive violence. He, his brothers, and so many of his friends lived in the shadow of a military base. We were witnessing a death that could be any of theirs. It was so deeply known that neither of us had to say it.

What does it mean that we were watching this unfold via surveillance camera? In the West Bank, death often arrives by way of a bullet at a protest. Here, the surveillance camera as a medium evoked the constancy of this violence. It was easy to feel that if one put up a camera for ordinary property protection, eventually it would catch soldiers hurting, harassing, or even killing a friend or a friend of a friend. If, in other contexts, security cameras activate the logic of the panopticon, here they provide the medium for a new exposure of sovereign power's killing with impunity, on camera, at potentially almost any moment. Indeed, the surveillance cameras for the youth center where we sat at that moment had caught Israeli army attacks too. It produced miniature action films featuring spirals of tear gas bouncing along the street in front of the youth center or invading the playground in back (or both);[13] it recorded the last glimpses community members had of youth being arrested in the middle of the night and taken away to the military base up the street; it had caught the flurry of activity after at least two recent Israeli army shootings of a teenager and a young man. That is to say, the odd angle of the surveillance camera was not one of the outsider, above and safe. It spoke more to the strange and uncomfortable positioning of Palestinian images and practices of Palestinian memory-making, like, as Edward Said once wrote, the peculiarly placed photos on the uneven walls of Palestinian refugees.[14] Images of Palestinian death punctured everyday life over and over again, across periods of calm or of turmoil, across generations of military occupation. Death was not a spectacle, as in systems where executions may have instantiated the vast power of the sovereign in a kind of theater; instead, the images of the dead accumulated as though someone were trying to enforce upon Palestinians that their lives were inconsequential. Watching this video together was not to stand outside and above the scene of violence; it was an embodied and intersubjective experience of witnessing.

In a different context, Sarah Luna writes about a shared and embodied sense of horror at hearing of increased violence in a city where she and her interlocutors had once lived. Writing from this moment, she argues, "in such atmospheres of terror, rumors of violence have a particular kind of contagious performativity that conditions affective responses and inculcates both fear and intimacy. These stories produce shared bodily intensities such as a rapid heart rate, a slowness of breath, and a hyperawareness."[15] Watching the video with my friend was this kind of a moment. Still, I knew our social location made our experience of such videos different. I might know the immediacy of the fear of military violence and, even more, the panic of worrying about those most vulnerable, but I also live with a basic condition of citizenship and residency abroad. I could only try to imagine the distinct terror and rage with which one might view such videos if one were living one's entire life under military occupation, feeling constantly under threat, with no place at all to seek refuge. Here, violence is highly structured by citizenship, gender, class, mobility privileges, and appearance, and so affective experiences of witnessing violence are as well.

On Facebook, Palestinians grieved for Nadeem and Mohammad, whether or not they knew them personally. A West Bank woman's share of a brief newspaper article, "The Evidence is in the Backpack of the Martyr," came with a comment re-stating the headline, and then a prayer: "May he rest in peace, dear God." *Allah yarḥamuhu yā rabb.* The brief article, translated from a Hebrew language Israeli newspaper, *Yediot Aharonot*, presented new evidence that Nadeem had been killed by live ammunition rather than by a rubber bullet, as the Israeli army had claimed. The bullet had been found in Nadeem's backpack, the article reported. Yet, I was almost certain that in her Facebook share, she was not trying to make an evidentiary point. My friend who wrote the post was a mother, and her brother and two of her cousins had also been shot and injured by Israeli soldiers. For her to reference how a child has been killed with one's backpack on was a way of alluding to children's utter vulnerability to occupation violence, to the pathos of dying so young. The backpack was a sign of innocence and hope. My friend's post had received several comments, all of them traditional sayings for offering comfort to those who grieve: "May he rest in peace," "May God give his family patience," and "God will hold them accountable." These were the same comments we might have heard at a mourning house: They were a way of drawing people together in loss.

Palestinians inside the Green Line were also following the story. A Palestinian woman from inside Israel wrote, "Palestine, may the death of your children bring life for those who seek it," followed by the hashtag, #ongoingnakba. Referencing a phrase that was common at Nakba Day commemorations, she asserted that the continued loss of Palestinian life to Israeli forces constitutes another layer of Palestinians' ongoing catastrophe. Indeed, there is a dynamic connection between what is said on the street and what is said (and resaid) on social media. These many posts and comments can be understood as phatic expression, a way of making connection[16] when people are not gathered for one of the annual commemorations. They are small commemorations of the everyday catastrophes of living under Israel's racist, militarized rule. In these posts, we read the word "Palestine" again and again. The word becomes an incantation invoking a unity of experience in the face of geographic and physical fragmentation.

While Palestinians inside the Green Line shared grief, they also wanted to critique the media that they heard from inside the Green Line, including Palestinian media. A woman commented with disgust that a radio host from a Palestinian station inside the Green Line, Radio Al-Shams, had asked the mourning father why he allowed his son to throw stones in protest. She closed her post with a sound word for spitting: "tfu tfu tfu." This idea, that Palestinians should control their children and prevent them from participating in resistance, is a common Zionist complaint, and for this woman, the journalist had broken those norms of public mourning through which Palestinians should address parents of martyrs in these times of loss. Even in digital space, she found a way to represent embodied disgust. The public was not a space for disembodiment but for a resolute assertion of expression through the body.

A similar video of the same incident was annotated and distributed by the prominent Israeli human rights organization B'Tselem. It was at the center of what Rebecca Stein names a "massive suspicion campaign" in Israel, in which, despite various evidence corroborating that Israeli troops killed the teenagers, video evidence was made to undercut the claims: "In the Israeli context," Stein writes, "images almost necessarily fail to persuade the public—often regardless of the precision of the images, the angle or number of cameras, and the manifest volume of substantiating images."[17] If, for many Jewish Israelis, these videos only perpetuate conversations that undermine public belief in these videos,[18] for Palestinians evidence is beyond the point for another reason. The larger truth of Israeli violence is already known, especially in the occupied territories. So it is that Palestinians respond to these videos instead with grief or dread, in religious or poetic traditions.

Later that summer, sitting in people's homes or in the same youth center where I watched the video with my friend, we were to witness much, much more Israeli violence unfold during the Gaza War of 2014. The UN estimates that 65 percent of the 2,251 Palestinians killed were civilians.[19] The deaths in those terrifying weeks of war came so fast that we hardly sat down to watch videos of one or two people being shot. People were killed mostly from the air, by missiles and bombs, often in large numbers. But as seems to happen in each such attack on Gaza, a few images broke through. This time, there was the terrible case of the Bakr boys, four children killed on July 16 while they were playing soccer on the beach.[20] A cameraperson working for French television captured three of them running away after the first was killed and moments before they themselves died. The image and reworkings of it became an internet meme: boys on a beach, running as though with innocent joy, but actually fleeing, futilely, for their lives. Their images joined those of Mohammad Al-Durra who was sheltered by his father as he was killed by an Israeli bullet in Gaza in 2000[21] and Huda Ghalia who grieved her father's killing on the beach in Gaza in 2006.[22] In the photograph of the Bakr boys, it is the juxtaposition between children's possibility for joy and the fact of these children's terrified flight before a bloody death—the excruciating resemblance between these things—that makes the image so cruel. Watching images of Palestinian death in Gaza from the West Bank, an hour way, utterly out of reach, evokes not only the agony of children dying and their parents, friends, and communities mourning them, but also the anguish and rage of watching something from afar, unable to do anything. And it reminds us of the incommensurability of watching a few minutes of video or taking in photographs that appear in a social media feed in relation to a decade and more lived under siege, cut off, in a severely degraded environment, and under constant military threat.[23]

Then, after this major Israeli attack on Gaza, the situation returned to its post-second Intifada norm of low-level violence against Palestinians, increasing Israeli racism, and sporadic, often uncoordinated, Palestinian resistance. Palestinians knew that their individual deaths were not attracting global attention, but they watched them unfold, too, as they had watched the bombs of the Gaza War. Indeed, social media and other digital technologies have made death visible in new ways.[24] For Palestinians, this means a nuanced shift in perceptions of Israeli sovereignty. Palestinians sit alone or together, around smart phones, televisions, or computer screens watching their people die at the hands of the state, in slightly different ways across the different spaces of Israeli rule.

Sovereign power now involves killing on camera with impunity. Watching is, today, a hand-held activity, done at home, in the office, in a café. Killing is no longer spectacular, and people may watch these deaths in passing as they go about other activities of their day. This is not just to say the violence is more intense than it once was, though some argue that it is, due to Israel's criminalization of Palestinians as a purportedly surplus population.[25] The difference I want to emphasize is that Palestinians must expect not only the death but also the watching. This has political consequences for human rights organizations, states, and Jewish Israeli and Palestinian publics.[26] It is from this imposed sense of the ordinariness of state violence against racialized subjects that emerges statements that should not have to be said, such as "Black Lives Matter." But this watching also opens space for analysis. As Palestinians witness these deaths, they notice that there is not a bright line between how Israel kills in Israel, in Jerusalem, in the rest of the West Bank, and in Gaza. This is fundamentally a lesson in racism, in how Israel makes Palestinian lives seem less worthy. Only in Gaza are these deaths obviously part of what can be termed "wars." In the West Bank and in Israel, the logics are somewhat different. But the continuity between these forms of violence is instructive, for Palestinians, and for those of us looking to understand racism, militarism, and settler colonialism in a broader global context.

In Gaza, death paradigmatically comes from above, from bombs or missiles, while in the West Bank it comes from a soldier's bullet. In Israel, police kill purportedly to preserve domestic order. Yet, these distinctions are not so clear, and so Palestinians are frequently looking over their shoulders with concern about the kind of violence that might be on the horizon. Those who remembered the second Intifada knew that Israel had also used airpower against them and knew it could again.[27] I often heard people in Aida Refugee Camp muse in recollection of the sight of F-16s or Apache helicopters over their community. The memories were dissonant as we ate sundaes in a café or sipped tea under a grapevine in someone's courtyard. So during the Gaza War, they watched the bombings not only with grief and anger, but also with fear.

The continuity between different kinds of state violence has long been recognized. W. E. B. Du Bois recognized the continuities between colonial wars abroad and internal violence, famously writing "There was no Nazi atrocity—concentration camps, wholesale maiming and murder, defilement of women, or ghastly blasphemy of childhood—which the Christian civilization of Europe had not long been practicing against colored folk in all parts of the world in the name of and for the defense of a Superior Race born to rule the world."[28] Ethnography opens the possibility of listening to colonized and otherwise racialized people with attention to the specificity and distinction of each case as well as to the intersections among them. For Palestinians, the relationship between state violence against external enemies and state violence against internal enemies is especially sharp, since Palestinians are posed as both the enemy abroad and the stigmatized group at home.[29] Palestinians sense and analyze this linkage between internal racism and external war, and the advent of social media allows them to do so more viscerally than ever, because the videos of killings circulate so pervasively among Palestinians inside the Green Line and in the occupied territories. Social media and other kinds of participant-observation also school me as an ethnographer about these interrelationships. The crucial point then is to question the very line between domestic and international forms of violence, by interrogating assumptions about state sovereignty. Studying Palestinians inside the Green Line and Palestinians in the West Bank together helps to interrogate just these assumptions. This is a problem that Indigenous people in struggle are often able to highlight, and they can offer a solution as well: to denaturalize and indeed challenge the assumed boundaries of settler colonial and even postcolonial states.[30] Such questions of territoriality and media bring us to publics and counterpublics.

Palestinian counterpublics and the limitations on deliberation

Palestinians' social media expressions about police and soldiers' killings can be regarded as constituting a kind of a public, a "large-scale political [subject]

. . . thinkable and practicable by means of mass-mediated communication."[31] Social media-circulated videos about deaths at the hands of soldiers and police are akin to the "one-day best-sellers" that newspapers were in an earlier era.[32] Palestinians know that other Palestinians are watching the same videos, following the news on a daily basis, and in this regard they have a similar sense of simultaneity.[33] In this way, this public, like others, is performative and self-actualizing.[34] Indeed, the internet has been a space for connection for Palestinians living in different countries.[35] Social media conjure a community of readers—in this case partially visible in the names of other people who have responded to a post that one is viewing.

Indeed, social media may seem on the surface to be ideal for the dominant text-centered approach to publics as "a space of discourse organized by nothing other than discourse itself."[36] When someone makes a post, we can almost imagine we are watching a public forming around it as people "like" (or otherwise emote about) it, comment on it, and share it. Yet, media ethnographers have urged us to go beyond the textual to consider the social and political worlds in which media are produced and circulated[37] and to see media as part of processes integrated with everyday life—to conduct internet ethnography that is "embedded, embodied, and everyday."[38] Thus, in analyzing Facebook, we should ask how this platform fits into other signifying practices for Palestinians, and we must be aware of the political and economic constraints of Facebook as a platform, in particular how states and state-like authorities have attempted to shape Facebook as a platform.

As we do this analysis, we will see that this is a particular kind of a public, a counterpublic. Counterpublics are not only oppositional to dominant ones due to their content, they also have different norms for communication, and they maintain "an awareness of [their] subordinate status" in relation to dominant publics.[39] Theories of the public first tended to presume the framework of a nation-state,[40] though scholars have elaborated the idea of global or transnational public spheres.[41] But these models do not confront the question of the role of the state in structuring publics, instead assuming that the public is set apart from the state. Here, such an assumption is untenable. We should think about how these counterpublic spaces relate both to dominant public spheres and to relevant state authorities. Palestinians have differently doubled consciousnesses, to build on Du Bois' concept of double consciousness as a mode of seeing one's self through the eyes of others because one is a racialized subject.[42]

Especially for Palestinian citizens of Israel, we might regard the counter-public of Palestinian social media as being in opposition to the dominant Israeli public. Israel has an active media world[43] made up of newspapers, television stations, and websites of many different political affiliations, but Palestinians are systematically marginalized from it.[44] Their double consciousness is shaped by a dynamic of constantly being aware of how they are being seen by the dominant Jewish Israeli public. Similar to the way in which African Americans have always been aware of a "white supremacist gaze,"[45] Palestinians in Israel know their place in Israeli society is mediated through a Zionist lens according to which Palestinians are consistently denigrated or neglected. Palestinians in Israel are also marginalized by Palestinian mainstream media in the occupied territories. Thus, in relation to both Israeli and Palestinian mainstream media, Palestinians in Israel become accustomed to reading against the grain as always-already outsiders.

The relationship of Palestinians in the West Bank to the Israeli dominant public is different. The dominant Israeli public is built on the erasure of the perspectives of Palestinians in the occupied territory, on treating them only as objects to be ruled or enemies to be defeated, rather than as citizens who might participate in public discussion. Still, Palestinians in the West Bank read a fair amount of news that has been translated from Israeli newspapers, and they also recirculate videos that have first appeared in Israeli outlets. I have argued elsewhere that Palestinians in the West Bank have a double consciousness structured in part by what they imagine to be the "international community"—how the world sees them.[46]

The Palestinian Facebook counterpublic must also be seen in relation to Palestinian "mainstream" media of newspapers and television. These media are restrictive in that they are subject to various forms of control and repression from the PA. They also follow some of the stylistic norms of liberal news, such as some reliance on professionalism, objectivity, and dispassion. Palestinian Facebook is also situated in relation to Arab satellite media, although perhaps somewhat less than during the second Intifada, when more of satellite media attention was oriented toward the Palestinian struggle.[47]

But again, it is not enough to situate the counterpublic that gathers around videos of killings in relation to dominant publics; we must also look at it in relation to states and other authorities that have governing powers. Publics and counterpublics near and across borders may reproduce or challenge state power, and so they should be evaluated for how they work on borders. Indeed, in a place of complex, overlapping, and limited sovereignties,[48] we must examine how media outlets and publics relate to more than one state or state-like entity.[49]

Israel has long restricted Palestinian speech, using different means ranging from shootings, to arrests, to censorship. Social media are only the newest terrain for longstanding restrictions on Palestinian expression. As with earlier restrictions, these impact both Palestinians of the West Bank and Palestinians carrying Israeli citizenship, though there are important differences. In the period of about a year in 2015 and 2016, Israel arrested more than four hundred Palestinians for their social media posts, most often on accusations of "incitement."[50] While the laws regarding incitement apply to both Palestinian citizens of Israel and Palestinians in the occupied territories, Palestinian citizens of Israel have been the primary targets of these arrests.[51] Moreover, Palestinian citizens of Israel have been at risk of losing their jobs for oppositional speech, especially on social media.[52]

Palestinians from the occupied territories are more likely to be put under administrative detention—held without charge under a British colonial rule still in effect—rather than being charged with incitement.[53] Moreover, it seems from some high-profile cases, such as that of the teenager Ahed Tamimi, that it is very easy for Israel to tack on incitement charges against those arrested for other charges.[54] It is easy to imagine that a great many people could be charged similarly. Cases like these can transform the atmosphere for expression, affecting many more people than just those legally charged.

Adding to restrictions, the PA is increasingly punishing online speech, as with its Electronic Crimes Law, adopted by presidential decree in July 2016. The law allows the fining and detention of online critics of the PA, and could also target people for sharing or retweeting news critical of the PA. Those deemed to have disturbed "public order," "national unity," or "social peace" through a crime online can be imprisoned and sentenced to up to fifteen years of hard labor.[55] The month after the law was passed, at least six journalists were arrested and detained for their social media posts, and a prominent activist was arrested for criticizing the arrests.[56] While the language of the law is somewhat different than the Israeli focus on incitement, it is clear that this law, like others, intensifies the complicity of the PA with Israeli rule. The PA is policing Palestinian speech at least partly according to Israeli standards of what kinds of speech are dangerous and perpetuating the crisis of Palestinian incarceration.

In the same year that Israel arrested about four hundred Palestinians for incitement, the Palestinian Authority arrested another four hundred based on information provided by Israel.[57] As Palestinian criticism of the PA has intensified, sometimes Israel conducts arrests on behalf of the PA. "Security coordination" thus goes in multiple directions, an insidious example of "sleight of hand sovereignty" by which Israel and the PA benefit from an interplay and melding of power. Thus, as we read Facebook posts, we must always remember that posters will be careful not to say certain things.

Finally, we must also account for how corporations such as Facebook shape expression according to statist and capitalist logics. YouTube and Facebook are "corporate spaces that are free to use at great cost to users' privacy and autonomy."[58] We must also position them within a world in which racialized security logics are always integrated with capitalist ones, as is especially true in Israel and the United States.[59] Facebook operates at requests from Israeli authorities and also under threats of lawsuits in the United States.[60] According to far right-wing Israeli Justice Minister Ayelet Shaked, Facebook granted 95 percent of her requests to close down accounts.[61] These include in September of 2016 the accounts of influential journalists, including four editors from the Shehab News Agency, which at the time had 6.3 million likes on Facebook, and three executives from Shabakat Al-Quds Al-Akhbariya (Quds News Network), which had 5.1 million likes.[62] Apparently one reason that Facebook complies with these requests is that Israel has threatened to pass laws requiring Facebook to comply with the requests, and fining or blocking the website if they do not do so.[63]

Complicating matters further, Facebook has a rule that states, "people must not praise, support, or represent a member . . . of a terrorist organization, or any organization that is primarily dedicated to intimidate a population, government, or use violence to resist occupation of an internationally recognized state."[64] This prejudices Facebook against Palestinians on a number of accounts. This rule would sanction Palestinian violence against Israel much more than the reverse because Israel is a fully internationally-recognized state. Statelessness effectively leads to limitations on expression, since dominant media—both news media and these large social media corporations—tend to see the world as one made up of states. As a UN Human Rights Council-commissioned expert commented about Facebook's definition of terrorist entities, "The definition is further at odds with international humanitarian law as it qualifies all non-state armed groups party to a non-international armed conflict as terrorists, even if these groups comply with international humanitarian law."[65] Since Facebook is a US-based company, we can expect they use US (legal or cultural) definitions of who is a terrorist. Those legal definitions include most major Palestinian political parties, including Hamas, with the exception of the dominant Fatah. Still, Facebook briefly shut down Fatah's page because of a posting of former President Yasser Arafat, who died in 2004, holding a rifle.[66] This case suggests the lack of transparency that guides Facebook's policies, relative to states with a rule of law that at least hypothetically are responsible to someone. Palestinians are aware of the risks of Facebook posts. Palestinian media cover such arrests, and several people I know have even had their accounts temporarily frozen. Perhaps these are some of the reasons that what is left to say on Facebook is sometimes less about substance or mobilization and more about a practice of mourning.

Emergent intimacies of mourning

Mass mediated death has played a major role in Palestinian political culture in the past and in recent uprisings around the world. The film *Off Frame AKA Revolution Until Victory* demonstrates the centrality of portraits of militancy to the Palestinian Revolution, with its archival shots of men, women, and children lovingly holding rifles.[67] During this time, Palestinians who died in struggle were regarded as heroes more than as victims, but in more recent years, martyrs—especially children—were seen as victims, as evidence of the need for human rights intervention.[68] During the second Intifada, martyrs' posters, with their formula of faces, names, and dates, transformed the streetscape into a reminder of loss and struggle, pasted in multiples.[69] Palestinians have a history of using visual media to appeal to international onlookers, as during the second Intifada.[70] For Israelis and Palestinians, the online world has clearly become a site of struggle in the conflict.[71]

In the wider Arab world, the role of social media in the 2011 Arab Revolts was first celebrated.[72] In Tunisia and Egypt, individual deaths and the media produced around them were viewed as the sparks of country-wide revolt. In Egypt, photos of the brutalized body of Khaled Said, a young man who was tortured and died in police custody, went viral, and the Facebook page "We are all Khaled Said" attracted hundreds of thousands of followers and mobilized protests. Many Egyptians used Khaled Said's smiling photo as their profile picture. Still, while the internet dimension of the protests attracted a great deal of attention, many have argued that many other factors led to the brave mobilizations of the Arab Revolts.[73] Looking to the period after the Arab Revolts, the potential for activist mobilization of images of violence has been more attenuated.[74] At issue here was not state racism but authoritarianism in which the preservation of the state and its hierarchies and privileges was of more value to those in power than respect for—or even the bare lives of—citizens.

In the United States, horrendous videos of racist murders of people like Ahmaud Arbery, images of the desecration of Black bodies like that of Michael Brown, and videos of Black people like George Floyd being killed by police have mobilized the Movement for Black Lives. Yet, we have also seen in the United States debates about whether or not we should or need to look at images of Black people being killed,[75] with many arguing that only Black dead bodies would be treated so cavalierly in news media.[76] For Rasul Mowatt, "use and reuse of the video and images serves as an e-lynching."[77] Here, mediations of killing at once bring to the fore questions of state racism and related cultural structures in which Black lives are consistently denigrated. Across these situations, the technologies are similar and, we can imagine, the suffering of friends, families, and communities are similar, but the political structures are different. Palestinians, especially those living under occupation, have especially low expectations of being able to influence political leaders. To put it in somewhat simplified terms, unlike in the Arab world, Israeli authorities claim no nationalist common ground with Palestinians (quite the contrary), and unlike in the United States, Israel extends no rights of citizenship to those living under military occupation, and so Palestinians under occupation can make no claims on this basis.

Therefore, while the posts I'm concerned with here include some attempts to encourage mobilizing for action (which is what we would expect in a classic liberal public sphere), even more than this we see an emphasis on expressing an emotion and on establishing and maintaining connections with other Palestinians. This is distinct from Judith Butler's arguments about the possibilities of mourning, vulnerability, and interconnectedness across social difference in the wake of the 9/11 attacks,[78] and it is also different from mourning in one take on the Black Lives Matter movement as "a strident form of resistance to the very same structures that took the deceased's life."[79] Moreover rather than thinking of social media as a kind of pressure valve—where people can let off steam rather than taking to the streets—it is useful to remember than there are many, many other reasons why Palestinian political organizing is currently at a nadir. Instead, we should look to Facebook posts as an expressive practice. In these posts, we find an engagement with Palestinian traditions through the poetics of the language and a prizing of local forms of speech. These qualities—these differences from standard news norms that arise from the platform and Palestinians' current political moment—make this a counterpublic (or counterpublics), distinct from the dominant publics. We see three major contents of such posts: poetry, prayers, and political analysis.

For many key theorists of the liberal public, "stranger sociability" is an important quality of publics.[80] In contrast, recent anthropological studies of publics have emphasized that people often interact in the public through and with people they know. We should be wary of what Francis Cody calls "the very ideological border that is maintained between the empty stranger/citizen of the public sphere and the marked, embodied subject."[81] Facebook is, of course, designed to be rooted in existing social relations, rather than relations with strangers. This quality can make Facebook especially appealing in certain situations of political repression, because people trust those whose identity they can verify—as long as they have some sense that privacy settings are reliable.[82] Moreover, the networked sociality of Facebook resembles in some ways that of Palestinian society as a whole. Conversations with a new acquaintance frequently begin with exchanges that render a new person knowable through familial, professional, political, or geographic links. A common introductory conversation might proceed with a series of questions: "Where are you from?" "Oh, from which family?" "Do you know so-and-so?" or, my favorite as a genealogically challenged anthropologist, "How are you related to so-and-so?" Facebook's algorithms do this work in a different but related way.

Edward Said wrote about a related form of Palestinian sociality as *al-dākhil*, or "the interior." For Said, this term had two meanings: first a geographic one, meaning the people who live under Israel rule (e.g., Palestinians in Israel before 1967 and both them and Palestinians in the West Bank and Gaza after 1967), and second a conceptual one. It is also "that region on the inside that is protected by both the wall of solidarity formed by members of the group, and the hostile enclosure created around us by the more powerful."[83] This is a Palestinian intimacy or interiority that is practiced on social media sites that are at once "intimate" sites of connection and expression of sentiment and also, users know, always surveilled. As Said wrote, "Yes, an open door is necessary for passing between inside and outside, but it is also an avenue used by others to enter. Even though we are inside our world, there is no preventing others from getting in, overhearing us, decoding our private messages, violating our privacy."[84] Facebook is a new platform on which this longstanding tension plays out.

Thus, one way in which Palestinian social media is a counterpublic distinct and oppositional to the dominant Israeli and Palestinian publics is that it is thick with interiorities and intimacies. But of what kind? If the cultural intimacy of nationalism[85] can often be read as a dominant form of intimacy, reinforcing the power of the nation-state, Lisa Lowe, building on Raymond Williams, suggests that we can identify "residual" and "emergent" forms of intimacy, produced in resistance to empire. She writes that residual and emergent intimacies are "less visible forms of alliance, affinity, and society among variously colonized peoples beyond the metropolitan national center."[86] I propose that we might identify here "emergent" intimacies that draw on traditional modes of expressing grief to draw close to martyrs who are actually strangers. These emergent intimacies can sometimes challenge hegemonic delineations of polities that isolate Palestinians in Israel and the West Bank from each other. Inside the Green Line, there is another engine for this Palestinian intimacy, Palestinians' sense that they are on the margins of both the Israeli and Palestinian mainstream. But sometimes they are intensely local, resisting colonial racisms simply by valuing Palestinian lives.

We see a kind of intimacy in these Palestinian publics also because death, injury, arrest, and other obviously political forms of suffering are never far off. Watching Palestinians in other political communities or in one's own political community dying at the hands of the state is a visceral reminder of this. Especially in the West Bank, people read the news to learn of arrests of neighbors and friends. Moreover, unlike in many parts of the United States and Europe,[87] death has not been distanced from everyday life. For Palestinians, death is traditionally absorbed by entire communities, with three or four days of mourning marked by large gatherings of people. As Aslı Zengin writes of Turkey, the embodied practices of burial are a domain of both intimacy and power in many Middle Eastern societies.[88] Online practices become an extension of this intense sociality. So it is that Palestinians often react to deaths online with the same responses that they might use when in a line of condolences. "May God have mercy upon him." "May God grant patience to his family."

Mourning Kufr Kanna's loss from Nablus

The Gaza War of 2014 had shocked Palestinians with Israel's furious violence, and Palestinians had protested it vigorously. By the fall, things were settling uneasily. Palestinians commemorated the fourteenth anniversary of the start of the second Intifada, which, inside the Green Line, involved a commemoration of the thirteen protesters killed in the Galilee in the first days of that uprising in 2000. Then, one day in November, Palestinians awoke to a new video of a police shooting. Khayr al-Din Hamdan, 22, was killed by police in his home village of Kufr Kanna in the Galilee, in Israel inside the Green Line, on November 8, 2014, in the middle of the night. The police had been in the neighborhood to arrest someone in a local dispute. In the black and white surveillance camera footage, a young man in white taps the front passenger window of the police van several times. The door to the van opens and closes, and Hamdan backs away. The door opens again, and an officer steps out. Within three seconds, he has shot Hamdan. The officers swiftly drag Hamdan, still alive, into the van, and then they drive off. He dies in police custody.[89]

The police van, the army jeep: The space of transport can be a site of terrible recklessness, violence, and neglect. Those who grieve Freddie Gray, of Baltimore, know this too well, as do those arrested from the West Bank who often experience a bad beating in those hours after their arrest, and those in the United States treated like cargo by for-profit prison transport companies.[90] For many of those who saw the video of Hamdan's detention, the video—the details of how his hurt body was treated—demonstrated Israeli police disregard for Palestinian life. The video was discussed in mainstream Israeli media. The Israeli newspaper *Haaretz* quoted a Kufr Kanna resident and Ph.D. student in political science, Hassan Amara, as saying of Hamdan's death:

> How could they have shown him such contempt and dragged him like that? You saw the film clip—it was not manslaughter. It was murder, the result of the racist policy of the public security minister and also of Minister Naftali Bennett, who says, "He's no citizen; he's a terrorist." His incitement is a policy of terrorists, a policy of murder, of incitement, of simply saying: He's an Arab, so he can be killed.[91]

A *Haaretz* op-ed by Odeh Bisharat, a life-long leftist activist, asked, "Why bother looking into the circumstances of the killing of Khayr ad-Din Hamdan of Kafr Kana? Just watching the police officers throwing him, like a sack of onions, onto the floor of the police car after he was mortally wounded says everything about the value of an Arab's life." "You saw the film clip," says Amara, and "Just watching," writes Bisharat—for these viewers, the video was incontrovertible—and note that in *Haaretz*, Palestinians wrote about it as evidence of a crime, somewhat differently than we will see on Facebook.[92]

The case against the officers who shot Hamdan was closed with no consequences for the officers, intensifying Palestinians' sense that their lives did not matter for Israeli police. Commented one Palestinian activist from inside the Green Line in a public post:

> 8/2012: The police execute Hazem Abu Al-Ba'aath in Tel Aviv, the investigations unit closes the case.

> 4/2013: The police execute 'Abed Al-Nasir 'Abd al-Qader in Al-Tiyrah, the Triangle, the investigations unit closes the case.

> 11/2014: The police execute Khayr ad-Din Hamdan in Kufr Kanna, the investigations unit closes the case.

> 6/2015 The Police kill the young man ". . . . . . ." from ". . . . . . ," the investigations unit closes the case.

> Who is next in line . . . . . .[93]

All three of these places are inside the Green Line. The blanks in the post and the ominous ellipses at the end give the sense of dread based on the sense that Palestinian citizens' lives are interchangeably expendable. The post gained almost two hundred likes and comments that included, "Can we expect anything else?" "God will hold them to account," and "We are all vulnerable to this fate."

In general, the story of Hamdan resonated more in Israel's 1948 territories than in the West Bank, as is often the case for events affecting Palestinian citizens of Israel. But for one Palestinian in Nablus, the West Bank, the killing inspired an assertion of Palestinian unity in grief. Perhaps the story resonated for Sa'ed Abu-Hijleh, a geography professor from Nablus, as it came during an annual season of grief for him and his family. His own mother, Shaden Abu-Hijleh, had been killed by Israeli soldiers as she sat doing embroidery on the steps of her veranda during the second Intifada, over ten years earlier on October 11, 2002. When she was killed, the prominent Jewish Israeli journalist Akiva Eldar commented, "This should be a turning point."[94] It had not been one. Abu-Hijleh posted two pictures of Hamdan that were commonly found on the internet along with his own poem. The poem links two placenames, one specific and small, Kufr Kanna, where Hamdan died, and Palestine, the unifying whole. For Abu-Hijleh's Facebook friends, the unspoken third place is surely Nablus, a great city of over 125,000 in the mountains of the West Bank known for its university, its sweets, and its magnificent old city. Kufr Kanna, a town of just over 20,000, is best known for a reference in the bible. The poem brings these places together, suggesting Kufr Kanna is as integral to Palestine as Nablus:

"Kufr Kanna"
We are of you and you are of us
Kufr Kanna
Your martyr is our martyr
By the grace of God and by his compassion
Hamdan is in heaven
Kufr Kanna . . .
We were and we continue to be
Dreaming and hoping
To be reunified
And to fulfill the meaning
Palestine is ours . . .
Palestine is ours . . .
Palestine is ours . . . [95]

The poem is written in a Palestinian spoken dialect, in particular its opening and closing lines, in which Abu-Hijleh marks the *kasra*, or opening "i" vowels, in the pronouns *iḥna*, *intu*, and *ilnā* to accentuate the dialect. It contains an invocation to God. We see two eternal temporalities, that of martyrdom and heaven and that of the nation, as in the lines, "we were and we continue to be / dreaming and hoping / to be reunified." For Abu-Hijleh, the death of Hamdan was an occasion on which to ponder both the specific—Hamdan's death, in the small village of Kufr Kanna—and the whole of the geography of Palestine and of the political cause of liberation. Abu-Hijleh evokes an emergent intimacy that links Palestinian citizens of Israel and Palestinians in the West Bank through this poem posted on a Facebook page, from one person mourning his mother in the city of Nablus, to a Galilee town mourning its son. The relationship he draws between the robust, storied city of Nablus and the much smaller town of Kufr Kanna also suggests that each of these places is a metonym for the larger regions of which they are a part: the West Bank, tough and self-assured in its sense of centrality in Palestinian politics, and Palestinian communities inside the Green Line, less well known, with no claim to centrality. The way in which Abu-Hijleh brings these places and these forms of violence together creates an intimacy in grief despite the fragmentation of settler colonialism.

Two views on a killing in Jerusalem

2014 had been the deadliest year for Palestinians since the Israeli occupation of the West Bank and Gaza began. While there was no war the next year, in the summer of 2015, Palestinians followed several killings with horror. In a village near Nablus in the West Bank, an Israeli settler firebombed the home of the Palestinian Dawabshe family in July, killing three people and leaving a toddler to recover slowly and painfully from severe burns and grieve the loss of his family. In September, soldiers killed an 18-year-old woman, Hadeel Hashlamoun, at a Hebron checkpoint. That fall of 2015, there was a series of mostly Hamas affiliated and lone wolf Palestinian stabbing attacks against Israeli soldiers and Jewish Israeli civilians. In October alone, there were eight Israeli fatalities and sixty-nine Palestinian fatalities.[96] Some of the incidents were captured in whole or in part on surveillance cameras or smart phones.

The most dramatic of the season's videos centered in Jerusalem, a city with great religious and political significance for Palestinians and Israelis that figures in a complicated way into an analysis of the relationship between Palestinians in the West Bank and those in Israel. East Jerusalem is part of the West Bank under international law, but it is part of Israel under Israeli law. Most Palestinians in East Jerusalem have residency status, but they have refused Israeli citizenship, and their residency status can be tenuous; they can receive some Israeli social services but cannot vote in Israeli national elections. For Palestinians, Jerusalem is meant to be the capital of a future state. While Israel claims Jerusalem as its capital, the international community has unanimously held firm in opposition to this claim because East Jerusalem is occupied territory taken in war. This shifted in late 2017 when US President Trump declared US recognition of the city of Jerusalem, though that declaration was widely condemned. While in Palestinian nationalist narratives Jerusalem stands consistently as a future capital and eternal religious center, Jerusalem means something slightly different to Palestinians of the occupied territories and those inside the Green Line. For Palestinian residents of Jerusalem, it is a site of struggle for housing itself, as became especially visible regarding the neighborhood of Sheikh Jarrah in 2021.[97] Some Palestinian Jerusalemites honor their city and its religious significance with practices of being present at its holy sites.[98] For Palestinian citizens of Israel, Jerusalem is a liminal space, more heavily militarized than other cities under Israeli civil rule, and a site of notorious settler violence that occupies—even terrorizes—Palestinian memory.[99] For Palestinians in the West Bank beyond East Jerusalem, Jerusalem is a space of longing or absence, since Palestinians have been forbidden from entering Jerusalem without a permit for decades. During some Muslim and Christian religious holidays, Israeli authorities allow some Palestinians—mostly women and elder men—from the West Bank to come to Jerusalem. Around these times one frequently sees Facebook posts of Palestinians in front of the Dome of the Rock or Al-Aqsa. That Jerusalem was at the center of events in 2015 was a result, then, of longstanding tensions in the city, and that so many people watched these events was indicative of Jerusalem's place in the Palestinian imaginary.

The killing of Fadi Alloun, a nineteen-year-old who worked in a bakery, on October 4, 2015, happened just outside of the Old City. The area of Damascus Gate or Bab Al-ʿAmoud and Al-Musrara is especially familiar to many Palestinians.[100] The area is bounded by an iconic section of the Old City's gates; it includes a bustling taxi stand and bus station, several famous bakeries, and a busy vegetable stand. It is an area where foreign tourists, Palestinian travelers, and Jerusalemites all rub shoulders, a site where protests occur and where Palestinians frequently pray when Israeli authorities prevent them from entering the Al-Aqsa Mosque. The area has long been heavily patrolled by Israeli police and border patrol soldiers, the former of whom carry pistols and the latter of whom carry M16 or similar assault rifles. In recent decades, the neighborhood increasingly has another addition: Israeli Jewish settlers, who often brandish weapons—including assault rifles—on these same streets.[101] The relatively new Jerusalem light rail, which became operational in 2011, also passes through this area.

On the early morning of Fadi Alloun's death, the grainy, nighttime video shows a man in white on the tracks of the light rail, darting back and forth to escape people chasing him. This time there is sound, because it is a smart phone video. We hear shouts in Hebrew: "Shoot him, the son of a bitch!" and to the young man himself, "You are going to die." When the police hesitate to shoot him, the shouting continues, "What kind of cops are you? Shoot him." The settler goads the police with a nightmarish vision of the police as petty sovereigns with the right—no, duty—to kill. Soon after, seven shots ring out, and the man falls to the ground. The mob continues to shout curses at Alloun, "Die! These sons of bitches! Whores!" Someone kicks at Alloun even as he lays dying.[102]

After his death, the incident unfolded with one video, first posted on Israeli news, and then a second. They are especially shocking to watch as one realizes that the people taking the video were apparently part of the mob, recording their own impunity.[103] Some Palestinian media outlets initially took the narrative from the crowd that called for his death that Alloun had just attacked someone. This demonstrated a revealing collusion between dominant Israeli narratives of Palestinian violence and some Palestinians' will to find resistance everywhere.

In the coming days, though, the Israeli newspaper *Haaretz* reported on the actual events leading up to the incident. A rally had gathered after a stabbing attack in which a Palestinian had killed two Jewish Israelis. The rally turned into a mob that marauded through the night with chants including "Death to the Arabs," until they encountered Alloun going to his work at a bakery at the break of dawn.[104] Palestinian media began to pick up this new narrative. The controversy drew the rebuke of a young woman from the West Bank who reposted the video and wrote in a longish Facebook post in the style of a poem:

Someone trying to be clever has claimed that #Fadi_Alloun wanted to carry out an operation

Is this someone who is carrying out an operation?

Where are the weapons!

. . . They surrounded him from all sides, and the occupation authorities shot him!

They are killing us in cold blood,

And then putting out news that it is an operation,

I know that you enjoy hearing that there has been an operation, especially in Jerusalem

But God have mercy upon you, Fadi

This is not an operation, stop taking anything from their news, which hurt us. The Israeli channels, they are after all called Israeli. It is impossible for them to publish something that benefits the Palestinian people . . .

This video burned my heart!

So how must it be for his mother and father and everyone who knows Fadi,

How would it be for them when they see this video, what would they feel!

God will account for this.

#the_martyr_killed_from_behind_Fadi_Alon

19 years old

Occupied Jerusalem—Palestine.[105]

This poem is a comment on media, both Palestinian social media and Israeli mainstream outlets. She reprimands people in her community who celebrated Alloun's death as an attempted attack on Jewish Israelis. She also warns people not to trust the Israeli media. Her commentary addresses a West Bank audience—rather than a Palestinian audience in Jerusalem or inside the Green Line—that has more options to turn its back on Israeli media and that is more inclined to celebrate such attacks. It also contains two common expressions of grief and political outrage, "May God have mercy upon you" and "God will hold them accountable." Both are the kinds of statements that one might hear in a house of mourning. She expresses pain at seeing someone killed with such hate—"this video burned my heart"—and voices her awareness that this must be wrenching for Alloun's family. Poetry, here and in Abu-Hijleh's case, seems a way to approach the hugeness of one's emotions that always escapes representation.

A reaction from Palestinians inside the Green Line was of a different kind of outrage. Another woman from the Galilee wrote about the same video that it was evidence of the racism of Israeli society and the impossibility of staying safely outside of national politics as a Palestinian. There, fewer people were inclined to celebrate the lone wolf stabbing attacks of the season. This kind of message would not resonate in the West Bank, where the threat of Israeli violence was never so veiled. No one under military occupation needed reminders of the possibility of Israeli violence. Jerusalem was a place that attracted the attention of people on both sides of the Green Line, and media about Alloun's death certainly went viral for both groups of Palestinians, but the conversations were different.

Commemorations in Haifa

That fall, activists and organizers commemorated older losses, as well. The intimacy of commemorating death in the digital age comes through in a social media campaign commemorating the police shooting of thirteen Palestinians who were at protests in 2000 in the Galilee. These deaths are a landmark in the recent history of Palestinian citizens of Israel.[106] The death of protesters in the West Bank is much more common than the death of protesters inside the Green Line, but events like this remind Palestinian citizens of Israel that it can happen in their communities, too. So, these thirteen protesters are remembered every year. Fifteen years after the killings, the political organization Baladna, the digital activism organization 7amleh, and the legal advocacy group Adalah launched a public campaign to commemorate these deaths. The campaign featured digital posters of people holding photographs of those killed over their own faces. The posters displayed the slogan "We carry the memory, we continue the struggle." These posters bear resemblance to martyrs' posters from an earlier age. This style evokes Palestinians' long history of protest. Yet, they are stylistically quite different from older martyrs' posters. They have a retro, analog feel, with a background of crumpled brown paper, and images of those killed that have the resolution of old prints.

For example, the poster for Eyad Lawabny of Nazareth reads, "Eyad Lawabny loved his nieces and nephews very much, and he used to leave change for them under his pillow. Whenever they came to sleep at their grandfather's house, they would race to make his bed to find the prize." This small story feels quintessentially Palestinian, describing someone who need be neither a revolutionary nor a privileged intellectual: sleeping at his natal home because he is unmarried, enjoying a long-running game with his nieces and nephews with both the generosity of an uncle and the playfulness of a cousin. Again, the text is written in a colloquial Palestinian dialect, such that one reads it and immediately hears a Palestinian dialect.[107] Conventional martyrs' posters in the West Bank—the dominant nationalist model—rarely present this personal information, and posters would not be in dialect but in modern standard Arabic. Using the dialect amplified the intimacy of these posters. Rather than making a hero out of these young men as in the older style of the Palestinian Revolution or even the second Intifada, the way in which a person holds the martyr's image over his own face suggests not only a sense of solidarity but also of interchangeability, that anyone holding the picture could die in the next protest. The poster refigures familiar Palestinian intimacies around the family and suggests a new kind of intimacy, perhaps a regional Palestinian one, around a Palestinian collective in struggle. Not only was this poster made to be shared on social media, but it was also designed in the same informal, intimate register of social media. If older martyrs' posters were standardized and impersonal, highlighting party affiliation over any element of the everyday, these were warm and personal.

Absence: Ya'qub Abu Al-Qi'an

Over a year later, perhaps it felt as though the situation had calmed down. Yet, the death of Ya'qub Abu Al-Qi'an—a math teacher and father who lived his life in a place Israel had been set upon extinguishing—was another kind of outrage. In the early hours of January 18, 2017, Israeli authorities came to the Bedouin village of Um Al-Hiran to destroy several of its houses, after a court struggle of more than a decade had finally concluded such that the Israeli Supreme Court allowed Israel to destroy the village to make way for a new Jewish town to be called Hiran. Abu Al-Qi'an had been driving out of the village to go to work when Israeli police shot him. Israeli officials claimed they had shot Abu Al-Qi'an because he was affiliated with the group the Islamic State and had carried out a car ramming operation in which an Israeli officer had been killed, but this immediately seemed implausible. Later in the day, as Israeli officials destroyed a group of homes, officers used tear gas and sponge-tipped bullets against protesters, including the highest-ranking Palestinian member of the Israeli Knesset, Ayman Odeh. Within a day, the Israeli organizations Active Stills, Forensic Architecture, and +972 Magazine published an analysis of two kinds of video that demonstrated that Abu Al-Qi'an's car had run into the officers after he had been shot and incapacitated.[108] That is, the Israeli shooting had caused the Israeli police officer to be killed by the teacher's car, rather than the reverse.

For the family of Abu Al-Qi'an, the atrocity of his shooting was compounded by the crimes, indignities and obvious lies that followed. Israeli authorities prevented an ambulance from reaching him for a half hour. He bled to death. Israeli authorities held his body for a week as a means of negotiating for a small funeral not held in the ruins of Um Al-Hiran, and not even held during the day. They only released his body for burial after orders of the Supreme Court demanded they do so.[109] Israeli authorities continued to claim that he had been carrying out an operation to kill police officers, and that he was affiliated with ISIS, but evidence for this did not pan out:

> [T]he only evidence they provided backing up that claim was the fact that three copies of the *Israel Hayom* newspaper with headlines about ISIS were found in his home. That claim now appears to have been quietly dropped.[110]

The killing was, for many, a brash example of Israeli authorities' sense of impunity and ability to lie about Palestinian deaths.[111] A year after the killing, a *Haaretz* editorial declared that this kind of incident and the lack of accountability for it could occur only because "in Prime Minister Benjamin Netanyahu's Israel, Arabs are presumed to be terrorists unless proven otherwise."[112] Though his death was at least as troubling as the other killings discussed in this chapter, it was less well incorporated into the litany of martyrs. Of public Facebook posts about him, almost all seem to come from Palestinian citizens of Israel, and disproportionately people from the Naqab / Negev, who called him "the martyr of the land and housing." Is this because, as an older man, he has less of an obvious cache on social media? He lacks the glamorous headshots of Fadi Alloun. He is not a child in need of protection. Is it because the videos themselves required some interpretation and analysis? Is it because his death happened well after the spate of killings I discuss in this chapter, when attention was turned elsewhere? Or is it because he was from a region with a poorer and more rural Palestinian population, where Palestinian Bedouins who are sometimes seen as being distinct from other Palestinians live? When we look at memorializations, it is also important to look at whose deaths are overlooked, even in counterpublic spaces.[113]

Conclusions

A Palestinian counterpublic of grief on social media is constituted in relation to Israeli and Palestinian mainstream media and existing hierarchies in Palestinian society; it courses in relation to currents of fury, attention, and energy that all surge and wane over time in these ongoing circumstances of dispossession. This counterpublic cites and comments upon mainstream media. However, like other counterpublics, it also has different norms for communication than the dominant publics. Its register is not so much one of analysis of events or a call to action—especially since too much commentary could land one in prison. Instead, the register is one of maintaining a certain sociality. We must think of this communicative practice in relation to other practices of grief as much as in relation to other practices of expression. Social media can be a space for emergent intimacies for commemorating Palestinian political deaths, as with the nearly endless echoing of condolences down the columns of Facebook posts that mirror, in digital form, the offerings of condolences in a line around a mourning house: *Allah yarḥamuhu, Allah yarḥamuhu, Allah yarḥamuhu.* May he rest in peace. People share bits of a story that help one to feel a new sadness in the face of so many other sadnesses and threats, as did the post about the bullet in the backpack. Sometimes the intimacies generated in Facebook commemorations of martyrs challenge the divide created by the Green Line, and sometimes they do not—but they do foster a sociality around a shared sense of loss and threat. They reconstitute the traditional condolence room in digital space.

But social media are not especially robust tools for connecting across the Green Line. We see here the success of Israeli policies of fragmentation and this is a reminder that—as we study counterpublics (or even transnational publics)—we need to think critically about the historical and political processes that lead to the "shape" of these spaces for conversation, to see these geographies of conversation not as naturally occurring, but as themselves the products of colonialism and militarism. Palestinians inside the Green Line and in the West Bank may be viewing the same videos, but they are friends primarily with people on their side of the Green Line, and their messages—other than the ubiquitous offering of condolences—often address members of their own community. If such videos give a glimpse of moments of terror that may be familiar, they can never fill out the everyday quality of politics—of Israeli repression—in each place. If publics and counterpublics are often imagined to be spherical or contiguous with the nation, here this is clearly not the case. All of this should be a reminder that whenever we study publics or counterpublics, we should also study how states shape and restrict them—through laws and policy—and how borders or apparent borders like the "Green Line" shape and limit publics. We should also examine the terrain of freedom of expression across borders or apparent borders to look at the spatial organization of expressivity. Facebook itself certainly does not exist outside of these geographies of state power—not for Palestinians or anyone else.

Finally, what does it mean that so many Palestinians have watched other Palestinians being killed? Being able to watch these deaths from various Palestinian communities provokes Palestinian analysis about the character of Israeli violence. These deaths become reminders of Israeli sovereignty, in its variation and its continuity across space. The project of looking at the environments of expression of Palestinian citizens of Israel and Palestinians in the West Bank involves a vertiginous movement across boundaries, a circling back, a recognition of both similarities and differences. We can see here that social media are deeply emplaced. Palestinians watch these videos of killings from specific places and with an awareness of their location.

I have argued here that that Palestinians recognize the particularity of the kinds of violence that they tend to face in each community, but that they also recognize that Israeli violence could also shift. Palestinians in the West Bank could again be bombed like Palestinians in Gaza, though they are usually shot by soldiers. Palestinians in Israel could again be killed as they protest, though police violence outside of this context is perhaps more familiar. Palestinians may have known this without the viral videos—but watching the videos of these deaths of other Palestinians in other places makes this knowledge more visceral.

If mourning on Facebook is one way in which Palestinians express a sense of connection across territory to take in the similarities and variation of the state violence that they face, imprisonment creates another set of challenges to Palestinians looking to speak together, to care for each other, and to bridge physical divides. Perhaps it is not a surprise that it is in and around prison that we find some of the most radical political connections between Palestinian citizens of Israel and Palestinians in the West Bank. Despite intense restrictions and multiple forms of violence, and despite the fact that political prison operates somewhat differently for Palestinian citizens of Israel than Palestinian subjects of military occupation in the West Bank, we will see that prison can be a profound site of connection among Palestinians across the Green Line. Can a small and transitory collective of bus riders also provide such care for each other?

Passage. Bethlehem to Jerusalem

By 2009, taking a bus from the main street of Bethlehem to a depot in East Jerusalem felt ordinary. These years after the shared taxi cabs of the second Intifada, when one had to wait for an old seven-passenger car to fill up, wondering whether there would be enough passengers for a car to embark in time, one could now get on a bus, exchange a few shekels for a little paper ticket, and choose a seat on a full-sized upholstered-seat bus. During the second Intifada, drivers took old vans and ancient Mercedes taxis off-roading through the mountains, but now there were established routes for the buses, even a de-facto lane for them at some of the checkpoints. At the Tunnel Checkpoint between Bethlehem and Jerusalem, everyone had to get off and wait in line for inspection. Sometimes exceptions were made for those who were quite old, had very young children with them, or were visibly foreigners. But the vast majority of us would file out of the bus into a line next to it, smelling the heavy, hot fumes from our bus or another one. Those at the end of the line would wait expectantly to reach the shade of the structure above the checkpoint. The bus, parked to the right in a multi-lane checkpoint, shielded us from seeing most of the cars pass through the checkpoint without even stopping. We'd show our papers to the soldier, usually with as little acknowledgement of the soldier as possible to quietly deny the soldier any sense of legitimacy, before climbing back into the bus and continuing on our way.

Travelers felt the segregation between Palestinian and Israeli forms of public transportation. As we made our way through Jerusalem's main roads, passing by the Jerusalem Cinematheque and the New Gate of the Old City, I looked at the people in the Israeli buses. We all stopped at the same traffic signals, and all started to move again at the same time. On occasion, though, soldiers would stop

the Arab vehicles, even after the shared taxis had given way to a more highly regu-
lated system of buses. Boarding the Arab buses in pairs of soldier-plus-rifle, they
would collect everyone's identity cards.

That summer, the buses I took traveled without being stopped for about a
month; then my buses were stopped twice in two days. On the second of the two
days, soldiers investigated our full, rush hour bus for a half hour as we waited next
to an Israeli bus stop. I wondered as I watched the Israeli buses coming and going:
Had I just been lucky before? Had something changed? I was not traveling that
route every day, and, because most of my social network in the region were West
Bankers who could not enter Jerusalem anyway or people who travelled in private
cars, I had few people with whom to compare notes. Fully appreciating knowledge
about movement required the context that came from routine or a social network.

But some elements of the power relations remained legible. A soldier admon-
ished an elderly Palestinian woman who said she was not carrying her identity
card: "You know you need to carry your identity card—how can you say, 'Of
course I will next time' when here you are without it!" Her impassive response
reminded me of a time when I had watched a pair of older women pretending to
sleep through such a stop. Soldiers did not bother waking them up to ask them for
their identity cards. Playing dumb. Lying low. These were good evasion tactics for
old women. The rest of us waited. The soldiers summoned a few young men off the
bus. The identity cards returned to us in a big pile. Someone in the middle held
them all and called out names. We passed them up and down the bus. It felt like
a small practice of collective trust and even care: The documents, our documents,
were back in our hands; we were doing something together. But then soldiers kept
the young men without proper identification, and the bus pulled away, leaving
them behind with the soldiers. What kind of a collective were we, with our permits
and passports?

6 Bonds of Care: Prison and the Green Line

THE PHOTOGRAPH SHOWED A WOMAN, her arms strained behind her in cuffs as officers surrounded her and pressed into a crowd of demonstrators. When I showed a photographer from Aida Refugee Camp this picture of the end of a 2014 demonstration against the Gaza War in Haifa, Israel, he focused on something small: the street sign indicating a traffic circle, with an arrow pointing in a circle. "If I were to take this picture," he said, "I would focus on that sign, somehow. To show, this is our lives. We get arrested again and again. It goes around and around to get everyone."[1] His words echoed the viewpoint expressed by a Haifa-based student activist when I interviewed her there: "If any Palestinian says that she does not expect arrest, then she is being unrealistic." For these two very differently located Palestinians—one a politically savvy photographer in a refugee camp, living and working practically in the shadow of a military watchtower and the separation wall, who could hardly turn away from politics if he had wanted to, and one an avid political activist who made a choice to put herself on the front lines of organizing in the Galilee—prison feels like an ever-present threat.

Among Palestinians, prison is where children accused of stone throwing lose their youth, where those who have taken part in armed resistance spend decades, where those caught inside the Green Line without permits are punished for being too mobile with outright confinement, where journalists go on hunger strikes until they can no longer speak, where those accused of nothing at all can be warehoused for months and months. Israel is, as Rashid Khalidi has recently written in the *Journal of Palestine Studies*, a "carceral state."[2] Prison is a crucible of Palestinian politics; it seems to concentrate and accentuate all of the dynamics of Palestinian politics writ large. As in other places that use prison for repression of dissent, it is part of a system of restriction that curdles lives and movements, and while the prison is a place that must be regarded in its material specificity, it has a far-reaching impact.[3] Support for political prisoners (*al-asrā*) is and has been essential to Palestinian politics and society for decades.

Prison also contains and constitutes a very specific set of expressive environments. Ways of communicating among prisoners, between prisoners and Israeli authorities, and between prisoners and their families and supporters are all tightly regimented.[4] Some of this communication relates to individual court cases, some is oriented around political activism, and some is oriented around efforts to maintain ordinary sociality and care in difficult circumstances. Palestinian women prisoners have been central to asserting the intersection of nationalist and feminist resistance[5]—one important way in which prisoners' activism has shaped and inspired activism outside of prison.[6] For Palestinian political prisoners, education and communication have been crucial practices of resistance in tightly controlled circumstances.[7] Prison can also be a space where alternative sovereignties are temporarily asserted through acts of resistance.[8] Among prisoners and between prisoners and their supporters, communication becomes a practice of care, just as isolation and silence are weapons the state uses against prisoners. Similar to the way that social media posts about Palestinians killed by police or soldiers are not quite about deliberation or mobilization, the connections cultivated between Palestinian citizens of Israel and Palestinians in the occupied territories that I discuss here are not primarily about policy debates, and they are not even necessarily about activism; instead, these interactions often foreground a certain practice of care that interrupts the violence of the settler colonial state and recreates anticolonial bonds of kin and community.[9] As Khalida Jarrar—who is again imprisoned as I complete this manuscript—writes, "Prison is comrades—sisters and brothers who, with time, grow closer to you than your own family. It is a common agony, pain, sadness and, despite everything, also joy at times."[10] Like the expressions of grief on Facebook discussed in the previous chapter, practices of care are grounded in Palestinian ways of being and relating, though they resemble also other modes prisoners establish in other places to draw people into relation despite incarceration.

The number of Palestinian citizens of Israel who are in prison is relatively small, as is the number of activists outside of prison who are citizens of Israel who cultivate direct connections with prisoners. Yet, the practices in and around prison that connect Palestinian citizens of Israel and Palestinians subject to military occupation in West Bank deserve our attention. They are fertile spaces of political practice in part because they are on the fringe. These norms stand outside a pattern of alignment between the state and patriarchy that is present in (but certainly not specific to) the PA and Israel.[11] By deliberately turning our heads away from party-oriented nationalist politics and often depoliticized NGO practices, we can identify tentative practices of kin-making as care that are rooted in Palestinian tradition but that disrupt Palestinian patriarchal norms around kinship and challenge Israeli policies of isolation and fragmentation. In rejecting a modality of care focused solely on bloodline and in disrupting other social hierarchies, they clear a ground for relations that may carry Palestinians forward to a more just and loving future.

Certainly, prison has been a prime mechanism of colonial control. For Palestinians this includes when prison is used directly as counterinsurgency[12] against Palestinian activists, and when Israel has employed fines and incarceration as a means of criminalizing Palestinian life. It is important not to draw too bright a line between "political" imprisonment and other kinds of imprisonment, though Palestinian activists have tended to focus on the former. It is also crucial to understand incarceration as a part of settler colonial violence of elimination. US historian Kelly Lytle Hernández writes in a book about the history of imprisonment in Los Angeles:

> Mass incarceration is mass elimination—Incarceration operates as a means of purging, removing, caging, containing, erasing, disappearing, and eliminating targeted populations from land, life, and society in the United States.[13]

Enclosure and imprisonment of Indigenous people in what is now Los Angeles was followed by systems of imprisonment of poor people, migrants, and African Americans. This examination of how a logic of elimination leads to prison as a systematic form of oppression is important as I try to bring arguments about what is called, in the Palestinian context, "political prison" into conversation with arguments about mass incarceration. Indeed, as I have learned in conversation with prison justice activists on two continents as well as from prison studies scholarship, all prison is political.[14] Also, incarceration rends kin ties in manifold ways. This breaking up of ways of caring is surely a modality of settler colonial elimination, as we see with other common settler colonial methods of breaking apart families, such as residential schools.

Looking across the Green Line regarding incarceration clarifies (again) the integral similarity between what is called mass incarceration and what is called political imprisonment. Writing in 1988, Elia Zureik emphasized how a racialized view of Palestinian citizens of Israel ("the Arab sector") and the framing of the Israeli settler colonialism as a national conflict produce intensified racialization and hatred toward Palestinians:

> [C]rime and deviance in the Arab sector must be understood in the context of (1) distorted patterns of urban development and social-class formations that are symptomatic of societies whose minorities lack access to the reward system and who are economically and politically dependent upon the dominant institutions in society; (2) state policies and a bureaucratic-administrative culture that are primarily designed to meet the needs of the Jewish population; (3) the Jewish majority's attitudes, which tend to endorse institutional closure and to withhold from the Arab citizens of the state principles of legal universalism and equality of opportunity; and (4) the presence of a territorial-national conflict between the Palestinians and Israelis where contest over resources, mainly land, is paramount, and in which the state resorts to instrumental use of the legal apparatus to criminalize what it considers to be threatening and politicized conduct on the part of the Palestinian.[15]

This is another way in which the Green Line enables a politics that compounds harm to all Palestinians under Israeli rule.

Indeed, the vast majority of Palestinian political prisoners are from the occupied territories. About 800,000 Palestinians in the occupied territories have been imprisoned since Israel's occupation began in 1967—roughly 40 percent of Palestinian men.[16] Inside the Green Line, Palestinians face disproportionately high rates of incarceration. In 2001, Israel incarcerated Palestinian citizens of Israel at about twice the rate that it incarcerated Jewish citizens of Israel.[17] Many Palestinians regard higher rates of crime in some Palestinian communities as being a result of Israeli official neglect of Palestinian communities, if they do not see it as a result of other even more blatant forms of criminalization.[18] While incarceration is an important issue for activist Palestinian citizens of Israel, the number of Palestinian political prisoners from inside the Green Line is relatively small. In July 2020, for example, out of 4,500 political prisoners, only 70 were citizens of Israel, while another 308 were from East Jerusalem.[19] Israel houses "security" prisoners together, though, so this means that prison is a rare space where Palestinian citizens of Israel live with Palestinians from the West

Bank and Gaza—and they do so inside the Green Line.[20] The fact of imprisonment together is central to the dynamic I explore in this chapter. At a site of the most restrictive repression, the connection between Palestinian citizens of Israel and Palestinians subject to military occupation in the occupied territories becomes sharply clear (even as differences in status are not entirely erased). The site of the most severe restriction also becomes a site of profound care. If settler colonialism operates in part through fragmentation through policies of imprisonment, Palestinians resist this fragmentation with determined connection.

Contesting the criminalization of expression

How does a settler colony with a strong investment in both being seen as a liberal state and maintaining an over half-century-old military occupation regulate political expression? It is difficult to determine how many Palestinians are detained for political expression, so an up-close look at a few cases is illuminating. Inside the Green Line, Israel has deemed more and more Palestinian political expression to be a threat to Israel. Israel places fewer direct limits on the content of what Palestinians in the occupied territories can say; rather these Palestinians are effectively banned from participating in the Israeli public sphere at all.[21] Following Israel's war on Gaza in 2014, Israel stepped up arrests against Palestinians for what it termed incitement. While arrests during the war targeted Palestinians at protests, arrests in the months and year that followed often focused on social media, especially for Palestinians who hold Israeli citizenship.

In this repressive atmosphere, Palestinians sometimes seem to regard court as expressive territory for contestation. Indeed, in their interviews with me, former prisoners, whose names here I use with their permission only when their cases are quite public, often spoke about the exchanges they had with interrogators or in court. Moments of arrest can provide a strange opportunity for interaction between Palestinians and the state made flesh, in the bodies of police, prison guards, prosecutors, and judges who are representing the state. These interactions occur under extreme duress and across a great power differential. Prisoners' freedom and even their bodily sanctity are at stake, and Israeli officials often have more access to information as well as the ability to define what counts as information. Still, these were revealing moments when Palestinians contested the logic of Israeli rule with peculiar immediacy. They spoke back to the interrogators and prosecutors, sometimes on their own terms and sometimes on the terms of the Israeli state, addressing a "state listening subject" that they understood to be hostile.[22] In my interviews, former prisoners recounted what they said or would have said to judges, guards, lawyers, and officers, often with a vehemence that demonstrates the stakes of all of this for them.

Here, then, I analyze a kind of metalingual communication. Former prisoners are talking to me about Israeli restrictions on speech; in some cases, they are talking to me about their conversations with state officials about Israeli restrictions on speech. We can see not only how Israeli restrictions on speech take subtly different forms inside the Green Line and under military occupation, but also how the Israeli logics behind restrictions on speech on each side of the Green Line seem to buttress each other, particularly in the assumption that Palestinian speech is, very often, equal to violence.[23] An important context to an analysis of incitement in the Palestinian context is that colonizers frequently perceive the colonized to be especially excitable and prone to violence or other embodied eruptions, to not regard the line between expression and action properly. These logics are racialized and enduring in a wide variety of colonial and postcolonial societies.[24] The history of colonialism tells us that colonizers often displace their violence onto the colonized.[25]

Three examples from inside the Green Line demonstrate how Israeli officials consistently read violence in Palestinian expression, even when the root of any violence comes from the Israeli state. Social media, protest, and poetry are interlinked domains for drawing Palestinians together that raise the concern of Israeli officials.[26] A theater student and Israeli citizen, Anas Khatib, was arrested when police officers came to his house one night, and he was charged with "incitement to violence and terrorism" for Facebook posts including "Jerusalem is Arab" and "Long live the Intifada." When I interviewed him at a Haifa café, I found him sincere, principled, and warm. He described how bravely his much younger brother had answered the door at the start of his nighttime arrest and tried to protect him with a fib. But soon the older brother was blindfolded with his hands and feet tied. His lawyers at Adalah, the most prominent Palestinian civil rights organization in Israel, questioned how his Facebook posts could be regarded as incitement since Israeli legal definitions of incitement are quite narrow.[27] In an October 2015 Facebook post, they compared his statement about Jerusalem to the overtly violent language of the Israeli minister of education and diaspora affairs, Naftali Bennett, who said, "I've killed many Arabs in my life, there's no problem with that," and later received 283,910 votes in a recent election. Bennett's statement had not been deemed incitement by Israel's attorney general following a case raised by Adalah. Anas

"I'VE KILLED MANY ARABS IN MY LIFE, THERE'S NO PROBLEM WITH THAT"
Minister Naftali Bennett. 283,910 votes in the last election. Attorney General said it was not incitement.

"WE MUST RAISE THE AXE AND CUT OFF THEIR HEADS"
Former Minister Avigdor Lieberman. 214,906 votes in the last election. Attorney General said it was not incitement.

"JERUSALEM IS ARAB, LONG LIVE THE INTIFADA"
19-year-old Anas Khateeb on Facebook. 70 'likes' on his post Arrested for incitement on 16/10/15, still in detention Attorney General approved an indictment.

Figure 23 In this graphic posted on Facebook, Palestinian human rights organization Adalah compared the violence and audience of different possible examples of incitement. Facebook page of Adalah—The Legal Center for Arab Minority Rights in Israel. Reprinted with permission.

Khatib had written "Jerusalem is Arab, Long live the Intifada," on Facebook, received 70 likes, and was still in detention, the graphic noted (Figure 23). As Adalah argued, "The aim of the continued detention of Mr. Khatib is to intimidate and deeply frighten Palestinian society from using social media to express support for their own people."[28] As Adalah lawyers pointed out, such claims that Jerusalem is Arab are a common political slogan. If this post could land someone in jail, then Israel was truly stifling the atmosphere of Palestinian expression. Moreover, we see Israel's racialized definition of violence in the disparate determinations of incitement: Violence against Palestinians is utterly normalized. That state officials are allowed such rhetoric—allowed both in that they are not legally sanctioned and in that these officials continue to have political careers—points to the way in which Israeli state violence, state policies, and politicians' rhetoric all align against Palestinians, criminalizing and threatening them, while young Palestinians making much more innocuous statements face the violence of arrest and incarceration. Naftali Bennett went on to become prime minister in 2021.[29]

Another activist's case is even stranger in its logic of displacing violence onto Palestinians. We met in a small Haifa café, off the beaten track of the more popular Palestinian restaurants, decorated with fabulous posters that seemed to represent decades of Arab activism and arts. Also an Israeli citizen, this young woman described how she was arrested at one in the morning from her home a few days before a demonstration was to take place because her phone number was listed as a contact for people wanting to come to that demonstration from her area. Like Anas Khatib, she was accused of incitement, and she was interrogated based on the idea that she had been involved with communication in order to instigate a riot. The evidence of her involvement in planning for a riot was that someone (not her) had written on the Facebook page planning for a demonstration that people should bring onions, a common antidote to teargas. Yet, as she pointed out to me, "Onions are a way to protect, we don't fight with them." In other words, Israeli prosecutors purportedly read violence into Palestinians' expectation of Israeli violence—all before a single person even arrived for a demonstration. In the end, this preemptive indictment did not stick for the judge. Yet, the prosecutor had successfully imprisoned the young woman and a number of other organizers for several days before the demonstration, resulting in it being much smaller. Here, again, Israeli state actions waylaid Palestinians' ability to express themselves.

The case of poet Dareen Tatour exhibited a similar set of assumptions from Israeli authorities. Israeli police came to arrest her from her home in the Galilee town of Reineh on October 11, 2015, at three-thirty in the morning, confiscating her computer and phone. I spoke with her about the experience in the summer of 2016, over rounds of coffee and tea in her family's small living room, while she was under house arrest. She was serious and tired, but her smile was the same radiant one I had seen in press coverage. As she remembers:

> All of a sudden, my family at home hear knocks at the door. They open the door and find a frightening police force. My mother and father start yelling, "They came to take you, they came to take you." I mean, I was sleeping, and didn't know what was going on. I opened the door and said, "Don't be afraid—they asked for me," I told my family. "Don't worry, I'll come back right away." They entered my room, took my computer and phone. One of the police that was

there even went into my room and found a guitar, and asked, "Is this guitar yours?" I told him yes.

He was surprised a woman in hijab would play guitar. She was surprised at the suddenness of their intrusion into her home.

She was not released that night, or even that week or that month. It was not until the fourth round of interrogations that she was told of what she was being accused. She recounted that she finally learned she was being accused of incitement of violence essentially because she expressed that she felt threatened by Israeli state and extrajudicial violence:

> It was around the end of October—the fourth interrogation—that they presented me with pictures, and I took in what they were talking about. It turns out that in 2014 I had put as my profile picture "I am the next martyr." That's what hundreds of young people put, in '48 Palestine and the West Bank. The meaning of "I'm the next martyr" took shape after the martyrdom of Mohammad Abu Khdeir, the Dawabshe family, and . . . Khayr Al-Din Hamdan, after they killed him . . . So this is, what can I call it, a type of expression of opinion, saying that any [Palestinian] person could be a victim of terrorism, meaning Jewish [Israeli] terrorism, violence, in cold blood . . . See how cheap an Arab person's blood is . . . "I'm the next martyr" is a clear expression. We Arabs can understand this, but for them using the word "martyr" itself is dangerous.

The names of those killed by settlers and Israeli police—invoked with passion by Tatour during my interview—evoke the pervasiveness of Israeli violence and the atmosphere of threat in which she lived. Notably, they include people killed both inside the Green Line and in the West Bank: Mohammad Abu Khdeir was lynched by settlers in Jerusalem, the Dawabshe family was firebombed by settlers in a village near Nablus in the West Bank, and Khayr Al-Din Hamdan was killed by police in a village in the Galilee quite near Tatour's own. As Tatour explained, Israeli authorities took her use of the word "martyr" as a threat that she would carry out an operation. For Palestinians, "martyr" (shahīd) refers to anyone who dies as a result of political oppression—whether they intended to resist that oppression or are victims of it. Calling someone a martyr is a way of dignifying the deaths not only of those who are active in resistance but also those who are killed while not engaged in political resistance.

In court, discussion continued about what part of her speech constituted incitement or violence. It again focused on the word shahīd, especially in relation to one of her poems. The poem named three young people killed by settlers or police: one in Jerusalem and two in the West Bank. In this hearing, the defense called on experts—especially Jewish Israeli ones that might carry authority with the court—to contest the prosecutors' translation of the poem into Hebrew, which translated the word *shuhadā'* (martyrs) into *shahidim*, a Hebraicized plural of the Arabic word *shahīd* (Arabic for martyr), which automatically evokes for Israelis the idea of someone carrying out an armed operation in which one is ready to lose one's life, rather than into the Hebrew word for martyr, *halalim*, which suggests the broader idea of someone dying for a cause, whether on purpose or not.[30] The literary translator Dr. Yoni Mendel confirmed in court the same argument that Tatour had made to me in an interview months earlier: "Mendel supported his interpretation of Tatour's poem by demonstrating that the poem doesn't celebrate the purveyors of violence but rather commemorates its victims, specifically 16-year-old Muhammed Abu Khdeir who was kidnapped and burned alive, baby Ali Dawabshe who was burned with his parents in his home in Duma, and Hadeel Al-Hashlamoun who was shot at an army checkpoint in Hebron (al-Khalil)."[31] Jewish Israeli literary figures also testified that Jewish poetry had included calls for violent resistance of oppression in the past. Still, the prosecutor questioned whether Dareen was truly a poet, asking "Should freedom of expression be given to anyone who claims to be a poet? What if someone has only written a single poem? How do we determine that Tatour is really a poet and that her writing is actually a poem?"[32] Generally speaking, and according to the Universal Declaration of Human Rights, freedom of expression is viewed as a universal human right, accorded to poets of all kinds as well as people who make no claim to poetry at all.

Throughout her trial, following an initial three months in prison, Tatour lived under house arrest with no access to the internet, according to the conditions of her arrest, as though her very access to the tools of expression was a threat to Israel. In July 2018, Tatour was found guilty of incitement, and was returned to prison until September 2018.[33] In May of 2019, the conviction related to her poem was overturned, though convictions related to the social media posts were allowed to stand. At any rate, years of her life had been lost to prison, house arrest, and worry over court dates. Importantly, the arrest of Tatour generated coverage in the Israeli press, in both English and Hebrew—another layer of discourse created by this arrest. This case was unusual enough that it warranted press attention. Inside the Green Line, under Israel's civil law, such cases became a news event.[34]

In contrast, in the West Bank, there was less textual exegesis surrounding similar arrests. These cases were generally not news events unless a prisoner was already prominent or unless a prisoner undertook a hunger strike. Such arrests were simply more ordinary, and there was significantly less burden of proof on the government, given the way that Israeli military law works.[35] This returns us to a key point we have seen throughout this book about the strange similarities and differences of Israeli rule over Palestinians inside the Green Line as opposed to under military occupation: In both places, people are arrested for what they may say, based on broad and racialized conceptions of what kinds of speech constitutes incitement, but inside the Green Line, legal arguments and press coverage matter more than they do under military occupation. These distinctions then shape how Palestinians address Israeli and other authorities.

Whether or not legal arguments made the news, I found that in my interviews about the arrests in the West Bank, people had a great deal to say about their own arrests. Mohammad Hammada of Beit Jala, who was arrested for his political expression, imagined a barrage of retorts to the Israeli army logic in my interview with him after his release. Mohammad Hamada, a relative of mine through marriage whose wireframed glasses suited his wiry frame, was no stranger to political imprisonment. Now in his mid-forties, he had been imprisoned about five times for political activity, including coordinated resistance to the occupation. Those imprisonments, all when he was much younger, affected him deeply. Though he worked as a health inspector, he poured much of his free time into activities to support prisoners and their families. He helped to greet prisoners who were being released, sometimes printing tchotchkes like mugs, chocolates, and t-shirts with a prisoner's name or face on it. He had a weekly radio show that allowed family members to send messages to prisoners, and he hosted a television show during Ramadan about how recently released prisoners were faring. Prison—its violence, its disruption, its injustice—had in so many ways structured his life, not only in terms of the years he spent in prison in his youth but also in terms of how he spent his time years later. But he never thought he would be arrested again. He had four children, he made sure to tell me during the recorded interview, though I knew each of these kids well: the oldest fourteen, and the youngest a preschooler, so "everything is different now," he told me. He also has health concerns that would make imprisonment especially dangerous for him. He explained, "Every other time I was arrested, I had expected it in some way. But this time, it wasn't on my mind. I didn't expect it at all. I was just working as a journalist. I present a show. I am involved in activities of civil society. All of this is inside the field of what is permitted." He was also surprised about how he was arrested in March 2016. "Those who came to my house were from the electronic engineering unit in the army. The soldiers did not even come in. They arrived at two in the morning, and they stayed for hours. They took every kind of electronics we had in the house," he said, including laptops, cameras, cell phones and twenty flash drives. This was a serious economic hit for him, as well as a loss of years of his work. None of these items have been returned to him.

Israeli prosecutors accused him of inciting violence with the radio show and through Facebook posts. On both accounts he was indignant and shocked, even when I interviewed him about this months later. "What did they say I said in the program? Did I say, 'Go kill Jews'?" He had not. His tone evoked the ridiculousness of this possibility. "What did I say?" And indeed, he said, the prosecutor could point to no specific statement from his radio show where he incited violence. It seemed just supporting and publicizing the stories of Palestinians who had been active in struggle and had been incarcerated— holding them up for the public to see—was enough to count as incitement. He was, if anything, even more infuriated at the logic behind the accusations that he incited via Facebook. He said that the social media engagement in question was of him "liking" or sharing videos of the deaths of Palestinians at the hands of Israeli police and soldiers—the kinds of videos discussed in the previous chapter. Yet, the videos in question were often from Israeli security cameras and broadcast by large media outlets. He recalled telling the judge, "When did the stabbings start and when did they increase? They increased after the video of Ahmed Manasra came forward." Ahmed Manasra was thirteen when he and his cousin left their homes with knives apparently with the aim of stabbing Jewish Israelis in a Jerusalem area settlement. His cousin stabbed and wounded two Israeli settlers, including a child. Immediately after the stabbings, his cousin was shot dead, and he was chased by other settlers and hit by a car, breaking his legs. A video taken by one of the settlers showed them taunting Manasra on camera while he was laying on the ground bleeding, shouting, "Die, you son of a whore."[36] The video went viral; later, another video of a harsh interrogation of him also went viral. Hamada asked, "Who broadcast that? I did? . . . .Who took the videos of Ahmed Al-Manasra? As a settler says, 'shoot him in the head.' They [the Israeli stations] broadcast it. Who broadcast the [leaked] video of the interrogations [of Manasara, which show him being yelled at]? Was I in that police station to take that video? They did it to terrify children. But it had the opposite reaction among the children . . . If those videos made it onto Facebook and I 'shared' or 'liked,' then I am the inciter? They just want to put something on people, force them to pay fines." How could it be a crime to circulate something that was already circulating widely? Implicit in Hamada's argument was Israeli prosecutors' assumption that certain media were acceptable for Israeli audiences and Israeli circulation, but unacceptable for Palestinian circulation, as though they could be spurred to violence all too easily.

Hamada was released after two weeks with the conditions of staying off of Facebook (they had already shut down his account) and staying off the radio show for six months. He paid six thousand shekels (about $1500) in bail, and he received a suspended sentence of eight months. If he broke the conditions of his release, the bail would turn into a fine, and he would immediately be imprisoned for the eight months. Though he adhered to the conditions of his release, he did not stop his activism. Each week, he still served as a producer for the radio show while a colleague served as the host. He continued to go to the protest tent in solidarity with prisoners on hunger strike outside the Church of the Nativity. At the very end of our interview, when I asked if he had anything else he wanted to add, he came to the crux of the matter, finally completely moving beyond the frame of the Israeli authorities that insisted that the videos were the problem: "About incitement, of course the media can have a role, but . . . it's not us who killed all of those [Palestinian] youth." Palestinian youth were angry because they were living under military occupation, and they watched videos of other youth being degraded, hurt, and killed. This, and not the videos, was the problem.

Also in the West Bank, Mohammad Al-Qeeq (also written Mohammad Al-Qiq), a journalist and former student leader, was arrested, he told me, at three in the morning on November 21, 2015. He would go on to carry out one of the longest hunger strikes in recent years. Like Mohammad Hamada, this was not his first imprisonment. He had been incarcerated as the elected president of the Birzeit student union in 2008. Also like Hamada, he described a settled domestic life that signaled how much of an interruption the arrest was: "I come home from work, I play with my kids, I spend time at home, I eat something delicious at night." Indeed, interviewing his wife and him in his home in the summer of 2016 just months after he was released, I felt welcomed into the family—and somewhat amazed by the spry energy of this man in a track suit whose story I had been following all spring as his health was collapsing due to the hunger strike.

The night of the arrest, he rushed to his door when he realized soldiers were there.[37] Soldiers were preparing to open it with a small explosive. He called out that he would open it, but they told him to stand back. It was too late. They used a small explosive to open the door. Al-Qeeq's wife, Fayha Shalash lamented how this interrupted the cozy, carpeted, winter home, and how she tried to protect her one-year-old daughter from the many soldiers who had intruded. The soldiers took two cell phones and a laptop. They did not let Al-Qeeq say goodbye to his daughter in his wife's arms.

Israeli authorities first interrogated Al-Qeeq insinuating that he was involved with military resistance, and then they turned to accusations of incitement. Eventually, though, they bypassed the textual exegesis that would have been necessary for an incitement case. They demanded that he sign a confession, and when he refused to do so, they gave him administrative detention, a policy dating back to the British Emergency Laws wherein people can be held without charge for three-month terms, indefinitely renewable.[38] Al-Qeeq described a conversation from the interrogation.

> [The Israeli officer] said, "Listen, either you sign here, and confess, or go to administrative detention." I said, "No, I'll go home." He said, "No, how will you do that?" I said, "I didn't do anything, and I refuse the administrative detention." He said, "How are you going to refuse administrative detention?" I said, "I'll go on a hunger strike." I told him, "I will die, but I will not be in illegitimate administrative detention." He started laughing. He said, "You want to strike, strike." Four days later, they brought me food, they said, "Ok, *khalas*, let's finish this up." ... The interrogator said, "It'll just be three months. You are killing your wife and children, staying in prison like this." I responded, "You have something against me, charge me, but who is killing my wife and children with this administrative detention, you or me?"

At the time, he was one of 750 Palestinians and five journalists held under administrative detention.[39] He, too, argued that Israeli policies were the source of the violence, not these Palestinians resisting occupation.

Al-Qeeq's health deteriorated as the strike continued, but he remained determined to reject administrative detention, as he told me.

I was ready to die in Israel prisons to send a cry to the world: A journalist is dying in Israeli prison. And he hasn't done anything. And the proof that he hasn't done anything is that he is imprisoned with administrative detention! . . . So I said, "I will refuse negotiations until I die . . . Give me an indictment. Other than that, I refuse."

His hunger strike lasted ninety-four days.[40] By February 6, 2016, he became so ill he could not speak[41]—as wrenching a statement about the communicative circumstances of Palestinian political imprisonment as any other.

We see from these cases that Palestinians inside the Green Line face more specific limitations on expression even as imprisoning them for expression requires much more exegesis. Prosecutors must meet more stringent requirements, and the news media will pay somewhat more attention to these arrests. Importantly, even an arrest that does not turn into a successful prosecution can be damaging for both movements and for individuals' lives. In the West Bank, the possibility of administrative detention and the arbitrariness of military law—under which 99.74 percent of people are found guilty in trials[42]—means that it is easier to penalize people for what they say without a great deal of textual analysis, and cases are so frequent that media pay little attention to most such cases. Still, for experienced activists in the West Bank, arrest itself can create a space for argument with otherwise inaccessible Israeli authorities. The arguments are not generally effective, neither as political advocacy to advance an end to the occupation nor even for the individual cases. But for those who have lived their entire lives under occupation, they open the black box of the military rule a sliver.

Youth arrests: Embodying pride and terror

One activist quipped in an interview in Haifa, "In the West Bank, people's knowledge of detention is deep. Is there anybody who has not experienced arrest? You don't scare anybody by arresting them in the West Bank. But if you arrest somebody in '48 [Israel], it's a crisis in the family. The aunts come from the North and the whole family gets together to discuss what they are going to do." I've certainly seen aunts and uncles (and brothers and sisters, and parents and grandparents) gathering with heavy heads after arrests in the West Bank. But underlying his quip is the serious point that political prison has a different social location for the two groups of Palestinians. Two videos about arrests of youth produced by two prominent Palestinian human rights organizations—one based in Haifa, Israel, and the other in Ramallah, the West Bank, each addressing their home communities—demonstrate an affective difference related to youth imprisonment in the two sites. The structures of feeling related to imprisonment are distinct even if the ideologies of Palestinian liberation are very similar.[43] For activist Palestinian citizens of Israel, prison is disruptive, terrifying, and certainly violent and unjust—but it also can be a place where one connects to a broader liberation project and where one's sense of oneself as an activist can gain strength. This can happen in the West Bank, as well—prison used to be known as the Palestinian "university"—but it seems that in more cases arrests are just another chapter in long experiences of Israeli occupation violence.

To understand the two videos under consideration, we should first understand more about the circumstances of their production. One of the producers, Adalah, a human rights organization based in Haifa, Israel, established as an independent NGO in 1997, has a mission "to promote human rights in Israel in general and the rights of the Palestinian minority, citizens of Israel, in particular."[44] Following the increase in arrests of Palestinians during street protests in 2014 and then the wave of arrests over Facebook posts based on what Israel regarded as "incitement" in 2015, Adalah initiated a "Protect the Protest" campaign, which included two brief videos about youth in detention.[45] One brief video that features the voices of the youth is called "Protect the Protest: Palestinian Child Detainees Speak."[46] The second is a video produced by Defense for International-Palestine (DCI-Palestine), a West Bank chapter of Defense for Children International whose mission is "securing a just and viable future for Palestinian children in the Occupied Palestinian Territory."[47] They have been addressing the issue of youth arrests in a sustained way for decades, but one of their recent videos on the topic is a brief video called "Palestinian Children in Israeli Military Detention," and it is a part of their international "No Way to Treat a Child" campaign.[48]

These are fact-based human rights video reports created by organizations with strong research records. In particular, the cruelty of arrest and interrogation techniques used against Palestinians in the occupied territories have been well documented over decades,[49] and the DCI-Palestine report is consistent with this research. There is somewhat less research on the treatment of Palestinian political detainees who are citizens of Israel. Just as importantly, these videos have an emotional politics.[50] So we can analyze them for the data they present as well as for how they present that data.

I also regard these documentaries as spaces of joint expression between youth featured in the videos and producers in those organizations. While the leaders of the organizations, the video producers, and the youth themselves might not have exactly the same opinions of political imprisonment, and they certainly do not have the same experiences of imprisonment, these videos allow them to speak together in a way that accommodates these gaps. In comparative terms, once again we find that political arrests across the Green Line share some similarities in terms of the Israeli tactics used, despite the different legal structures under civil and military authority. At least as important, we find that the attitudes of these youth—and implicitly the tone of the advocates—are subtly different.

Most fundamentally, the videos demonstrate that youth can be targets of Israeli political repression on both sides of the Green Line. Scholars have argued and Palestinians frequently theorize that targeting young people has the political purpose of recruiting new waves of collaborators and intimidating a new generation into submission.[51] Children—legally, anyone under the age of eighteen—also have special rights under international law. The "Protect the Protest" video notes that of 250 Palestinian protesters in Israel detained from October 1 until the video was published on December 28, 2015, half were children. A companion video by Adalah notes that only 21 were charged, indicating an aggressive approach to arrests. The video produced by DCI-Palestine starts with an intertitle that declares, "700 Palestinian children are arrested and prosecuted in the Israeli military court system each year." While among Palestinian citizens of Israel, 2015 saw an intense wave of arrests, in the West Bank, the arrests happened all the time with a similar frequency. Throughout the videos we get a sense of the different scope of the problem in the two communities: The dataset is much smaller inside the Green Line.

According to these reports, the violence Israeli authorities deploy in arrests on either side of the Green Line was uncannily similar, given that one area is under civilian rule and the other is under military rule. In both cases, violence at the time of arrest serves to intimidate young detainees, priming them for interrogation. Sujood, a 14-year-old girl in Israel, remembers, "The moment that affected me the most was when a policeman threw me on the ground with his hand and then stepped on my neck. With his leg." Abed, a fourteen-year-old boy in the West Bank, recalled, "The series of beatings began in the car. They were beating me until all I felt was pain." In both places, children are separated from their parents under interrogation. In the West Bank, according to a

DCI-Palestine intertitle, "88% of children are arrested without Israeli forces informing parents of the reason for arrest or location of detention." For advocates, such an argument appeals to viewers' deeply held sense that parents should be able to protect their children.

Physical abuse continued while detainees were being interrogated in both locations, though perhaps with more intensity in the occupied territories. Anas, the young man discussed above who was nineteen at the time of his arrest and a Palestinian from Israel, recalls in the video, "I was seated on a low chair. Which is very uncomfortable for the body. It was a chair without a backrest. Light was shone in front of my eyes so that I couldn't open my eyes, and all this without sleeping. The sleep deprivation was also hard. The air-conditioning blew in my face and on my body. At times it blew cold air, at times hot air, all of which was going to [get] me sick at some point." As Mohammad, 16, Palestinian from the West Bank recalls, "They stripped me of all my clothes and searched them. Then they put me in a small room. I stayed there with no clothes on for about four hours. In those four hours, it was so cold. My body felt like an ice cube." In both places, too, Palestinian young people are coerced into confessing. Mohammad continues, "At first, I didn't confess to anything. He then brought in this really big, strong guy. He started hitting my injured leg until he got a confession. Eventually I confessed to throwing a few stones." Sujood, the 14-year-old girl in Israel, said, "only in court did I learn that I had signed a confession that said I had hit a riot policeman and was accused of throwing stones." All of this can happen as youth are isolated from their parents. As DCI-Palestine reports, for West Bank children, "97% have no parent or lawyer present during their interrogation." Inside Israel, as Sujood reports in the Adalah video, "They didn't tell us that our parents or lawyers ought to be there with us, and they made me sign documents that I couldn't understand." Again, these and other similar abusive techniques are well-documented.[52] While torture was on the rise once again during this period,[53] a recent survey found that inside Israel there is a high level of acceptance of the idea that an "enemy combatant" can be tortured to obtain important information.[54]

The emotional politics of the videos matter too. Both videos send the message that these youth and their families have big hopes for the future. In the Adalah video, each youth is introduced by a title card that gives their names and a brief description of their aspirations or vocations: "Shaymaa, 15. Aspires to be a journalist," "Sujood, 14. Hopes to be a hairdresser," "Raya, 17. Community Organizer," and "Anas, 19. Wishes to study theatre." In the DCI-Palestine video, a father reflects on watching his son in the aftermath of prison, "It is a very bad feeling. When you know you have bright children. You feel like they collapse in front of you. And you can't do anything." Though both videos appeal to expectations about youth and hopes for the future, it is important to recognize how hope can be differently situated for those facing various kinds of precarity and threat.[55]

The children and parents in the two videos had very different affects as they described (or listened to) the heartbreaking moments of arrest. When asked what moment from her arrest she would never forget, Shaymaa, a Palestinian from Israel, replied, "The look in my grandma's eyes. It will never leave me. Not now, not ever" (*shayli shayli*). Shaymaa, with her long, straight hair, cherubically round face, and a shirt that sparkled, wiped away a tear. Not only is Shaymaa emotional, but the filmmakers are vested in her being emotional, lingering on her gesture. At the end of the video, after the credits, comes another closeup of her visibly moved, as though to underscore that these arrests hurt.

In contrast, watching the video from the West Bank, I felt (somewhat despite myself) that documenting these arrests is a struggle against the mundane, because arrest stories are so repetitive. Childhood is so pervasively taken from youth through arrest that Nadera Shalhoub-Kevorkian has called the phenomenon "unchilding."[56] In the DCI-Palestine video, the affect is despairing but at times strangely flat. Being or having been a political prisoner is supposed to be an esteemed social category.[57] Yet, with a growth in trauma-related approaches to imprisonment and the NGO-ification of Palestinian politics, Palestinians are increasingly likely to see former child prisoners as passive victims.[58] Some of this came through in the DCI-Palestine production—yet even this level of emotion was difficult to muster. Amir, 16, describes his arrest in a matter-of-fact tone: "There was a confrontation [between the Israeli army and Palestinians] one evening. I was watching and out of nowhere I was attacked by an Israeli army dog." In the same flat tone, his father continues, "Doctors arrive at the scene. The first thing they did was perform a check up on the dog. Then they grabbed Amir and threw him into the jeep." His tone betrays no outrage or surprise. But his eyes fluttered downward in describing the prioritized treatment of the dog (Figure 24).

Even the mode of editing of the DCI-Palestine video seemed to contribute to this flat, sad affect. Mohammad, 16, Palestinian from the West Bank, comes across as old beyond his years. He is filmed wearing a gray sweatshirt that looks like he could have worn it working construction. He describes being

Figure 24   A father describes the medical neglect of his son that preceded his son's arrest. Video stills from Defense for Children International Palestine (DCI-Palestine) video, "Detaining Dreams." Reprinted with permission.

strip-searched and held in a cold room for hours with a dismissive wave of his own hand—the only animation he exhibits. The cutaway the videographers select as he describes this is of him sipping tea. While youth do drink tea, this read to me as another adult gesture. It is as though neither he nor the videographers can muster a sense of outrage, or even as though they are actively trying to communicate how ordinary it all is.

In the Adalah video from Haifa, we have the sense that the children believe in the possibility of effective political expression even if it happens under threat of violence. The opening of the Adalah video includes the most political statement by a child in either of the videos. "In this state, whoever wants to go out and demonstrate has to expect suppression at any moment, but that's not going to silence us," says Shaymaa. She continued, "You don't know the value of freedom until you lose it" (Figure 25). She is here invited to be a political analyst and activist, and her statement suggests that before she was arrested, she felt that she had at least some measure of freedom. In contrast, in the video from the West Bank, the closest we get to abstract political statements is one boy declaring, "The life of a Palestinian child is nothing but fear, humiliation, and rage. Everything is a burden" (Figure 26). He looks away from the camera, despondent. These are feelings that I recognized from my ethnographic work in Aida Refugee Camp, where generation after generation of youth has faced arrest.[59]

We see that while child political prisoners faced similar (though not identical) forms of violence, imprisonment was met with different structures of feeling. Inside Israel, young activists proudly embodied the role of activist and spoke in powerful and abstract ways about their political values.[60] In the West

That you don't know the value
of freedom until you lose it

Figure 25 A teenaged girl who had experienced arrest for her political expression is invited to be a political analyst in an advocacy video. Adalah—The Legal Center for Arab Minority Rights in Israel. Reprinted with permission.

Figure 26 A teenaged boy who had experienced imprisonment offers a grim view of life and politics as his mother looks on. Video stills from Defense for Children International Palestine (DCI-Palestine) video, "Detaining Dreams." Reprinted with permission.

Bank, it was as though this idealistic political project was out of reach. In the West Bank, Palestinians are up against not only Israel's militarized occupation that systemically refuses to engage politically with them as a collective and instead uses force to repress them, but also the PA, which is in collaboration with Israeli authorities.[61] As more and more people are co-opted into the PA and into the neoliberal structures of debt and quietism, it is harder to imagine a resistance that might pay off, and so it is harder to dignify and honor the pain and terror of prison, perhaps especially when young people are imprisoned in high numbers for minor infractions. Moreover, they and their parents and grand-parents have been facing military occupation for generations now. For Palestinian political prisoners inside the Green Line—a relatively small group—arrests and imprisonments follow somewhat explicit political actions. Prison strengthens the connections Palestinian citizens of Israel have to a larger project of collective liberation struggle. Children imprisoned in the West Bank often feel like just another child who has had a bad experience, while those arrested inside Israel's 1948 territories are exceptional, and some seemed proud to have passed through this painful experience.

The criminalization of Palestinian life and defiant bonds of care

In dyadic images of mother and son or father and son in the DCI-Palestine video from the West Bank, we see the camera frame remaking kin relations that are so drastically riven when children are taken from their homes by the army. Stealing parents' ability to nurture is another profound and widespread violence of the occupation.[62] These videos mark a tentative re-establishment of a more normal parenting relationship. The children were alone in prison. Now in the aftermath of violence, they share a couch with their parents. The parent cannot protect the child, but at least the parent can listen, bear witness, help the child to narrate a painful experience. One father acknowledges his own agony. The parent implicitly protects the terrorized child from this new (much gentler) interrogation, that of the filmmaker and the camera. When, in the Adalah video, children are alone on camera, we can glean a kind care from the camera lens itself. Despite it all, we see a young man expressing deep emotions. We see a girl's sparkle, the kind of distinct charm that one loves in a child or sister or good friend. They suggest a relationship between the filmmaker and those in front of the screen. These evanescent dynamics suggest that in their production, these films were a way of expressing care.

The way prison rends kin connection is painfully familiar to Palestinians, as indeed it is for other groups subject to the ache of mass incarceration. In the summer of 2021, in a twist on the sad practice of watching Palestinians be killed on camera, Palestinians took in the unspeakable grief of an incarcerated mother, Khalida Jarrar—a member of the Palestinian parliament imprisoned under administrative detention—as she was not allowed to attend her daughter's funeral after her sudden death. This time, there was no video to see but photographs of the mother and daughter together when Jarrar had last been released from prison and wreaths of flowers from her daughter's funeral. On social media, people looked at these photographs and read Jarrar's words smuggled from prison:

> Suha came to life while her father was imprisoned, and now she is "leaving life" while her mother is imprisoned. This is an intense human summary of the life of the Palestinian who loves life, hope and freedom and hates slavery and colonialism. This occupation robs us of everything, even the oxygen we breathe. It deprives us as it denied me farewell to my little bird, Suha, so I bid her farewell with a rose that grew in the soil of the homeland, so Rest In Peace the bird of my heart.[63]

Many Palestinians shared her message on social media. What could anyone say or do in the face of such grief and such isolation?

But prison was also sometimes a site of new kinds of kinship. In the fiction film *3000 Nights*, a 2015 film by Mai Masri, the main character, a woman from the West Bank, has a baby in prison and raises her son for years among women from across a geography that would be divided outside of prison, including a Palestinian prisoner from Lebanon and a Jewish woman convicted for a criminal offense.[64] The documentary *Naila and the Uprising* chronicles how, at the start of the first Intifada in the late 1980s, a student activist loses a pregnancy in prison, then has a baby only to lose her husband to deportation, a form of Israeli punishment more common in the first Intifada.[65] Then she is imprisoned again herself, and her son is soon sent into prison to be raised by her and the women. He takes is first steps there, among these incarcerated women. This dynamic of making and remaking bonds of care despite prison is the theme of the rest of the chapter. The word "bond" here is fertile because, even as its negative connotation points back to prison, it also suggests both connection and a promise.

In the "security" wing of Israeli prisons, there is little distinction between Palestinian citizens of Israel and subjects of military occupation in the West Bank, so prisoners from either side of the Green Line may live together and communicate relatively freely. However, controlling access to communication in prison is nevertheless a complex endeavor. Not only are political prisoners isolated from the general population, they can be punished with various levels of further isolation. Prison officials strictly regulate visitors, usually allowing only parents, spouses, children, and sometimes siblings for 45-minute, biweekly visits. Letters and photographs are also restricted. As a former long-term prisoner from Al-Lidd / Lod explained to me in the summer of 2018, "The human, in order to live his humanity, must be social. So when they put you in the isolation, this is very difficult. They make you lose one of the most important parts of your humanity." I felt the truth of his words as I spoke to him in his modest living room, with his two young children and wife nearby, and knowing that he was now part of a larger community of extended family and friends. Maintaining connections is a vital project for prisoners, and the struggle to make kin is one way in which these connections are conceived.

Kinship systems can reaffirm patriarchy and reinstate hierarchies, but kin can also be sources of solidarity and love. Sometimes the line between repressive and liberatory forms of love, or between traditional forms of love and radical new ones, is not entirely clear.[66] For Palestinians, extended kin networks of aunts, uncles, cousins, in-laws, and more (second) cousins are an integral form of social organization.[67] Even beyond the family, a language of kinship is a dominant mode for Palestinians to think about relationality, and it is engrained in Palestinian nationalism.[68] Although prison is a space where Israel regulates kinship ties down to its barest formations, for example by limiting who can visit a prisoner and for how long, and although Palestinian society has strong traditions of valuing kin as blood relations, I write here of an expansive and expanding notion of kin-making as care: an idea of kin that is rooted in Palestinian values of belonging in large extended families, yet that is not based in blood relations, but instead in a sense of being together in struggle and caring for people in prison whether or not they are your blood kin. If the jailer wishes to attenuate kin and other social connections, the Palestinian response is to enrich them through the Palestinian modality of kin. If, in earlier chapters, I have written about ways in which Palestinians make bridges across fragmentation that are about connections sketched but not fleshed out, imagined, almost missed, or occurring through digital rituals, here, finally, we see Palestinians from across the Green Line caring for each other in crisis, over years, inside prison and out. Certainly practices of care among prisoners and between prisoners and those outside are not distinct to Palestinians;[69] I want to emphasize, though, the Palestinian sensibility of these forms of care.

This expansive practice of care exists in opposition to the Israeli logic of arrests and incarceration. Not only do these logics fragment families through separation and severely limit how people can stay in touch with each other, but they also presume and rearticulate patriarchy. For the Haifa woman arrested for advising people to bring onions to a protest discussed above, this demonstrated the inextricability of colonialism and patriarchal logics:

It is important for me to say that they arrested the young women with their fathers. This also points to the patriarchy of colonialism. We can't distinguish between patriarchy and colonialism. This shows two things: First Israel knows that we are a patriarchal society, and it tries to take advantage of this—an eastern, rural [qarawī], patriarchal society. It tries to use this to make us feel shame [ʿār]—that because of me my father was arrested. And the second element of this is that Israeli rule reinforces that patriarchy. If we want to describe a patriarchal system and a colonial system, we will use the same phrases: They both use repression.

In contrast to the patriarchal and colonial logic of kin within which, she argued, Israel operates, we will see how prisoners, their families, and other activists reasserted Palestinian bonds of care. These practices of care are often rooted in ideas of Palestinian kinship. Living in prison is, of course, to live in an artificial, imposed social structure—one that is, among prisoners, gender segregated. Prisoners established social orders based on Palestinian social orders and nurturing. Inside prison, gender roles and the established relationship between Palestinian citizens of Israel and Palestinian subjects of military occupation are both disrupted.

Imprisonment created a sense of cohesion among the prisoners that can overcome the Green Line. Khalida Jarrar told me in 2018,

In my own experience in captivity, women prisoners were united from all over Palestine. . . . I mean we had from inside '48, from Gaza, from Jerusalem. . . . There you feel like your identity is reinforced; their goal is to punish us, but there you feel that your identity is enhanced because we were all suffering from the same occupation. . . . We were living together as Palestinian women. . . . So in the end there are things that keep us feeling strongly that we are one people.

This sense of being in political struggle while physically together was quite unusual: It happened neither at protests nor at Nakba commemorations nor as each person sat over their Facebook accounts, but co-presence in struggle did happen in prison.

Unlike outside of prison, where no elected parties encompass both Palestinian citizens of Israel and Palestinians of the West Bank, inside prison there is one system of representing prisoners that includes both citizens of Israel and subjects of military occupation. Dareen Tatour, the poet from Reineh, became the representative of her division in particular because, as an Israeli citizen, her

Hebrew was fluent. This meant that all communications with the prison administration went through her. This right to organize itself was secured through prisoners' protests and hunger strikes of the past.[70] This was a powerful experience for Tatour, a new prisoner in this women's division. As the representative,

> The person gains confidence, not just from regular people, but from people who are accused in security issues, in large security issues too. To win their confidence is not easy. For me it was a big responsibility. In this period, I forgot even that I was a prisoner myself . . . I forgot that in two weeks I could also be sentenced. I forgot all of this. One stops thinking of herself, and starts to think of those around her.

In that capacity, she advocated for health care for other women in prison, including for a woman who was in cardiac arrest. These were immense and novel forms of responsibility to what was for her a new kind of collective.

While all prisoners struggle against isolation on a personal level, for people from inside Israel, imprisonment means taking on a higher political profile in terms of Palestinian national politics. One young prisoner recalled the honor he felt in living for a few weeks with political prisoners he had only heard of. He described the ritual of greeting all of the prisoners in his division after weeks of isolation and terror in interrogation. Suddenly, he was with other prisoners. "There are 120 people in the unit. You and 119 others. And you have to greet each one of them. This takes time." Then, he described, there is a week when you are regarded as a guest, a time of recuperation: "People make you food. They leave you alone. They say, you are coming from the solitary confinement cells, you have to rest. They bring you clothes. It's a family." From guest to family member, the men find ways to nurture a new prisoner in crisis. These rituals are based in embodied Palestinian habits of hospitality that are foundational to Palestinian traditions, such as the greeting of each person in a circle.

This young man was surprised to meet not only prisoners from inside Israel who were legendary long-term prisoners but also a prisoner from the Nablus area with whom he had corresponded in the past. Upon introducing himself, the prisoner said, "I still have your letters in my room." He reflected on what it meant to be a new prisoner with high confidence that he would soon be free among much longer-term prisoners: "As much as it was a horrible experience, it was very powerful, too. To be a guest among people who are sentenced to life. Or to 10, 12 life sentences. To greet a person, to give him a hug, and he has been in prison for 18 years. I would feel humbled that I am going to get out of there.

I don't want to be in prison. But you go, and there are 120 prisoners in a unit, and they all want to talk to you, to greet you." The feeling was overwhelming.

The former prisoner from Al-Lidd / Lod, told a similar story from decades earlier. He was imprisoned for almost thirty years, but he harbored intense memories of his first, brief incarceration in the early 1980s.

> I remember in 1982, I was twenty years old, they put me in Ma'var Ramla [a prison for transport], and there were names of people that I can still remember today. Because I was a young man, and it was the first time that I met people who, at that time, had spent fourteen years in prison. And in those days, that was something unbelievable. I remember those days: I was a young man coming from inside [Israel], . . . and in my imagination and in our culture, there was the figure of the armed resistor, and there I was, standing in front of them . . . We're talking 1982, so they'd been in prison since like 1968. It was astonishing, and it wasn't just amazing because of the amount of time. They'd been in prison for fourteen years, and their health was good. That their culture was rich, their morale was high, that they dealt with you with humility, they received you with love. You feel like you're here, and you don't want to leave the room. And you know what that room is? It's very narrow. It has three times the number that should be there. And despite this, people are living in a way that is very organized and very respectable. . . . Everyone wants to serve each other. It was something from the highest feelings of comfort. And most of those prisoners were from the West Bank, Gaza, Jerusalem.
>
> I was only there for about two or three weeks . . . Then they sent me to Damoun, where I mixed again with prisoners from Dheisheh [Refugee Camp in the West Bank] and Al-Azrariyya [in the West Bank] . . . So again, this was an experience . . . These were people who of course I would not have gotten to know under ordinary circumstances. And it was a true experience living with them.

In these accounts, Palestinian values of hospitality and humility come forward. The methodical greetings along a long line of people are of a sort that Palestinians would practice at a wedding or funeral. A Palestinian sociality is recreated inside prison, and it is one in which "everyone wants to serve each other"— where the values of caring override hierarchy. And again, for Palestinian citizens of Israel, being in prison for the first time was to come close to people that they would have trouble meeting on other occasions.

This sense of solidarity that challenged the Green Line extended to those who were visiting prisoners. As they wait to see their relative, families develop relationships with each other. As the former long-term prisoner from Al-Lidd / Lod recalled, "Families meet together in the visits. There will be friendships. Until today, there are families from Gaza that my mom knows from visits, and every once in a while they get in touch with her. Many prisoners send letters to my mom, just to be in touch with her. So my mom used to say, 'Thanks to [my son], I have hundreds of children.' " These letters, too, answered that fundamental desire of prisoners to maintain and widen their social circle and circle of kin, and in this practice the Green Line dissolved entirely.

These connections endured well after releases. For Khaled Al-Azraq, a Palestinian from the West Bank (and my brother-in-law), being released after twenty-nine total years of imprisonment meant leaving behind people he cared about, among them Kareem Yunis, the longest serving political prisoner. Kareem is from the village of ʿArʿara in the Triangle region in Israel, and he was sentenced to forty years in prison. When, several years after his release, Khaled had his first children, twin boys, he named one of them Kareem. As he explained to me,

Kareem is special symbolically. First, he is a friend. He is a sincere person, and he is a genuine fighter. When I was released and left them behind, I felt guilty. How can we come back and leave them behind? Of course, this is not in our hands. So [naming my son after Kareem] is a kind of an act of devotion. And Kareem and his family really appreciated it. They really did. Those people are in need of people to honor them. So that they stay in people's memories, so we don't forget them.

Naming a child after his friend from prison was one of the greatest gestures he could make as a released prisoner.

Palestinian prisoners who are released under agreements with Israeli authorities—before their full sentences have ended—usually have restrictions on movement. Former prisoners from Israel are not allowed to enter the occupied territories. Former prisoners from the West Bank are not allowed to enter Israel or East Jerusalem or to leave the country. Thus Khaled cannot even apply for a permit to visit Kareem's family. Nor can Khaled's family easily visit Kareem's family, due to the strict permit regime. However, Kareem's mother and sister have visited Khaled's family several times, both before and after Khaled's release, and again after the babies were born. A show from Palestine TV about Palestinian prisoners, *Giants of Patience*, produced a segment about the babies, celebrating the joy of a long-suffering former prisoner and recognizing his act of honoring Kareem Yunis.[71] The episode featured the two tiny newborns held by Khaled, an older father in his mid-fifties. He thanked God for the gift of two children, saying, "So much of the pain of life can be erased in those first moments" of holding the babies. He expressed hope that "every prisoner and older prisoner can live this joy and can be among us. They are prisoners of life, not of death." On his act of naming, he said, "Kareem Yunis represents something great. A story that must be told not just to Palestinians, but to other Arabs and globally. Our human, political, national story. Maybe in the 1970s, stories like this were told in stories and poetry. But the stories, the specific circumstances . . . we tell these less . . . So the least we can do is to name a child Kareem Yunis." It adds another subtle layer of dignifying Palestinian political prisoners' experience that "Kareem" means generous, suggesting here someone who has given something great to the struggle.

Inside prison is one of the few places where Palestinians from more than one place—inside the Green Line, East Jerusalem, the rest of the West Bank, Gaza, and even refugee communities beyond historic Palestine—fall under the same structures of representation to Israeli authorities. With their collective representation they challenge Israeli authorities, and they have won concrete victories over the administration at various times.[72] It is also crucial to recognize the ways in which prisoners cultivate bonds of care with other prisoners with whom they are living or used to live. Naming a child after a friend in prison brings that friend into one's life in a loving and permanent way; it is a practice of kin-making as care. Palestinian traditions often ask oldest sons to name their own first son after their father. A naming practice that honors a different kind of relationship, one forged in struggle, is generous and hopeful, looking to the future. Rooted in a more traditional Palestinian kinship, these practices challenge the fragmentation of Israeli settler colonialism as well as the isolation of prison.

Activism and art

In another mode of drawing close to political prisoners in a way that challenges the Green Line, Palestinian citizens of Israel engage in activism on behalf of prisoners, whether by organizing protests or by, in recent years, attending to prisoners on hunger strike when they are held in hospitals in Israel. One artist and activist has nurtured prisoners during their trials, during hunger strikes, and during sentences. This activism has, in turn, fed both public art and her gallery exhibitions. Rana Bishara, my cousin, grew up in the Galilee town of

Tarshiha. In the late 2000s, she decided to move to the Bethlehem area. In 2009-2010, she had a student who was the wife of a prisoner. Bishara encouraged her to begin an art project of a 100-meter-long letter to her husband—another reflection on the affective intensity of labor of maintaining relations with imprisoned loved ones. When her work attracted attention, her husband's family demanded that she stop what she was doing. Bishara helped her to continue. The letter was an expression of the labor involved with loving and supporting someone in prison, of her desire to remain bonded despite a distance that could not be spanned. This experience was one catalyst for Bishara to do more activist and artistic work on prisoners.

Soon she turned to supporting individual prisoners in crisis. When a young teenager was arrested a Jerusalem-area village in 2015, he was one of the youngest political prisoners. He came from a village located in the part of the West Bank that was annexed by Israel, but which is on the West Bank side of the separation wall. He and his cousin were arrested for carrying a knife with the intention of using it against soldiers near the Jerusalem light rail, though they never used it or even pulled it out of their bags. He and his family, fearing a harsh sentence, accepted a plea deal after he had already spent months in prison. It involved an additional two-year sentence at a youth detention and "rehabilitation" facility in the northern part of the country. Because it is not an ordinary prison, it was especially difficult and expensive for his mother to go there and visit him. Thus Bishara, who had attended many of the boy's court hearings and established a strong relationship with the family, visited him often. She spoke of how clever he was, and how young he was, too. She commented that the intimacy of her activism—visiting prisoners, meeting with families of prisoners—"makes you feel these prisoners are your sons and daughters." For her to have these familial ties broke so many political boundaries and challenged social rules as well: She was a Christian woman from the Galilee from a middle-class family, drawing close to a poorer Muslim family from the East Jerusalem area. In the Palestinian context, these rules often enforce the preservation of women's status and the maintenance of community boundaries. Unlike certain kinds of humanitarian work or official NGO work, which are feminized in a different way in this context,[73] Bishara established a fundamentally personal connection. She told me she felt she was lucky to be doing this work, possible only because of her Israeli citizenship, but it was also clear that this was very difficult work emotionally. When the boy was released, she was there to help welcome him back.

Such relationships have inspired her artwork on behalf of child prisoners, including an abacus made of barbed wire, a giant ball made of barbed wire, and a robe made of plastic ties like those used with handcuffs. The ball and the robe are both woven through with toys. These artworks suggest how the violence of occupation intrudes upon all aspects of childhood. She also thematizes how she herself cannot escape injury as she addresses occupation. Caring about people in this state hurts. But this would never stop her from doing her work. Carrying out this and other similar performances in the United States and Europe, she further uses the mobility linked to her Israeli passport to highlight prisoners' stories (Figure 27).

Another realm of her prison-related activism has been perhaps even more wrenching. She has befriended and visited prisoners on hunger strikes. Prisoners have engaged in individual hunger strikes over the last several years, especially to protest administrative detention, Israel's policy of detaining people without charge. When one man went on a long hunger strike in recent years, a deal had been made to move him to a non-prison hospital. However, he remained out of reach for his family. Bishara could again play a special role because of her Israeli citizenship. While there were often multiple checkpoints in the hospital blocking access to prisoners on hunger strike, Bishara and others who were involved in a demonstration on his behalf outside the facility managed to see him. Bishara visited him as much as she could.

Bishara was a steady presence and a conduit to his family, whom she also visited frequently. Interactions with women in his family in the West Bank were facilitated because she was also a woman. Trust and friendship take strange shapes when one is on a hunger strike in prison. When the prisoner was only drinking water and worried that authorities would give him nutrients in the water, thus breaking his strike, Bishara told me that there were times when he trusted only her to refill his water bottle. To care for someone who is so ailing is the treasured obligation of a family member. But he was cut off from this care. In an Israeli hospital, weak and under the custody of the enemy, he was profoundly isolated and vulnerable. His wife was a vocal advocate for him outside, but she could not come to see him. For Bishara, an unrelated woman, to stand in to care for him in this time was to establish something like kinship, a truly distinctive relationship of nurturing.

So profound and so difficult are these experiences that Bishara returns to them in her artwork. Bishara has made portraits in the leaves of cactus that she finds near her home (Figure 28). She scrapes off the top layer of the cactus'

Figure 27 Rana Bishara brought her art about youth imprisonment to Washington Square Park in New York City. Courtesy of Rana Bishara. Reprinted with permission.

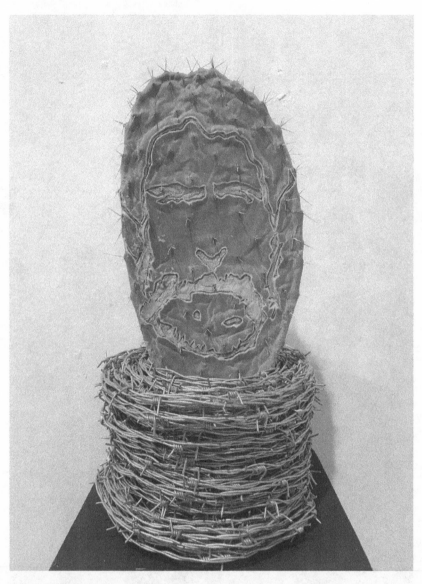

Figure 28 Rana Bishara's portrait of a prisoner on hunger strike carved into the leaf of a cactus. Courtesy of Rana Bishara. Reprinted with permission.

skin. She lets the leaves dry over time, and records how they change color and shape. Cactus is a symbol of Palestinian fortitude and connection to the land. But beyond its symbolism, we must think of its material qualities. It hurts the artist as she works with it. Bishara's use of materials like barbed wire and cactus is another kind of bricolage, a mode of expression deeply rooted in place and the materials that are at hand. Whether they are pleasant in their associations, like cactus, or unpleasant, like barbed wire, the materials Bishara uses in this work are sharp and difficult. Her materials necessarily wound her in their acts of creation. The pain of the prisoners and of drawing close to them—a privilege and a challenge to both Israeli and Palestinian rules about who should care for whom—is evident. Bishara's art and activism is a testament to the possibility of creating new kin ties as a pillar of strength in the face of Israel's policies of in-carceration and fragmentation. Her artwork is an extension and expression of this kinship that can be seen around the world through her gallery exhibitions as well as on social media, where she has an active presence.

Conclusions

The weight of the images of formerly incarcerated children from the West Bank—their matter-of-fact misery—has stayed with me through the many months of writing and reviewing this chapter. They see nothing emerging out of their sacrifice, only being regarded as less valuable than the army dog. For young Palestinians inside the Green Line and those who advocate for them, a wave of arrests was terrifying but perhaps gave some of the youth whose arrests and detentions were brief a stronger sense of their place in a larger struggle. The structures of feeling around incarceration were different. Both groups could be sanctioned for what they said, as Israeli authorities gave the concept of "incitement" an especially wide definition when Palestinians were involved; still Israeli citizenship did blunt some of the violence, recklessness, and capri-ciousness experienced by those arrested inside Israel. For those on both sides of the Green Line who faced longer periods of incarceration, prison is a space of violence and the ultimate dispossession of freedom over body and space. Yet, prisoners have found ways to organize their time, their voices, and their space to create kinds of hospitality and care that, among other things, smudge the Green Line. For those who support prisoners outside of prison, privileges associated with Israeli citizenship are important tools for supporting prisoners. Importantly, the politics of care I have described here escape Palestinian party politics (despite the fact that prisoners organize themselves by party), social movement politics, and NGO practices.

The environment for expression in and around prison is extremely constrained, and in its extremity, it elucidates three major themes of this book: first, how Israeli rule is similar but different in the West Bank and inside Israel; second, how Palestinians perceive that rule and are affected by those differences; and third, how Palestinians draw close to each other despite Israel's politics of fragmentation. It suggests a pair of contradictory dynamics. First, being a citizen of Israel still provides some legal protections against arbitrary and violent arrest, but arrests in Israel's 1948 territories and the 1967 occupied territories can share dynamics in common because of Israel's racist assumptions about Palestinians and violence and based on its fundamentally colonial legal system. Second, it may be surprising that it is only in this last chapter that we see Palestinian citizens of Israel and Palestinians from the West Bank living together and caring for each other. This suggests that being regarded as an enemy by Israel (rather than attempting always to fit in and get by) can be liberating in small ways even as it can also irrevocably disrupt one's life. After all, it is in prison that Palestinian citizens of Israel and Palestinians in the occupied territories cohabitate and establish modes of interacting based in Palestinian traditions and values.

We have seen throughout this book that one primary mode of Israeli repression is control of Palestinian movement, not only within the occupied territories but also across the Green Line. Isolation in prison is another dimension of this modality of repression. Nevertheless, prison is a surprising space of connection among Palestinians inside the Green Line and Palestinians in the West Bank. At this critical juncture for Palestinians, when official leadership is so devoid of vision and so directionless, this may be an especially important time to examine how Palestinians maintain connection and how they nurture each other through some of the worst moments of Israeli violence. In these stories we see how an approach to politics that looks to new, tentative practices of kin-making as care can decenter our assumptions about what politics are and refocus our attention on process, on cultivating a ground for liberation and survival.

Passage. Driving North

If being together in prison is one way that Palestinians experience collectivity by being outside the law, there are others as well. Friends had made it into Israel's 1948 territories from Bethlehem in the West Bank for nothing more than a few days away: a shamit hawa, *a breath of fresh air. Permits be cursed, they wanted to feel the ocean and the air of the green mountains of the north. They had taken a risk for nothing but a little adventure. So what could I do but drive to meet them with my children in the backseat: north and then east along the very edge of the country. The road was narrow and hilly. Just out the window to our left was Lebanon, sometimes just beyond a few wire fences. The Israeli military presence here was unavoidable. I felt like we could fall off: off the hill, off of this last bit of civilian space. Off the last edge of legality upon which we perched. I wondered who was watching us. And I felt bad for the drivers caught behind me as I edged along the road, leaning forward a little too much and moving a little too slowly. We arrived at a small shopping mall on the edge of the Golan Heights, an appointed meeting spot before we were to take a hike along a rare river in the region. It felt like an outpost in the old frontier sense of the word. There was a hiking goods store and a coffeeshop, both empty. We bought drinks and an REI hat and sat outside in the hot sun, because this felt more private than sitting inside. We avoided speaking Arabic and waited nervously for our friends' arrival. And suddenly, they piled out of a car, having been almost clownishly squeezed in to make the most of the rented vehicle. Their arrival felt improbable, like a small miracle, and so did the hours that followed, out of range of the centers of Palestinian and Israeli political power, just a little unsure of the turns we took, but elated at the fact of being together, there. We were on the edge, and yet we were also deeply in community: with Palestinian loved ones, taking part in Arab places and Palestinian pleasures.*

Conclusion

IN THE SPRING OF 2018, as Palestinians in Gaza were challenging Israeli expulsion and siege in the Great March of Return, the Palestinian anthem "Mawtani" announced itself in a number of surprising places from my Facebook feed. On May 15, 2018, Nakba Day, Palestinian students stood at the entrance to Tel Aviv University and sang "Mawtani" as some Palestinian members of Knesset stood in front. Many held their hands to their hearts. Others stood solemnly with their hands folded. A sound system projected the song with a backup orchestra. A banner at the front of the gathering declared in Hebrew and Arabic the context of Nakba. The video was posted by a page identified with the Palestinian community of Jaffa, and it was shared over four thousand times, with over three hundred thousand views.

A few days later, Palestinians staged a protest in Haifa in memory of the more than fifty Palestinian protesters in Gaza whom Israeli forces had massacred on Nakba Day. Protests like these were broken up by arrests and beatings.[1] They were risky gatherings on the edge of the law. Still, these protesters, too, waved Palestinian flags beneath the great Bahai temple of Haifa, and they, too, sang "Mawtani," this time with no backdrop, no sound system, only a clapped beat to hold them together. Again, the video was posted on Facebook by a longtime activist, and it gained nearly five thousand views.

These occasions of singing such a Palestinian national anthem in Israel's 1948 territories—at a formal gathering at an Israeli institution and at a protest in the heart of one of Israel's largest cities in the aftermath of a massacre—suggest that at nearly any time Palestinian citizens of Israel could break into song and constitute and assert their collectivity, using only their voice and their will. No wonder, as Mairav Zonszein observed in the *Washington Post* around this time, "Within Israel's 1948 borders, for the most part, when Jewish citizens protest, it's tolerated; when Palestinian citizens protest, it's 'disturbing the peace' or worse."[2] If the Palestinian collectivity as an encompassing whole has indeed been fragmented, then what does it mean that a group of people outside their university or in a public square can invoke that whole just by singing?

Perhaps the most moving rendition of the anthem I heard via Facebook that spring was from April 19, at the 2018 March of Return in ʿAtlit, a demolished village just outside of Haifa and overlooking the Mediterranean Sea. After a long day of marching wound down, a group of young people sat in a circle on the beach. One went live with a video on Facebook using the account of the Association for the Defense of the Rights of the Internally Displaced (ADRID), as another played "Mawtani" on an *oud*, a fretless lute that is the backbone of Palestinian music. Voices rose in song, with people taking turns leading the lyrics as they knew them. The volume rose on the chorus. They clapped and whistled for each other as the song ended. The cameraperson panned around the circle as if to affirm individual and collective presence. Some people stood up and placed their hands on their hearts as they sang. It was remarkable also because of who had been there: I saw the video because it was shared by friends from the West Bank who had illegally entered Israel's 1948 territories in order to attend the march. For them, marking the Nakba there had been a risky act. They were not themselves from ʿAtlit, so their attendance was not a literal return, but it was, for them, an assertion of their belonging to all of historic Palestine, and a rejection of Israel's restrictions on movement. It was the quietest of the three singings of "Mawtani," the least public, and it was another moment of emergent intimacy[3] among Palestinians from different places, another kind of temporary collective that could help Palestinians envision new futures. Watching the video with some relief that by then my friends had safely returned to the West Bank, I wondered: Is it possible that what this time demands more than anything else is a willingness to break Israeli law, in careful ways, to reject fragmentation and the demonization of Palestinians with one's body? If Palestinian pleasure can lead to a "self-liberation,"[4] these moments of being together, of appreciating voices not quite in unison, were a brief manifestation of what liberation could feel like.

It may also be that just speaking together may be an important start. During the spring of 2021, as hundreds of Palestinians in the Jerusalem neighborhood of Sheikh Jarrah stood against their collective eviction and in the midst of another

Figure 29 Nidal Al-Azza (center) sits among a group of children and youth in the Aida Refugee Camp in Bethlehem as part of a community sit-in for the General Strike in Palestine on Tuesday, May 18, 2021. Photo by Yumna Patel / Mondoweiss. Reprinted with permission.

ferocious Israeli attack on Gaza, Palestinians organized an unprecedented day of general strike. Stores closed, school was suspended, and people gathered for protests. They chanted for popular uprising in Haifa. A widely circulated image showed a woman at a Ramallah protest in a kaffiyeh holding a sign that read, "Every Israeli City was once Sheikh Jarrah." Once again, what happened before and after the main protests was at least as important as the protests themselves. In Aida Refugee Camp, a group of youth, older community activists, and activists from the Galilee discussed Israeli colonialism in its many forms, some of which were visible from there: the wall that loomed nearby, the settlements like the one that grew beyond the wall (Figure 29).[5] In Haifa, shops closed, and people gathered around a drum and an *oud* to sing Palestinian songs, called to gather by posters layered on top of posters (Figure 30).[6]

A Manifesto of Dignity and Hope circulated widely that day. Unsigned and addressed simply to the "People of Palestine," it proposed a vision for the future that would struggle against fragmentation:

> In these days, we write a new chapter, a chapter of a united Intifada that seeks our one and only goal: reuniting Palestinian society in all of its different parts; reuniting our political will, and our means of struggle to confront Zionism throughout Palestine.

This long Intifada is, at its heart, an Intifada of consciousness. It is an Intifada to overthrow off the filth of quietude and defeatism. Because of it, the brave generations to come will have been raised, once again, on the fundamental principle of our unity. It will stand in the face of all the elites working to deepen and entrench the divisions in and between our communities.[7]

This Intifada of consciousness would reach beyond the longstanding divisions into which both Israel and the Palestinian Authority have long been vested.

It was a historic day, a variety of mainstream outlets and many Palestinian analysts agreed. The *New York Times* reflected, "Since hundreds of thousands of Palestinians fled or were expelled from their homes in 1948, they have been divided not only by geography, but also by lived experience." The article quoted Mustafa Barghouti, a prominent independent Palestinian politician, calling the day "very significant" and saying, "It reflects how Palestinians now have a unified struggle against the same system of apartheid."[8] But it was also an outcome of years—decades—of efforts to transcend or even breach the Green Line. And even if this one day did not directly lead to fundamental political change, it was

Figure 30 Posters in Halisa, Haifa, for the general strike in May 2021 were layered on top of other posters and graffiti. Yoav Haifawi / Mondoweiss. Reprinted with permission.

an act that sustained not only visions of a shared past and shared future, but also many local communities' strength and confidence in their own collectivities, as people gathered in so many different places from Haifa to Hebron.

USA! USA!

The United States as a global presence could validate a historic day of strikes, as in the *New York Times* article, but the specter of the United States could also threaten collective action. It is worth returning to that man in the USA t-shirt whom I encountered in Tarshiha at the protest against the war on Gaza (Figure 4). He had used his camera to take photos of demonstrators and of me photographing him back, with my doubled sense of anger and impunity. What does the US stand for to Palestinians and how does it shape the signification of Palestinian protest? In that protest in Tarshiha, certainly, the US flag was a flag not of liberty but of force, the kind of force that masks itself preposterously in a language of liberal democracy, as if to say: Because we are the free ones, we have the right to use violence against you and the right to determine whether what you say is violence. It was a deployment of the US flag fully aligned with the Israeli state (indeed, I could only wonder who was paying this man, both directly and indirectly, given the United States' long history of aid to Israel). This alignment was the reason why Israel had both the military might and the political impunity to hit Gaza so ferociously, once again. It was the flag of one militarized settler colonial state wielded in another. It was also undeniably the flag of my country, as I felt only too strangely when I was doing fieldwork: the country whose passport I carried in my bag as a talisman against violence, the passport that many other Palestinian Americans have wielded as though it would protect them from Israeli violence, whether or not it has.[9] And it was the country that has claimed to be the major exporter of democracy around the world. Certainly that last point did not ring true in Tarshiha or Al-Lidd / Lod or Bethlehem. I am quite sure it did not ring true in Gaza either.

But the appearance of that flag at the Tarshiha protest brings forth other questions, too: How does a comparative vantage on protests in the US help us to reflect on the same themes of place, population, and struggle that we have examined here? In November 2014, the fall after that war on Gaza, I was at a Black Lives Matter protest held in Washington, DC (during the annual American Anthropological Association meetings, no less) after a judge failed to indict the police officer in Staten Island who choked and killed Eric Garner, detained for selling untaxed cigarettes. It was an unpermitted protest, and we were perhaps

200 people, walking through the wide avenues of a mostly deserted downtown. We closed intersections, chanting. We lay down in the street. The ground was cold and hard, and the night was dark, but I felt comforted by my friends and by the crowd, and it was hard to imagine any harm would come to us. As we were doing this, police more or less stopped traffic for us. They were protecting us from ordinary oncoming traffic, and not, notably, from racists who would have threatened harm on ideological terms, for there were no counterdemonstrators here. They did this despite the fact that we were in an unlicensed protest, presumably because they did not want the conflict or bad publicity of shutting down this protest, and because they did not perceive us to be a threat.

As we stood there in the street, the protest chants drew out long into the night. A Black man held a megaphone to shout out, "If I can't breathe" and the crowd responded, "you can't breathe." Our speech was embodied in that essential, universal act of breath, breath that led to speech. The chant was referring to the video recording that showed that Eric Garner had called out eleven times that he was suffocating in the officer's chokehold. I thought, too, of Al-Lidd / Lod, and evocation of a radical Palestinian collectivity that could extend from there to Dheisheh in the West Bank to the Galilee, to Shatila Camp in Lebanon. I also thought of Bethlehem, where tear gas often meant that protesters could not breathe, and Ferguson, where US police officers deployed tear gas abundantly. The chant in DC evoked for me a sense that our collective and individual survivals were interdependent. We felt, in those months, that taking the streets in one place was a reminder to people elsewhere that they could do the same.

Spread out across an intersection, the young man turned to another chant: "Tell me what democracy looks like!" and then let the crowd answer, "This is what democracy looks like." He passed the megaphone around the circle so many could lead the chant—demonstrating in a new way what democracy might look like, right there. The different timbres and accents of our voices rang out across the square we had made—demonstrating again how protests can be a way of remaking space and of creating a collectivity. If the hegemonic vision of democracy is headquartered in the Capitol Building and the White House, this gathering, it seemed, was schooling any passing congressperson that democracy was something made and remade in the street.

It was an inspiring moment, but for me it was also strange. At the end of one of the rounds of "This is what democracy looks like," I heard myself call out, "Only in the very center of the empire!" My friend whipped around to give me a sharp look. I felt peculiarly—indeed uncomfortably—safe (just as I felt immediately guilty for undercutting the protest chant). If democracy is meant to be synonymous with rule by the consent of the governed and not by force, were we participating in some kind of a play of nonviolence with the police when we knew that the US rules by force in different ways in poor communities of color in the US and around the world? Were we at one of the few sites around the world at which protesters could both not be met with violence and dream to influence media and politicians?

What does democracy look like when it exists in real space rather than utopic spheres? And what about democracy becomes clear once we interrogate the shapes that publics take—too often isolated islands—rather than just imagining them to be round and even? Or when we denaturalize borders revealing that they do not legitimately rope off concerns and conversations? We should be skeptical of how news outlets tend to define publics and audiences. On July 4, 2021, I had a "driveway moment" when National Public Radio's Lulu Garcia-Navarro interviewed Iraqi poet Sinan Antoon about the death a few days earlier of former US Defense Secretary Donald Rumsfeld, who had overseen the invasion of Iraq in 2003. Antoon spared no words:

> GARCIA-NAVARRO: What was your reaction to hearing the news that Donald Rumsfeld had died?
> ANTOON: I thought of hell and if there is a special place in hell for war criminals. In a more ideal world, everyone would acknowledge that Donald Rumsfeld was a war criminal whose actions are responsible for the deaths of hundreds of thousands of Iraqis. So I don't know how to describe my feeling, but it just brought back the tragedy of the destruction of a country called Iraq and the fact that millions of Iraqis suffer the consequences of some of Donald Rumsfeld's decisions.[10]

Antoon went on to talk about text messages of righteous anger he was receiving from other Iraqis: a reminder on NPR that there are other everyday conversations going on about US foreign policy in places where that policy is domestic life. It is only our acceptance of national borders—an acceptance that occludes colonial and imperial power—that means we hear so much less from Iraqis or Afghans than from Americans at moments like these.

If most of this book addresses the relationship of two Palestinian groups to each other, a relationship shaped both by Israeli modes of violence and PA complicity with fragmentation, I want to reflect here on the interrelationship among militarized settler colonies and on flows of global power that set the norms for political expression. Following the traffic of weapons and rhetoric, watching how legal systems operate, we can see that in states driven by racism, the violence of police is related to the violence of soldiers.[11] Traveling from the occupied West Bank to Palestinian gatherings inside the Green Line, we encounter more of a spectrum of police and soldiers than a clear divide between them. The kinds of weapons they have are not simply divided into two categories. The roles they play are not so distinct. And in the United States, we know that US militarism has its own trickle-down effects in police forces in cities and towns.

While we may imagine protest to be a global practice with common rules or norms, in the same way that democracy itself is imagined as a universal,[12] modes of protest are context specific, shaped not only by the laws and traditions of states, but also by what state authorities want others to believe about the boundaries of their rule. If the trick of Israeli sovereignty is to hide its own rule in the occupied territories (to act as if it fights an enemy there rather than ruling over racialized subjects), the trick in the United States is that what seems in law like one kind of rule over fifty states is in fact more than one: one set of rules in that federal part of DC, and another in Ferguson or Baltimore.[13] In both cases, subterfuges related to boundaries and law are masked in part by blaming protesters' "cultures" for their internal violence: their problematic tendencies to rioting or terrorism.

On a more positive note, though, we might think about how modes of protest are nevertheless interrelated and even interdependent. We see how in Al-Lidd / Lod and Bethlehem chants resonated with similar themes and slogans and faced related threats of violence. We also saw—in the furious, sad summer of 2014—how Palestinians and Black Lives Matter protesters shared tips on how to manage tear gas.[14] How are protesters connected in less immediate ways? How can we promote an awareness of how protest practices are both overlapping and distinct? How can we help each protest in one place make room for protests in another? We must make more expansive the assertion, "if I can't breathe, you can't breathe," because political expression depends not on individual ability but upon an environment of expression—and environments of expression, like environments in the natural sciences, are never hermetically sealed from each other. They are distinct but connected. I think of Ross Gay's poem for Eric Garner, who had worked for the Horticultural Department of the New York City Department of Parks and Recreation. Gay imagines that some of Garner's plantings are still alive, that they "continue / to do what such plants do

... like making it easier / for us to breathe."[15] We are all surviving based on metaphorical plantings of other people, including those who are no longer with us.

This is one reason why activism that bridges difference is important both
for Palestinians in various locations and for people suffering under different
but related racialized settler colonial regimes. The point is not only to identify
sameness but to hold ground open, to make paths for expression and protest.
Mark Lamont Hill makes a similar point:

> While pedagogically helpful for highlighting the global nature of systemic op-
> pression and practically useful for developing broader networks of resistance,
> an exclusive focus on sameness is . . . problematic. By focusing on shared op-
> pression as a means of creating networks of solidarity, we also obscure other
> forms of oppression that are equally significant to particular members of an
> oppressed group.[16]

Activism across difference is not only about marking other and sometimes
more evident forms of suffering—it is about recognizing how struggles link
up or why they fail to. The United States is a backdrop to this book as a related
settler colonial enterprise, as well as a global hegemon that has a loud voice in
determining how politics elsewhere—and especially for Palestinians and Israelis—will happen.[17] Examining environments for expression in multiple locations is one element of the work of linking places and of seeing these different
forces and frameworks in action.

Embodied environments of expression, contained by states

Beyond important but somewhat abstract ideas of privilege that shape concepts of voice, we can think of the material comforts and risks, deprivations
and injuries, joys, terrors, and grief that people experience and express in acts
of expression. We can think of how the "street" is not only a metaphorical place
but also one that is peopled by specific neighbors and adorned by graffiti in one
language or another, policed or patrolled by one kind of authority or another
who carry one set of weapons or another (even if those arsenals do overlap).
A walk with the threat of tear gas poses different risks than a walk where the
homes of one's ancestors have been demolished and replaced by skyscrapers.
This is not to diminish the risks of the latter.

We must consider how what are usually called publics are shaped by state
authorities: by laws, borders, and the possibility of state or non-state violence.

These dynamics are especially pronounced when the state is settler colonial, racist, or highly militarized, three intersecting but distinct political forms. When we look broadly at the relationship between political expression and the state, we will by necessity examine the traditional practices of the public—such as newspaper reading and television viewing—alongside practices that bring people out in public spaces for acts of expression, such as protests and commemorations, and expressions on new(er) social media platforms.

With this integrative look at environments for expression, grounded in place and the body, we may explore more how political expression can be an act of bricolage based on the materials available: poetry, slogans, barbed wire, cactus, posts and reposts on social media. None of these are neutral mediums, but all can be repurposed to craft a message. When we think of political expression as a kind of collage, it is easier to recognize both its limits and its poetics. To truly understand limitations to speech, we must not look only at individual speakers but at communities and conversations, at how figures of speech travel even when people (mostly) do not. While social media may gather people around the same videos, they do not erase the political boundaries of fragmentation created by Israel's maintenance of the occupation. Though Palestinian political practice has sustained and innovated ways of thinking about dispossession in the past and the present, as through the concept of *al-nakba al-mustamirra*, or "the ongoing Nakba," the Palestinian publics gathered around these kinds of phrases are not always in conversation, and the phrase can mean something different in one Palestinian place than another. The jagged, overlapping, asymmetrical quality of Palestinian publics on either side of the Green Line emerges when we look at what counts as Palestinian news or "local" news or at counterpublics of grief on Facebook.

As we recognize these irregularly shaped publics, we can look beyond concepts of "national narratives" to consider how people speak together but not in unison in a particular vein of "partial connection":[18] how a pair of photographs might mean more than each one separately. It is possible that someone with one kind of privilege may help another to say something, even if they do not fully agree with it or seek to say it themselves. We see this as Jewish people and others with diverse views on the boycott, divestment, and sanctions (BDS) movement stand up strongly for the right to boycott. Yet, given the uncomfortable terrain of expression on Palestine even in the United States,[19] even those who seem to have some kinds of representational privileges—based on their religious or racial positions or as members of Congress or Parliament or as college professors—can still be vulnerable. For those of us with relative comforts and privileges, whatever our identity, this should nevertheless help us to ask: How can I say something with someone else with whom I share something or to whom I am somehow connected? The practice of doing this itself illuminates communicative terrain anew, and remakes that terrain, whatever the medium or space of that expression. Indeed, this book centers on Palestinian perspectives and experiences, but it has depended on such communicative collaborations with activists, scholars, and journalists of many backgrounds and political orientations.

Reflections for Palestinians and Palestine Studies

In 2003, just weeks after I arrived in the West Bank as a PhD student for my first long period of fieldwork, my aunt in the Galilee—in the far north of Israel's 1948 territories, a three-hour drive from Jerusalem—looked at me seriously over our small cups of Arabic coffee and asked how things were, really, in the West Bank. I did not know what to say. In that moment, I wondered how it was that a woman who had lived her whole life in the Galilee would possibly ask me, who had never lived in the Galilee or the West Bank, for a report just weeks after I had arrived. What could I possibly have to contribute? This moment stuck with me enough that years later it was one of the moments that inspired me to think through the lived experiences of Palestinian geopolitical fragmentation. In the years that followed, I often found that friends in the West Bank were curious about life in the Galilee too—and they were eager to visit, when they could make that possible.

This book can be considered as one entry point for more robust conversations among Palestinians. Arguably, these conversations and forms of shared action are happening more and more. It is critical that, as they do, they do not reproduce forms of exclusion based on class, education, gender, geography, sexuality, or other social hierarchies. As Palestinians commit to these kinds of conversations, even key terms like "Palestine" and "liberation" will be contested. They will sometimes have dominant meanings that sit in service of existing hierarchies, but other possible meanings will emerge as well. Ethnographic research and other social and political modes of being engaged in more than one Palestinian place—feeling always off-center as a researcher and, in my case, also as a Palestinian—can help to uncover and map out when "Palestine" is being used to repress democratic possibilities and entrench both Israeli occupation and a Palestinian elite. If Palestinian activists, writers, readers, and viewers assume that "publics" will take unusual shapes, they will do more work not only to listen but also to extend, deviate, wander, patch together. I regret that this book project has not taken me to Lebanon or to Gaza, or to other Palestinian places, except as a mediated onlooker or reader of ethnographies and other scholarship. However, I hope that other researchers, writers, activists, and artists will continue to explore in an open-ended way what Palestine means to people in different Palestinian places. In careful work of looking at two or more places in relation, in recognizing the specificity of Palestinian struggles, accomplishments, and experiences, we can continue to build ethnographic and other portraits of Palestinian lives today that themselves can come together in a kind of collage.

To a more concrete point, scholars of Palestinians should be precise in their language so that we are clear about what we are including and what we must exclude in a particular study, and why. While no project can address all places relevant to Palestinians and Jewish Israelis, a project for justice and rights for Palestinians cannot only be based in the occupied territories without acknowledging the specificity of that project. Justice for Palestinians and Jewish Israelis (for they will be interrelated) must include all of historic Palestine and the refugee and diaspora communities where Palestinians live today, as well as other communities with meaningful connections to this land.

For scholars of settler colonialism, racism, militarism, capitalism, and displacement, Israel offers rich territory for analysis. It calls for an examination of the interrelationship of these phenomena, and of different stages and forms of colonialism. A study like this begins to show how military occupation in the territory Israel has controlled since 1967 impacts the territory Israel has controlled since 1948, entrenching racism against Palestinians as an enemy, perpetuating the possibility that all territory can be a site for a border dispute. But Palestinian citizens of Israel will remind us that military occupation predates 1967, because most of them lived under military occupation from 1948 to 1966. The problem of military occupation introducing lawlessness and violence within Israel's 1948 boundaries is not a problem only of the last half century but a symptom of Israel's constitutive injustices. It is crucial to recognize the different kinds of racism, legal and military threats, and violence faced by Palestinian citizens of Israel and Palestinians living under military occupation in the West Bank. Issues of identity come to the fore more for Palestinians in Israel's 1948 territories, while Palestinians in the occupied territories face more intense risks of military violence. But even as we recognize these differences among Palestinian experiences of dispossession and Israeli violence, we can see that these forms of racism and violence are interrelated; they work together not only to fragment Palestinians in different locations but also to threaten them. Palestinian citizens of Israel may worry that the violence that those in the West Bank have faced might be just around the corner, while those in the West Bank may fear that the violence endured by those in Gaza looms for them. While Palestinian citizens of Israel must constantly manage being pushed to the margins of the nationalist project, Palestinians in the West Bank face the challenge of not having their nationalism be co-opted or repressed by the PA's floundering state project.

If this book is a loose comparison of the environments for expression for two groups of Palestinians, much recent scholarship on Palestinians is guided by other kinds of comparison. Recent scholarship in Palestine studies has focused on the lens of settler colonialism studies, and on whether and how Palestinians fit into the category of indigeneity. Scholarship has also traced solidarity between Palestinians and Black Americans, recognizing that some Palestinians face similar kinds of state violence and state racism. Palestinians are also placed in a framework of displacement and refugee studies. All of these are relevant and rich frames for discussion and analysis. While Palestinians have a structural and historical similarity with Indigenous people through their experiences of displacement and dispossession, their experiences have been distinct in part because the Palestinian story of dispossession is so new and because it began in a profoundly different legal, media, biopolitical, and military context than that of Indigenous people in the larger settler colonies. It is important to look at experiential, legal, and social similarities and differences between Palestinian groups and other oppressed groups with a variety of structural positions. We look at similarities and differences to understand more about how settler colonialism, racism, militarism, and displacement operate, interact, and compound each other today; we do this to highlight the generative connections activists have made across movements; we do this to shine lights from one part of the world to another so that we can deepen our readers' senses of understanding and solidarity of lesser-known places. Scholars studying Palestinians and living in larger settler colonies also must do this connective work to attend to their own responsibilities to the Indigenous communities where they live.[20] But these theorizations, connections, and allusions should never be allowed to reduce the specificity of people's struggles and life experiences.

Geopolitical fragmentation and control over mobility are key modes of settler colonial violence and threats to collectivity. Checkpoints and permit regulations—the physical and bureaucratic infrastructures of closure—prohibit the movement of people through territory controlled by a single sovereign, Israel. They inhibit Palestinian citizens of Israel and Palestinians of the West Bank from conversing with one another in the easy way that neighbors might otherwise do. Fragmentation can be perpetuated through geographic and legal division, and these can ossify or become naturalized as cultural formations. Geopolitical fragmentation and "sleight of hand sovereignty" are a pair of strategies through which states like Israel that purport to be democracies continue to make this claim despite their segregationist logics. Similar dynamics limit political possibilities for those in US territories like Puerto Rico and Guam. Indian citizens in Kashmir and other Muslim minorities there face a different but related set of designations regarding who can be part of the Indian democracy and on what terms. In all of these cases, the designation of the territory that belongs and the territory that should be excluded is also rooted in racialized exclusions of certain populations as undeserving, uncivilized, or threats to democracy. We should be wary indeed when states cordon off areas where the rule of law operates from those where it does not and call the result a "democracy."

Although activists in both Palestinian communities share political practices and texts—slogans, a memorial calendar, outrage over Israeli violence—living separately, they develop distinct political habitus, or embodied, everyday understandings and ways of maneuvering under Israeli sovereignty, and different structures of feelings take shape. People fear different things. Protesters and writers are emboldened in different ways. Journalists delimit local news differently. Activists look over their shoulders slightly differently, whether when they are stopped by police or looking out for where a soldier's gun is pointed, or where the next round of tear gas might fall. There is no doubt that Palestinians in Israel have deeply compromised citizenship; yet they are taught to think of themselves as citizens, even if as excluded or neglected ones. So Palestinian children incarcerated because of a protest may see this as a heroic opportunity for expression. For the second or third generation to grow up under Israeli military occupation in the West Bank, prison is often just another ordeal, a disruption, an everyday terror. Many living under this regime feel there is less to say and less reason to say anything at all to Jewish Israeli audiences. This illuminates why understanding the dynamics among Palestinians is crucial to fostering understanding of relations between Palestinians and Jewish Israelis.

Palestinian citizens of Israel have grown adept at seeing themselves at once through their own eyes and through the eyes of the Israeli public. They are also often aware of how Palestinians in the occupied territories—those at the center of the current national project—view them. These distinct double and triple views are differently disorienting. Palestinian citizens of Israel seem adept at adaptation and resignification, at adjusting the meanings of Palestinian dominant national culture. What practices can help us to recognize geopolitical fragmentation without idealizing a concept of unity that erases difference? To bring forward the voices of feminists, poor people, and others who tend to be shut out by the PA's neoliberal elite? To create Palestinian-centered collectivities that are nonetheless open to others who embrace justice? To nurture the time we have, given that liberation seems so far away? The Tal'at movement against violence against women has creatively bridged the Green Line to challenge Israeli oppression and patriarchy.[21] Small NGOs have found creative ways to bring Palestinians and sometimes Palestinians and Jewish Israelis together across the Green Line to learn about their histories.

At the 2021 March of Return, the artist Rana Bishara brought out one of her older works of art: a three-dimensional puzzle of historic Palestine over a meter long, made of wood and painted the color of rich dirt that she had made so carefully two decades earlier. Like much of her work, the large pieces invited engagement, including from children at the event. On them were placenames of hundreds of cities and villages, written in her own attentive hand. Perhaps one would imagine the goal was for the puzzle to be put together as one Palestine. Perhaps the purpose was something else: that the children could sit on it, that they could move its pieces playfully around, that they could find their hometown and many other places. That they could walk away from it and come back. That it was here this Nakba Day, and that next Nakba Day, they would gather with something else to explore.

Notes

Prologue

1. Increasing the Jewish population of the Galilee, which was supposed to be part of a Palestinian state as part of the United Nations partition plan and which has had a stubbornly high percentage of Palestinians, has been an enduring goal of Israeli planners (Falah 1991; Ghanem 2001; Y. Jabareen 2017).

2. Tawil-Souri 2012.

3. See Silvia Pasquetti's analysis of a similar dynamic in Al-Lidd / Lod (Pasquetti 2013, 472).

4. Berda 2017, 47.

5. Berda 2017, 54.

6. Pasquetti 2013.

7. Lior 2017a.

8. Haraway 1988.

9. Stewart 2007, 4.

10. Berry et al. 2017.

11. This complexity gives new meanings to what it means to be a feminist, "halfie" anthropologist in the field (Abu-Lughod 1991). I am also inspired by other Palestinian writing about class, exile, family history, and privilege, including that of Sherene Seikaly (Seikaly 2018).

12. Bourdieu 1993; Hirschkind 2006.

13. Williams 1977.

14. Gilroy 2001; Hammami 2019; Larkin 2013; Peteet 2017; Yazıcı 2013.

15. Dalakoglou 2010.

16. A. A. Bishara 2015. In this regard, Palestinians are like other Indigenous people who diagnose and contest settler colonialism in and through transit (Byrd 2011).

17. Cattelino 2008; Rutherford 2012; A. Simpson 2014.

18. Anghie 2006.

19. Deeb and Winegar 2016.

20. Said 1979, 1981.

21. Bayoumi 2008; Deeb and Winegar 2016; Mamdani 2004.

22. Erakat 2019.

23. Atshan 2021; Furani and Rabinowitz 2011.

24. A. Y. Davis 2016; Lamont Hill 2018.

25. Beliso-De Jesús and Pierre 2020, 65.

26. As Shu-mei Shih writes, "Comparison as relation means setting into motion historical relationalities between entities brought together for comparison, and bringing into relation terms that have traditionally been pushed apart from each other due to certain interests...The excavation of these relationalities is what I consider to be the ethical practice of comparison, where the workings of power are not concealed but necessarily revealed" (Shih 2013, 79).

27. E.g., Said 1992; Zureik 1979.

28. Bhandar and Ziadah 2016; S. Bishara 2018; Pappé 2018; Tatour 2019.

29. Allen 2018; A. Y. Davis 2016; K. P. Feldman 2015; Fischbach 2018; Lamont Hill 2018; Lubin 2014.

30. Al-Bulushi, Ghosh, and Tahir 2020.

31. Strathern 2004, xxi.

Introduction

1. Though I heard him earlier in this year, a similar performance by Sbeit was recorded on another evening after a protest in solidarity with prisoners (Hungry4Freedom 2011).

2. UNRWA 2019. 470,000 Palestinian refugees are registered with UNRWA in Lebanon, and the total population is much larger.

3. Darwish wrote, "We have on this land what makes life worth living" (Darwish 2007).

4. See Karkabi 2017 for more on reggae in Walaa Sbeit's music and its political significance, and *Geographies of Liberation* (Lubin 2014) for more on shared Afro-Arab political imaginaries.

5. Palestinian refugees are defined as "persons whose normal place of residence was Palestine during the period 1 June 1946 to 15 May 1948, and who lost both home and means of livelihood as a result of the 1948 conflict" (UNRWA, n.d.d). In general, internally displaced people are "persons or groups of persons who have been forced or obliged to flee or to leave their homes or places of habitual residence, in particular as a result of or in order to avoid the effects of armed conflict, situations of generalized

violence, violations of human rights or natural or human-made disasters, and who have not crossed an internationally recognized border" (OHCHR n.d.).

6. Palestinians and others have long recognized that Israel is a settler colonial state (Abowd 2014; Abu-Lughod 2020; Hanafi 2009; Rashid Khalidi 2020; Lustick 1993; Rouhana and Sabbagh-Khoury 2015; Salaita 2006; Salamanca et al. 2012; Said 1992; Shihade 2012; Sayegh 2012; Zureik 1979). In the 1950s and 1960s, journalists, poets, and other writers saw the Palestinian struggle as one for liberation against colonialism, drawing inspiration both from anticolonial struggles in Africa and Asia and from their own struggle against the British Mandate (Nassar 2017). Writing in the 1970s, Elia Zureik termed Israel's rule there to be "internal colonialism" (Zureik 1979). In recent years, the settler colonial framework has (re)emerged in European and US-based scholarship as an alternative to that of an Israeli-Palestinian or Arab-Israeli conflict, though it has not consistently acknowledged the history of the idea among Palestinians (Bhandar and Ziadah 2016).

7. See Klein 2014 for another perspective on the different dynamics of copresence in different locations under Israeli sovereignty.

8. Levi-Strauss writes of the bricoleur as someone who works with the heterogenous and contingent tools at hand (Lévi-Strauss 1962, 17–18).

9. Feld 1982, 15.

10. I am drawing here on ideas of habitus developed by scholars like Pierre Bourdieu and Charles Hirschkind (Bourdieu 1977; Hirschkind 2006), and on the concept of structures of feelings developed by Raymond Williams (Williams 1977).

11. De la Cadena 2015, 32-33.

12. A. Bishara 1997; Y. Sayigh 2011.

13. Buttu 2014b.

14. *Memories of Revolt* is a foundational study that does this in the Palestinian context (Swedenburg 1995).

15. Harrison 1997.

16. Scholarly literature addresses this diversity historically and today; see e.g., Bowman 2000; Doumani 1995; Lybarger 2007; Tamari 2008; Nasasra 2017.

17. Constantin Zureiq, a Syrian intellectual and important Arab nationalist thinker, first used the term to describe these events of dispossession in 1948 (Zureiq 1948). For other landmark scholarship on Al-Nakba see Walid Khalidi's *All That Remains* (1992), which was a major force in beginning the revision of the events of 1948, as well as Masalha (1992), on the history of the concept of transfer in Zionist thought. There is a growing literature on the Nakba as event and as a key Palestinian political concept (Al-Hardan 2015; Ghanim 2011; Pappé 2006; Sa'di 2003; Sa'di and Abu-Lughod 2007).

18. Allan 2014; I. Feldman 2018; Gabiam 2016.

19. As Julie Chu writes of people waiting on papers or smugglers to be able to migrate in a swiftly changing China, "It was actually *immobility* that was experienced as the definitive form of displacement" (Chu 2010, 11). For more on how this operates in Palestine, see Berda 2017; Hammami 2010; Hammami 2019; Peteet 2017.

20. Peteet 2015.

21. Wolfe 2006.

22. In the North American context, we might think of blood quantum laws (Kauanui 2008; Tallbear 2013) and tensions among those Native American groups who have gained Federal recognition and those who have not, and authenticity claims regarding "reservation," "urban," and "praying" Indians as products of a similar logic of settler colonial fragmentation that works toward elimination of Indigenous people as made up of collectives. Failing to recognize Indigenous peoples' interconnectedness as well as their connectedness to each other through land and movement has diminished and disrupted Indigenous forms of collectivity and sovereignty (L. Brooks 2018; L. Brooks and C. Brooks 2010; Estes 2019b; Goeman 2013). Ayesha Jalal's history of Muslim identities under British rule in South Asia is also formative research on this subject (Jalal 2000). Mahmoud Mamdani's work on the tactic of "define and rule" as an instrument of the British Empire is an important related example of how fragmentation operates (Mamdani 2012). His exploration of "territorial indirect rule" exemplifies how people are categorized through physical isolation to exacerbate legal difference (Mamdani 2020).

23. As a comparative example, US colonialism also operates differently across various spaces, making it harder to characterize the overarching system (A. Goldstein 2014). While, because of its enormous scope, the cumulative effect of US colonialism is less about fragmenting one people into many parts, US colonialism is similar to Israeli colonialism in that it creates different legal structures across the spaces it controls, ranging from domestic space, non-state territories, and military bases of different kinds. As in Israel, parts of the United States can appear to be a formal democracy, even if in other places where these states are sovereign there is little possibility for democratic practice.

24. Notable exceptions include discussions through organizations like the refugee resource center Badil that address fragmentation through programing and publications (Badil 2013); Sa'ed Atshan's research on queer Palestine (Atshan 2020); Silvia Pasquetti's research on connections between Palestinians in Al-Lidd / Lod, in Israel, and Jalazon Refugee Camp (Pasquetti 2013, 2015); Hassan Amara's research on language in "border villages" (Amara 1990); and Guy Burton's recent work on activism (Burton 2015; 2017).

25. Falk and Tilley 2017a.

26. Falk and Tilley 2017b.

27. See Englund 2006, 54.

28. Al-Haq 2019; B'Tselem 2021; HRW 2021a.

29. HRW 2021a.

30. Marcus 1998.

31. Deeb and Winegar 2016; Perez et al. 2015.

32. In 2011, Israel's civil administration issued 101 types of movement permits (Levinson 2011).

33. Hass 2013.

34. Erakat 2011.

35. Wimmer and Nina Glick Schiller 2002, 304; see also Li 2019, 31–33. As Lisa Lowe recently observed, "the modern division of knowledge into academic disciplines, focused on discrete areas and objects of interest to the modern national university, has profoundly shaped the inquiry into . . . connections" among single societies, peoples and regions (Lowe 2015, 1). While her work addresses the relationships among continents, it reveals something about the politics of nation-states that it is also difficult to study a single group (Palestinians) as they live across two adjacent areas.

36. Anzaldúa 1987; Ghosh 2019; Li 2019; Mahajan 2019; Maqsood 2019; A. Simpson 2014; Yıldız 2013.

37. Pappé 2017, 2. Yet, despite this caveat, the book from which this framing remark was taken focuses only the occupation of the West Bank and Gaza.

38. Abrams 1988.

39. Note the difference between a policy of assimilation as Patrick Wolfe (2006) identifies as a common technique of settler colonies and the cultural erasure of Palestinians. Palestinian citizens of Israel cannot be assimilated into Israel because in hegemonic Israeli discourse and in law, Israel is defined as a Jewish state.

40. Mamdani 2020, 35.

41. Yarimar Bonilla (@yarimarbonilla), "Dear allies: when feeling the need to assert that Puerto Ricans are 'fellow US citizens.'" Twitter, July 29, 2019. https://twitter.com/yarimarbonilla/status/1155854246195150848?lang=en. See e.g., Holston 2011; Ong 2006; Paz 2018; Robinson 2013.

42. De la Cadena 2015; Strathern 2004.

43. De la Cadena 2015, 32.

44. Malkki 1992.

45. Adalah 2015a.

46. Importantly, this is not the case for Palestinians living in unrecognized and threatened Bedouin encampments in the West Bank. Israel's treatment of Bedouins in the Negev and in rural areas of the West Bank resemble each other (Adalah 2013).

47. Mbembe 2003.

48. Foucault 1975, 1991. Mbembe and Foucault acknowledge that these forms of rule interact. As I think about necropolitics for Palestinian citizens of Israel, I am also thinking comparatively with Carolyn Rouse's important argument about necropolitics as a mode of rule of Black people in the United States (Rouse 2021).

49. Díaz-Barriga and Dorsey 2020; Jones 2016; Rosas 2012; De León 2015; McAtackney and McGuire 2020.

50. Azoulay and Ophir 2013. Asserting Israel's one-state reality and challenging its claims to being Jewish and democratic is by now not a new conversation, including in US journalistic outlets; see e.g., Li 2011; Lustick 2019; Masri 2014; Remnick 2014.

51. A. A. Bishara 2017.

52. See I. Feldman 2008.

53. Hamdan 2018; Khamaisi 2008.

54. B'Tselem 2017. The separation wall is generally made up of walls in populated areas and fences in outlying areas.

55. Maidhof 2016.

56. See e.g., Al-Bulushi 2020; Lutz and Enloe 2009; Tahir, Touhouliotis, and Sogn n.d.; Vine 2009.

57. Ralph 2020.

58. Gingrich and Fox 2002; Shih 2013; Strathern 2004.

59. Bäuml 2017.

60. Pappé 2006, xiii.

61. Peteet 2015.

62. Gal and Irvine 2000, 38.

63. Jamal 2017, 64.

64. Pappé 2006, xiii.

65. Wakim 2001. Today, these displaced people number approximately 384,200, according to the Palestinian NGO Badil (N. Al-Azza and Al-Orzza 2015, 8).

66. Nasasra et al. 2014, 131.

67. Nassar 2017; Robinson 2013.

68. Adalah 2017.

69. Rouhana and Sultany 2003, 5.

70. Firro 2001.

71. Kanaaneh 2008, 10.

72. Jamal 2011, 2; Rabinowitz and Abu-Baker 2005; Rouhana and Sabbagh-Khoury 2015.

73. M. Berger 2019; Ghanem 2002; Makhoul 2015.

74. Nassar 2017, 100.

75. Mada al-Carmel 2007, 7–8.

76. National Committee for the Heads of the Arab Local Authorities in Israel 2006, 3.

77. Adalah 2007, 4.

78. Jamal 2011, 161–86.

79. Adalah Justice Project 2021.

80. Saʿdi 2017; Zreik 2003.

81. Sultany 2012, 197.

82. Adalah 2013; Eghbariah 2021.

83. H. Jabareen and S. Bishara 2019.

84. Bandel 2021.

85. Lynk 2017, 7.

86. Pappé 2017, 4.

87. Francis 2014.

88. Buttu 2019, 32.

89. Abu-Zahra and Kay 2013; Berda 2017; A. A. Bishara 2015; Hammami 2010, 2019; Hass 2002; Peteet 2017.

90. Buttu 2019, 22.

91. Amnesty International 2011; Jamal 2005; Nossek and Rinnawi 2016; UNESCO and Birzeit University Media Development Center 2014.

92. Y. Sayigh 2011; Usher 1996.

93. Buttu 2014a.

94. Shalhoub-Kevorkian 2015; Zureik 2001.

95. Bornstein 2002; Farsakh 2005.

96. Nassar 2021.

97. Karkabi 2013.

98. Furani 2012.

99. For example, the organization of Palestinian anthropologists and anthropologists of Palestine, Insaniyyat, embraces anthropologists on both sides of the Green Line and beyond.

100. S. Bishara 2016.

101. Berda 2017, 18; Nassar 2017; Robinson 2013; Shenhav and Berda 2009. Specifically, some of Israel's limitations on Palestinian expression in Israel's 1948 territories and forms of penalties against Palestinians there rely on the British Emergency Laws from the time of the British Mandate and thus on Israel's maintenance of a state of emergency, which has been in place since Israel's establishment. Israel is working to regularize these regulations. In 2016, Israel passed a new Counterterrorism Law that applies only inside Israel, not in the West Bank, which replaces many of the emergency regulations and perpetuates limitations on expression, as with its stipulations against identifying with a terrorist organization and incitement to terrorism (Lis 2016b). This is a mode of bringing some of the longstanding British colonial law into regular domestic law, further blurring the line between Israel's 1948 territories and the occupied territories.

102. Lis 2013; Sultany 2017, 218.

103. Jamal 2017; Nassar 2017.

104. Nassar 2017.

105. Nassar 2017, 76; see also Jamal 2009.

106. Nassar 2017, 100.

107. Schejter 2009, 66.

108. Peled 1992; Sultany 2017.

109. Schejter 2009, 92–93.

110. Schejter 2009.

111. Friedman 1983; Wolfsfeld and Rabihiya 1988.

112. CPJ 1988.

113. Jamal 2005, 83.

114. Jamal 2005, 101.

115. Amnesty International 2019b; HRW 2018b; Kurd 2020; Parsons 2010; Y. Sayigh 2011; Zureik, Lyon, and Abu-Laban 2013.

116. Amnesty International 2017.

117. Hill 2016.

118. This was a refinement of earlier language; the previous version of the law had read, "A list of candidates shall not participate in the elections for the Knesset if its aims or actions, expressly or by implication, point to one of the following: (1) denial of the existence of the State of Israel as the state of the Jewish people; (2) denial of the democratic nature of the state; and (3) incitement to racism" (Adalah n.d.b).

119. Adalah n.d.a.

120. Quoted in Strickland 2015.

121. Sultany 2017, 223.

122. Takriti 2019.

123. S. Bishara 2016; Masri, Rouhana, and Sabbagh-Khoury 2015; Nassar 2017; Sultany 2015.

124. Sultany 2017, 212.

125. S. Bishara 2015; Ravid 2015.

126. Addameer 2017.

127. Addameer 2017.

128. Take, for example, a survey from the late 2000s in which Palestinian citizens were asked whether they agreed with the following statement: "Israel should stop being a Jewish state and become a state for two peoples": 57.9 percent said, "I agree and work should start immediately to implement this demand"; 21.3 percent said "I agree, but this is a demand that can only be partially implemented right now"; 16.3 percent said "I agree, but this is a demand that can't be implemented right now." Only 4.5 percent said "I don't agree" (Ghanem and Mustafa 2009, 63). The gradations of pragmatism stand revealingly in contrast to the overall consensus, demonstrated not only by the responses to the survey but by the design of it by two Palestinian researchers situated in Israeli universities.

129. Amnesty International 2014.

130. For example, in 2020, 355 people were held under administrative detention, down from 584 in 2015 (B'Tselem 2020).

131. Khoury, Breiner, and Hasson 2021.

132. A. Bishara 2001; Hawari 2021.

133. Said 1984.

134. Spivak 2010.

135. E.g., Allen 2013; A. A. Bishara 2013; Dabashi 2006; Erakat 2019.

136. A. Simpson 2014, 104; see also Dowell 2013; Robertson 2018.

137. Allan 2018; Erakat 2019; Gabiam 2018; Kauanui 2008; Massad 2018b; Salih and Richter-Devroe 2018; A. Simpson 2014; Sturm 2017.

138. Habermas 1989.

139. Anderson 1991.

140. Paz 2019, 78.

141. To put this in different terms, according to this ideal, "as speakers of the law, the people exercise power as the sovereign; as addressees, they submit to the law as citizens" (Slotta 2017, 330).

142. Jakobson 1960.

143. Slotta 2017, 2015.

144. See for example Rihan Yeh's formulation of two border publics in Tijuana, Mexico: one constituted around the middle class "I" and another around a more diffuse "we" of working class and less mobile residents of Tijuana (Yeh 2018); see also Alejandro Paz's conception of *chisme* in undocumented, working class Latinx publics in Israel (Paz 2018).

145. For example, PA regulations have made it difficult for Palestinian citizens of Israel to serve on the boards of Palestinian NGOs in the West Bank.

146. Lowe 2015.

147. Boym 1998, 499.

Passage: Aida Refugee Camp to the Haifa Bridge

1. Anderson 1996.

Chapter 1

1. There is a robust scholarly discussion about Palestinians' aspirations toward statehood and what might come after them (Erakat 2019; Farsakh 2017, 2021; Massad 2018a; Salih and Richter-Devroe 2018). I am also inspired here by works in critical Indigenous studies and elsewhere about the constraints and oppressiveness of state sovereignty as a goal (Kauanui 2018; Bonilla 2015, 2017), the prehistories of nationalism in West Asia (Kia 2020), and the possibility that resurgence and renewal can be "nation building, not nation-state building, but nation building" (L. B. Simpson 2016, 22).

2. Kayyal n.d.

3. Doumani 2007, 51.

4. Silverstein 1976, 29.

5. Hanks 1990, 4, 15.

6. Hanks 1990, 4.

7. I am inspired in this chapter by Andrew Graan's writing on statecraft and branding (Graan 2013). The PA and other Palestinians are involved in this performance of statehood across a variety of practices, including human rights, journalism, and even waste management (Allen 2013; A. A. Bishara 2013; Stamatopoulou-Robbins 2020).

8. Schulthies 2015.

9. Bachelard 1994; Basso 1996; Feld and Basso 1996; Gupta 1992; Lefebvre 1991.

10. Bakhtin 1981.

11. While these categories of dominant, residual, and emergent are useful for analysis, there is a dynamism among them. Williams recognizes the cultural as a site of contestation and dynamism: "The complexity of a culture is to be found not only in its variable processes and their social definitions—traditions, institutions, and formations—but also in the dynamic interrelations, at every point in the process, of historically varied and variable elements" (Williams 1977, 121).

12. Chu 2010.

13. Soussi 2019.

14. Lis 2016a.

15. Jacir 2018.

16. Malkki 1995; see also Gupta 1992.

17. Anzaldúa 1987; Díaz-Barriga and Dorsey 2020; Ghosh 2019; Koyagi 2019; Luna 2020; Mahajan 2019; Yıldız 2013.

18. Bonilla 2015, 2017.

19. Kauanui 2018.

20. Kauanui 2019.

21. Wilder 2015.

22. Anghie 2006.

23. R. Khalidi 1997; Tamari 2008.

24. R. Khalidi 1997.

25. Banko 2012, Doumani 2007. Legal scholar Susan Akram argues that since then Palestinian nationality has continued to exist, and that this can be an important means of claiming rights for Palestinians (Akram 2017).

26. First Palestinian Conference 1964.

27. Y. Sayigh 2000; Irfan 2020.

28. Ibrahim 1988.

29. Rutherford 2012.

30. Salih and Richter-Devroe 2018, 3.

31. Segal 2017.

32. Abbas 2011.

33. Permanent Observer Mission of Palestine to the United Nations 2021.

34. Mbembe 2003.

35. Scholarship in the anthropology of infrastructure has especially contributed to this perspective (Anand 2017; Beck, Klaeger, and Stasik 2017; Stamatopoulou-Robbins 2020).

36. Graan 2016.

37. Notably, the PA is not alone in its receipt of international funds for such basic services, pointing to the way in which entities do not need to be legally devoid of sovereignty, as is the PA, for critiques of the bounds and meaning of sovereignty to be applicable (A. A. Bishara 2015).

38. Bhabha 1983.

39. Rutherford 2012.

40. Cattelino 2008.

41. Kauanui 2017, 328.

42. A. A. Bishara 2017.

43. B. Anderson 1991; R. Khalidi 1997.

44. A. A. Bishara 2013; Velthuis 2006.

45. Jusionyte 2015; Cody 2011a.

46. Yeh 2018, 12.

47. We can find these other journalisms organized around Indigenous, migrant, diasporic, or radical communities (Bernal 2014; Fisher 2016; Juris 2012; Paz 2018).

48. I focus on those outlets that are most popular according to the Alexa ranking of website traffic in Israel and in what Alexa, a website ranking program, calls the "Palestinian Territory," and on looking at sources from a variety of political orientations. I confirmed that the layouts of the websites analyzed here had not changed significantly over time, first looking at these organizations starting in 2017 and re-checking these categorizations in June 2019 and July 2020.

49. It was the top ranked news webpage in the Palestinian Territory on the Alexa measure of website traffic per country June 2021, and in July 2021, it was the second most trafficked site overall.

50. Donya Al-Watan 2020.

51. Specifically, on June 19, 2019, it listed under "Local News" the following categories, in this order: Ramallah, Gaza, Jerusalem, Nablus, Jenin, Hebron, Tulkarem, Bethlehem, Tubas, Qalqilya, Salfit, Jericho, and the prisoners; the listing on July 8, 2020, started with Jerusalem and then Ramallah, Gaza, Bethlehem and other West Bank districts, with the exclusion of the category of prisoners.

52. Ma'an was the second most popular newssite and fifth overall on July 3, 2021.

53. The full list comprised of two columns, the first reading Jerusalem, Ramallah, Gaza, Jericho, Qalqiliya, and Tubas, and the second reading Hebron, Bethlehem, Jenin, Salfit, and Tulkarem. At the bottom of both columns was the category "'48 Palestine." A

similar organization dates to at least August 2017, though the inclusion of "'48 Palestine" as part of the local happened between June 2019 and June 2020; it had previously been its own category. In 2011, it was even more PA-specific, organized by the administrative "districts" of Jerusalem, Bethlehem, Ramallah, Hebron, Nablus, Jenin, Tubas, Tulkarem, Qalqilya, Jericho, Salfit, and Gaza.

54. This was the organization on July 9, 2020, and a year later on July 3, 2021. Generally speaking, the lower placement of '48 Palestine on the webpage has been consistent over years.

55. Writing in 2000, Avraham, Wolfsfeld, and Aburaiya observe, "apart from one exception, none of the major news media in Israel have ever assigned a permanent reporter to cover the Arab population on a long-term basis" (Avraham, Wolfsfeld, and Aburaiya 2000, 123).

56. Panet 2019. Panet was ranked ninth on Alexa in Israel, and incidentally eleventh on Alexa for the Palestinian Territory in June 2019; in July 2021, it ranked thirty-seven in Israel and was not in the top fifty in the Palestinian Territory.

57. I first observed this on August 8, 2017, and I confirmed this on July 3 2021.

58. For example, some of its subheadings read: "This is Nazareth," "Akka and the region," "Tarshiha and the region," and "Al-Lydd, Al-Ramla, and Yaffa."

59. This was as of July 7, 2020, and continued to be true on July 3, 2021. Previously it had been listed as Palestinian news.

60. According to Alexa, Arab48 was not in the top fifty most popular sites in Israel in June 19, 2019 nor on July 3, 2021. In the Palestinian Territory, it was the twelfth most popular site, just after Panet in 2019 and the tenth most popular in 2021. If *Haaretz*, often called the *New York Times* of Israel, ranked thirty-third in Israel in 2021, it is hardly surprising that Arab48 (perhaps the *New York Times* for Palestinians in Israel in terms of its quality journalism) does not rank at all.

61. Balad 2017.

62. Rasgon 2019.

63. See Yurchak 2005 on how complex nominalizations made it difficult to counter certain semi-official writing in late Soviet socialism.

64. Mazzarella 2003.

65. See for example *The Wanted 18* on Israeli military responses to this strategy during the Intifada of the late 1980s (Shomali and Cowan 2014).

66. There is a robust and growing literature on neoliberalism in the occupied territories, some of which conceives of neoliberal capitalism as a second occupation (Clarno 2017; Haddad 2018; Raja Khalidi and Samour 2011; Rabie 2021; Tayeb 2019).

67. Haddad 2018, 8.

68. I am inspired by Julie Chu's thinking about mobility as a quality that signifies (Chu 2010).

69. Sienkiewicz 2012.

70. This is a familiar joke (A. A. Bishara 2015, 44).

71. Stamatopoulou-Robbins 2020.

72. Wedeen 1999; Yurchak 2005.

73. I am using C. S. Peirce's definition of an icon as something that resembles what it represents (Peirce 1985).

74. "Aḥyā, Uḥibb, Ataḥada, Wa A ʿūd, Li-akūn."

75. Williams 1977, 129.

76. De Certeau 1984, 99.

77. Kuttab 2016; Ihmoud 2019.

78. De Certeau 1984, 92.

79. De Certeau 1984.

80. "*Alān fi-l-manfā, na ʾm fi-l-bayt*" (Darwish 2009). A range of Palestinian writers have addressed this condition of exile at home over many decades (Said 1986; Shalhoub-Kevorkian and Ihmoud 2014; Shalhoub-Kevorkian 2008).

81. Karkabi 2018.

82. Adalah n.d.c.

83. Williams 1977, 113.

84. Williams 1977, 122.

85. Williams 1977, 123.

Passage. Aida Refugee Camp to the Northern Galilee

1. Suleiman and Kayyal 2020.

2. Adalah 2018; Hovel and Khoury 2014.

3. For more on processes of encroachment on such Galilee villages, see Yiftachel 1996.

Chapter 2

1. In Israel's early years especially, development towns served the purpose of settling marginal areas with non-European Jewish immigrants (Rabinowitz 1997, 7).

2. Raphael 2011.

3. As part of my research on the barriers to Palestinian political engagement across the Green Line, the 1948 armistice line that divides Israel and the West Bank, I went to several protests against the war both inside Israel and in the West Bank. I also followed protests and vigils through news and social media and conducted interviews with activists about these protests. In addition, before the war began, I had been attending other Palestinian protests in Israel and the West Bank that summer. Inside Israel's 1948 territories, the anti-war protests I attended included one in Haifa that ended in multiple arrests, as described at the end of Chapter 1, and the standout in Tarshiha. In the West Bank, I went to several of the nightly protests on the main street in Bethlehem, encountered the regular protests in Aida in my daily life there, attended a children's vigil against

the war in Manger's Square in Bethlehem, and participated in a drive for bottled water and other donations in Aida Refugee Camp. I also interviewed protest organizers, especially in Haifa and in Aida Camp, and I spoke to lawyers at the Palestinian human rights organization Adalah, which represented many of those who were arrested at the protests inside Israel during this period.

4. OCHA 2015a.

5. Fiona Wright observes in her research on the radical Jewish left in Israel, "a suitable diagnostic for whether a particular group might appear within this loose definition of "left radical" activism is its stance on the attacks on Gaza in Operation Cast Lead and the later assaults of November 2012 and July–August 2014" (Wright 2018, 8).

6. Tilly 2006.

7. See Lila Abu-Lughod's classic critique of the culture concept (Abu-Lughod 1991).

8. C. W. Anderson 2013, 2021; Banko 2016; Swedenburg 1995.

9. For example, those participating in the Standing Rock movement have refused a language of "protest" in favor of calling themselves water protectors (Estes 2019).

10. Cody 2015, 2011b; Mazzarella 2010.

11. Warner 2002, 67.

12. Habermas 1989, 27.

13. Fraser 2007.

14. Mitchell 1999.

15. See, however, Naomi Schiller's important critiques of the concept of liberal independence in the press (Schiller 2018).

16. Tilly 2006, 35.

17. Tilly 2006, 35.

18. Tilly 2006, 16.

19. A. A. Bishara 2017.

20. Freedom House 2021.

21. Jamal 2009; Robinson 2013; Rouhana and Huneidi 2017.

22. Tilly 2006, 16.

23. Takriti 2019, 59.

24. Baumgarten-Sharon 2010, 4–5.

25. Lior 2017b.

26. Shaindlinger (2019) makes a similar point about generational difference.

27. See also Zonszein 2018.

28. Berda 2017.

29. However, raising a Palestinian flag is viewed as a threat in East Jerusalem and in Israel today and can attract police action (Konrad 2019).

30. B'Tselem 2018.

31. Amnesty International 2014, 6.

32. Baumgarten-Sharon 2010, 11.

33. Baumgarten-Sharon 2010, 3.

34. Amnesty International 2019a; J. Cook 2020; Wermenbol 2019.

35. King-Irani 2000.

36. A. Bishara 2001.

37. A. Feldman 1991, 163.

38. Tilly 2006.

39. Monterescu and Rabinowitz 2007; Pasquetti 2015.

40. Pasquetti 2015, 2.

41. Bardawil 2020, xv-xvi.

42. My translation. The Hebrew and English versions of the invitation were briefer and did not include this full statement.

43. Bakhtin 1981, 342; see also Yurchak 2005, 61.

44. Pasquetti 2015.

45. Busailah 1981, 135; Pappé 2006, 166–67.

46. Trilling 2020.

47. Compare with de Velasco (2019).

48. Berda 2017; Hammami 2010; Peteet 2017.

49. Bornstein 2002; Farsakh 2005.

50. "Ana ṣāmed, ṣāmed / Law qatalū khayye / Ṣāmed / Law qatalū bayye / Ṣāmed / Law qaṣafū ḥayyi / Ṣāmed / Shaʿbi bi-Ghazza / Ṣāmed / Fī al-Lid wa Ramle / Ṣāmed / Bi-Yāffā wa ʿAkkā / Ṣāmed."

51. Colla 2013, 38.

52. "ʿAlī ʿalī ʿalī ṣawt / Min il-Lidd li-bayrut / Allī byihtif mā biymut." Colla heard a chant similar to this one during the January 2011 protests in Egypt (Colla 2013, 41).

53. Colla 2013, 39.

54. Adalah 2014a.

55. Ticktin 2017.

56. "Waleʿ Waleʿ Waleʿ Waleʿ / Al-yawm taskīr al-shawāreʿ."

57. Casumbal-Salazar 2017; Estes 2019a; Obamsawin 1993.

58. "Yā fidāʾī yā ḥabīb / Iḍrub, Iḍrub Tel Abīb."

59. Adalah 2015c; Berman and staff 2014.

60. Abou Shahadeh 2021; Al-Jazeera 2021; Hasson 2015.

61. Dorsey and Díaz-Barriga 2015; Hernández 2010; Junaid 2020a; Schrader 2019. During the May 2021 protests of Israel's next major attack on Gaza, Israeli authorities again deployed border police widely in Israel's 1948 territories, and then Prime Minister Netanyahu urged security forces "not to be afraid" of future potential inquiries, thereby further encouraging their violence (HRW 2021b).

62. Tilly 2006.

63. "ʿAlimnā ʿalim filasṭīn / wājib ʿalaynā nerfaʿ hā."

64. Askew 2002, 23.

65. Arab48 2014.

66. Frank Cody's research offers an important exploration of this phenomena (2015).

67. Cody 2011b, 38.

68. "Weḥda weḥda waṭaniyya / Kul al-quwwa thawriyya."

69. "Irfa īdak wa ʿallī / Al-mawt walla al-madhalleh."

70. "Li-l-Quds rayḥīn / Shuhadāʾ bi-l-malāyīn."

71. For more on the separation wall, especially in and around Bethlehem, see A. A. Bishara 2020; Lagerquist 2004; Lynk 2005.

72. HRW 2014.

73. "ʿAn Ghazza mā fī badīl / Idrub, iqṣuf Israʾel."

74. Tilly 2006.

75. While I did not get the full text of the chant due to the distance between myself and the small group that was chanting it, other similar chants included "Our experience with [PA and Israeli] security coordination has fucked us over" (tajāribnā bi-l-tansīq jābat ilnā khawāzīq).

76. These commonly include "Fuck your mother" and "son of a whore."

77. Colla 2013, 44.

78. Dabashi 2006, 133.

79. Dabashi 2006, 133.

80. Simmons 2017.

81. Butler 2011.

82. Jawad 2011, 138.

83. Jawad 2011, 141.

84. See Takriti 2019 for a similar argument about struggle and confrontation related to the boycott, divestment, and sanctions movement.

85. Spivak 2010, 62.

86. For more explication on the local logics of popular resistance in a West Bank refugee camp, see the author's article on protests in Aida (2020).

87. Sheizaf and Jabareen 2015.

88. I draw on Patrick Wolfe's insight that settler colonialism operates with many different logics of elimination (Wolfe 2006).

89. Tilly 2006, 35.

Passage. Bethlehem to Lubya

1. Israel has a long history of trying to separate Druze from other Arabs, and has had mixed success in doing so (Firro 2001; Hajjar 2000).

2. B'Tselem 2011.

3. Bardenstein 2000; HRW 2011; McKee 2014.

Chapter 3

1. UNRWA n.d.c.

2. Slyomovics 1998.

3. ARIJ 2010. In Area C of the West Bank (about 60 percent), Israel maintains full control over security and civil matters, such that Israel would need to issue permits for buildings. Israel "views the area as there to serve its own needs, such as military training, economic interests and settlement development," and "Israel practically bans Palestinian construction and development" in Area C (B'Tselem n.d.a.).

4. UNRWA n.d.c.

5. See Braverman 2019 on Refa'im Stream National Park. Examples of other villages that have become national parks include Al-Qabu, now Begin National Park (Zochrot 2011), and Beit Jibreen, now Beit Govrin National Park (Zochrot n.d.a), both places where residents of Aida came from, and Ber'am in the Galilee.

6. See De Cesari 2019 and Abu-Lughod 2020 on recent developments in Palestinian museums.

7. Abu El-Haj 2001; Awayed-Bishara 2020; Benvenisti 2000.

8. Sorek 2015, 6.

9. Katriel 2016; Lentin 2010.

10. E.g., Allen 2006; R. Davis 2011, 2016; Khalili 2007; Khleif and Slyomovics 2008; R. Sayigh 2015, 1979; Sorek 2015.

11. R. Davis 2011. Rashid Khalidi has called this a kind of "local patriotism" (Rashid Khalidi 1997, 21).

12. Bahloul 1996; Connerton 1989; Halbwachs 1980; Shaw 2002.

13. Maha Nassar notes that gathering people together despite movement restrictions has been a longstanding strategy of Palestinian resistance inside Israel (Nassar 2017, 5).

14. Basso 1996; Feld 1996; Gordillo 2004; Myers 1991.

15. Bonilla 2015, 134.

16. Peteet 2005, 94. See also Abu Hatoum 2020; Peteet 2017 on place making in extremely circumscribed circumstances.

17. In contrast, outside of historic Palestine, commemorations can alienate Palestinians from the immediacy of politics around them. Diana Allan shows that in Lebanon commemorations can disempower newer generations whose experiences and histories are sidelined by such events. As she writes, commemorations "created a hierarchy of experiences deemed worthy of retention and fostered the belief that daily life . . . is always a direct reflection of larger political forces. The net result is that macrohistories masquerade as microhistories" (Allan 2014, 41).

18. Shira Robinson writes about this phenomenon in Kufr Qasim (2006, 116).

19. Al-Hardan 2015; Sa'di 2003; Sa'di and Abu-Lughod 2007.

20. Robinson 2006.

21. If an institution receiving public funding commemorates Israel's Independence Day as a day of mourning, this can lead to legal sanction (Adalah n.d.a). See Shalhoub-Kevorkian 2017 for more on the criminalization of Nakba Day.

22. Commemorations can also be occasions for factionalism in the occupied territories (Browne 2013).

23. This is also the case in commemorations of the Kufr Qasim massacre and was true of the 2011 Nakba Day March of Return at the Lebanese-Israeli border (Allan 2016; Robinson 2006, 116, 122).

24. For example, in 2011, I attended two Land Day events, one in Al-ʿAraqeeb in the Naqab / Negev, inside the Green Line, and the other in Bethlehem, the West Bank. In 2014, I went to three Land Day events, one in the town of Qalansawe inside the Green Line, one in Bethlehem in the West Bank, and a third in Al-Khader, also in the West Bank. In 2011, I went to four Nakba Day events: in Haifa, Jaffa, and Al-Damoun and Al-Ruways inside the Green Line, and Aida Refugee Camp and Al-Walaja in the West Bank. In 2014, I attended Nakba Day events in Lubya inside the Green Line, and in Aida Refugee Camp and Al-Walaja in the West Bank. During both years, these were just a few of the many events—small and large—planned for these days of commemoration.

25. Allen 2006.

26. Askew 2002; Feld 1989; Stokes 2000.

27. Shaw 2002, 5.

28. See Glass 2008 for more on t-shirt wearing as political and commemorative practice in another Indigenous community living under settler colonialism.

29. Sorek 2015, 67.

30. Sorek 2015, 69.

31. Rouhana and Sabbagh-Khoury 2017, 417.

32. Simri Diab 2014. Translation mine.

33. Mishal and Aharoni 1994, 96.

34. "Yawm istiqlālkum yawm nakbitnā."

35. The National Day of Mourning resonates deeply with Nakba Day commemorations in that it is both a day of grief and a day of asserting collectivity, presence, and strength. As organizers write, "We are mourning our ancestors and the genocide of our peoples and the theft of our lands. NDOM is a day when we mourn, but we also feel our strength in action" ("2020 National Day of Mourning Livestream" 2021).

36. Allan 2014, 40.

37. Peteet 2017; Hass 2002; Berda 2017; Hammami 2010, 2019.

38. Pfeffer 2011.

39. Pfeffer 2011.

40. Pfeffer 2011.

41. Reuters 2011.

42. A. A. Bishara 2020.

43. Haar and Ghannam 2018.

44. I am thinking here not only of Patrick Wolfe's (2006) writing on settler colonialism as a structure but also of Julie Chu's writing of the slow effects and ambiguous signs of government neglect for residents fighting eviction in urban China (Chu 2014).

45. B'Tselem n.d.b.

46. Tilly 2006.

47. See the story of Ahed Tamimi's slapping of a soldier who violently invaded her home after soldiers had just shot and seriously injured her cousin; see also Chapter 5 in *Back Stories* about another Palestinian teenager's confrontational stance toward an Israeli soldier that was caught by an Associated Press photographer (A. A. Bishara 2013).

48. Adalah n.d.a.

49. Sultany 2017.

50. Shalhoub-Kevorkian 2017, 355.

51. The video about the day produced by Zochrot, which advocates for Jewish Israeli memory and learning about the Nakba, likewise emphasizes the natural beauty of the surroundings, and even the act of moving, as the handheld quality of the camera work as the camera moves through the landscape is pronounced (Zochrot n.d.c). Picking such plants has been criminalized in Israel (Eghbariah, Asad, and Mansour 2021).

52. Bardenstein 2000.

53. W. Khalidi 1992.

54. Lior 2011.

55. Monterescu 2015, 303.

56. Monterescu 2015, 303.

57. Arab48 2010.

58. Kanafani 2000.

59. "What Is BDS?" 2016.

60. One does see this phrase used by Palestinians in the occupied territories as well. Tawfiq Zayyad's poetry is part of a larger national literature not specific to Palestinian citizens of Israel.

61. Wakim 2001, 33.

62. Abu-Rabia 2008.

63. Monterescu 2015.

64. "Al-Lidd / Rāje' / Haifa wa Yāfā / Rāje'."

65. Zochrot n.d.b.

66. 'Aql 2014.

67. Abu Artema 2018.

68. Abu Artema 2018.

69. Al-Jazeera News 2018.

70. Human Rights Watch 2018a.

71. Breiner 2018.

72. Nasr-Mazzawi and Al-Azza 2018. Translation mine.

73. "Laysh nuḥāṣir Ghazza laysh / Ma bikfī ḥiṣār al-jaysh?"

74. Arab48 2018.

75. Maʿan News Agency 2018.

76. "Ghazza tuwaḥidna #irfa3u_al_3aqabat."

77. Maʿan News 2018.

78. "Marra al-sulṭa, marra al-jaysh."

79. N. Al-Azza 2018. Translation mine.

80. N. Al-Azza 2018. Translation mine.

81. This is an important theme in both scholarly writing about Indigenous resistance (Estes 2019) and in popular representations, as with the iconic t-shirt or poster that declares, "Homeland Security: Fighting Terrorism since 1492," and features a photograph of Apache Chief Geronimo and three of his warriors.

82. UNRWA n.d.b.

83. UNRWA n.d.e.; Y. Berger and Khoury 2018.

84. Silverstein 1976.

85. Sorek 2015, 136. Sorek also notes that there has been a decline in the address of a Jewish Israeli audience, as signaled by a decreasing use of Hebrew in these commemorations in recent years (Sorek 2015, 86).

86. Allan 2014, 53.

Passage. Jaffa to Aida Refugee Camp

1. TOI Staff 2013.

Chapter 4

1. Wang and Burris 1997. I thank Tracy Zhang for honing my thinking around this distinction.

2. Asthana and Havandjian 2016; Hart 2007; Norman 2009; Sawhney, Yacoub, and Norman 2009.

3. Norman 2009.

4. Allen 2013.

5. Hanafi and Tabar 2005.

6. Asthana and Havandjian 2016; Norman 2009.

7. For more on how this distinction between humanitarian work and political work has been developed and contested, see I. Feldman 2018.

8. Bourdieu 1977; Hirschkind 2006.

9. Stewart 2007; Williams 1977. Stewart recognizes the resemblance between these concepts (Stewart 2007, 2–3).

10. Andén-Papadopoulos 2014, 756.

11. Westmoreland 2015, 3.

12. Butler 2015.

13. Rouch and Feld 2003, 185.

14. LeVine 2005.

15. Monterescu 2015, 8.

16. Monterescu 2015, 8.

17. UNRWA n.d.

18. Monterescu and Rabinowitz 2007.

19. Monterescu 2015, 303.

20. Monterescu 2015; Abu Shehadeh and Shbaytah 2008; Tamari and Hammami 1998. The song "Hymn to Gentrification," performed by Faraj Suleiman and with lyrics by Majd Kayyal, treats this topic and its far-reaching social consequences focusing on Haifa (Suleiman and Kayyal 2020).

21. For more on the complexity of Rachel's Tomb as a military base and a religious site, see Bowman 2013.

22. See Kanaaneh 2008 for a complex analysis of the motivations and experiences of Palestinian citizens of Israel who join the Israeli army.

23. Monterescu 2015, 299.

24. Shani and Copti 2009.

25. Refugees from Aida would not be "returning" to Jaffa, for example, because they were not from there. But on the other hand, for those in Aida, "returning" to Jaffa might hold some appeal: Jaffa had the beach and the city, while their villages were set in the mountains, away from the thrum of the city.

26. I am thinking here with Judith Butler's writing on the politics and risks involved in certain kinds of public appearances (Butler 2015).

27. A focus on process is a longstanding concern of anthropology of media, which has, for a generation or more, illuminated processes of media production (Abu-Lughod 2005; Ginsburg, Abu-Lughod, and Larkin 2002; Dornfeld 1998; Pedelty 1995).

28. Monterescu 2015, 139–40.

29. Butler 2015, 52.

30. See Monterescu 2015, 197–199 for more on Andromeda.

31. See Roth 2016 for more on this case.

32. Clarno 2017.

33. Berda 2017, 46–47.

34. After all "violent wartime noise can immunize those who become inured to it" (Daughtry 2014, 44).

35. In situations like these "when one looks, one looks quickly, tactically . . . The sounds of combat, by contrast, are more readily continuously available" (Daughtry 2014, 26).

36. Wolfe 2006.

37. Abu Shehadeh and Shbaytah 2008.

38. Williams 1977, 130–31.

39. Zani 2019, 108.

40. Kaplan 2009, 313.

41. For more on the pervasiveness of this logic of security, see Ochs 2011. In a similar vein, Audra Simpson (A. Simpson 2014) writes about Mohawk refusal of the use of the US passport—a striking refusal of what is presumed to be an unparalleled gift—and she and others conceptualize refusal as not exactly resistance; instead it is reproductive of community and a mode of restructuring political relations between people and state (McGranahan 2016).

42. Ferber 2013.

43. Coussin 2005; Livneh 2012; Maltz 2014.

44. Ferber 2013.

45. Maltz 2014.

46. Kanaaneh 2008; Robson 2010; Sa'ar 1998; Shihade 2011.

47. Monterescu 2015, 65.

48. Isaac 2010, 28.

49. Gopinath 2018. One way to think of curating is as "care-taking . . . a kind of intimate, intersubjective, interrelational obligation" (Lehrer, Milton, and Patterson 2011, 4).

50. This contrasts with a "photovoice" approach in which community-produced images might be used to send a message to policy makers, because here there was no presumption that policy makers were concerned or listening (Wang and Burris 1997). For similar reasons, this practice of taking photographs was also distinct from that you would find when a civil contract is created through photography (Azoulay 2008).

51. Rose 2009.

52. Abu Shehadeh and Shbaytah 2008.

53. Masarwa 2020; Shezaf 2018; Watad 2020.

Passage. Jerusalem to Nablus

1. Abdelhadi 2004.

2. Abu-Assad 2002.

Chapter 5

1. Bonilla and Rosa 2015; Lamont Hill 2016.

2. Abusidu 2020; 7amleh 2017.

3. Rankine 2015.

4. Byrd 2011, xv. See also Mora 2017.

5. Zia 2016.

6. Mariana Mora makes these connections powerfully in writing about the forced disappearances of forty-three peasant and Indigenous students in Mexico (Mora 2017).

7. Wolfe 2016, 5.

8. Gilmore 2007, 28.

9. Ralph 2020; Schrader 2019.

10. Zuboff 2019.

11. Barghuthy and Carmel 2019, 16.

12. Defense for Children International Palestine 2014.

13. M. Al-Azza and A. A. Bishara 2016.

14. Said 1986, 58.

15. Luna 2018, 59.

16. Jakobson 1960.

17. Stein 2017, 61.

18. Stein and Kuntsman 2015.

19. OCHA 2015a.

20. Van Esveld 2014.

21. Abu Rahma 2020.

22. Mousa 2020.

23. Salamanca 2011.

24. Malkowski 2017.

25. Abu-Manneh 2020.

26. Stein 2021.

27. I am thinking comparatively with Sami Hermez's writing on Lebanon (2017).

28. Du Bois 2014, 15.

29. For a similar case we can also look to Kashmiris and other Muslims in India (Junaid 2020b).

30. Byrd 2011; Simpson 2014.

31. Cody 2011b, 38.

32. B. Anderson 1991, 35.

33. Anderson writes of the sense of simultaneity of this ritual of reading the morning paper (B. Anderson 1991, 35).

34. Warner 2002, 113–14.

35. Aouragh 2012.

36. Warner 2002, 67.

37. Ginsburg, Abu-Lughod, and Larkin 2002.

38. Hine 2015.

39. Warner 2002, 119.

40. B. Anderson 1991; Habermas 1989.

41. Fraser 2007.

42. Du Bois 2004.

43. The concept of media worlds helps us to think about the relationship among media and the relationship between media and other social practices (Ginsburg, Abu-Lughod, and Larkin 2002).

44. Jamal 2009; Schejter 2009.

45. hooks, cited in Smith 2000, 581.

46. A. A. Bishara 2013.

47. Zayani 2007.

48. McKee 2019; Stamatopoulou-Robbins 2020.

49. For other global examples of this approach, see Jusionyte 2015; Yeh 2012.

50. J. Brown 2017b.

51. Kane 2016.

52. Adalah 2015b.

53. Addameer 2016.

54. Y. Berger and Kubovich 2018.

55. Amnesty International 2017.

56. Rosenfeld 2017.

57. J. Brown 2017b.

58. Juhasz 2015.

59. D. Goldstein 2010; Ochs 2011.

60. Social media companies like Facebook and Twitter are facing lawsuits for failing to stop attacks that killed Americans in Israel (Associated Press 2017), though experts dismissed such cases as unmeritorious. Another class action lawsuit of 20,000 Israelis filed in 2015 held that Facebook was obliged to prevent incitement from appearing on its pages (JTA 2015). Such lawfare is an intimidating weapon that supporters of Israel are increasingly using to repress dissent and stigmatize Palestinians.

61. Gostoli 2016.

62. Gostoli 2016.

63. Greenwald 2017.

64. N. Nashif 2017.

65. OHCHR 2018.

66. Greenwald 2017.

67. Yaqubi 2015.

68. Khalili 2007.

69. Allen 2006.

70. Allen 2009.

71. Aouragh 2012; Allan and Brown 2010; Stein 2012, 2021.

72. Abukhater 2012; Khamis, Gold, and Vaughn 2012.

73. Aouragh 2016; Fuchs 2012; Khamis, Gold, and Vaughn 2012.

74. Andén-Papadopoulos 2020.

75. Juhasz 2016; Fain 2016.

76. K. J. Brown 2018.

77. Mowatt 2018, 798. One key difference in contexts may be that in the United States, discussions revolve around what it means that so many people—implicitly white—are viewing Black bodies in denigrated situations, while in the West Bank Palestinians watch these videos somewhat separately from Jewish Israelis, even if they know that videos can circulate in Israel, too.

78. Butler 2004.

79. Mowatt 2018, 802.

80. B. Anderson 1991; Warner 2002.

81. Cody 2015, 61.

82. Zayani 2015, 170.

83. Said 1986, 52.

84. Said 1986, 53.

85. Herzfeld 2005.

86. Lowe 2015, 19.

87. Malkowski 2017. Foucault likewise observed that death "has ceased to be one of those spectacular ceremonies in which individuals, the family the group, and practically the whole of society took part;" death "has become, in contrast, something to be hidden away" (Foucault 2003, 247).

88. Zengin 2019.

89. Adalah 2014b.

90. A. A. Bishara and Al-Azraq 2010; C. Cook, Hanieh, and Kay 2004; Hager and Santo 2016.

91. Khoury 2014.

92. Bisharat 2014.

93. Abu Raya 2014. Translation mine.

94. Gaouette 2003.

95. Abu-Hijleh 2014. Translation mine.

96. Zonszein 2015; OCHA 2015b.

97. Ihmoud 2021.

98. Ihmoud 2019.

99. Ihmoud 2015.

100. The specific territory of neighborhoods and cities and their histories of racism, violence, and gentrification are important contexts for understanding incidents of racist violence (Lamont Hill 2016).

101. For more on these settlers, see e.g., Paz 2014.

102. J. Brown 2015.

103. This is, unfortunately, a familiar phenomenon when people feel empowered in their virulent racism, as in the case of the white men who recorded themselves shooting Ahmaud Arbery as he went on a jog in the US state of Georgia (Yankah 2021).

104. Hasson 2015.

105. Al-Azraq 2015. Translation mine.

106. A. Bishara 2001.

107. There is not one single Galilee dialect, but the use of one points to the multiplicity of Palestinian places and modes of expression.

108. Active Stills and Forensic Architecture 2017.

109. Noy 2017.

110. J. Brown 2017a.

111. J. Cook 2017.

112. Haaretz Editorial 2018.

113. I thank Thayer Hastings for suggesting I address this killing here.

Chapter 6

1. M. Al-Azza and A. A. Bishara 2016.

2. R. I. Khalidi 2014.

3. Munif 2020, 40

4. E. Nashif 2008, 52.

5. Abdo 2014.

6. Norman 2021.

7. E. Nashif 2008.

8. Bargu 2014; A. A. Bishara 2017.

9. I am inspired by feminist Indigenous studies scholarship that recognizes how settler colonial states have redefined "family" in narrow models—and fragmented Indigenous families—while Indigenous models of kin and connection are sometimes much thicker (Kauanui 2018; Povinelli 2006; Shalhoub-Kevorkian 2008).

10. Jarrar 2019, 2.

11. W. Brown 1992.

12. Khalili 2012.

13. Hernández 2017. See I. Feldman's (2019) historicization of incarceration and Palestinian dispossession and Nichols 2015.

14. My thinking about prison has been shaped by US-based conversations as well as Palestinian and other global conversations. US exploitation and incarceration of Black people over four centuries is part of a racialized system of settler colonial exploitation (Gilmore 2007; Wacquant 2001). Indigenous people experience high rates of incarceration across various settler colonies, whether due to their direct political resistance,

because settler colonial governments criminalize Indigenous lifeways, or because these governments harm Indigenous communities in ways that push them to break the law (Fisher 2016; Nichols 2015). It is crucial to see how the possibility of democracy is undermined by incarceration driven by both racism and empire (A. Y. Davis 2005).

15. Zureik 1988, 412.

16. R. I. Khalidi 2014, 5–6.

17. Korn 2003, 46.

18. Hassanein 2016.

19. Addameer 2020.

20. In contravention of the Fourth Geneva Convention, Israel moves imprisoned people into its own territory.

21. Notably, Palestinians in the West Bank have also faced increasing threats of arrest from the PA, which places different but related restrictions on expression (Hill 2016).

22. Vincent Pak thinks of the state listening subject as "a nonhuman, multi-actor entity that does not have a sole representative, but a host of state-representative actors that listen, perceive, and rearticulate on behalf of the larger state" (Pak 2021, 14).

23. A complement to this point is that in fact Israel's advocates deem non-Palestinian critique of Israel as constituting terrorism, as well, as in accusations that actions supporting the boycott, divestment, and sanctions movement are terrorism. For example, Israeli President Isaac Herzog called the decision of Ben and Jerry's ice cream not to sell in Israeli settlements of the occupied territories "a new kind of terrorism" (Serhan 2021).

24. Keane 2009; Mazzarella 2013.

25. Fanon 1965.

26. See Furani 2012 on poetry and 7amleh 2017 on social media.

27. They argued: "The criminal charge of incitement has very clear legal grounds, including that the incitement has to be clear, specific and concrete . . . Also, the law provides that conduct only constitutes incitement when there is a real and strong possibility that others will be encouraged to commit violent acts based on this speech" (Adalah 2015c).

28. Adalah 2015c.

29. Ofir 2021.

30. Jensen and Haifawi 2017. This is by no means the only case in which Islamophobic translations have led to legal and other attacks on people advocating for Palestine. Atiqa Hachimi's analysis of a prayer at first deemed to be anti-Semitic revealed that the initial translation hinged on a mistranslation of the word *danas* (profane) (Hachimi 2019).

31. Jensen and Haifawi 2017.

32. Jensen and Haifawi 2017.

33. Shpigel 2018; Ziv 2018.

34. I thank Frank Cody for helping me to think about the "eventness" of news and its effects in particular circumstances.

35. Hajjar 2005; Kelly 2006.

36. G. Brooks 2017.

37. His wife has written a fuller account of his arrest and detention (Baroud and Shalash 2019).

38. A variety of human rights organizations, social scientists, and legal scholars have addressed this policy (B'Tselem 2010; Hajjar 2005, 110; Pacheco 1989).

39. Al-Jazeera 2016.

40. Al-Jazeera 2016.

41. Ma'an News 2016.

42. Sheizaf 2011.

43. Raymond Williams' concept of structures of feeling (Williams 1977) is useful here because the feelings about imprisonment discussed here are indeed structured by Israeli political institutions and forms of violence, and they are also related to institutionalized forms of Palestinian nationalism, but they are also deeply personal, irreducible to Palestinian nationalist prizing of the heroism of imprisonment or a blunt reaction to Israeli vilification of it.

44. Adalah n.d.d.

45. While the videos include hashtags in three languages—English, Arabic, and Hebrew—the speaking in them is all in Arabic and the titling and subtitling in them is almost all in English, suggesting an audience made up of Palestinians, English-speaking people in Israel, and a global human rights audience.

46. Adalah 2015d.

47. DCI Palestine n.d.

48. (*Palestinian Children in Israeli Military Detention* 2015). I quote the English language subtitles from both of the videos, rather than presenting my own translations of the Arabic.

49. C. Cook, Hanieh, and Kay 2004; Hawari 2019; Shoughry-Badarne 2011.

50. Tate 2007, 146.

51. C. Cook, Hanieh, and Kay 2004.

52. Addameer 2019; B'Tselem and HaMoked 2017; HRW 2015; Levinson 2017.

53. Levinson 2015.

54. An ICRC survey found that 50 percent of Israelis agreed with this idea, more than in any of the sixteen countries surveyed (International Committee of the Red Cross 2016, 10).

55. I am drawing here on Ayse Parla's discussion of precarity (Parla 2019).

56. Shalhoub-Kevorkian 2019.

57. Abdo 2014; Peteet 2000.

58. Bornstein 2001; Jad 2004.

59. M. Al-Azza 2013; A. A. Bishara and Al-Azraq 2010.

60. I recognized a similar dynamic in my work on journalism during the second Intifada, when I found that Palestinian journalists from inside Israel who worked in the West Bank were often making a decision to draw closer to national politics in one of the few routes available to them at that time, while some journalists from the West Bank were in fact moving away from more direct political involvement (A. A. Bishara 2013).

61. Tartir 2017a; 2017b.

62. Shalhoub-Kevorkian 2014.

63. Jarrar 2021.

64. Masri 2015.

65. Bacha 2017.

66. For example, Suad Joseph (1994) writes about the under-analyzed brother-sister relationships in Borj Hammoud, Lebanon, as having a paradoxical dynamic of both being rooted in love and nurturing and also reinstating patriarchy. Sarah Pinto writes of how families cared for women who were confined in mental hospitals or decided to bring them home: "when things have come undone, care became—necessarily—indistinguishable from constraint" (Pinto 2014, 3). Sarah Luna (2020) writes about love relationships among sex workers, Christian missionaries, and God that exhibit both elements of care and also repression. In the Palestinian context, Lena Meari writes of the pain of maintaining and attenuating kin ties based on the pressures of being steadfast in the face of imprisonment (Meari 2014).

67. King-Irani 2008; Taraki 2006.

68. Kanaaneh 2002.

69. See for example Buntman 2003 on practices like food sharing that stood against racist categorization of prisoners in South Africa.

70. For more on such hunger strikes, see Nashif 2008 and Norman 2021.

71. Radio and television shows can be crucial means with which prisoners stay in touch with people outside of prison (Fisher 2016); however, in 2016 Israel banned this show from being seen in prisons based on a claim that the show was inciting of violence.

72. Norman 2021.

73. Jad 2004.

Conclusion

1. Shpigel and Khoury 2018; TOI Staff 2019.

2. Zonszein 2018.

3. Lowe 2015.

4. Karkabi 2020. I am also inspired by Lara Deeb and Mona Harb's writing on the sociopolitical importance of leisure (Deeb and Harb 2013).

5. Patel 2021.

6. Haifawi 2021.

7. Adalah Justice Project 2021.

8. Kingsley and Nazzal 2021.

9. A. A. Bishara 2010.

10. Antoon and Garcia-Navarro 2021.

11. A. Y. Davis 2005; Ralph 2020.

12. Paley 2008.

13. Alexander 2012; Hernández 2011. I also am inspired here in part by US Congress-woman Alexandria Ocasio-Cortez's tweeted answer to what it would mean to defund the police: "The good thing is that it actually does not take a lot of imagination. It looks like a suburb. Affluent white communities already live in a world where they choose to fund youth, health, housing etc more than they fund police. These communities have lower crime rates not because they have more police, but bc they have more resources to support healthy society in a way that reduces crime." [https://twitter.com/ashley_quan/status/1271179469382979584/photo/1 https://www.marieclaire.com/politics/a32849383/alexandria-ocasio-cortez-defund-the-police/].

14. A. Y. Davis 2016, 42, 85; Mackey 2014.

15. Gay 2015.

16. Lamont Hill 2018, 954.

17. I am inspired here by Alejandro Paz's thinking about how discourse circulates in relation to the North Atlantic's democratic empires.

18. De la Cadena 2015; Strathern 2004.

19. Palestine Legal and Center for Constitutional Rights 2015; Beinart 2021.

20. I thank J. Kēhaulani Kauanui for emphasizing this crucial point.

21. Marshood and Alsanah 2020.

Bibliography

7amleh. 2017. "Istitlāʿ Maydānī: Al-Amin al-Raqami Wa al-Shebāb al-Filastīnī" [Field Observation: Digital Security and Palestinian Youth]. Haifa: 7amleh- The Arab Centre for Social Media Advancement.

"2020 National Day of Mourning Livestream." 2021. United American Indians of New England-UAINE. 2021. http://uaine.org/.

Abbas, Mahmoud. 2011. "Statement by H. E. Mr. Mahmoud Abbas before United Nations General Assembly Sixty-Sixth Session." New York, September 23. https://gadebate.un.org/sites/default/files/gastatements/66/PS_en.pdf.

Abdelhadi, Amer. 2004. "Surviving Siege Closure, and Curfew: The Story of a Radio Station in Nablus." *Journal of Palestine Studies* 34 (1): 51–67.

Abdo, Nahla. 2014. *Captive Revolution: Palestinian Women's Anti-Colonial Struggle within the Israeli Prison System.* London: Pluto Press.

Abou Shahadeh, Sami. 2021. "'Death to Arabs': Palestinians Need International Protection from Israel's Racist Jewish Thugs | Opinion." *Haaretz*, April 26, 2021. https://www.haaretz.com/middle-east-news/.premium-death-to-arabs-palestinians-need-protection-from-israel-s-racist-jewish-thugs-1.9747860.

Abowd, Thomas Philip. 2014. *Colonial Jerusalem: The Spatial Construction of Identity and Difference in a City of Myth, 1948-2012.* Syracuse: Syracuse University Press.

Abrams, Philip. 1988. "Notes on the Difficulty of Studying the State." *Journal of Historical Sociology* 1 (1): 58–89.

Abu Artema, Ahmed. 2018. "I Helped Start the Gaza Protests. I Don't Regret It." *New York Times*, May 14, 2018, sec. Opinion. https://www.nytimes.com/2018/05/14/opinion/gaza-protests-organizer-great-return-march.html.

Abu El-Haj, Nadia. 2001. *Facts on the Ground: Archaeological Practice and Territorial Self-Fashioning in Israeli Society.* Chicago: University of Chicago Press.

Abu Hatoum, Nayrouz. 2020. "For 'A No-State Yet to Come': Palestinian Displacement and Place-Making in Jerusalem's Settler-Colonial Frontiers." *Environment and Planning E: Nature and Space*. https://doi-org.ezproxy.library.tufts.edu/10.1177/2514848 620943877.

Abu Rahma, Talal. 2020. "Behind the Lens: Remembering Muhammad al-Durrah, 20 Years on." Al-Jazeera. September 30, 2020. https://www.aljazeera.com/fea tures/2020/9/30/behind-the-lens-remembering-muhammad-al-durrah.

Abu Raya, Jihad. 2014. "08/2012: The Police Execute Hazem Abu Al-Ba'ath." Facebook. November 11, 2014.

Abu Shehadeh, Sami, and Fadi Shbaytah. 2008. "Jaffa: From Eminence to Ethnic Cleansing." *Al-Majdal*, no. 39–40 (Autumn-Winter 2009). http://www.badil.org/en/pub lication/periodicals/al-majdal/item/4-jaffa-from-eminence-to-ethnic-cleansing .html.

Abu-Assad, Hany, dir. *Ford Transit*. 2002. Amsterdam: Augustus Film.

Abu-Hijleh, Sa'ed. 2014. "Kufr Kanna." Facebook. November 8, 2014.

Abukhater, Jalal. 2012. "Hashtagging Khader Adnan: A Global Protest on Twitter." Al Akhbar English. February 20, 2012. http://english.al-akhbar.com/content/hash tagging-khader-adnan-global-protest-twitter.

Abu-Lughod, Lila. 1991. "Writing Against Culture." In *Recapturing Anthropology: Working in the Present*, edited by Richard Fox, 137–62. Santa Fe: School of American Press.

———. 2005. *Dramas of Nationhood: The Politics of Television in Egypt*. Chicago: University of Chicago Press.

———. 2020. "Imagining Palestine's Alter-Natives: Settler Colonialism and Museum Politics." *Critical Inquiry* 47 (1): 1–27. https://doi.org/10.1086/710906.

Abu-Manneh, Bashir. 2020. "Two Decades After the Second Intifada, Palestine Still Has No Partner for Peace." *Jacobin Magazine*, September 28, 2020. https://jacobinmag .com/2020/09/second-intifada-palestine-israel-occupation.

Abu-Rabia, Safa. 2008. "Between Memory and Resistance, an Identity Shaped by Space: The Case of the Naqab Arab Bedouins." *Hagar; Beer-Sheva* 8 (2): 93-119, 253.

Abusidu, Eman. 2020. "Social Media Is the Bridge to the World for Palestinian Youth." Middle East Monitor. April 11, 2020. https://www.middleeastmonitor.com/20200411 -social-media-is-the-bridge-to-the-world-for-palestinian-youth/.

Abu-Zahra, Nadia, and Adah Kay. 2013. *Unfree in Palestine: Registration, Documentation, and Movement Restriction*. London: Pluto Press.

Active Stills, and Forensic Architecture. 2017. *Visual Investigation: Police Shooting, Car Ramming at Umm El-Hiran*. Jerusalem: +972 Magazine. YouTube video. https:// www.youtube.com/watch?v=AEPMrh7TXAM.

Adalah. n.d.a. "'Nakba Law' - Amendment No. 40 to the Budgets Foundations Law." Adalah. https://www.adalah.org/en/law/view/496.

——. n.d.b. "Basic Law: The Knesset." Adalah. https://www.adalah.org/en/law/view/530.

——. n.d.c. "Protect the Protest in Palestine & Israel." GlobalGiving. Accessed July 10, 2020b. https://www.globalgiving.org/projects/protecttheprotest/.

—— n.d.d. "About Adalah." Accessed June 19, 2011. http://www.adalah.org/eng/about.php

——. 2007. "The Democratic Constitution." Adalah. https://www.adalah.org/uploads/oldfiles/Public/files/democratic_constitution-english.pdf.

——. 2013. "From Al-Araqib to Susiya." Adalah. May 14, 2013. https://www.youtube.com/watch?v=HtF3rOdSbr4&t=8s.

——. 2014a. "Adalah Demands That Israeli Academic Institutions and Employers Retract Punitive Measures Taken." Adalah. August 6, 2014. http://www.adalah.org/en/content/view/8315.

——. 2014b. "Adalah Statement on the Killing of Kheir Hamdan by Israeli Police." Adalah. September 11, 2014. https://www.adalah.org/en/content/view/8403.

——. 2015a. "Deliberate Obstacles, Not Failures: Adalah's Response to the State Comptroller's Report on the Housing Crisis in Israel." Adalah. April 28, 2015. http://www.adalah.org/en/content/view/8536.

——. 2015b. "Silencing the Opposition: Israeli Law Enforcement's Restrictions on Freedom of Expression in Israel during 'Operation Protective Edge' in Gaza." Haifa: Adalah.

——. 2015c. "10 Days after Arrest for Facebook Post: Akka Court Extends Detention of 19-Year-Old Anas Khateeb." Adalah. October 27, 2015. http://www.adalah.org/en/content/view/8673.

——. 2015d. Protect the Protest: Palestinian Child Detainees Speak. YouTube video. https://www.youtube.com/watch?v=PdtAxSQyZ4o.

——. 2017. "The Discriminatory Laws Database." Adalah. 2017. https://www.adalah.org/en/content/view/7771.

——. 2018. "Israeli Town Halts Sale of New Home Plots as More than 50% of Buyers Are Arab Citizens." Adalah. March 18, 2018. https://www.adalah.org/en/content/view/9434.

Adalah Justice Project (@adalahjustice). 2021. "The Manifesto of Dignity and Hope." Twitter. May 18, 2021. https://twitter.com/adalahjustice/status/1394658944618962948.

Addameer. 2016. "Daring to Post: Arrests of Palestinians for Alleged Incitement." Addameer. August 24, 2016. http://www.addameer.org/publications/daring-post-arrests-palestinians-alleged-incitement.

——. 2017. "Detained Palestinian Legislative Council Members." Addameer. July 25, 2017. http://www.addameer.org/publications/detained-palestinian-legislative-council-members-0.

———. 2019. "Addameer Collects Hard Evidence on Torture and Ill-Treatment Committed against Palestinian Detainees at Israeli Interrogation Centers." Addameer. December 23, 2019. http://www.addameer.org/news/addameer-collects-hard-evidence-torture-and-ill-treatment-committed-against-palestinian.

———. 2020. "Statistics." Addameer. July 2020. http://www.addameer.org/statistics.

Agamben, Giorgio. 1998. *Homo Sacer: Sovereign Power and Bare Life.* Translated by Daniel Heller-Roazen. Stanford: Stanford University Press.

Akram, Susan. 2017. "Palestinian Nationality, 'Jewish' Nationality and the Balfour Declaration." Public talk at conference, Balfour's Legacy: Confronting the Consequences, Nov. 11, 2017. Cambridge, MA.

Al-Azraq, Yasmine. 2015. "Someone Trying to Be Clever Has Claimed." Facebook. October 9, 2015.

Al-Azza, Mohammad. 2013. *Just a Child.* Documentary, 11 minutes. Bethlehem: Lajee Center. https://vimeo.com/57369678.

Al-Azza, Mohammad, and Amahl A. Bishara. 2016. *Take My Pictures for Me.* Documentary, 32 minutes. Bethlehem: Lajee Center.

Al-Azza, Nidal. 2018. "Masīrat Al-ʿAwda Nuqṭa Taḥawul Istrātījī fī Mashrūʿ Al-Taḥarur." [The March of Return Is Strategic Turning Point in the Liberation Project]. Shabkat Al-Quds Al-Ikhbāriyya. April 1, 2018. https://qudsn.net/post/144697/ مسيرة-العودة-نقطة-تحول-استراتيجي-في-مشروع-التحرر.

Al-Azza, Nidal, and Amaya Al-Orzza. 2015. "Survey of Palestinian Refugees and Internally Displaced Persons, 2013-2015." Bethlehem: Badil Resource Center for Palestinian Residency and Refugee Rights. https://www.badil.org/phocadownloadpap/badil-new/publications/survay/Survey2013-2015-en.pdf.

Al-Bulushi, Samar. 2020. "Making Sense of the East African Warscape." *POMEPS STUDIES 40 Africa and the Middle East: Beyond the Divides*: 40–43.

Al-Bulushi, Samar, Sahana Ghosh, and Madiha Tahir. 2020. "American Anthropology, Decolonization, and the Politics of Location." *American Anthropologist*, May 28, 2020. https://www.americananthropologist.org/commentaries/al-bulushi-ghosh-and-tahir.

Alexander, Michelle. 2012. *The New Jim Crow: Mass Incarceration in the Age of Colorblindness.* New York: The New Press.

Al-Haq. 2019. "Palestinian, Regional, and International Groups Submit Report on Israeli Apartheid to UN Committee on the Elimination of Racial Discrimination." Al-Haq. 2019. https://www.alhaq.org/advocacy/16183.html.

Al-Hardan, Anaheed. 2015. "Al-Nakba in Arab Thought: The Transformation of a Concept." *Comparative Studies of South Asia, Africa and the Middle East* 35 (3): 622–38. https://doi.org/10.1215/1089201x-3426457.

Al-Jazeera. 2016. "Israel Frees Palestinian Journalist Mohammed Al-Qeeq." Al-Jazeera. May 19, 2016. https://www.aljazeera.com/news/2016/05/israel-frees-palestinian -journalist-mohammed-al-qeek-160519141834952.html.

———. 2018. "Second Journalist Covering Gaza Rally Killed by Israeli Forces." April 25, 2018. https://www.aljazeera.com/news/2018/04/journalist-covering-gaza-rally-killed-israeli-forces-180425163003132.html.

———. 2021. "Israeli Far-Right Groups March through Occupied East Jerusalem." Al-Jazeera. June 16, 2021. https://www.aljazeera.com/news/2021/6/15/tensions-high -in-jerusalem-ahead-of-hardline-israeli-march.

Allan, Diana. 2014. *Refugees of the Revolution: Experiences of Palestinian Exile*. Stanford Studies in Middle Eastern and Islamic Societies and Cultures. Stanford: Stanford University Press.

———. 2016. "Watching Photos in Shatila: Visualizing Politics in the 2011 March of Return." *Visual Anthropology* 29 (3): 296–314. https://doi.org/10.1080/08949468.2016.1 154762.

———. 2018. "'This Is Not a Politics': Solidarity and Subterfuge in Palestinian Refugee Communities in Lebanon." *South Atlantic Quarterly* 117 (1): 91–110.

Allan, Diana, and Curtis Brown. 2010. "The Mavi Marmara at the Frontlines of Web 2.0." *Journal of Palestine Studies* 40 (1): 63–77.

Allen, Lori. 2006. "The Polyvalent Politics of Martyr Commemorations in the Palestinian Intifada." *History and Memory* 18 (2): 107–38.

———. 2009. "Martyr Bodies in the Media: Human Rights, Aesthetics, and the Politics of Immediation in the Palestinian Intifada." *American Ethnologist* 36 (1): 161–80.

———. 2013. *The Rise and Fall of Human Rights: Cynicism and Politics in Occupied Palestine*. Stanford: Stanford University Press.

———. 2018. "What's in a Link? Transnational Solidarities Across Palestine and Their Intersectional Possibilities." *South Atlantic Quarterly* 117 (1): 111–33.

Amara, Muhammad Hasan. 1990. *Politics and Sociolinguistic Reflexes: Palestinian Border Villages*. Amsterdam: John Benjamins Publishing Company.

Amnesty International. 2011. "State of Palestine: Alarming Attack on Freedom of Expression." London: Amnesty International. https://www.amnesty.org/download/ Documents/MDE1569832017ENGLISH.pdf.

———. 2014. "Trigger-Happy: Israel's Use of Excessive Force in the West Bank." London: Amnesty International.

———. 2017. "State of Palestine: Alarming Attack on Freedom of Expression." August 23. London: Amnesty International. https://www.amnesty.org/en/documents/mde15/ 6983/2017/en/.

————. 2019a. "Elected But Restricted: Shrinking Space for Palestinian Parliamentarians in Israel's Knesset." London: Amnesty International. https://www.amnesty.org/download/Documents/MDE1508822019ENGLISH.PDF.

————. 2019b. "Everything You Need to Know about Human Rights in Palestine." 2019. https://www.amnesty.org/en/countries/middle-east-and-north-africa/palestine-state-of/report-palestine-state-of/.

Anand, Nikhil. 2017. *Hydraulic City: Water and the Infrastructures of Citizenship in Mumbai*. Durham, NC: Duke University Press.

Andén-Papadopoulos, Kari. 2014. "Citizen Camera-Witnessing: Embodied Political Dissent in the Age of 'Mediated Mass Self-Communication.'" *New Media & Society* 16 (5): 753–69. https://doi.org/10.1177/1461444813489863.

————. 2020. "Image Activism After the Arab Uprisings | The 'Image-as-Forensic-Evidence' Economy in the Post-2011 Syrian Conflict: The Power and Constraints of Contemporary Practices of Video Activism." *International Journal of Communication* 14: 5072–5091.

Anderson, Benedict. 1991. *Imagined Communities: Reflections on the Origin and Spread of Nationalism*. New York: Verso.

Anderson, Charles W. 2013. "From Petition to Confrontation: The Palestinian National Movement and the Rise of Mass Politics, 1929–1939." Ann Arbor: MI: ProQuest Dissertations Publishing. http://search.proquest.com/docview/1468938822/?pq-origsite=primo.

————. 2021. "Other Laboratories: The Great Revolt, Civil Resistance, and the Social History of Palestine." *Journal of Palestine Studies* 50 (3): 47–51. https://doi.org/10.1080/0377919X.2021.1938483.

Anderson, Mike B., director. 1996. "Treehouse of Horror VII." *The Simpsons*, October 27, 1996, Season 8, Episode 1.

Anghie, Antony. 2006. "The Evolution of International Law: Colonial and Postcolonial Realities." *Third World Quarterly* 27 (5): 739–53.

Antoon, Sinan, and Lulu Garcia-Navarro. 2021. "Iraqi Poet Sinan Antoon Looks Back on Donald Rumsfeld's Career." NPR, July 4, 2021, sec. National. https://www.npr.org/2021/07/04/1012978311/iraqi-poet-sinan-antoon-looks-back-on-donald-rumsfelds-career.

Anzaldúa, Gloria. 1987. *Borderlands/La Frontera: The New Mestiza*. San Francisco: Spinsters/Aunt Lute.

Aouragh, Miriyam. 2012. *Palestine Online: Transnationalism, the Internet and the Construction of Identity*. New York: Bloomsbury Academic.

————. 2016. *Social Media, Mediation and the Arab Revolutions*. Leiden: Brill. https://doi.org/10.1163/9789004291393_016.

'Aql, Mohammad. 2014. "Bi-Munāsibat Masīrat Al-'Awda: Ta'ruf Ila Qariyat Lūbiya Al-Muhajira." Arab48. May 2, 2014. https://www.arab48.com/لوبيا-المهجرة-.-د.محمد-عقل فلسطينيات/النكبة:-مقالات-وبراسات-/2014/05/02/بمناسبة-مسيرة-العودة-تعرف-إلى-قرية-لوبية-

Arab48. 2010. "Taḥt Shʿār ʿAna Mish Khādimʾ: ʿAnʿaqād Muʿatamar Ḍid Makhaṭaṭ al-Khīdma al-Medinīa Yawm al-Sabt al-Qādim Fī Haifa.'" Arab48. October 31, 2010. https://www.arab48.com/حيفا-في-القادم-السبت-يوم-المدنية-الخدمة-مخطط-ضد-مؤتمر-إنعقاد
محليات/أخبار-محلية/2010/10/31, /تحت-شعار-أنا-مُش-خادم-- .

———. 2014. "Al-Lidd Is in Cohesion with Gaza in a Major Demonstration." Arab48, August 3, 2014. http://www.arab48.com/حاشدة-مظاهرة-في-غزة-مع-تلتحم-اللد/
محليات/أخبار-محلية/2014/08/03. -

———. 2018. "Irfaʿū Al-ʿuqūbāt: Al-Ālāf Yunāṣirūn Ghazza fī Rām Allah" [Lift the Sanctions: Thousands Stand with Gaza in Ramallah]. June 10, 2018. https://www .arab48.com/2018/06/10/ رام-الله-تتظاهر-ضد-الإجراءات-العقابية-على-قطاع-غزة/فلسطينيات/أخبار.

ARIJ. 2010. "Al Walaja Village Profile." Bethlehem: ARIJ, The Applied Research Institute, Jerusalem.

Askew, Kelly. 2002. *Performing the Nation: Swahili Music and Cultural Politics in Tanzania.* Chicago: University of Chicago.

Associated Press. 2017. "Lawsuits Blame Facebook and Twitter in Terror Attacks in Paris, Brussels." *Los Angeles Times*, January 19, 2017. http://www.latimes.com/business/technology/la-fi-tn-lawsuits-social-media-terror-20170119-story.html.

Asthana, Sanjay, and Nishan Havandjian. 2016. *Palestinian Youth Media and the Pedagogies of Estrangement.* New York: Palgrave Macmillan.

Atshan, Saʿed. 2020. Queer Palestine and the Empire of Critique. Stanford: Stanford University Press.

———. 2021. "The Anthropological Rise of Palestine." *Journal of Palestine Studies.* 50 (4): 3–31. https://doi.org/10.1080/0377919X.2021.1969806.

Avraham, Eli, Gadi Wolfsfeld, and Isaam Aburaiya. 2000. "Dynamics in the News Coverage of Minorities: The Case of the Arab Citizens of Israel." *Journal of Communication Inquiry* 24 (2): 117–33.

Awayed-Bishara, Muzna. 2020. *EFL Pedagogy as Cultural Discourse: Textbooks, Practice, and Policy for Arabs and Jews in Israel.* London: Routledge.

Azoulay, Ariella. 2008. *The Civil Contract of Photography.* New York: Zone Books.

Azoulay, Ariella, and Adi Ophir. 2013. *The One-State Condition: Occupation and Democracy in Israel/Palestine.* Stanford: Stanford University Press.

Bacha, Julia, dir. *Naila and the Uprising.* 2017. Washington, D.C.: Just Vision. Documentary, 76 minutes.

Bachelard, Gaston. 1994. *The Poetics of Space.* Boston: Beacon Press.

Badil. 2013. "Toward a Prognosis: Diagnosing Fragmentation and Problems of Representation in Palestinian Politics." *Al-Majdal*, no. 52 (Spring).

Bahloul, Joëlle. 1996. *The Architecture of Memory: A Jewish-Muslim Household in Colonial Algeria 1937-1962* [La Maison de Mémoire]. Translated by Catherine Du Peloux Ménagé. Cambridge: University of Cambridge Press.

Bakhtin, Mikhail M. 1981. *The Dialogic Imagination*. Austin: University of Texas Press.

Balad. 2017. "Principles of Al-Tajamuʻa [Mabādiʾ Al-Tajamuʻ]." Al-Tajamoa Website. April 1, 2017. http://www.altajamoa.org/التجمع-مبادئ / 2017/04/01/مؤسسة-نصوص.

Bandel, Netael. 2021. "Israel's Top Court Rules the Nation-State Law Is Constitutional, Denies Petitions against It." *Haaretz*, July 8, 2021. https://www.haaretz.com/israel -news/.premium-high-court-rules-nation-state-law-is-constitutional-denies-peti tions-against-it-1.9982856.

Banko, Lauren. 2012. "The Creation of Palestinian Citizenship Under an International Mandate: Legislation, Discourses, and Practices, 1918-1925." *Citizenship Studies* 16 (5–6): 641–55. https://doi.org/10.1080/13621025.2012.698487.

———. 2016. "Citizenship Rights and the Semantics of Colonial Power and Resistance: Haifa, Jaffa, and Nablus, 1931-1933." In *Violence and the City in the Modern Middle East*, 75–94. Stanford: Stanford University Press.

Bardawil, Fadi A. 2020. *Revolution and Disenchantment: Arab Marxism and the Binds of Emancipation*. Durham, NC: Duke University Press.

Bardenstein, Carol B. 2000. "Trees, Forests, and the Shaping of Palestinian and Is- raeli Collective Memory." In *Acts of Memory: Cultural Recall in the Present*, ed- ited by Mieke Bal, Jonathan Crewe, and Leo Spitzer, 148–68. Hanover: Dartmouth College.

Barghuthy, Eyad, and Alison Carmel. 2019. "Silenced Networks: The Chilling Effect among Palestinian Youth in Social Media." 7amleh—The Arab Centre for Social Media Advancement.

Bargu, Banu. 2014. *Starve and Immolate: The Politics of Human Weapons*. New York: Columbia University Press.

Baroud, Ramzy, and Fayha Shalash. 2019. "A Palestinian Hunger Strike: 'Bury Me in My Mother's Grave.'" Al-Jazeera. April 23, 2019. https://www.aljazeera.com/opin ions/2019/4/23/a-palestinian-hunger-strike-bury-me-in-my-mothers-grave.

Basso, Keith. 1996. *Wisdom Sits in Places: Landscape and Language among the Western Apache*. Albuquerque: University of New Mexico Press.

Baumgarten-Sharon, Naama. 2010. "The Right to Demonstrate in the Occupied Ter- ritories." B'Tselem. https://www.btselem.org/download/20100715_right_to_demo nstrate_eng.pdf.

Bäuml, Yair. 2017. "Israel's Military Rule over Its Palestinian Citizens (1948-1968): Shap- ing the Israeli Segregation System." In *Israel and Its Palestinian Citizens: Ethnic Privi- leges in the Jewish State*, edited by Rouhana, Nadim N. and Sahar S. Huneidi, 103–36. Cambridge: Cambridge University Press.

Bayoumi, Moustafa. 2008. *How Does It Feel to Be a Problem? Being Young and Arab in America*. New York: Penguin Press.

Beck, Kurt, Gabriel Klaeger, and Michael Stasik. 2017. *The Making of the African Road.* Leiden: Brill.

Beinart, Peter. 2021. "It's Time to Name Anti-Palestinian Bigotry." *Jewish Currents* (blog). July 16, 2021. https://jewishcurrents.org/its-time-to-name-anti-palestinian -bigotry/.

Beliso-De Jesús, Aisha M., and Jemima Pierre. 2020. "Anthropology of White Suprem- acy." *American Anthropologist* 122 (1): 65–75. https://doi.org/10.1111/aman.13351.

Benvenisti, Meron. 2000. *Sacred Landscape: The Buried History of the Holy Land Since 1948.* Berkeley: University of California Press.

Berda, Yael. 2017. *Living Emergency: Israel's Permit Regime in the Occupied West Bank.* Stanford: Stanford University Press.

Berger, Miriam. 2019. "Palestinian in Israel." *Foreign Policy* (blog). 2019. https:// foreignpolicy.com/2019/01/18/palestinian-in-israel/.

Berger, Yotam, and Jack Khoury. 2018. "How Many Palestinians Live in Gaza and the West Bank? It's Complicated." *Haaretz*, March 28, 2018. https://www.haaretz.com/ israel-news/how-many-palestinians-live-in-gaza-and-the-west-bank-it-s-com plicated-1.5956630?utm_campaign=newsletter-daily&utm_medium=email&utm _source=smartfocus&utm_content=https%3A%2F%2Fwww.haaretz.com%2Fisrael -news%2Fhow-many-palestinians-live-in-gaza-and-the-west-bank-it-s-compli cated-1.5956630.

Berger, Yotam, and Yaniv Kubovich. 2018. "Ahed Tamimi, Palestinian Teen Who Slapped Israeli Soldier in Video, Charged With Assault." *Haaretz*, January 1, 2018. https:// www.haaretz.com/israel-news/1.832424.

Berman, Lazar, and Times of Israel staff. 2014. "Palestinians Charged with Incitement over Facebook Posts." *Times of Israel.* December 22, 2014. http://www.timesofisrael .com/palestinians-charged-with-incitement-over-facebook-posts/.

Bernal, Victoria. 2014. *Nation as Network: Diaspora, Cyberspace, and Citizenship.* Chi- cago: University of Chicago Press.

Berry, Maya, Claudia Chávez Argüelles, Shanya Cordis, Sarah Ihmoud, and Elizabeth Velásquez Estrada. 2017. "Toward a Fugitive Anthropology: Gender, Race, and Vio- lence in the Field." *Cultural Anthropology* 32 (4): 537–65.

Bhabha, Homi K. 1983. "Of Mimicry and Man: The Ambivalence of Colonial Discourse." *October* 28 (Spring): 125–33. https://doi.org/10.2307/778467.

Bhandar, Brenna, and Rafeef Ziadah. 2016. "Acts and Omissions: Framing Settler Colonialism in Palestine Studies." *Jadaliyya.* January 14, 2016. http://www.jadali yya.com/Details/32857/Acts-and-Omissions-Framing-Settler-Colonialism-in -Palestine-Studies.

Bishara, Amahl A. 2010. "Weapons, Passports, and News: Palestinian Perceptions of U.S. Power as a Mediator of War." In *Anthropology and Global Counterinsurgency*, edited by John Kelly, Beatrice Jauregui, Sean T. Mitchell, and Jeremy Walton, 125–36. Chicago: University of Chicago Press.

———. 2013. *Back Stories: U.S. News Production and Palestinian Politics*. Stanford: Stanford University Press.

———. 2015. "Driving While Palestinian in Israel and the West Bank: The Politics of Disorientation and the Routes of a Subaltern Knowledge." *American Ethnologist* 42 (1): 33–54.

———. 2017. "Sovereignty and Popular Sovereignty for Palestinians and Beyond." *Cultural Anthropology* 32 (3): 349–58. https://doi.org/10.14506/ca32.3.04.

———. 2020. "An Ongoing Violence, a Sustained Resistance: Israel's Racist Separation Wall at Aida Refugee Camp." In *Walling In and Walling Out: Why Are We Building New Barriers to Divide Us?*, edited by Laura McAtackney and Randall H. McGuire, 85–107. New Mexico: University of New Mexico Press.

Bishara, Amahl A., and Nidal Al-Azraq, directors. *Degrees of Incarceration*. 2010. Documentary, 32 minutes. https://vimeo.com/514413925.

Bishara, Azmi. 1997. "Bridging the Green Line: The PA, Israeli Arabs, and Final Status. An Interview with ʿAzmi Bishara." *Journal of Palestine Studies* 26 (3): 67–80. https://doi.org/10.2307/2538158.

———. 2001. "Reflections on October 2000: A Landmark in Jewish-Arab Relations in Israel." *Journal of Palestine Studies* 30 (3): 54–67. https://doi.org/10.1525/jps.2001.30.3.54.

Bishara, Suhad. 2015. "Returning to the Days of Military Rule in Israel." Al-Jazeera. December 24, 2015. https://www.aljazeera.com/indepth/opinion/2015/12/returning-days-military-rule-israel-151223131305852.html.

———. 2016. "Discourse and Dispossession." *The Nakba Files* (blog). June 15, 2016. https://nakbafiles.org/2016/06/15/discourse-and-dispossession/.

———. 2018. "Distorting Awareness and Dispelling Historical Conflict Indigenous Framework and the Palestinians." *The Nakba Files* (blog). November 12, 2018. https://nakbafiles.org/2018/11/12/distorting-awareness-and-dispelling-historical-conflict-indigenous-framework-and-the-palestinians/.

Bisharat, Odeh. 2014. "If You're an Arab, They Shoot First." *Haaretz*, November 10, 2014. https://www.haaretz.com/opinion/.premium-if-you-re-an-arab-they-shoot-first-1.5326341.

Black for Palestine. 2015. "2015 Black Solidarity Statement with Palestine." Black for Palestine. 2015. http://www.blackforpalestine.com/.

Black-Palestinian Solidarity. 2015. "When I See Them I See Us." *Washington Post*. October 14, 2015. https://www.washingtonpost.com/video/world/when-i-see-them-i-see-us/2015/10/15/c8f8aa40-72c2-11e5-ba14-318f8e87a2fc_video.html.

Bonilla, Yarimar. 2015. *Non-Sovereign Futures: Politics in the Wake of Disenchantment*. Chicago: University of Chicago Press.

———. 2017. "Unsettling Sovereignty." *Cultural Anthropology* 32 (3): 330–39.

Bonilla, Yarimar (@yarimarbonilla). 2019. "Dear allies: when feeling the need to assert that Puerto Ricans are 'fellow US citizens.'" Twitter. July 29, 2019. https://twitter .com/yarimarbonilla/status/1155854246195150848?lang=en.

Bonilla, Yarimar, and Jonathan Rosa. 2015. "#Ferguson: Digital Protest, Hashtag Ethnography, and the Racial Politics of Social Media in the United States." *American Ethnologist* 42 (1): 4–17.

Bornstein, Avram S. 2001. "Ethnography and the Politics of Prisoners in Palestine-Israel." *Journal of Contemporary Ethnography* 30 (5): 546–74.

———. 2002. *Crossing the Green Line between Palestine and Israel.* Philadelphia: University of Pennsylvania Press.

Bourdieu, Pierre. 1977. *Outline of a Theory of Practice.* Cambridge: Cambridge University Press.

———. 1993. *The Field of Cultural Production.* New York: Columbia University Press.

Bowman, Glenn. 2000. "Two Deaths of Basem Rishmawi: Identity Constructions and Reconstructions in a Muslim-Christian Palestinian Community." In *Perplexities of Identification: Anthropological Studies in Cultural Differentiation and the Use of Resources,* edited by Henk Driessen and Ton Otto, 56–94. Aarhus: Aarhus University Press.

———. 2013. "A Weeping on the Road to Bethlehem: Contestation over the Uses of Rachel's Tomb." *Religion Compass* 7 (3): 79–92.

Boym, Svetlana. 1998. "On Diasporic Intimacy: Ilya Kabakov's Installations and Immigrant Homes." *Critical Inquiry* 24 (2): 498–524.

Braverman, Irus. 2019. "Nof Kdumim: Remaking the Ancient Landscape in East Jerusalem's National Parks." *Environment and Planning E: Nature and Space.* https://doi .org/10.1177/2514848619889594.

Breiner, Josh. 2018. "Attorney Says Policeman Struck, Humiliated Rights Activist Arrested in Haifa Protest." *Haaretz,* May 24, 2018. https://www.haaretz.com/israel -news/.premium-attorney-police-struck-humiliated-activist-arrested-in-haifa-pro test-1.6115987.

Brooks, Geraldine. 2017. "The Dovekeeper and the Children's Intifada." *The New Yorker.* May 27, 2017. https://www.newyorker.com/books/page-turner/the-dove keeper-and-the-childrens-intifada.

Brooks, Lisa. 2018. *Our Beloved Kin: A New History of King Philip's War.* New Haven and London: Yale University Press.

Brooks, Lisa, and Cassandra Brooks. 2010. "The Reciprocity Principle and Traditional Ecological Knowledge: Understanding the Significance of Indigenous Protest on the Presumpscot River." *International Journal of Critical Indigenous Studies.* June 1, 2010. https://doi.org/10.5204/ijcis.v3i2.49.

Brown, John. 2015. "New Video Shows Accused Stabber Posed No Threat When Shot." +972 Magazine. October 10, 2015. http://972mag.com/new-video-shows-accused -stabber-posed-no-threat-when-shot/112593/.

———. 2017a. "Video Contradicts More Police Claims in Umm El-Hiran Killing." +972 Magazine. February 1, 2017. https://972mag.com/video-contradicts-more-police -claims-in-umm-el-hiran-killing/124950/.

———. 2017b. "Arrest of Palestinians for Potential Terror Attacks Brings New Meaning to 'Minority Report.'" *Haaretz*, April 24, 2017. http://www.haaretz.com/opinion/. premium-1.785470.

Brown, Kimberly Juanita. 2018. "Mortevivum: Black Photography and Politics of the Visual." Public talk. Center for the Humanities at Tufts. January 24.

Brown, Wendy. 1992. "Finding the Man in the State." *Feminist Studies* 18 (1): 7–34.

Browne, Brendan. 2013. "Commemoration in Conflict Comparing the Generation of Solidarity at the 1916 Easter Rising Commemorations in Belfast Northern Ireland and the 1948 'Nakba' Commemorations in Ramallah, Palestine." *Journal of Comparative Research in Anthropology and Sociology* 4 (2): 143–63.

B'Tselem. n.d.a. "Area C." Accessed April 26, 2018. http://www.btselem.org/topic/area_c.

———. n.d.b. "Refaʾim Stream National Park." Accessed July 19, 2019. https://www.bt selem.org/jerusalem/national_parks_refaim_stream.

———. 2010. "Statistics on Administrative Detention." B'Tselem. 2010. http://www.bt-selem.org/english/Administrative_Detention/Statistics.asp.

———. 2011. "Route 443 – West Bank Road for Israelis Only." B'Tselem. January 1, 2011. https://www.btselem.org/freedom_of_movement/road_443.

———. 2017. "The Separation Barrier." B'Tselem. November 11, 2017. https://www.bt selem.org/separation_barrier.

———. 2018. "With No Cause or End in Sight: Administrative Detention a Routine Matter." B'Tselem. 2018. https://www.btselem.org/administrative_detention/20180730 _no_case_and_no_end_in_sight.

———. 2020. "Statistics on Palestinians in the Custody of the Israeli Security Forces." B'Tselem. June 30, 2020. https://www.btselem.org/statistics/detainees _and_prisoners.

———. 2021. "A Regime of Jewish Supremacy from the Jordan River to the Mediterranean Sea: This Is Apartheid." B'Tselem. January 2021. https://www.btselem.org/ publications/fulltext/202101_this_is_apartheid.

B'Tselem, and HaMoked. 2017. "Unprotected: Detention of Palestinian Teenagers in East Jerusalem." Jerusalem: B'Tselem and HaMoked. https://www.btselem.org/ publications/summaries/201710_unprotected.

Buntman, Fran Lisa. 2003. *Robben Island and Prisoner Resistance to Apartheid*. Cambridge: Cambridge University Press.

Burton, Guy. 2015a. "Beyond Fragmentation: The Ties That Bind Palestinians in the 1967 and 1948 Territories." In *Critical Readings of Development Under Colonialism*, 87–134. Palestine: Rosa Luxemburg Stiftung Regional Office Palestine, Center for Development Studies, Birzeit University.

———. 2017. "Building Ties Across the Green Line: The Palestinian 15 March Youth Movement in Israel and Occupied Palestinian Territory in 2011." *Third World Quarterly* 38 (1): 169–184. https://doi.org/10.1080/01436597.2015.1135398.

Busailah, Reja-e. 1981. "The Fall of Lydda, 1948: Impressions and Reminiscences." *Arab Studies Quarterly* 3 (2): 123–51.

Butler, Judith. 2004. *Precarious Life: The Powers of Mourning and Violence*. London: Verso.

———. 2011. "Bodies in Alliance and the Politics of the Street." European Institute for Progressive Cultural Policies. September 2011. http://www.eipcp.net/transversal/1011/butler/en.

———. 2015. *Notes Toward a Performative Theory of Assembly*. Cambridge, MA: Harvard University Press.

Buttu, Diana. 2014a. "Behind Israel's Demand for Recognition as a Jewish State." *Journal of Palestine Studies* 43 (3): 42–45. https://doi.org/10.1525/jps.2014.43.3.42.

———. 2014b. "Blaming the Victims." *Journal of Palestine Studies* 44 (1): 91–96. https://doi.org/10.1525/jps.2014.44.1.91.

———. 2019. "The Oslo Agreements—What Happened?" In *From the River to the Sea: Palestine and Israel in the Shadow of "Peace,"* edited by Mandy Turner, 17–40. Lanham, MD: Rowman & Littlefield.

Byrd, Jodi A. 2011. *The Transit of Empire: Indigenous Critiques of Colonialism*. Minneapolis: University of Minnesota Press.

Casumbal-Salazar, Iokepa. 2017. "A Fictive Kinship: Making 'Modernity,' 'Ancient Hawaiians,' and the Telescopes on Mauna Kea." *Native American and Indigenous Studies* 4 (2): 1–30. https://doi.org/10.5749/natiindistudj.4.2.0001.

Cattelino, Jessica. 2008. *High Stakes: Florida Seminole Gaming and Sovereignty*. Durham, NC: Duke University Press.

Chu, Julie Y. 2010. *Cosmologies of Credit: Transnational Mobility and the Politics of Destination*. Durham, NC: Duke University Press.

———. 2014. "When Infrastructures Attack: The Workings of Disrepair in China." *American Ethnologist* 41 (2): 351–67. https://doi.org/10.1111/amet.12080chut.

Clarno, Andy. 2017. *Neoliberal Apartheid: Palestine/Israel and South Africa after 1994*. Chicago: University of Chicago Press.

Cody, Francis. 2011a. "Echoes of the Teashop in a Tamil Newspaper." *Language and Communication* 31: 243–54. https://doi.org/10.1016/j.langcom.2011.02.005.

———. 2011b. "Publics and Politics." *Annual Review of Anthropology* 40: 37–52.

———. 2015. "Populist Publics: Print Capitalism and Crowd Violence beyond Liberal Frameworks." *Comparative Studies of South Asia, Africa and the Middle East* 35 (1): 50–65.

Colla, Elliott. 2013. "In Praise of Insult: Slogan Genres, Slogan Repertoires and Innovation." *Review of Middle East Studies* 47 (1): 37–48.

Connerton, Paul. 1989. *How Societies Remember*. Cambridge: Cambridge University Press.

Cook, Catherine, Adam Hanieh, and Adah Kay. 2004. *Stolen Youth: The Politics of Israel's Detention of Palestinian Children*. London: Sterling Press.

Cook, Jonathan. 2017. "Police Lied to Me over Umm Al-Hiran Deaths." *Jonathan Cook's Blog*. February 2, 2017. https://www.jonathan-cook.net/blog/2017-02-02/police-lied-to-me-over-umm-al-hiran-deaths/.

———. 2020. "Gantz Fears Something More than Coronavirus or Netanyahu: Palestinians." Middle East Eye. April 1, 2020. http://www.middleeasteye.net/opinion/israels-no-arabs-consensus-restored-gantz-joins-netanyahu-government.

Coussin, Orna. 2005. "Waging War Against The McDonald's of Books." *Haaretz*. April 8, 2005. http://www.haaretz.com/waging-war-against-the-mcdonald-s-of-books-1.155468.

CPJ. 1988. *Journalism Under Occupation: Israel's Regulation of the Palestinian Press*. New York: Committee to Protect Journalists.

Dabashi, Hamid. 2006. "In Praise of Frivolity: On the Cinema of Elia Suleiman." In *Dreams of a Nation: On Palestinian Cinema*, edited by Hamid Dabashi, 131–60. New York: Verso.

Dabashi, Hamid, ed. 2006. *Dreams of a Nation: On Palestinian Cinema*. New York: Verso.

Dalakoglou, Dimitris. 2010. "The Road: An Ethnography of the Albanian-Greek Cross-Border Motorway." *American Ethnologist* 37 (1): 132–49. https://doi.org/10.1111/j.1548-1425.2010.01246.x.

Darwish, Mahmoud. 2007. "On This Earth." In *Subjective Atlas of Palestine*, by Annelys de Vet, 10–11. Rotterdam: 010 Publishers.

———. 2009. *Almond Blossoms and Beyond*. Northampton, MA: Interlink Books.

Daughtry, J. Martin. 2014. "Thanatosonics: Ontologies of Acoustic Violence." *Social Text* 32 (2): 25–51. https://doi.org/10.1215/01642472-2419546.

Davis, Angela Y. 2005. *Abolition Democracy: Beyond Empire, Prisons, and Torture*. New York: Seven Stories Press.

———. 2016. *Freedom Is a Constant Struggle: Ferguson, Palestine, and the Foundations of a Movement*. Chicago: Haymarket Books.

Davis, Rochelle. 2011. *Palestinian Village Histories: Geographies of the Displaced*. Stanford: Stanford University Press.

De la Cadena, Marisol. 2015. *Earth Beings: Ecologies of Practice across Andean Worlds*. Durham: Duke University Press.

De Certeau, Michel. 1984. *The Practices of Everyday Life*. Berkeley: University of California.

De Cesari, Chiara. 2019. *Heritage and the Cultural Struggle for Palestine*. Stanford: Stanford University Press.

De León, Jason. 2015. *The Land of Open Graves: Living and Dying on the Migrant Trail*. Oakland: University of California Press.

Deeb, Lara, and Mona Harb. 2013. *Leisurely Islam: Negotiating Geography and Morality in Shiʿite South Beirut*. Princeton: Princeton University Press.

Deeb, Lara, and Jessica Winegar. 2016. *Anthropology's Politics: Disciplining the Middle East*. Stanford: Stanford University Press.

Defense for Children International Palestine. n.d. "Who We Are." Defense for Children Palestine. Accessed December 16, 2020. https://www.dci-palestine.org/who_we_are.

———. 2014. *Unlawful Killing of Two Palestinian Teens Outside Ofer*. YouTube video. https://www.youtube.com/watch?v=CaibEqx2m_k.

———. 2017. *Palestinian Children in Israeli Military Detention*. YouTube video. https://www.youtube.com/watch?v=g8RhyAqTS5I&t=24s.

Diaz-Barriga, Miguel, and Margaret E. Dorsey. 2020. *Fencing in Democracy: Border Walls, Necrocitizenship, and the Security State*. Durham, NC: Duke University Press.

Dornfeld, Barry. 1998. *Producing Public Television, Producing Public Culture*. Princeton: Princeton University Press.

Dorsey, Margaret, and Miguel Díaz-Barriga. 2015. "The Constitution Free Zone in the United States: Law and Life in a State of Carcelment." *Political and Legal Anthropology Review* 38 (2): 204–25. https://doi.org/10.1111/plar.12107.

Doumani, Beshara. 1995. *Rediscovering Palestine: Merchants and Peasants in Jabal Nablus*. Berkeley: University of California Press.

———. 2007. "Palestine Versus the Palestinians? The Iron Laws and Ironies of a People Denied." *Journal of Palestine Studies*, 36 (4): 49-64, https://doi.org/10.1525/jps.2007.36.4.49.

Dowell, Kristin L. 2013. *Sovereign Screens: Aboriginal Media on the Canadian West Coast*. Lincoln: University of Nebraska Press.

Du Bois, W. E. B. 2004. *The Souls of Black Folk*. Boulder, CO: Paradigm Publishers.

———. 2014. *The World and Africa and Color and Democracy*. Oxford: Oxford University Press.

Donya Al-Watan. 2020. "Facebook Page for Donia Al-Watan." Facebook. July 8, 2020. https://www.facebook.com/alwatanvoice/.

Eghbariah, Rabea. 2021. "Jewishness as Property under Israeli Law." LPE Project. July 9, 2021. https://lpeproject.org/blog/jewishness-as-property-under-israeli-law/.

Eghbariah, Rabea, Cher Asad, and Lena Mansour. 2021. "Palestine In Between, Episode 2." Center for Palestine Studies | Columbia University. 2021. http://palestine.mei.columbia.edu/events-spring-2021/criminalfoodspodcast.

El Kurd, Dana. 2020. *Polarized and Demobilized: Legacies of Authoritarianism in Palestine*. Oxford: Oxford University Press.

Englund, Harri. 2006. *Prisoners of Freedom: Human Rights and the African Poor*. Berkeley: University of California Press.

Erakat, Noura. 2011. "It's Not Wrong, It's Illegal: Situating the Gaza Blockade between International Law and the UN Response." *UCLA Journal of Islamic and Near Eastern Law* 11: 37–84.

———. 2019. *Justice for Some: Law and the Question of Palestine*. Stanford: Stanford University Press.

Estes, Nick. 2019. *Our History Is the Future: Standing Rock versus the Dakota Access Pipeline, and the Long Tradition of Indigenous Resistance*. London: Verso.

Fain, Kimberly. 2016. "Viral Black Death: Why We Must Watch Citizen Videos of Police Violence." *JSTOR Daily* (blog). September 1, 2016. https://daily.jstor.org/why-we-must-watch-citizen-videos-of-police-violence/.

Falah, Ghazi. 1991. "Israeli 'Judaization' Policy in Galilee." *Journal of Palestine Studies* 20 (4): 69–85.

Falk, Richard, and Virginia Tilley. 2017a. "Israeli Practices towards the Palestinian People and the Question of Apartheid." *Palestine - Israel Journal of Politics, Economics, and Culture* 22 (2/3): 191–96.

———. 2017b. "Open Letter to UN Ambassador Nikki Haley on Our Report on Apartheid in Israel." *The Nation*, April 25, 2017. https://www.thenation.com/article/open-letter-to-un-ambassador-nikki-haley-on-our-report-on-apartheid-in-israel/.

Fanon, Frantz. 1965. *The Wretched of the Earth*. New York: Grove Press.

Farsakh, Leila. 2005. *Palestinian Labour Migration to Israel: Labour, Land and Occupation*. London: Routledge.

———. 2017. "The 'Right to Have Rights': Partition and Palestinian Self-Determination." *Journal of Palestine Studies* 47 (1): 56–68. https://doi.org/10.1525/jps.2017.47.1.56.

———, ed. 2021. Rethinking Statehood in Palestine: Self-Determination and Decolonization Beyond Partition. California: University of California Press. DOI: https://doi.org/10.1525/luminos.113

Feld, Steven. 1982. *Sound and Sentiment: Birds, Weeping, Poetics, and Song in Kaluli Expression*. Philadelphia: University of Pennsylvania Press.

———. 1989. "Aesthetics as Iconicity of Style, or 'Lift-Up-Over Sounding': Getting into the Kaluli Groove." *Yearbook for Traditional Music* 20: 74–113.

———. 1996. "Waterfalls of Song: An Acoustemology of Place Resounding in Bosavi, Papua New Guinea." In *Senses of Place*, edited by Keith Basso and Steven Feld, 91–136. Santa Fe: School of American Research Press.

Feld, Steven, and Keith Basso, eds. 1996. *Senses of Place*. Santa Fe: School of American Research Press.

Feldman, Allen. 1991. *Formations of Violence: The Narrative of the Body and Political Terror in Northern Ireland*. Chicago: University of Chicago Press.

Feldman, Ilana. 2008. *Governing Gaza: Bureaucracy, Authority and the Work of Rule, 1917-1967*. Durham, NC: Duke University Press.

———. 2018. *Life Lived in Relief: Humanitarian Predicaments and Palestinian Refugee Politics*. Berkeley: University of California.

———. 2019. "Elimination Politics: Punishment and Imprisonment in Palestine." *Public Culture* 31 (3): 563–580.

Feldman, Keith P. 2015. *Shadow over Palestine: The Imperial Life of Race in America*. Minneapolis: University of Minnesota Press.

Ferber, Alona. 2013. "At a Jaffa Bookstore-Cafe, Writing the Story of Co-Existence." *Haaretz*, April 17, 2013. http://www.haaretz.com/israel-news/culture/leisure/at-a -jaffa-bookstore-cafe-writing-the-story-of-co-existence.premium-1.515980.

Firro, Kais M. 2001. "Reshaping Druze Particularism in Israel." *Journal of Palestine Studies* 30 (3): 40–53.

First Palestinian Conference. 1964. "Palestine National Charter." Permanent Observer Mission of Palestine to the United Nations. 1964. https://web.archive.org/ web/20101130144018/http://www.un.int/wcm/content/site/palestine/pid/12363.

Fischbach, Michael. 2018. *Black Power and Palestine*. Stanford: Stanford University Press.

Fisher, Daniel. 2016. *The Voice and Its Doubles: Media and Music in Northern Australia*. Durham, NC: Duke University Press.

Foucault, Michel. 1975. *Discipline and Punish: The Birth of the Prison*. New York: Vintage.

———. 1991. "Governmentality." In *The Foucault Effect: Studies in Governmentality*, edited by Graham Burchell, Colin Gordon, and Peter Miller, 87–104. Chicago: University of Chicago.

———. 2003. *Society Must Be Defended*. New York: Picador.

Francis, Sahar. 2014. "Status of Palestinian Prisoners in International Humanitarian Law." *Journal of Palestine Studies* 43 (4): 39–48. https://doi.org/10.1525/jps.2014.43.4.39.

Fraser, Nancy. 2007. "Transnationalizing the Public Sphere: On the Legitimacy and Efficacy of Public Opinion in a Post-Westphalian World." In *Identities, Affiliations, and Allegiances*, edited by Seyla Benhabib, Ian Shapira, and Danilo Petranovic, 45–66. Cambridge: Cambridge University Press.

Freedom House. 2021. "Israel: Freedom in the World 2021 Country Report." https:// freedomhouse.org/country/israel/freedom-world/2021.

Friedman, Robert I. 1983. "Israeli Censorship of the Palestinian Press." *Journal of Palestine Studies* 13 (1): 93–101.

Fuchs, Christian. 2012. "Social Media, Riots, and Revolutions." *Capital & Class* 36 (3): 383–91. https://doi.org/10.1177/0309816812453613.

Furani, Khaled. 2012. *Silencing the Sea: Secular Rhythms in Palestinian Poetry*. Stanford: Stanford University Press.

Furani, Khaled and Dan Rabinowitz. 2011. "The Ethnographic Arriving of Palestine." *Annual Review of Anthropology*. 40: 475–491. https://doi.org/10.1146/annurev-anthro -081309-145910.

Gabiam, Nell. 2016. *The Politics of Suffering: Syria's Palestinian Refugee Camps*. Bloomington: Indiana University Press.

———. 2018. "Mapping Palestinian Identity in the Diaspora: Affective Attachments and Political Spaces." *South Atlantic Quarterly* 117 (1): 65–90. https://doi.org/10.1215/00382876-4282046.

Gal, Susan, and Judith T. Irvine. 2000. "Language Ideology and Linguistic Differentiation." In *Regimes of Language: Ideologies, Polities, and Identities*, edited by Paul V. Kroskrity, 35–83. Santa Fe, NM: School of American Research Press.

Gaouette, Nicole. 2003. "Attention Builds over a Slain Civilian." *Christian Science Monitor*, January 10, 2003. https://www.csmonitor.com/2003/0110/p01s04-wome.html.

Gay, Ross. 2015. "A Small Needful Fact." Text. Poets.Org. 2015. https://poets.org/poem/small-needful-fact.

Ghanem, As'ad. 2001. *The Palestinian-Arab Minority in Israel, 1948-2000*. Stonybrook: State University of New York Press.

———. 2002. "The Palestinians in Israel: Political Orientation and Aspirations." *International Journal of Intercultural Relations* 26 (2): 135–52.

Ghanem, As'ad, and Mohanad Mustafa. 2009. "Coping with the Nakba: The Palestinians in Israel and the 'Future Vision' as a Collective Agenda." *Israel Studies Review* 24 (2): 52–66. https://doi.org/10.3167/isf.2009.240203.

Ghanim, Honaida. 2011. "The Nakba." In *The Palestinians in Israel: Readings in History, Politics, and Society*, edited by Nadim N. Rouhana and Areej Sabbagh-Khoury, 16–25. Haifa: Mada al-Carmel.

Ghosh, Sahana. 2019. "Security Socialities: Gender, Surveillance, and Civil-Military Relations in India's Eastern Borderlands." *Comparative Studies of South Asia, Africa and the Middle East* 39 (3): 439–450. https://doi.org/10.1215/1089201X-7885389.

Gilmore, Ruth Wilson. 2007. *Golden Gulag: Prisons, Surplus, Crisis, and Opposition in Globalizing California*. Berkeley: University of California Press.

Gilroy, Paul. 2001. "Driving While Black." In *Car Cultures*, edited by Daniel Miller, 81–104. Oxford: Berg.

Gingrich, Andre, and Richard Fox, eds. 2002. *Anthropology, By Comparison*. London: Routledge.

Ginsburg, Faye, Lila Abu-Lughod, and Brian Larkin, eds. 2002. *Media Worlds: Anthropology on New Terrain*. Berkeley: University of California Press.

Glass, Aaron. 2008. "Crests on Cotton: 'Souvenir' T-Shirts and the Materiality of Remembrance Among the Kwakwaka'wakw of British Columbia." *Museum Anthropology* 31 (1): 1–18. https://doi.org/10.1111/j.1548-1379.2008.00001.x.

Goeman, Mishuana. 2013. *Mark My Words: Native Women Mapping Our Nations*. Minneapolis: University of Minnesota Press.

Goldstein, Alyosha. 2014. *Formations of United States Colonialism*. Durham, NC: Duke University Press.

Goldstein, Daniel. 2010. "Toward a Critical Anthropology of Security." *Current Anthropology* 51 (4): 487–517.

Gopinath, Gayatri. 2018. *Unruly Visions: The Aesthetic Practices of Queer Diaspora*. Durham, NC: Duke University Press.

Gordillo, Gastón R. 2004. *Landscapes of Devils: Tensions of Place and Memory in the Argentinean Chaco*. Durham, NC: Duke University Press.

Gostoli, Ylenia. 2016. "Is Facebook Neutral on Palestine-Israel Conflict?" Al-Jazeera. September 26, 2016. http://www.aljazeera.com/news/2016/09/facebook-neutral -palestine-israel-conflict-160921115752070.html.

Graan, Andrew. 2013. "Counterfeiting the Nation? Skopje 2014 and the Politics of Nation Branding in Macedonia." *Cultural Anthropology* 28 (1): 161–79. https://doi .org/10.1111/j.1548-1360.2012.01179.x.

———. 2016. "The Nation Brand Regime: Nation Branding and the Semiotic Regimentation of Public Communication in Contemporary Macedonia." *Signs and Society* 4 (S1): S70–105. https://doi.org/10.1086/684613.

Greenwald, Glenn. 2017. "Facebook Says It Is Deleting Accounts at the Direction of the U.S. and Israeli Governments." *The Intercept* (blog). December 30, 2017. https:// theintercept.com/2017/12/30/facebook-says-it-is-deleting-accounts-at-the-direc tion-of-the-u-s-and-israeli-governments/.

Gupta, Akhil. 1992. "The Song of the Nonaligned World: Transnational Identities and the Reinscription of Space in Late Capitalism." *Cultural Anthropology* 7 (1): 63–79.

Haar, Rohini, and Jess Ghannam. 2018. "No Safe Space: Health Consequences of Tear Gas Exposure Among Palestine Refugees." University of California Berkeley: Human Rights Center, School of Law. https://www.law.berkeley.edu/wp-content/up loads/2017/12/NoSafeSpace_full_report22Dec2017.pdf.

Haaretz Editorial. 2018. "What Israel's State Prosecutor Ignored at Umm al-Hiran | Opinion." *Haaretz*, June 12, 2018. https://www.haaretz.com/opinion/editorial/ what-israel-s-state-prosecutor-ignored-at-umm-al-hiran-1.6171016.

Habermas, Jürgen. 1989. *The Structural Transformation of the Public Sphere*. Translated by Thomas Burger. Cambridge, MA: MIT Press.

Hachimi, Atiqa. 2019. "The War on Translation: Arabic and the Global Islamophobic Network." Public talk at *Digital Israel/Palestine: An International Symposium*. Toronto: University of Toronto.

Haddad, Toufic. 2018. *Palestine Ltd.: Neoliberalism and Nationalism in the Occupied Territory*. SOAS Palestine Studies. London: I. B. Tauris.

Hager, Eli, and Alysia Santo. 2016. "Inside the Deadly World of Private Prisoner Transport." The Marshall Project. July 6, 2016. https://www.themarshallproject.org/2016/ 07/06/inside-the-deadly-world-of-private-prisoner-transport.

Haifawi, Yoav. 2021. "Haifa Intifada Diary: The General Strike." Mondoweiss. May 21, 2021. https://mondoweiss.net/2021/05/haifa-intifada-diary-the-general-strike/.

Hajjar, Lisa. 2000. "Speaking the Conflict, or How the Druze Became Bilingual: A Study of Druze Translators in the Israeli Military Courts in the West Bank and Gaza." *Ethnic and Racial Studies* 23 (2): 299–328. https://doi.org/10.1080/014198700329060.

———. 2005. *Courting Conflict: The Israeli Military Court System in the West Bank and Gaza.* Berkeley: University of California Press.

Halbwachs, Maurice. 1980. *The Collective Memory.* Translated by F. Ditter. New York: Harper and Row.

Hamdan, Hashem. 2018. "Isra'il Tarfuḍ Al-Kashf 'An Al-Khaṭ Al-Akhḍar Li-Asbāb Amniya." *Arab48.* February 21, 2018. https://www.arab48.com/أمنية-أسباب-لـ-الأخضر-الخط-عن-الكشف-ترفض-إسرائيل/2018/02/21/أخبار/إسرائيليات-.

Hammami, Rema. 2010. "Qalandiya: Jerusalem's Tora Bora and the Frontiers of Global Inequality." *Jerusalem Quarterly* 41: 29–51.

———. 2019. "Destabilizing Mastery and the Machine: Palestinian Agency and Gendered Embodiment at Israeli Military Checkpoints." *Current Anthropology* 60 (S19): S87–97. https://doi.org/10.1086/699906.

Hanafi, Sari. 2009. "Spacio-Cide: Colonial Politics, Invisibility, and Rezoning in Palestinian Territory." *Contemporary Arab Affairs* 2 (1): 106–21.

Hanafi, Sari, and Linda Tabar. 2005. *The Emergence of Palestinian Globalized Elite: Donors, International Organizations, and Local NGOs.* Jerusalem: Institute of Jerusalem Studies.

Hanks, William. 1990. *Referential Practice: Language and Lived Space Among the Maya.* Chicago: University of Chicago Press.

Hansen, Thomas Blom, and Finn Stepputat. 2001. "Introduction: States of Imagination." In *States of Imagination: Ethnographic Explorations of the Postcolonial State,* edited by Thomas Blom Hansen and Finn Stepputat, 1–38. Durham, NC: Duke University Press.

Haraway, Donna. 1988. "Situated Knowledges: The Science Question in Feminism and the Privilege of Partial Perspective." *Feminist Studies* 14 (3): 575–99.

Harrison, Faye. 1997. "Ethnography as Politics." In *Decolonizing Anthropology: Moving Forward Toward an Anthropology for Liberation,* 88–110. Arlington, VA: Association of Black Anthropologists.

Hart, Jason. 2007. "Empowerment or Frustration? Participatory Programming with Young Palestinians." *Children, Youth, and Environments* 17 (3): 1–28.

Hass, Amira. 2002. "Israel's Closure Policy: An Ineffective Strategy of Containment and Repression." *Journal of Palestine Studies* 31 (3): 5–20.

———. 2013. "State Bars Westerners Living in West Bank from Entering Israel, East Jerusalem." *Haaretz,* January 2, 2013. https://www.haaretz.com/.premium-foreigners-in -wb-barred-from-israel-1.5286128.

Hassanein, Sohail Hossain. 2016. "Crime, Politics, and Police in the Palestinian's Society in Israel." *Social Identities* 22 (4): 376–96. https://doi.org/10.1080/13504630.2015.110 6312.

Hasson, Nir. 2015. " 'Let the People of Israel Enter the Gates and Kill Arabs.' " *Haaretz*, October 4, 2015. http://www.haaretz.com/israel-news/.premium-1.678800.

Hawari, Yara. 2019. "The Systematic Torture of Palestinians in Israeli Detention." *Al-Shabaka* (blog). November 28, 2019. https://al-shabaka.org/briefs/the-systematic -torture-of-palestinians-in-israeli-detention/.

———. 2021. "Defying Fragmentation and the Significance of Unity: A New Palestinian Uprising." *Al-Shabaka* (blog). June 29, 2021. https://al-shabaka.org/commentaries/ defying-fragmentation-and-the-significance-of-unity-a-new-palestinian-uprising/.

Hermez, Sami. 2017. *War Is Coming: Between Past and Future Violence in Lebanon*. Philadelphia: University of Pennsylvania Press.

Hernández, Kelly Lytle. 2010. *Migra!: A History of the U.S. Border Patrol*. Berkeley: University of California Press.

———. 2011. "Amnesty or Abolition?" *Boom: A Journal of California* 1 (4): 54–68. https:// doi.org/10.1525/boom.2011.1.4.54.

———. 2017. *City of Inmates: Conquest, Rebellion, and the Rise of Human Caging in Los Angeles, 1771-1965*. Chapel Hill: University of North Carolina Press.

Herzfeld, Michael. 2005. *Cultural Intimacy: Social Poetics in the Nation-State*. 2nd Edition. New York: Routledge.

Hill, Thomas W. 2016. "From the Small Zinzana to the Bigger Zinzana: Israeli Prisons, Palestinian Prisons." *Journal of Palestine Studies* 45 (3): 7–23. https://doi.org/10.1525/ jps.2016.45.3.7.

Hine, Christine. 2015. *Ethnography for the Internet: Embedded, Embodied, and Everyday*. London: Bloomsbury.

Hirschkind, Charles. 2006. *The Ethical Soundscape: Cassette Sermons and Islamic Counterpublics*. New York: Columbia University Press.

Holston, James. 2011. "Contesting Privilege with Right: The Transformation of Differentiated Citizenship in Brazil." *Citizenship Studies* 15 (3–4): 335–52. https://doi.org/10.1 080/13621025.2011.565157.

Hovel, Revital, and Jack Khoury. 2014. "High Court Upholds Residential Screening Law, Enabling Jewish Villages to Keep Arabs Out." *Haaretz*, September 17, 2014. https:// www.haaretz.com/.premium-court-allows-villages-to-veto-residents-1.5302588.

Human Rights Watch (HRW). 2011. "Erasing Links to the Land in the Negev." Human Rights Watch. March 11, 2011. https://www.hrw.org/news/2011/03/11/erasing-links -land-negev.

———. 2014. "Israel: Shooting Deaths after West Bank Protest." Human Rights Watch. August 3, 2014. https://www.hrw.org/news/2014/08/03/israel-shooting-deaths-after -west-bank-protest.

———. 2015. "Israel: Security Forces Abuse Palestinian Children." Human Rights Watch. July 19, 2015. https://www.hrw.org/news/2015/07/19/israel-security-forces -abuse-palestinian-children.

———. 2018a. "Israel: Apparent War Crimes in Gaza." Human Rights Watch. June 13, 2018. https://www.hrw.org/news/2018/06/13/israel-apparent-war-crimes-gaza.

———. 2018b. "Two Authorities, One Way, Zero Dissent." Human Rights Watch. October 23, 2018. https://www.hrw.org/report/2018/10/23/two-authorities-one-way-zero-dissent/arbitrary-arrest-and-torture-under.

———. 2021a. "A Threshold Crossed: Israeli Authorities and the Crimes of Apartheid and Persecution." Human Rights Watch. April 27, 2021. https://www.hrw.org/report/2021/04/27/threshold-crossed/israeli-authorities-and-crimes-apartheid-and-persecution.

———. 2021b. "Israel: Border Police Shouldn't Use Excessive Force." Human Rights Watch. May 14, 2021. https://www.hrw.org/news/2021/05/14/israel-border-police-shouldnt-use-excessive-force.

Hungry4Freedom. 2011. *Hungry for Freedom, Wala' Sbeit, Handala.* YouTube video. https://www.youtube.com/watch?v=8FML1QG-2XM&feature=related.

Ibrahim, Youssef M. 1988. "PLO Proclaims Palestine to Be an Independent State; Hints at Recognizing Israel." *New York Times*, November 15, 1988, sec. World. https://www.nytimes.com/1988/11/15/world/plo-proclaims-palestine-to-be-an-independent-state-hints-at-recognizing-israel.html.

Ihmoud, Sarah. 2015. "Mohammed Abu-Khdeir and the Politics of Racial Terror in Occupied Jerusalem." *Borderlands* 14 (1): 1–28.

———. 2019. "Murabata: The Politics of Staying in Place." *Feminist Studies* 45 (2): 512–40. https://doi.org/10.15767/feministstudies.45.2-3.0512.

———. 2021. "Sheikh Jarrah: The Question Before Us." *Jadaliyya.* May 16, 2021. https://www.jadaliyya.com/Details/42757.

International Committee of the Red Cross (ICRC). 2016. "People on War: Perspectives from 16 Countries." Geneva: ICRC.

Irfan, Anne. 2020. "Palestine at the UN: The PLO and UNRWA in the 1970s." *Journal of Palestine Studies* 49 (2): 26–47. https://doi.org/10.1525/jps.2020.49.2.26.

Isaac, Rami Khalil. 2010. "Alternative Tourism: New Forms of Tourism in Bethlehem for the Palestinian Tourism Industry." *Current Issues in Tourism* 13 (1): 21–36. https://doi.org/10.1080/13683500802495677.

Jabareen, Hassan, and Suhad Bishara. 2019. "The Jewish Nation-State Law." *Journal of Palestine Studies* 48 (2): 43–57. https://doi.org/10.1525/jps.2019.48.2.43.

Jabareen, Yosef. 2017. "Controlling Land and Demography in Israel: The Obsession with Territorial and Geographic Dominance." In *Israel and Its Palestinian Citizens: Ethnic Privileges in the Jewish State*, edited by Nadim N. Rouhana, with the assistance of Sahar S. Huneidi, 238–66. Cambridge: Cambridge University Press.

Jacir, Annemarie, dir. *Wajib.* 2018. Palestine: Philistine Films.

Jad, Islah. 2004. "The NGO-Isation of Arab Women's Movements." *IDS Bulletin* 35 (4): 34–42. https://doi.org/10.1111/j.1759-5436.2004.tb00153.x.

Jakobson, Roman. 1960. "Linguistics and Poetics." In *Style in Language*, edited by Thomas A. Sebeok, 350–77. Cambridge: MIT Press.

Jalal, Ayesha. 2000. *Self and Sovereignty: Individual and Community in South Asian Islam Since 1850*. London: Routledge.

Jamal, Amal. 2005. *Media, Politics and Democracy in Palestine*. Sussex: Academic Press.

———. 2009. *The Arab Public Sphere in Israel: Media Space and Cultural Resistance*. Bloomington: Indiana University Press.

———. 2011. *Arab Minority Nationalism in Israel: The Politics of Indigeneity*. Abingdon, Oxon: Routledge.

———. 2017. "Mechanisms of Governmentality and Constructing Hollow Citizenship: Arab Palestinians in Israel." In *Israel and Its Palestinian Citizens: Ethnic Privileges in the Jewish State*, edited by Nadim N. Rouhana, with the assistance of Sahar S. Huneidi, 159–90. Cambridge: Cambridge University Press.

Jarrar, Khalida. "Foreword." In *These Chains Will Be Broken: Palestinian Stories of Struggle and Defiance in Israeli Prisons*. Ramzy Baroud, Khalida Jarrar, and Richard Falk, eds. 2019. Atlanta: Clarity Press.

———. 2021. "Risālat al-Asīra Khalida Jarrar." *Al-Multaqā Al-Filastīnī* (blog). July 19, 2021. https://www.palestineforum.net/رسالة-الأسيرة-خالدة-جرار/.

Jawad, Rania. 2011. "Staging Resistance in Bil'in: The Performance of Violence in a Palestinian Village." *TDR: The Drama Review* 55 (4): 128–43.

Jensen, Kim, and Yoav Haifawi. 2017. " 'With Furious Cruelty'—Palestinian Poet Dareen Tatour Still Facing Prosecution in Israel." Mondoweiss. April 13, 2017. http://mondoweiss.net/2017/04/furious-palestinian-prosecution/.

Jones, Reece. 2016. *Violent Borders: Refugees and the Right to Move*. London: Verso Books.

Joseph, Suad. 1994. "Brother Sister Relationships: Connectivity, Love, and Power in the Reproduction of Patriarchy in Lebanon." *American Ethnologist* 21 (1): 50–73.

JTA. 2015. "20,000 Israelis Reportedly Sue Facebook for Failing to Stop Incitement to Terror." *Haaretz*, October 27, 2015. https://www.haaretz.com/israel-news/1.682485.

Juhasz, Alexandra. 2015. "Ev-Ent-Anglement 3: One Current Shape for Internet Feminism and Its Many Discontents." *MEDIA PRAXIS* (blog). July 3, 2015. https://aljean.wordpress.com/2015/07/03/ev-ent-anglement-3-one-current-shape-for-internet-feminism-and-its-many-discontents/.

———. 2016. "How Do I (Not) Look? Live Feed Video and Viral Black Death." *JSTOR Daily* (blog). July 20, 2016. https://daily.jstor.org/how-do-i-not-look/.

Junaid, Mohamad. 2020a. "The Price of Blood." *Comparative Studies of South Asia, Africa and the Middle East* 40 (1): 166–79. https://doi.org/10.1215/1089201X-8186159.

———. 2020b. "Laughter and Leaked Memos: Debating State Violence at a Kashmiri Baker's Shop." *Association for Political and Legal Anthropology* (blog). August 25,

2020. https://politicalandlegalanthro.org/2020/08/25/laughter-and-leaked-memos
-debating-state-violence-at-a-kashmiri-bakers-shop/.

Juris, Jeff S. 2012. "Frequencies of Transgression: Notes on the Politics of Excess and Constraint among Mexican Free Radios." In *Radio Fields: Anthropology and Wireless Sound in the 21st Century*, edited by Daniel Fisher and Lucas Bessire, 160–78. New York City: New York University Press.

Jusionyte, Ieva. 2015. *Savage Frontier: Making News and Security on the Argentine Border*. Oakland: University of California Press.

Kanaaneh, Rhoda Ann. 2002. *Birthing the Nation: Strategies of Palestinian Women in Israel*. Berkeley: University of California Press.

———. 2008. *Surrounded: Palestinian Soldiers in the Israeli Military*. Stanford: Stanford University Press.

Kanafani, Ghassan. 2000. *Palestine's Children: Returning to Haifa and Other Stories*. Translated by Barbara Harlow and Karen E. Riley. Three Continents Book. Boulder, CO: Lynne Rienner Publishers.

Kane, Alex. 2016. "Israel Targeting Palestinian Protesters on Facebook." *The Intercept* (blog). July 7, 2016. https://theintercept.com/2016/07/07/israel-targeting-palestinian
-protesters-on-facebook/.

Kaplan, Danny. 2009. "The Songs of the Siren: Engineering National Time on Israeli Radio." *Cultural Anthropology* 24 (2): 313–45. https://doi.org/10.1111/j.1548-1360.2009.01133.x.

Karkabi, Nadeem. 2013. "Staging Particular Difference: Politics of Space in the Palestinian Alternative Music Scene." *Middle East Journal of Culture and Communication* 6 (3): 308–28. https://doi.org/10.1163/18739865-00603004.

———. 2017. "Electro-*Dabke*: Performing Cosmopolitan Nationalism and Borderless Humanity." *Public Culture* 30 (1): 173-196. https://doi.org/10.1215/08992363-4189215.

———. 2018. "How and Why Haifa Has Become the 'Palestinian Cultural Capital' in Israel." *City and Community* 17(4): 1168-1188.

———. 2020. "Self-Liberated Citizens: Unproductive Pleasures, Loss of Self, and Playful Subjectivities in Palestinian Raves" Anthropological Quarterly 93 (4): 679–708. https://doi.org/doi:10.1353/anq.2020.0071.

Katriel, Tamar. 2016. "Memory to Action." *Journal of International and Intercultural Communication* 9 (3): 264–67. https://doi.org/10.1080/17513057.2016.1193935.

Kauanui, J. Kēhaulani. 2008. *Hawaiian Blood: Colonialism and the Politics of Sovereignty and Indigeneity*. Durham, NC: Duke University Press.

———. 2017. "Sovereignty: An Introduction." *Cultural Anthropology* 32 (3): 323–29.

———. 2018. *Paradoxes of Hawaiian Sovereignty: Land, Sex, and the Colonial Politics of State Nationalism*. Durham, NC: Duke University Press.

———. 2019. "Decolonial Self-Determination and 'No-State Solutions.'" *Humanity Journal* (blog). July 2, 2019. http://humanityjournal.org/blog/decolonial-self-determina-tion-and-no-state-solutions/.

Kayyal, Majd. n.d. "Oslo Īdiolojiya wa Laysat Itifāqiya" [Oslo Is an Ideology and Not an Agreement]. *Jabhat Al-Niḍāl Al-Sha ʿbī Al-Filasṭīnī* (blog). Accessed June 14, 2021. https://www.nedalshabi.ps/?p=90059.

Keane, Webb. 2009. "Freedom and Blasphemy: On Indonesian Press Bans and Danish Cartoons." *Public Culture* 21 (1): 47–76.

Kelly, Tobias. 2006. *Law, Violence, and Sovereignty Among West Bank Palestinians.* Cambridge: Cambridge University Press.

Khalidi, Raja, and Sobhi Samour. 2011. "Neoliberalism as Liberation: The Statehood Program and the Remaking of the Palestinian National Movement." *Journal of Palestine Studies* 40 (2): 6–25. https://doi.org/jps.2011.XL.2.6.

Khalidi, Rashid. 1997. *Palestinian Identity: The Construction of Modern National Consciousness.* New York: Columbia University Press.

———. 2014. "Israel: A Carceral State." *Journal of Palestine Studies* 43 (4): 5–10. https://doi.org/10.1525/jps.2014.43.4.5.

———. 2020. *The Hundred Years' War on Palestine: A History of Settler Colonialism and Resistance, 1917–2017.* New York: Metropolitan Books.

Khalidi, Walid, ed. 1992. *All That Remains: The Palestinian Villages Occupied and Depopulated by Israel in 1948.* Washington: Institute of Palestine Studies.

Khalili, Laleh. 2007. *Heroes and Martyrs of Palestine: The Politics of National Commemoration.* Cambridge: Cambridge University Press.

———. 2012. *Time in the Shadows: Confinement in Counterinsurgencies.* Stanford: Stanford University Press.

Khamaisi, Rassem. 2008. "From Imposed Ceasefire Line to International Border: The Issue of the Green Line between Palestine and Israel." *Journal of Borderlands Studies* 23 (1): 85–102. https://doi.org/10.1080/08865655.2008.9695690.

Khamis, Sahar, Paul B. Gold, and Katherine Vaughn. 2012. "Beyond Egypt's 'Facebook Revolution' and Syria's 'YouTube Uprising': Comparing Political Contexts, Actors, and Communication Strategies." *Arab Media & Society*, no. 15. http://www.arabmediasociety.com/?article=791.

Khleif, Waleed, and Susan Slyomovics. 2008. "Palestinian Remembrance Days and Plans: Kafr Qasim, Fact and Echo." In *Modernism and the Middle East*, edited by Sandy Isenstadt and Kishwar Rizvi, 186–218. Architecture and Politics in the Twentieth Century. Seattle: University of Washington Press. https://www.jstor.org/stable/j.ctvctoozn.14.

Khoury, Jack. 2014. "Hundreds of Israeli Arabs Protest: 'The Charge: Being Arab; the Sentence: Death.'" *Haaretz*, November 9, 2014. http://www.haaretz.com/israel-news/1.625480.

Khoury, Jack, Josh Breiner, and Nir Hasson. 2021. "Gantz Signs Administrative Detention Order for Arab Citizen over Rioting in Mixed City." *Haaretz*, June 23, 2021. https://www.haaretz.com/israel-news/.premium-jewish-arab-city-resident-put-under-administrative-detention-after-riots-last-month-1.9932732.

Kia, Mana. 2020. *Persianate Selves: Memories of Place and Origin Before Nationalism.* Stanford: Stanford University Press.

King-Irani, Laurie. 2000. "Land, Identity and the Limits of Resistance in the Galilee." *Middle East Report* 216: 40–44.

———. 2008. "Kinship, Class, and Ethnicity." In *Understanding the Contemporary Middle East*, edited by Jillian Schwedler and Deborah Gerner. Boulder, CO: Lynne Rienner Publishers.

Kingsley, Patrick, and Rami Nazzal. 2021. "Palestinians Strike Across West Bank, Gaza and Israel." *New York Times*, May 18, 2021. https://www.nytimes.com/2021/05/18/world/middleeast/palestine-strike.html.

Klein, Menachem. 2014. *Lives in Common: Arabs and Jews in Jerusalem, Jaffa and Hebron.* Oxford: Oxford University Press.

Konrad, Edo. 2019. "WATCH: Israeli Police Snatch Palestinian Flags from Protesters in Jerusalem." +972 Magazine. February 24, 2019. https://www.972mag.com/watch-israeli-police-snatch-palestinian-flags-protesters-jerusalem/.

Korn, Alina. 2003. "Rates of Incarceration and Main Trends in Israeli Prisons." *Criminal Justice* 3 (1): 29–55.

Koyagi, Mikiya. 2019. "Drivers across the Desert: Infrastructure and Sikh Migrants in the Indo-Iranian Borderlands, 1919–31." *Comparative Studies of South Asia, Africa and the Middle East* 39 (3): 375–88. https://doi.org/10.1215/1089201X-7885334.

Kuttab, Daoud. 2016. "How Damascus Gate Became the Symbol of the Intifada." Al-Monitor. February 19, 2016. https://www.al-monitor.com/pulse/originals/2016/02/jerusalem-damascus-gate-israel-arrests-journalists.html.

Lageman, Thessa. 2016. "Mohamed Bouazizi: Was the Arab Spring Worth Dying For?" Al-Jazeera. January 3, 2016. https://www.aljazeera.com/news/2015/12/mohamed-bouazizi-arab-spring-worth-dying-151228093743375.html.

Lagerquist, Peter. 2004. "Fencing the Last Sky: Excavating Palestine After Israel's 'Separation Wall.' " *Journal of Palestine Studies* 33 (2): 5–35.

Lamont Hill, Marc. 2016. *Nobody: Casualties of America's War on the Vulnerable, from Ferguson to Flint and Beyond.* New York: Simon and Schuster.

———. 2018. "From Ferguson to Palestine: Reimagining Transnational Solidarity Through Difference." *Biography* 41 (4): 942–57. https://doi.org/10.1353/bio.2018.0086.

Larkin, Brian. 2013. "The Politics and Poetics of Infrastructure." *Annual Review of Anthropology* 42: 327–43.

Lefebvre, Henri. 1991. *The Production of Space.* Oxford: Blackwell.

Lehrer, Erica, Cynthia E. Milton, and Monica Eileen Patterson, eds. 2011. *Curating Difficult Knowledge: Violent Pasts in Public Places.* Houndmills, UK: Palgrave Macmillan.

Lentin, Ronit. 2010. *Co-Memory and Melancholia: Israelis Memorialising the Palestinian Nakba.* Manchester: Manchester University Press.

LeVine, Mark. 2005. *Overthrowing Geography: Jaffa, Tel Aviv, and the Struggle for Palestine, 1880-1948*. Berkeley: University of California Press.

Levinson, Chaim. 2011. "Israel Has 101 Different Types of Permits Governing Palestinian Movement." *Haaretz*, December 22, 2011. https://www.haaretz.com/1.5222134.

———. 2015. "Torture of Palestinian Detainees by Shin Bet Investigators Rises Sharply." *Haaretz*, March 6, 2015. https://www.haaretz.com/.premium-torture-by-shin-bet-investigators-rises-sharply-1.5332951.

———. 2017. "Torture, Israeli-Style - as Described by the Interrogators Themselves." *Haaretz*, January 24, 2017. https://www.haaretz.com/israel-news/.premium-israeli-style-torture-as-described-by-the-interrogators-themselves-1.5489853.

Lévi-Strauss, Claude. 1962. *The Savage Mind*. Chicago: University of Chicago Press.

Li, Darryl. 2011. "Occupation Law and the One-State Reality." *Jadaliyya*. August 2, 2011. https://www.jadaliyya.com/Details/24275.

———. 2019. *The Universal Enemy: Jihad, Empire, and the Challenge of Solidarity*. Stanford: Stanford University Press.

Lior, Ilan. 2011. "Hundreds in Jaffa Take to the Streets to Mark Nakba Day." *Haaretz*, May 14, 2011. https://www.haaretz.com/1.5012028.

———. 2017a. "New Guideline Permits Israel to Deny Entry to Visitors Over 'BDS Activity.' " *Haaretz*, July 6, 2017. https://www.haaretz.com/israel-news/.premium-new-guideline-permits-israel-to-deny-entry-to-visitors-over-bds-activity-1.5492085.

———. 2017b. "Israeli Court: Protesters Outside Attorney General's Home Don't Need Police Permit." *Haaretz*, October 9, 2017. https://www.haaretz.com/israel-news/.premium-israeli-high-court-protesters-at-ag-s-home-dont-need-permit-1.5456408.

Lis, Jonathan. 2013. "Israel Extends Official State of Emergency, Again." *Haaretz*, April 23, 2013. http://www.haaretz.com/israel-news/israel-extends-official-state-of-emergency-again-1.516991.

———. 2016a. "Israeli Lawmaker Says Palestinian Nation Doesn't Exist, Because Arabic Doesn't Have 'P.' " *Haaretz*, February 10, 2016. https://www.haaretz.com/israel-news/likud-lawmaker-no-p-no-palestine-1.5402938.

———. 2016b. "Knesset Passes Sweeping Anti-Terrorism Law." *Haaretz*, June 15, 2016. https://www.haaretz.com/israel-news/1.725225.

Livneh, Neri. 2012. "Farewell, Dear Friend." *Haaretz*, April 11, 2012. http://www.haaretz.com/israel-news/farewell-dear-friend-1.423817.

Lowe, Lisa. 2015. *The Intimacies of Four Continents*. Durham, NC: Duke University Press.

Lubin, Alex. 2014. *Geographies of Liberation: The Making of an Afro-Arab Political Imaginary*. Chapel Hill: University of North Carolina Press.

Luna, Sarah. 2018. "Affective Atmosphere of Terror on the Mexico-U.S. Border: Rumors of Violence in Reynosa's Prostitution Zone." *Cultural Anthropology* 33 (1): 58–84. https://doi.org/10.14506/ca33.1.03.

———. 2020. *Love in the Drug War: Selling Sex and Finding Jesus on the Mexico-US Border*. Austin: University of Texas Press.

Lustick, Ian S. 1993. *Unsettled States, Disputed Lands: Britain and Ireland, France and Algeria, Israel and the West Bank-Gaza*. Ithaca, NY: Cornell University Press.

———. 2019. *Paradigm Lost: From Two-State Solution to One-State Reality*. Philadelphia: University of Pennsylvania Press.

Lutz, Catherine, and Cynthia Enloe, eds. 2009. *The Bases of Empire: The Global Struggle against U.S. Military Posts*. New York: New York University Press.

Lybarger, Loren D. 2007. *Identity and Religion in Palestine: The Struggle Between Islamism and Secularism in the Occupied Territories*. Princeton: Princeton University Press.

Lynk, Michael. 2005. "Down by Law: The High Court of Israel, International Law, and the Separation Wall." *Journal of Palestine Studies* 35 (1): 6–24. https://doi.org/10.1525/jps.2005.35.1.6.

———. 2017. "Report of Special Rapporteur on Situation of Human Rights in Palestinian Territories." United Nations General Assembly. https://www.un.org/unispal/document/report-of-special-rapporteur-on-situation-of-human-rights-in-palestinian-territories-michael-lynk-advance-unedited-version/.

Ma'an News. 2016. "Imprisoned Hunger Striker Al-Qiq Refuses Israeli Offer to Be Released in May." Ma'an News Agency. February 7, 2016. http://www.maannews.com/Content.aspx?ID=770170.

———. 2018. "Ajhiza al-Amin Tamna' Taẓāhira fī Rām Allah wa Taqmi' al-Mushārikīn" [Security Forces Forbid Protests in Ramallah and Repress Protesters]. Ma'an News Agency. June 13, 2018. http://www.maannews.net/Content.aspx?ID=952247.

Ma'an News Agency. 2018. "Abu Jaysh: Al-Faṣā'il Lā 'Alm Lahā Bi-Masīrat Nāblus" [Abu Jaysh: The Factions Have No Knowledge of the Protest in Nablus]. Ma'an News Agency. June 13, 2018. http://www.maannews.net/Content.aspx?ID=952222.

Mackey, Robert. 2014. "Advice for Ferguson's Protesters from the Middle East." *New York Times*, August 14, 2014, sec. World. https://www.nytimes.com/2014/08/15/world/middleeast/advice-for-fergusons-protesters-from-the-middle-east.html.

Mada al-Carmel. 2007. "The Haifa Declaration." Mada al-Carmel. https://www.adalah.org/uploads/oldfiles/newsletter/eng/may07/haifa.pdf.

Mahajan, Nidhi. 2019. "Dhow Itineraries: The Making of a Shadow Economy in the Western Indian Ocean." *Comparative Studies of South Asia, Africa and the Middle East* 39 (3): 407–19. https://doi.org/doi 10.1215/1089201X-7885356.

Maidhof, Callie. 2016. "A House, A Yard, and A Security Fence: Israel's Secular Settlers in the West Bank." Dissertation. University of California at Berkeley.

Makhoul, Manar. 2015. "Palestinian Citizens of Israel—Evolution of a Name." In *The Palestinians in Israel: Readings in History, Politics, and Society*, edited by Nadim N. Rouhana and Areej Sabbagh-Khoury. Haifa: Mada al-Carmel.

Malkki, Liisa. 1992. "National Geographic: The Rooting of Peoples and the Territorialization of National Identity among Scholars and Refugees." *Cultural Anthropology 7* (1): 24–44.

———. 1995. "Refugees and Exile: From 'Refugee Studies' to the National Order of Things." *Annual Review of Anthropology* 24: 495-523.

Malkowski, Jennifer. 2017. *Dying in Full Detail: Mortality and Digital Documentary.* Durham, NC: Duke University Press.

Maltz, Judy. 2014. "In Jaffa, Rockets and Conflict Threaten a Delicate Jewish-Arab Coexistence." *Haaretz,* July 14, 2014. http://www.haaretz.com/israel-news/.premium -1.605141.

Mamdani, Mahmood. 2004. *Good Muslim, Bad Muslim: America, The Cold War, and the Roots of Terror.* New York: Three Leaves Press Doubleday.

———. 2012. *Define and Rule: Native as Political Identity.* Cambridge, MA: Harvard University Press.

———. 2020. *Neither Settler nor Native: The Making and Unmaking of Permanent Minorities.* Cambridge, MA: Harvard University Press.

Maqsood, Ammara. 2019. "The Social Life of Rumors: Uncertainty in Everyday Encounters between the Military, Taliban, and Tribal Pashtun in Pakistan." *Comparative Studies of South Asia, Africa and the Middle East* 39 (3): 462–74. https://doi .org/10.1215/1089201X-7885414.

Marcus, George. 1998. "Ethnography in/of the World System: The Emergence of Multi-Sited Ethnography." In *Ethnography Through Thick and Thin,* edited by George Marcus, 79–104. Princeton: Princeton University Press.

Marshood, and Riya Alsanah. 2020. "Tal'at: A Feminist Movement That Is Redefining Liberation and Reimagining Palestine." Mondoweiss. February 25, 2020. https:// mondoweiss.net/2020/02/talat-a-feminist-movement-that-is-redefining-liberation -and-reimagining-palestine/.

Masalha, Nur. 1992. *Expulsion of the Palestinians: The Concept of "Transfer" in Zionist Political Thought 1882-1948.* Washington, D.C.: Institute for Palestine Studies.

Masarwa, Lubna. 2020. "Palestinian Citizens of Israel Protest to Save Jaffa Cemetery." Middle East Eye. June 19, 2020. http://www.middleeasteye.net/news/israel -palestinian-jaffa-cemetery-protest-planned-demolition.

Masri, Mazen. 2014. *The Dynamics of Exclusionary Constitutionalism: Israel as a Jewish and Democratic State.* United Kingdom: Hart Publishing.

Masri, Mai, dir. *3000 Nights.* 2005. Montreal: Cinema Politica. Fiction Film, 1 hr 34 minutes.

Masri, Mazen, Nadim N. Rouhana, and Areej Sabbagh-Khoury. 2015. "The Limits of Electoral Politics: Section 7A of Basic Law: The Knesset." In *The Palestinians in Israel: Readings in History, Politics, and Society,* 2:129–38. Haifa: Mada al-Carmel.

Massad, Joseph. 2018. "Against Self-Determination." *Humanity: An International Journal of Human Rights, Humanitarianism, and Development* 9 (2): 161–91. https://doi.org/10.1353/hum.2018.0010.

Mazzarella, William. 2003. *Shoveling Smoke: Advertising and Globalization in Contemporary India*. Durham, NC: Duke University Press.

———. 2010. "The Myth of the Multitude, or, Who's Afraid of the Crowd?" *Critical Inquiry* 36 (Summer): 697–727.

———. 2013. *Censorium: Cinema and the Open Edge of Mass Publicity*. Durham, NC: Duke University Press.

Mbembe, Achille. 2003. "Necropolitics." *Public Culture* 15 (1): 11–40.

McAtackney, Laura, and Randall H. McGuire, eds. 2020. *Walling In and Walling Out: Why Are We Building New Barriers to Divide Us?* Albuquerque: University of New Mexico Press.

McGranahan, Carol. 2016. "Theorizing Refusal: An Introduction." *Cultural Anthropology* 31 (3): 319–25. https://doi.org/10.14506/ca31.3.01.

McKee, Emily. 2014. "Performing Rootedness in the Negev/Naqab: Possibilities and Perils of Competitive Planting." *Antipode* 46 (5): 1172–89. https://doi.org/10.1111/anti.12013.

———. 2019. "Water, Power, and Refusal: Confronting Evasive Accountability in a Palestinian Village." *Journal of the Royal Anthropological Institute* 25 (3): 546–65. https://doi.org/10.1111/1467-9655.13082.

Meari, Lena. 2014. "Sumud: A Palestinian Philosophy of Confrontation in Colonial Prisons." *South Atlantic Quarterly* 113 (3): 547–78.

Mishal, Shaul, and Reuben Aharoni. 1994. *Speaking Stones Intifada: Communiqués from the Intifada Underground*. Syracuse: Syracuse University Press.

Mitchell, Timothy. 1999. "Society, Economy, and the State Effect." In *State/Culture: State-Formation after the Cultural Turn*, edited by George Steinmetz, 76–97. Ithaca, NY: Cornell University Press.

Monterescu, Daniel. 2015. *Jaffa Shared and Shattered: Contrived Coexistence in Israel/Palestine*. Bloomington: Indiana University Press.

Monterescu, Daniel, and Dan Rabinowitz, eds. 2007. *Mixed Towns, Trapped Communities: Historical Narratives, Spatial Dynamics, Gender Relations and Cultural Encounters in Palestinian-Israeli Towns*. Hampshire: Ashgate.

Mora, Mariana. 2017. "Ayotzinapa and the Criminalization of Racialized Poverty in La Montaña, Guerrero, Mexico." *Political and Legal Anthropology Review* 40 (1): 67–85.

Mousa, Ola. 2020. "Never Flinch until Justice Is Served." Electronic Intifada. March 26, 2020. https://electronicintifada.net/content/never-flinch-until-justice-served/29821.

Mowatt, Rasul. 2018. "Black Lives as Snuff: The Silent Complicity in Viewing Black Death." *Biography* 41 (September): 777–806. https://doi.org/10.1353/bio.2018.0079.

Munif, Yasser. 2020. *The Syrian Revolution: Between the Politics of Life and the Geopolitics of Death*. London: Pluto Press.

Myers, Fred. 1991. *Pintupi Country, Pintupi Self: Sentiment, Place and Politics among Western Desert Aborigines*. Berkeley: University of California Press.

Nasasra, Mansour. 2017. *The Naqab Bedouins: A Century of Politics and Resistance*. New York: Columbia University Press.

Nasasra, Mansour, Sophie Richter-Devroe, Sarab Abu-Rabia-Queder, and Richard Ratcliffe, eds. 2014. *The Naqab Bedouin and Colonialism: New Perspectives*. London, New York: Routledge.

Nashif, Esmail. 2008. *Palestinian Political Prisoners: Identity and Community*. New York: Routledge.

Nashif, Nadim. 2017. "Surveillance of Palestinians and the Fight for Digital Rights." *Al-Shabaka* (blog). October 23, 2017. https://al-shabaka.org/briefs/surveillance-palestinians-fight-digital-rights/.

Nasr-Mazzawi, Rula, and Nidal Al-Azza. 2018. "Ḥirāk Ḥaifa: Naẓra ʿala Muʾasharāt al-Taghyīr" [The Haifa Movement: A Look at Signs of Change]. Tajammuʿ (National Democratic Assembly). August 29, 2018. http://www.altajamoa.org/مؤشرات-التغيير/مقالات/2018/08/29/حراك-حيفا-نظرة-على-.

Nassar, Maha. 2017. *Brothers Apart: Palestinian Citizens of Israel and the Arab World*. Stanford: Stanford University Press.

———. 2021. " ʿAl-Aqsa Is in Danger': How Jerusalem Connects Palestinian Citizens of Israel to the Palestinian Cause." Berkley Center for Religion, Peace & World Affairs. August 6, 2021. https://berkleycenter.georgetown.edu/responses/al-aqsa-is-in-danger-how-jerusalem-connects-palestinian-citizens-of-israel-to-the-palestinian-cause?fbclid=IwAR1Ujxdi3I3uSFTLdNX1RPiuaJpqlNNyLKLeOZm6DPpPJlYeokM_XLT_B6w.

National Committee for the Heads of the Arab Local Authorities in Israel. "The Future Vision of the Palestinian Arabs in Israel." 2006. https://www.adalah.org/uploads/oldfiles/newsletter/eng/dec06/tasawor-mostaqbali.pdf.

Nichols, Robert. 2015. "The Colonialism of Incarceration." *Radical Philosophy Review* 17 (2): 435–55. https://doi.org/10.4324/9781315747699-4.

Norman, Julie. 2009. "Creative Activism: Youth Media in Palestine." *Middle East Journal of Culture and Communication* 2: 251–74.

———. 2021. *The Palestinian Prisoners Movement*. London: Routledge.

Nossek, Hillel, and Khalil Rinnawi. 2016. "Censorship and Freedom of the Press Under Changing Political Regimes: Palestinian Media from Israeli Occupation to the Palestinian Authority." *International Communication Gazette* 65 (2): 183–202. https://doi.org/10.1177/0016549203065002005.

Noy, Orly. 2017. "When the High Court Has to Intervene so a Palestinian Family Can Mourn." +972 Magazine. January 24, 2017. https://972mag.com/when-the-high -court-has-to-intervene-so-a-palestinian-family-can-mourn/124737/.

Obamsawin, Alanis, dir. *Kanehsatake: 270 Years of Resistance*. 1993. National Film Board, Canada. Documentary, 1hr 59 mins. https://www.nfb.ca/film/kanehsatake _270_years_of_resistance/.

OCHA. 2015a. "Key Figures on the 2014 Hostilities, Gaza One Year On." United Nations Office for the Coordination of Humanitarian Affairs - Occupied Palestinian Territory. 2015. http://gaza.ochaopt.org/2015/06/key-figures-on-the-2014-hostilities/.

———. 2015b. "Wave of Violence across the oPt and Israel Results in Record Casualties." United Nations Office for the Coordination of Humanitarian Affairs - Occupied Palestinian Territory. November 11, 2015. https://www.ochaopt.org/content/ wave-violence-across-opt-and-israel-results-record-casualties.

Ochs, Juliana. 2011. *Security and Suspicion: An Ethnography of Everyday Life in Israel*. Philadelphia: University of Pennsylvania Press.

Ofir, Jonathan. 2021. "The Israel Hasbara Machine Is Attempting to Sanitize Naftali Bennett's 'I Killed Many Arabs' Quote." Mondoweiss. June 18, 2021. https://mon doweiss.net/2021/06/the-israel-hasbara-machine-is-attempting-to-sanitize-naftali -bennetts-i-killed-many-arabs-quote/.

OHCHR. n.d. "Questions and Answers about IDPs." Accessed July 5, 2020. https://www .ohchr.org/EN/Issues/IDPersons/Pages/Issues.aspx.

———. 2018. "UN Human Rights Expert Says Facebook's 'Terrorism' Definition Is Too Broad." September 3, 2018. https://www.ohchr.org/EN/NewsEvents/Pages/Dis playNews.aspx?NewsID=23494&LangID=E.

Ong, Aihwa. 2006. *Neoliberalism as Exception: Mutations in Citizenship and Sovereignty*. Durham, NC: Duke University Press.

Pacheco, Allegra A. 1989. "Occupying an Uprising: The Geneva Law and Israeli Administrative Detention Policy during the First Year of the Palestinian General Uprising." *Columbia Human Rights Law Review* 21 (2): 515–64.

Pak, Vincent. 2021. "(De)Coupling Race and Language: The State Listening Subject and Its Rearticulation of Antiracism as Racism in Singapore." *Language in Society*, 1–22. https://doi.org/10.1017/S0047404521000373.

Palestine Legal, and Center for Constitutional Rights. 2015. "The Palestine Exception to Free Speech: A Movement Under Attack in the US." Center for Constitutional Rights. 2015. https://ccrjustice.org/node/5281.

Paley, Julia, ed. 2008. *Democracy: Anthropological Approaches*. Santa Fe: School for Advanced Research Press.

Panet. 2019. "Panet: Who Are We [Man Naḥnu]." Panet. June 19, 2019. https://www.pa-net.co.il.

Pappé, Ilan. 2006. *The Ethnic Cleansing of Palestine*. Oxford: Oneworld Publications.

———. 2017. *The Biggest Prison on Earth: A History of the Occupied Territories*. Oxford: Oneworld Publications.

———. 2018. "Indigeneity as Cultural Resistance: Notes on the Palestinian Struggle within Twenty-First-Century Israel." *South Atlantic Quarterly* 117 (1): 157–78. https:// doi.org/10.1215/00382876-4282082.

Parla, Ayşe. 2019. *Precarious Hope: Migration and the Limits of Belonging in Turkey*. Stanford: Stanford University Press.

Parsons, Nigel. 2010. "Israeli Biopolitics, Palestinian Policing: Order and Resistance in the Occupied Palestinian Territories." In *Policing and Prisons in the Middle East: Formations of Coercion*, edited by Laleh Khalili and Jillian Schwedler, 57–76. London: Hurst and Company.

Pasquetti, Silvia. 2013. "Legal Emotions: An Ethnography of Distrust and Fear in the Arab Districts of an Israeli City." *Law and Society Review* 47 (3): 461–92.

———. 2015. "Subordination and Dispositions: Palestinians' Differing Sense of Injustice, Politics, and Morality." *Theory and Society* 44: 1–31.

Patel, Yumna. 2021. "'We Are United as a People': Palestinians Celebrate a Historic Strike, Urge Supporters to 'Keep Momentum Going.'" Mondoweiss. May 18, 2021. https://mondoweiss.net/2021/05/we-are-united-as-a-people-palestinians-celebrate -a-historic-strike-urge-supporters-to-keep-momentum-going/.

Paz, Alejandro I. 2014. "Guiding Settler Jerusalem: Voice and the Transpositions of History in Religious Zionist Pilgrimage." *Religion and Society* 5 (1): 128–42. https://doi .org/10.3167/arrs.2014.050108.

———. 2018. *Latinos in Israel: Language and Unexpected Citizenship*. Bloomington: Indiana University Press.

———. 2019. "Communicating Citizenship." *Annual Review of Anthropology* 48 (1): 77– 93. https://doi.org/10.1146/annurev-anthro-102317-050031.

Pedelty, Mark. 1995. *War Stories: The Culture of Foreign Correspondents*. New York: Routledge.

Peirce, Charles. 1985. "Logic as Semiotic: The Theory of Signs." In *Semiotics: An Introductory Anthology*, edited by Robert E. Innis, 1–23. Bloomington: Indiana University Press.

Peled, Yoav. 1992. "Ethnic Democracy and the Legal Construction of Citizenship: Arab Citizens of the Jewish State." *American Political Science Review* 86 (2): 432–43.

Perez, Ramona, Niko Besnier, Patrick Clarkin, Hugh Gusterson, John Jackson, and Katherine Spielmann. 2015. "Report to the Executive Board: The Task Force on AAA Engagement on Israel-Palestine." Arlington, VA: American Anthropological Association.

Permanent Observer Mission of Palestine to the United Nations. 2021. "Diplomatic Relations." Permanent Observer Mission of Palestine to the United Nations. 2021. https://palestineun.org/about-palestine/diplomatic-relations/.

Peteet, Julie. 2000. "Male Gender and Rituals of Resistance in the Palestinian Intifada: A Cultural Politics of Violence." In *Imagined Masculinities: Male Identity and Culture in the Modern Middle East*, edited by Mai Ghoussoub and Emma Sinclair-Webb, 103–26. London: Saqi Books.

———. 2005. *Landscape of Hope and Despair: Palestinian Refugee Camps*. Philadelphia: University of Pennsylvania Press.

———. 2016. "Camps and Enclaves: Palestine in the Time of Closure." *Journal of Refugee Studies* 29 (2): 208–228. https://doi.org/10.1093/jrs/fev014.

———. 2017. *Space and Mobility in Palestine*. 2017 ed. Bloomington: Indiana University Press.

Pfeffer, Anshel. 2011. "Fourteen Killed as Northern Border Breached by Palestinians During Nakba Day Demonstrations." *Haaretz*, May 16, 2011. https://www.haaretz.com/1.5012507.

Pinto, Sarah. 2014. *Daughters of Parvati: Women and Madness in Contemporary India*. Philadelphia: University of Pennsylvania Press.

Povinelli, Elizabeth A. 2006. *The Empire of Love: Toward a Theory of Intimacy, Genealogy, and Carnality*. Durham, NC: Duke University Press.

Rabie, Kareem. 2021. *Palestine Is Throwing a Party and the Whole World Is Invited: Capital and State Building in the West Bank*. Durham, NC: Duke University Press.

Rabinowitz, Dan. 1997. *Overlooking Nazareth: The Ethnography of Exclusion in Galilee*. Cambridge: Cambridge University Press.

Rabinowitz, Dan, and Khawla Abu-Baker. 2005. *Coffins on Our Shoulders: The Experience of the Palestinian Citizens of Israel*. Berkeley: University of California Press.

Ralph, Laurence. 2020. "The Making of Richard Zuley: The Ignored Linkages between the US Criminal In/Justice System and the International Security State." *American Anthropologist* 122 (1): 133–42. https://doi.org/10.1111/aman.13356.

Rankine, Claudia. 2015. "'The Condition of Black Life Is One of Mourning.'" *New York Times*, June 22, 2015. http://www.nytimes.com/2015/06/22/magazine/the-condition-of-black-life-is-one-of-mourning.html.

Raphael, Gaelle. 2011. "Al-Shabbi's 'The Will to Life.'" *Jadaliyya*. May 1, 2011. https://www.jadaliyya.com/Details/23935.

Rasgon, Adam. 2019. "A Brief History of Balad, the Renegade Joint List Faction That Passed on Gantz." *Times of Israel*. September 24, 2019. https://www.timesofisrael.com/a-brief-history-of-balad-the-renegade-joint-list-faction-that-passed-on-gantz/.

Ravid, Barak. 2015. "Israel Outlaws Islamic Movement's Northern Branch." *Haaretz*, November 17, 2015. http://www.haaretz.com/israel-news/1.686521.

Remnick, David. 2014. "Israel's One-State Reality." *The New Yorker*. November 10, 2014. https://www.newyorker.com/magazine/2014/11/17/one-state-reality.

Reuters. 2011. " 'It Was Always My Dream to Reach Jaffa', Syrian Infiltrator Says." *Haaretz*, May 16, 2011. https://www.haaretz.com/1.5012965.

Robertson, Joseph Carver. 2018. "The Impact of Data Sovereignty on American Indian Self-Determination: A Framework Proof of Concept Using Data Science." Dissertation. South Dakota State University. https://openprairie.sdstate.edu/etd/2485.

Robinson, Shira. 2006. "Commemoration under Fire: Palestinian Responses to the 1956 Kafr Qasim Massacre." In *Memory and Violence in the Middle East and North Africa*, edited by Ussama Samir Makdisi and Paul A. Silverstein, 103–32. Bloomington: Indiana University Press.

———. 2013. *Citizen Strangers: Palestinians and the Birth of Israel's Liberal Settler State*. Stanford: Stanford University Press.

Robson, Laura C. 2010. "Palestinian Liberation Theology, Muslim–Christian Relations and the Arab–Israeli Conflict." *Islam and Christian–Muslim Relations* 21 (1): 39–50. https://doi.org/10.1080/09596410903481846.

Rosas, Gilberto. 2012. *Barrio Libre: Criminalizing States and Delinquent Refusals of the New Frontier*. Durham, NC: Duke University Press.

Rose, Steve. 2009. "Peace Centre with a Panic Room." *The Guardian*, February 17, 2009. http://www.theguardian.com/artanddesign/2009/feb/17/peace-house-israel-architecture.

Rosenfeld, Jesse. 2017. "The Palestinian Authority Is Using a New Cyber-Crimes Law to Crack Down on Dissent." *The Intercept* (blog). December 18, 2017. https://theintercept.com/2017/12/18/palestinian-authority-cyber-crimes-law-dissent-issa-amro/.

Roth, Natasha. 2016. "Wiping Palestinian History off the Map in Jaffa." *+972 Magazine*. June 4, 2016. https://972mag.com/wiping-palestinian-history-off-the-map-in-jaffa/119688/.

Rouch, Jean, and Steven Feld. 2003. *Ciné-Ethnography*. Translated by Steven Feld. Minneapolis: University of Minnesota Press.

Rouhana, Nadim N., and Sahar Huneidi, eds. 2017. *Israel and Its Palestinian Citizens: Ethnic Privileges in the Jewish State*. Cambridge: Cambridge University Press.

Rouhana, Nadim N., and Areej Sabbagh-Khoury. 2015. "Settler-Colonial Citizenship: Conceptualizing the Relationship Between Israel and Its Palestinian Citizens." *Settler Colonial Studies* 5 (3): 205–25.

———. 2017. "Memory and the Return of History in a Settler-Colonial Context." In *Israel and Its Palestinian Citizens: Ethnic Privileges in the Jewish State*, 393–432. Cambridge: Cambridge University Press.

Rouhana, Nadim N., and Nimer Sultany. 2003. "Redrawing the Boundaries of Citizenship: Israel's New Hegemony." *Journal of Palestine Studies* 33 (1): 5–22. https://doi.org/10.1525/jps.2003.33.1.5.

Rouse, Carolyn M. 2021. "Necropolitics versus Biopolitics: Spatialization, White Privilege, and Visibility during a Pandemic." *Cultural Anthropology* 36 (3): 360–367. https://doi.org/10.14506/ca36.3.03.

Rutherford, Danilyn. 2012. *Laughing at Leviathan: Sovereignty and Audience in West Papua*. Chicago: University of Chicago Press.

Sa'ar, Amalia. 1998. "Carefully on the Margins: Christian Palestinians in Haifa between Nation and State." *American Ethnologist* 25 (2): 215–39.

Sa'di, Ahmad H. 2003. "Catastrophe, Memory and Identity: Al-Nakbah as a Component of Palestinian Identity." *Israel Studies* 7 (2): 175–98.

———. "Palestinian Social Movement and Protest within the Green Line: 1949-2001." In *Israel and Its Palestinian Citizens: Ethnic Privileges in the Jewish State*, edited by Nadim N. Rouhana, with the assistance of Sahar S. Huneidi, 369–92. Cambridge: Cambridge University Press.

Sa'di, Ahmad H., and Lila Abu-Lughod, eds. 2007. *Nakba: Palestine, 1948, and the Claims of Memory*. New York: Columbia University Press.

Said, Edward W. 1978. *Orientalism*. New York: Vintage Books.

———. 1981. *Covering Islam: How the Media and the Experts Determine How We See the Rest of the World*. New York: Pantheon Books.

———. 1984. "Permission to Narrate." *Journal of Palestine Studies* 8 (3): 27–48.

———. 1986. *After the Last Sky: Palestinian Lives*. New York: Pantheon.

———. 1992. *The Question of Palestine*. New York: Vintage Books.

Salaita, Steven. 2006. *The Holy Land in Transit: Colonialism and the Quest for Canaan*. Syracuse: Syracuse University Press.

Salamanca, Omar Jabary. 2011. "Unplug and Play: Manufacturing Collapse in Gaza." *Human Geography* 4 (1): 22–37. https://doi.org/10.1177/194277861100400103.

Salamanca, Omar Jabary, Mezna Qato, Kareem Rabie, and Sobhi Samour. 2012. "Past Is Present: Settler Colonialism in Palestine." *Settler Colonial Studies* 2 (1): 1–8.

Salih, Ruba, and Sophie Richter-Devroe. 2018. "Palestine beyond National Frames: Emerging Politics, Cultures, and Claims." *South Atlantic Quarterly* 117 (1): 1–20. https://doi.org/10.1215/00382876-4282019.

Sawhney, Nitin, Raed Yacoub, and Julie M. Norman. 2009. "Jerusalem and Belfast: Envisioning Media Arts for Urban Renewal and Cultural Identity in Divided Cities." *The Jerusalem Quarterly Journal* 39: 62–80.

Sayegh, Fayez. 2012. "Zionist Colonialism in Palestine (1965)." *Settler Colonial Studies* 2 (1): 206–25. https://doi.org/10.1080/2201473X.2012.10648833.

Sayigh, Rosemary. 1979. *Palestinians: From Peasants to Revolutionaries, A People's History*. London: Zed Press.

———. 2015. "Oral History, Colonialist Dispossession, and the State: The Palestinian Case." *Settler Colonial Studies* 5 (3): 193–204. https://doi.org/10.1080/22014 73X.2014.955945.

Sayigh, Yezid. 2000. *Armed Struggle and the Search for State: The Palestinian National Movement, 1949-1993*. Oxford: Oxford University Press.

———. 2011. "Policing the People, Building the State: Authoritarian Transformation in the West Bank and Gaza." Washington, D.C.: The Carnegie Endowment for International Peace.

Schejter, Amit. 2009. *Muting Israeli Democracy: How Media and Cultural Policy Undermine Free Expression*. Urbana: University of Illinois Press.

Schiller, Naomi. 2018. *Channeling the State: Community Media and Popular Politics in Venezuela*. Durham, NC: Duke University Press.

Schrader, Stuart. 2019. *Badges without Borders: How Global Counterinsurgency Transformed American Policing*. Oakland: University of California Press.

Schulthies, Becky. 2015. "Do You Speak Arabic? Managing Axes of Adequation and Difference in Pan-Arab Talent Programs." *Language and Communication* 44: 59–71. https://doi.org/10.1016/j.langcom.2014.10.010.

Segal, Jerome. 2017. " 'Land of the Three Faiths:' The Little-Known History of the Palestinian Declaration of Independence." *Haaretz*, November 15, 2017. https://www.haaretz.com/middle-east-news/palestinians/the-1988-declaration-of-independence-1.5150321.

Seikaly, Sherene. 2018. "How I Met My Great-Grandfather." *Comparative Studies of South Asia, Africa and the Middle East* 38 (1): 6–20. https://doi.org/10.1215/1089201x-4389931.

Serhan, Yasmeen. 2021. "What the Ben & Jerry's Decision Reveals About Israel." *The Atlantic*, July 23, 2021. https://www.theatlantic.com/international/archive/2021/07/ben-jerrys-decision-israel-settlements/619537/.

Shaindlinger, Noa. 2019. "Wishful Landscapes: Protest and Spatial Reclamation in Jaffa." *Comparative Studies of South Asia, Africa and the Middle East* 39 (2): 313–27. https://doi.org/10.1215/1089201X-7586819.

Shalhoub-Kevorkian, Nadera. 2008. "Counter-Spaces as Resistance in Conflict Zones: Palestinian Women Recreating a Home." *Journal of Feminist Family Therapy* 17 (3–4): 109–41. https://doi.org/10.1300/J086v17n03_07.

———. 2014. "Criminality in Spaces of Death: The Palestinian Case Study." *The British Journal of Criminology* 54 (1): 38–52.

———. 2015. *Security Theology, Surveillance and the Politics of Fear*. Cambridge: Cambridge University Press.

———. 2017. "Settler Colonialism, Surveillance, and Fear." In *Israel and Its Palestinian Citizens: Ethnic Privileges in the Jewish State*, edited by Nadim N. Rouhana, with the assistance of Sahar S. Huneidi, 336–66. Oxford: Oxford University Press.

———. 2019. *Incarcerated Childhood and the Politics of Unchilding*. Cambridge: Cambridge University Press.

Shalhoub-Kevorkian, Nadera, and Sarah Ihmoud. 2014. "Exiled at Home: Writing Return and the Palestinian Home." *Biography* 37 (2). https://muse.jhu.edu/article/576904.

Shani, Yaron, and Scandar Copti, directors. *Ajami.* 2009. New York: Kino Lorber. Fiction film, 2 hours.

Shaw, Rosalind. 2002. *Memories of the Slave Trade: Ritual and the Historical Imagination in Sierra Leone.* Chicago: University of Chicago Press.

Sheizaf, Noam. 2011. "Conviction Rate for Palestinians in Israel's Military Courts: 99.74%." +972 Magazine. November 29, 2011. https://972mag.com/conviction-rate -for-palestinians-in-israels-military-courts-99-74-percent/28579/.

Sheizaf, Noam, and Hassan Jabareen. 2015. "'The Problem Isn't Arab Protesters, It's the Society That Sees Them as an Enemy.'" *+972 Magazine.* October 6, 2015. http:// 972mag.com/the-problem-isnt-arab-protesters-its-the-society-that-sees-them-as -an-enemy/112371/.

Shenhav, Yehouda, and Yael Berda. 2009. "The Colonial Foundations of the State of Exception: Juxtaposing the Israeli Occupation of the Palestinian Territories with Colonial Bureaucratic History." SSRN Scholarly Paper ID 2296861. Rochester, NY: Social Science Research Network. http://papers.ssrn.com/abstract=2296861.

Shezaf, Hagar. 2018. "Saving Tel Aviv-Jaffa's Only Muslim Cemetery." *Haaretz*, March 18, 2018. https://www.haaretz.com/israel-news/.premium-saving-tel-aviv-jaffa-s-only -muslim-cemetery-1.5910776.

Shih, Shu-mei. 2013. "Comparison as Relation." In *Comparison: Theories, Approaches, Uses*, edited by Rita Felski and Susan Stanford Friedman, 79–98. Baltimore: Johns Hopkins University Press.

Shihade, Magid. 2011. *Not Just a Soccer Game: Colonialism and Conflict among Palestinians in Israel.* Syracuse: Syracuse University Press.

———. 2012. "Settler Colonialism and Conflict: The Israeli State and Its Palestinian Subjects." *Settler Colonial Studies* 2 (1): 108–23. https://doi.org/10.1080/22014 73X.2012.10648828.

Shomali, Amer, and Paul Cowan, directors. *The Wanted 18.* 2014. New York: Kino Lorber. Animated documentary, 1 hr 15 minutes.

Shoughry-Badarne, Bana. 2011. "A Decade after the High Court of Justice 'Torture' Ruling, What's Changed?" In *Threat*, edited by Abeer Baker and Anat Matar, 114–22. Palestinian Political Prisoners in Israel. London: Pluto Press. https://doi.org/10.2307/j .ctt183p121.15.

Shpigel, Noa. 2018. "Israeli Arab Poet Dareen Tatour Gets Five-Month Sentence for Incitement on Social Media." *Haaretz*, July 31, 2018. https://www.haaretz.com/ israel-news/israel-hands-palestinian-poet-dareen-tatour-five-month-prison-sen tence-1.6335232.

Shpigel, Noa, and Jack Khoury. 2018. "21 Israeli Arabs Arrested during Haifa Protest against Gaza Killings." *Haaretz*, May 19, 2018. https://www.haaretz.com/israel-news/ 21-israeli-arabs-arrested-in-northern-israeli-city-in-gaza-killing-pro-1.6097975.

Sienkiewicz, Matt. 2012. "Out of Control: Palestinian News Satire and Government Power in the Age of Social Media." *Popular Communication* 10 (1–2): 106–18. https://doi.org/10.1080/15405702.2012.638575.

Silverstein, Michael. 1976. "Shifters, Linguistic Categories, and Cultural Description." In *Meaning in Anthropology*, edited by Keith Basso and Henry Selby, 11–55. Albuquerque: University of New Mexico Press.

Simmons, Kristen. 2017. "Settler Atmospherics." *Society for Cultural Anthropology* (blog). November 20, 2017. https://culanth.org/fieldsights/settler-atmospherics.

Simpson, Audra. 2014. *Mohawk Interruptus: Political Life across the Borders of Settler States*. Durham, NC: Duke University Press.

Simpson, Leanne Betasamosake. 2016. "Indigenous Resurgence and Co-Resistance." *Critical Ethnic Studies* 2 (2): 19–34.

Simri Diab, Najwan. 2014. "Ilā Mīlād Abī Al-Jadīd" [To My Father's New Birthday]. Arab48. April 15, 2014. https://www.arab48.com/دياب-سمري-نجوان--الجديد-أبي-ميلاد-إلى/
مقالات-وآراء/15/04/2014.

Slotta, James. 2015. "Phatic Rituals of the Liberal Democratic Polity: Hearing Voices in the Hearings of the Royal Commission of Aboriginal Peoples." *Comparative Studies in Society and History* 57 (1): 130–60. https://doi.org/10.1017/S001041751400 00620.

———. 2017. "Can the Subaltern Listen? Self-Determination and the Provisioning of Expertise in Papua New Guinea." *American Ethnologist* 44 (2): 328–40. https://doi.org/10.1111/amet.12482.

Slyomovics, Susan. 1998. *Object of Memory: Arab and Jew Narrate the Palestinian Village*. Philadelphia: University of Pennsylvania Press.

Smith, Shawn Michelle. 2000. "'Looking at One's Self through the Eyes of Others': W. E. B. Du Bois's Photographs for the 1900 Paris Exposition." *African American Review* 34 (4): 581–99.

Sorek, Tamir. 2015. *Palestinian Commemoration in Israel: Calendars, Monuments, and Martyrs*. Stanford: Stanford University Press.

Soussi, Alasdair. 2019. "The Mixed Legacy of Golda Meir, Israel's First Female PM." Al-Jazeera. March 18, 2019. https://www.aljazeera.com/indepth/features/mixed-legacy-golda-meir-israel-female-pm-190316050933152.html.

Spivak, Gayatri Chakravorty. 2010. "Can the Subaltern Speak? Revised Edition." In *Can the Subaltern Speak?: Reflections on the History of an Idea*, edited by Rosalind C. Morris, 21–79. New York: Columbia University Press.

Stamatopoulou-Robbins, Sophia. 2020. *Waste Siege: The Life of Infrastructure in Palestine*. Stanford: Stanford University Press.

Stein, Rebecca L. 2012. "StateTube: Anthropological Reflections on Social Media and the Israeli State." *Anthropological Quarterly* 85 (3): 893–916.

———. 2017. "GoPro Occupation: Networked Cameras, Israeli Military Rule, and the Digital Promise." *Current Anthropology* 58 (Supplement 15): S56–64. https://doi.org/10.1086/688869.

———. 2021. *Screen Shots: State Violence on Camera in Israel and Palestine.* Stanford: Stanford University Press.

Stein, Rebecca L., and Adi Kuntsman. 2015. *Digital Militarism: Israel's Occupation in the Social Media Age.* Stanford: Stanford University Press.

Stewart, Kathleen C. 2007. *Ordinary Affects.* Durham, NC: Duke University Press.

Stokes, Martin. 2000. "'Beloved Istanbul': Realism and the Transnational Imaginary in Turkish Popular Culture." In *Mass Mediations: New Approaches to Popular Culture in the Middle East and Beyond,* edited by Walter Armbrust, 224–42. Berkeley: University of California Press.

Strathern, Marilyn. 2004. *Partial Connections.* Walnut Creek, CA: Rowman Altamira.

Strickland, Patrick. 2015. "Israel Continues to Criminalise Marking Nakba Day." Al-Jazeera. May 14, 2015. https://www.aljazeera.com/news/2015/05/israel-nakba-palestine-150514080431980.html.

Sturm, Circe. 2017. "Reflections on the Anthropology of Sovereignty and Settler Colonialism: Lessons from Native North America." *Cultural Anthropology* 32 (3): 340–48.

Suleiman, Elia, dir. *The Time that Remains.* 2009. Paris: Le Pacte. Fiction film, 105 minutes.

Suleiman, Faraj, vocalist. "Hymn to Gentrification." YouTube video, 2020. Lyrics by Majd Kayyal. Haifa. https://www.youtube.com/watch?v=jXohY3fgC7k.

———. "Questions on My Mind." YouTube video, 2020. Lyrics by Majd Kayyal. Haifa. https://www.youtube.com/watch?v=FZ8HH9aQ12U.

Sultany, Nimer. 2012. "The Making of an Underclass: Palestinian Citizens in Israel." *Israel Studies Review* 27 (2): 190–200. https://doi.org/10.3167/isr.2012.270210.

———. 2015. "The National Democratic Assembly." In *The Palestinians in Israel: Readings in History, Politics, and Society,* edited by Nadim N. Rouhana and Areej Sabbagh-Khoury, 215–29. Haifa: Mada al-Carmel.

———. 2017. "The Legal Structure of Subordination: The Palestinian Minority and Israeli Law." In *Israel and Its Palestinian Citizens: Ethnic Privileges in the Jewish State,* edited by Rouhana, Nadim N. and Sahar S. Huneidi, 191–238. Cambridge: Cambridge University Press.

Swedenburg, Ted. 1995. *Memories of Revolt: The 1936-1939 Rebellion and the Palestinian National Past.* Minneapolis: University of Minnesota Press.

Tahir, Madiha, Vasiliki Touhouliotis, and Emily Sogn. n.d. "The Military Present, Episode Two." *Anthropological Airwaves.* Accessed November 29, 2021. https://www.americananthropologist.org/podcast/military-present-episode2-madiha-tahir

Takriti, Abdel Razzaq. 2019. "Before BDS: Lineages of Boycott in Palestine." *Radical History Review* 2019 (134): 58–95. https://doi.org/10.1215/01636545-7323408.

Tallbear, Kim. 2013. *Native American DNA: Tribal Belonging and the False Promise of Genetic Science.* Minneapolis: University of Minnesota Press.

Tamari, Salim. 2008. *Mountain Against the Sea: Essays on Palestinian Society and Culture*. Berkeley: University California Press.

Tamari, Salim, and Rema Hammami. 1998. "Virtual Returns to Jaffa." *Journal of Palestine Studies* 27 (4): 65–79.

Taraki, Lisa, ed. 2006. *Living Palestine: Family Survival, Resistance, and Mobility under Occupation*. Syracuse: Syracuse University Press.

Tartir, Alaa. 2017a. "Criminalizing Resistance: The Cases of Balata and Jenin Refugee Camps." *Journal of Palestine Studies* 46 (2): 7–22. https://doi.org/10.1525/jps .2017.46.2.7.

———. 2017b. "The Palestinian Authority Security Forces: Whose Security?" *Al-Shabaka* (blog). May 16, 2017. https://al-shabaka.org/briefs/palestinian-authority -security-forces-whose-security/.

Tate, Winifred. 2007. *Counting the Dead: The Culture and Politics of Human Rights Activism in Colombia*. Berkeley: University of California Press.

Tatour, Lana. 2019. "The Culturalisation of Indigeneity: The Palestinian-Bedouin of the Naqab and Indigenous Rights." *The International Journal of Human Rights* 23 (10): 1569–93. https://doi.org/10.1080/13642987.2019.1609454.

Tawil-Souri, Helga. 2012. "Uneven Borders, Coloured (Im)Mobilities: ID Cards in Palestine/Israel." *Geopolitics*, 17 (1): 153–176. https://doi.org/10.1080/14650045.2011 .562944.

Tayeb, Sami. 2019. "The Palestinian McCity in the Neoliberal Era." *Middle East Research and Information Project* (MERIP) 290 (Spring 2019). https://merip.org/2019/07/ the-palestinian-mccity-in-the-neoliberal-era/.

Ticktin, Miriam. 2017. "A World without Innocence." *American Ethnologist* 44 (4): 577–90. https://doi.org/10.1111/amet.12558.

Tilly, Charles. 2006. *Regimes and Repertoires*. Chicago: University of Chicago Press.

TOI Staff. 2013. "Iconic Armored Vehicles Moved from Highway." *Times of Israel*. November 27, 2013. https://www.timesofisrael.com/iconic-armored-vehicles-to-be -moved-from-highway/.

———. 2019. "Policeman Indicted for Beating, Breaking Knee of Arab Protester in Haifa." *Times of Israel*. June 2, 2019. https://www.timesofisrael.com/policeman-in dicted-for-beating-breaking-knee-of-arab-protester-in-haifa/.

Trilling, Claire. 2020. "A Day in Lod: Separate Lives in Mixed Cities." *Times of Israel*. March 22, 2020. https://blogs.timesofisrael.com/a-day-in-lod-separate-lives-in-mixed-cities/.

UNESCO, and Birzeit University Media Development Center. 2014. "Assessment of Media Development in Palestine." Ramallah: UNESCO.

UNRWA. n.d.a. "Aida Refugee Camp." UNRWA (United Nations Relief and Works Agency). Accessed December 28, 2010b. http://www.unrwa.org/sites/default/files/ aida_refugee_camp.pdf.

———. n.d.b. "Gaza Strip." UNRWA. Accessed August 25, 2019. https://www.unrwa.org/ where-we-work/gaza-strip.

———. n.d.c. "Mini Profile: Al Walaja, Bethlehem Governorate." West Bank: UNRWA (United Nations Relief and Works Agency). https://www.unrwa.org/userfiles/image/articles/2013/The_International_Court_of_Justice_AlWalaja_mini_profile.pdf.

———. n.d.d. "Palestine Refugees." UNRWA. https://www.unrwa.org/palestine-refugees.

———. n.d.e. "West Bank." UNRWA. Accessed August 25, 2019. https://www.unrwa.org/where-we-work/west-bank.

———. 2019. "Where We Work: Lebanon." UNRWA (United Nations Relief and Works Agency). 2019. https://www.unrwa.org/where-we-work/lebanon.

Usher, Graham. 1996. "The Politics of Internal Security: The PA's New Intelligence Services." *Journal of Palestine Studies* 25 (2): 21–34.

Van Esveld, Bill. 2014. "Dispatches: Explaining Four Dead Boys on a Gaza Beach." Human Rights Watch. July 17, 2014. https://www.hrw.org/news/2014/07/17/dispatches-explaining-four-dead-boys-gaza-beach.

Velasco, Antonio de. 2019. " 'I'm a Southerner, Too': Confederate Monuments and Black Southern Counterpublics in Memphis, Tennessee." *Southern Communication Journal* 84 (4): 233–45. https://doi.org/10.1080/1041794X.2019.1636129.

Velthuis, Olav. 2006. "Inside a World of Spin." *Ethnography* 7 (1): 125–50.

Vine, David. 2009. *Island of Shame: The Secret History of the U.S. Military Base on Diego Garcia*. Princeton: Princeton University Press.

Wacquant, Loïc. 2001. "Deadly Symbiosis: When Ghetto and Prison Meet and Mesh." *Punishment & Society* 3 (1): 96–134.

Wakim, Wakim. 2001. "The 'Internally Displaced': Seeking Return within One's Own Land." *Journal of Palestine Studies* 31 (1): 32–38.

Wang, Caroline, and Mary Ann Burris. 1997. "Photovoice: Concept, Methodology, and Use for Participatory Needs Assessment." *Health Education & Behavior* 24 (3): 171–86. https://doi.org/10.1177/109019819702400309.

Warner, Michael. 2002. *Publics and Counterpublics*. New York: Zone Books.

Watad, Mohammad. 2020. "Maqbarat Al-Is'āf Fī Yāfā . . . Al-Jurḥ Al-Nāzif Li-Awqāf Wa Muqadisāt Filasṭīn" [The Is'āf Cemetery in Jaffa . . . The Bleeding Wound of the Islamic Properties and Palestine's Holy Sites]. *Al-Jazeera Net* (blog). December 6, 2020. https://www.aljazeera.net/news/politics/2020/6/12/مقبرة-الإسعاف-في-يافا-الجرح-النازف.

Wedeen, Lisa. 1999. *Ambiguities of Domination: Politics, Rhetoric, and Symbols in Contemporary Syria*. Chicago: University of Chicago Press.

Wermenbol, Grace. 2019. "The Ongoing Divide: Palestinian Participation in Israeli Elections." Middle East Institute. 2019. https://www.mei.edu/publications/ongoing-divide-palestinian-participation-israeli-elections.

Westmoreland, Mark. 2015. "Mish Mabsoota: On Teaching with a Camera in Revolutionary Cairo." *Journal of Aesthetics and Culture* 7 (1): 1–11. https://doi.org/10.3402/jac.v7.28253.

"What Is BDS?" 2016. BDS Movement. April 25, 2016. https://bdsmovement.net/what-is-bds.

Wilder, Gary. 2015. *Freedom Time: Negritude, Decolonization, and the Future of the World*. Durham, NC: Duke University Press.

Williams, Raymond. 1977. *Marxism and Literature*. Oxford: Oxford University Press.

Wimmer, Andreas, and Nina Glick Schiller. 2002. "Methodological Nationalism and Beyond: Nation-State Building, Migration, and The Social Sciences." *Global Networks* 2 (4): 301–34. https://doi.org/10.1111/1471-0374.00043

Wolfe, Patrick. 2006. "Settler Colonialism and the Elimination of the Native." *Journal of Genocide Research* 8 (4): 387–409.

———. 2016. *Traces of History: Elementary Structures of Race*. London: Verso Books.

Wolfsfeld, Gadi, and Yitzhak Rabihiya. 1988. "Communication and Control in Times of Crisis: Israeli Censorship in the Occupied Territories." *Canadian Journal of Communication* 13 (6): 96–101. https://doi.org/10.22230/cjc.1988v13n6a3164.

Wright, Fiona. 2018. *The Israeli Radical Left: An Ethics of Complicity*. Philadelphia: University of Pennsylvania Press.

Yankah, Ekow N. 2021. "Ahmaud Arbery, Reckless Racism and Hate Crimes: Recklessness as Hate Crime Enhancement." *Arizona State Law Journal* 53 (2): 681–706.

Yaqubi, Mohanad, dir. *Off Frame AKA Revolution Until Victory*. 2015. Paris: Momento! Films Ltd. Documentary, 62 minutes.

Yazıcı, Berna. 2013. "Towards an Anthropology of Traffic: A Ride Through Class Hierarchies on Istanbul's Roadways." *Ethnos* 78 (4): 515–42.

Yeh, Rihan. 2012. "Two Publics in a Mexican Border City." *Cultural Anthropology* 27 (4): 713–34.

———. 2018. *Passing: Two Publics in a Mexican Border City*. Chicago: University of Chicago Press.

Yiftachel, Oren. 1996. "The Internal Frontier: Territorial Control and Ethnic Relations in Israel." *Regional Studies* 30 (5): 493–508. https://doi.org/10.1080/00343409612331349808.

Yıldız, Emrah. 2013. "Fugitive Markets, Arrested Mobilities: Gaziantep's Iranian Bazaar." *Jadaliyya*. November. https://www.jadaliyya.com/Details/29807.

Yurchak, Alexei. 2005. *Everything Was Forever, Until It Was No More: The Last Soviet Generation*. Princeton: Princeton University Press.

Zani, Leah. 2019. "Blast Radius." In *Bomb Children: Life in the Former Battlefields of Laos*. Durham, NC: Duke University Press.

Zayani, Mohamed. 2007. "Witnessing the Intifada: Al Jazeera's Coverage of the Palestinian-Israeli Conflict." In *The Al Jazeera Phenomenon: Critical Perspectives on New Arab Media*, edited by Mohamed Zayani, 171–82. Boulder, CO: Paradigm Publishers.

———. 2015. *Networked Publics and Digital Contestation: The Politics of Everyday Life in Tunisia*. Oxford: Oxford University Press.

Zengin, Aslı. 2019. "The Afterlife of Gender: Sovereignty, Intimacy, and Muslim Funerals of Transgender People in Turkey." *Cultural Anthropology* 34 (1): 78–102. https://doi.org/10.14506/ca34.1.09.

Zia, Ather. 2016. "The Spectacle of a Good Half-Widow: Women in Search of their Disappeared Men in the Kashmir Valley." *Political and Legal Anthropology Review*. 39 (2): 164-175.

Ziv, Oran. 2018. "Palestinian Poet Dareen Tatour Set Free." +972 Magazine (blog). September 20, 2018. https://972mag.com/palestinian-poet-dareen-tatour-set-free/137840/.

Zochrot. n.d.a "Bayt Jibrin." Accessed June 23, 2020a. https://zochrot.org/en/village/49055.

———. n.d.b. "Lubya." Accessed May 1, 2018b. http://www.zochrot.org/en/village/49244.

———. n.d.c. *March of Return to Al-Ruways and al-Damoun*. YouTube video. Accessed May 1, 2018c. https://www.youtube.com/watch?v=z4OcUSVU5O4.

———. 2011 "Al-Qabu Tour Report." https://zochrot.org/en/tour/50075.

Zonszein, Mairav. 2015. "Israel Killed More Palestinians in 2014 than in Any Other Year since 1967." *The Guardian*, March 27, 2015. http://www.theguardian.com/world/2015/mar/27/israel-kills-more-palestinians-2014-than-any-other-year-since-1967.

———. 2018. "Israel Lets Jews Protest the Occupation. It Doesn't Let Palestinians." *Washington Post*, May 31, 2018, sec. Outlook, Perspective. https://www.washingtonpost.com/outlook/israel-lets-jews-protest-the-occupation-it-doesnt-let-palestinians/2018/05/30/5e95e5b4-636f-11e8-a69c-b944de66d9e7_story.html.

Zreik, Raef. 2003. "The Palestinian Question: Themes of Justice and Power: Part I: The Palestinians of the Occupied Territories." *Journal of Palestine Studies* 32 (4): 39–49. https://doi.org/10.1525/jps.2003.32.4.39.

Zuboff, Shoshana. 2019. *The Age of Surveillance Capitalism: The Fight for a Human Future at the New Frontier of Power*. New York: PublicAffairs.

Zureik, Elia. 1979. *The Palestinians in Israel: A Study in Internal Colonialism*. London: Routledge and Kegan Paul.

———. 1988. "Crime, Justice, and Underdevelopment: The Palestinians under Israeli Control." *International Journal of Middle East Studies* 20 (4): 411–22.

———. 2001. "Constructing Palestine through Surveillance Practices." *British Journal of Middle East Studies* 28 (2): 205–27.

Zureik, Elia, David Lyon, and Yasmeen Abu-Laban, eds. 2013. *Surveillance and Control in Israel/Palestine: Population, Territory and Power*. London: Routledge.

Zureiq, Constantin. 1948. *The Meaning of the Nakba*. Beirut: Center for Arab Unity Studies.

Index